THE CENTURY HISTORICAL SERIES
WILLIAM E. LINGELBACH, *Editor*

Iron Out of Calvary

Iron Out of Calvary

AN INTERPRETATIVE HISTORY OF THE SECOND WORLD WAR

BY

WALTER PHELPS HALL, Ph.D

Dodge Professor of History

Princeton University

STUDENT'S EDITION

NEW YORK AND LONDON

D. APPLETON-CENTURY COMPANY, INC.

446

TO

*Walter Phelps Hall, Jr., Technical Sergeant,
Eighty-fifth Mountain Infantry, Tenth Mountain
Division. Killed in action near Mt. Belvedere,
Italy, February 20, 1945*

AND

*Edward Buckley Van Zile, Jr., Private First
Class, Fifth Amphibious Corps, Fourth Marines.
Killed in action, Iwo Jima, February 24, 1945*

❋   ❋   ❋

*Conceived in liberty . . . full measure of devo-
tion . . . honored dead—the words of Lincoln haunt
the memory still.*

*By Norman beaches and in Leyte swamps,
beyond the Rhine and beneath the Seven Seas,
in Pacific jungles and African deserts, under the
volcanic ash of Iwo Jima and high amid the
rugged Apennines, lie our honored dead.*

CONTENTS

ACKNOWLEDGMENT

For skillful and generous assistance in preparing this book for the printer, the author wishes to thank Miss Elisabeth D'Arcy of Lawrenceville, New Jersey, and his colleague at Princeton University, Professor Walter Lincoln Whittlesey.

W. P. H.

Iron Out of Calvary

FOREWORD

"For iron—cold iron—is master of men all." Thus the medieval baron of Kipling's gnomic poem, as he besieged the castle of his sovereign lord. Justice, truth, kindliness were craft-words for weak monks; steel out of iron was for men.

Did ten years' war from Ethiopia in October, 1935, to Japan in August, 1945, prove the baron wrong; show the aimless impotence of brute force? Did the empty, immeasurable waste of this global mêlée rouse deaf ears to the possibility, always latent in mankind, of good tidings, of a world ruled by reason and compromise, by tempered mercy, God's compassion? Or, quite the other way, do such successive lunacies show the baron sane? Crude cannon on walls besieged were the undoing of armored knights, but larger artillery soon laid those walls in dust and rubble. Arquebus gave way to musket, the matchlock to Marlborough's Brown Bess, and that lethal beldame to the crude rifle of the Crimean War. Cutlass and landing net yielded to torpedo and submarine. War was no longer on one plane only, but on all three, with the ominous blast from skies above in August, 1945, at Hiroshima and Nagasaki. Oil and gas, the ships, the planes, bombs, manpower and Satan-power were in war the overmastering and uniting possessions of the United Nations, not of their disjointed adversaries. Iron, as conceived by Kipling's baron and his heirs since then, with all that grim symbol ever stood for, was both slave and master of men all.

To pessimists, any chirping hope of blessed deliverance from human strife was necessarily ridiculous. "And why," said they, "stand we in jeopardy every hour?" Because we live! The last war was like other wars before it, only worse. They were sure no good could ensue therefrom. Even before the end in 1945 they chattered like the "banderlog" of a new and a third World War, foresaw Soviet Russia in global conflict with the capitalistic West while Asia's teeming millions knifed each others' throats.

There were some more optimistic, and being not unmindful that one after another Italy, Germany and Japan lay in ruins, they per-

1

ceived the immediate task fulfilled. They knew that the poisoned and poisonous roots of chauvinistic nationalism, as well as of deadly economic greed, had withstood the scorching flames of war, perhaps to be fertilized into fuller fungus growth by its very ashes; they realized only too well that absence of clear thinking, want of faith, and lack of any unified philosophy of human life, combined to paralyze the vague aspirations of even the best intentioned. But most desperately they hoped this ghastly sacrifice of the young and old, of greatness and of littleness, had not been in vain; that somehow, in some way, the frightful shock beneath which all mankind was reeling might force a final issuance to better things, etch so vividly in sharp outline the iron need of coöperatively sharing in humanity's rehabilitation that the gates of War-hell might close forevermore.

"Iron out of Calvary is master of men all." Thus the poem ends. What Kipling meant by this last line is a problem in exegesis which perhaps cannot be solved. But of this we may be sure; the poet of imperialism, the author of "Keep ye the law, be swift in all obedience," was not one to renounce authority, to suborn discipline, to substitute soft pleadings for legitimate commands. He still had use for iron. It alone, however, he seemed to sense would fail unless mansuetude and selflessness and sacrifice, which meant Calvary, were reflected in the spirit and the temper of those who made the laws and of those who executed them.

Yet iron was iron still, and spikes forged thereof had nailed God-Man fast to Calvary's bloody tree. Iron was fact. So also Calvary. In the war now ended they were curiously commingled, inseparable comrades. Iron out of Calvary had once worked miracles in this world. Could it do so again?

1. CONFUSION TO CHAOS

THERE was neither security nor faith on earth as the fourth decade of this century opened. America had been far more prosperous than her sister democracies, but rumors of impending revolution were not altogether absent in 1931, as workmen without jobs milled around in city streets and a deluge of foreclosures made banks own farms they did not want. The flood-tide of the great depression had not yet engulfed France, but unsavory politicos and politics without honesty were steadily undermining the prestige of the Third Republic, soon to be hollowed out further by Fascist termites. Soviet Russia was said to be forging ahead, but an iron tyranny as complete as the Tsar's gripped the Russian people, and many went hungry in Sovietland despite coöperative farms and multitudes of tractors. In Germany Hitler's Brown Shirts mocked law, order, decency. England was not as badly off as Germany, but depressed areas along Tyneside, in South Wales and Lancashire cast just as murky a shadow, in some ways an even darker one, than those threatening an eclipse of civilization in the Reich. Railroads, it was said, now ran on time in Italy. But Italians had no assurance that either peace or bread would be their lot. On the pampas of South America plots innumerable were hatching against democracy and Yankee imperialism. In India smoldering antagonism to the British raj broke out in riot. Young army officers in Japan, ignorant of history and common sense, plotted their raid upon the world. War lords in Chinese provinces did as they saw fit, giving small obedience to the Chinese Republic, torn as it was by Communist and anti-Communist propaganda, its sheer instability inviting attack. Uncertainty, disillusionment, conflicting faiths and loyalties played havoc with men's minds in Chicago, Calcutta, Cairo, London and Shanghai.

Soon the seemingly incredible came to pass; evil incarnate marched from victory to victory; broad areas of this world, considered civilized, sank into barbarism; while those in high authority in lands not yet dangerously ill were, for the most part, blind

3

guardians of the blind, without wisdom, without fortitude. Surely history's annals contain no decade as ruinous as this, commencing with economic blight which covered the globe, ending in universal war wherein every race of mankind, brown and white, black and yellow, was engulfed. And this but twenty years after the war to end war!

Why? Despite unparalleled disasters, domestic confusion, international anarchy, ordinary folk stuck intuitively to their daily tasks. Boys and girls fell in love, married, had children because they wanted them; and these they fed, clothed, and protected because it was their instinct so to do. Most men and women worked at useful occupations—when there was work available. Carpenters built homes, farmers ploughed, miners dug, fishermen drew nets, lumbermen swung axes, teachers taught, policemen walked their beats, and business men paid their debts. There were illnesses and accidents, cold, heat, storms, and now and again discouragement, bitter and hard to endure. But most folks took those things in their stride and died as they had lived, not without dignity. How could they know that civilization was undermined and a second world war around the corner? They were not responsible for its coming.

As fair a bill of health can be given scientists, technicians, and most entrepreneurs who encouraged them. Between World War I and World War II they made astonishing advances. Machines, the children of their brains, were more universally used, cheaper to operate, more helpful in lessening toil, more potent in production, more effective in ministering to our well-being in 1940 than in 1920. And this was true whether we think of agriculture, manufacture, transportation, bridges, domestic appliances, scientific apparatus to explore opaque substances or the conquest of the ether by electrons. One need but compare the plane in which Wendell Willkie flew to England in 1941 with the *Spirit of St. Louis* flown by Lindbergh in his solo flight of 1927, the clumsy farm tractors of the early twenties with their mammoth rubber-tired counterparts of the late thirties, the first radio apparatus for the deaf with the latest hearing aid, the engine room of the *Queen Mary* with that of the now forgotten *Mauretania*. Ships steered without hands, doors opened by shadows cast upon an electric eye, airconditioned homes, cloth spun from glass, cows inseminated by life substance taken from prize bulls thousands of miles distant. These discoveries showed the restless energy of our human intellect.

To be sure, there were no equivalent victories in human relationships—quite the contrary. Danger lurked here; the new technology unloosed powers of destruction as well as of construction. But from that it did not follow that the hard-won conquests of science were in themselves injurious. It was not the fault of chemists, engineers and physicists that economists, statesmen, teachers and humanists made such little headway (if any) in pulling humanity out of the obscurantism, defeatism, greed, vanity and cowardice into which it was sinking.

Who then was responsible for the war of wars which began so informally in 1931 with the Japanese occupation of Manchuria and which ended in 1945 with the American occupation of Tokyo? Since humanity dearly loves its scapegoats, many have been suggested; sometimes whole groups: Japanese army officers, reactionary Nazis, revolutionary Communists; more frequently individuals; Mussolini for starting the Fascist march, Chamberlain for appeasement, Roosevelt for aiding Britons and Chinese, and, most of all, Hitler, seen as incarnate spirit of evil. But this does not hit the heart of the matter. World War II was not caused primarily by the stupidities of individuals nor by malevolent prophets of evil entrancing the multitude. It is both superficial and unhistorical to lay it simply on the doorstep of Prussian militarism or to analyze its causes in terms of Fascist ideology alone, whether nursed in Berlin, Rome or Tokyo.

The truth is the prevailing distempers of the age poisoned men's minds everywhere, more virulently in France than in Britain, in Germany than in France, in Japan than in China. The disease, or diseases, which came so close to killing civilization in our own time were indigenous to no single country, confined to no continent.

Just what were these diseases? A complete answer is today impossible, perhaps tomorrow also. But certain symptoms can be traced, checked, analyzed. Among them three seem outstanding: economic maladjustments on a larger, more global scale than ever in the past; an intensified feverish nationalism sweeping the earth, accompanied by an ever growing anger of yellow, brown and black against white domination; and the steady disintegration of confidence and faith in the liberal heritage of the nineteenth century.

ECONOMIC MALADJUSTMENTS

One major fact of international anarchy in the period between the two world wars was economic maladjustment. The free market, the free exchange of commodities between the various peoples of the earth, never completely operative, broke down so miserably in ten years as seriously to threaten world trade, finance and commerce, thus on the one hand diminishing prosperity and on the other heightening nationalistic hate.

Nothing could be more ironic now than the speeches of Richard Cobden, that fiery international pacifist of the nineteenth century, so superbly confident that free trade, free competition, free enterprise and the free market would link together in human brotherhood all people who on earth do dwell. It seemed so clear, so obvious. Surely business was business, a science like physics or chemistry. Religion, politics concerned it not; to tinker with it was harmful; also, in the long run, useless. Left to itself it would enrich the world materially, but more important it would strengthen it spiritually. Inefficiency would be weeded out, the rewards won by sobriety, steadfastness, honesty, hard work, intelligence.

To Cobden, trade and commerce were not weighed and valued only in terms of comfortable living, although he did not scorn such; to him the exchange of goods and the endless flow of commodities in a free market meant that all nations and all continents would become closer and closer linked, and that something resembling a world community based on economic interests serving human life would wax stronger and stronger until armies, navies, and war itself became mere history.

Cobden's dream did not come true. By the end of his century almost all nations except Britain had walled themselves in behind tariff barriers, a precedent reluctantly followed by his own country by the 1930s. Instead of free trade and widespread competition, business men found it paid to consolidate, to combine their holdings with those of others, to form trusts which grew into monopolies. Whether this practice was encouraged by the law, as in Germany, or discountenanced, as in the United States, made no difference. The man with little capital saw the handwriting on the wall and ducked for cover, preferring safety and some profit to lone adventure and the risk of losing all.

This did not mean, as the Marxists asserted, that the rich were growing richer, the poor, poorer. What was taking place was not so much concentration of capital as concentration of management, partly by interlocking directorates, partly by modern banking methods, partly because widely diffused ownership made it futile for those with a few shares of stock to unite with thousands of other small stockholders to wrest control from the big fellow.

By 1930 some four families lorded it over the shipping and textile industries of Japan, while one Japanese company, the Southern Manchurian Railway, became economic dictator of the old Chinese provinces which comprised Manchuria. In France, banking became more highly concentrated than anywhere else, the Bank of France, with more than 30,000 stockholders, being controlled by some two hundred families. In Germany, pyramiding directorates in the steel, chemical, and electrical industries put their future at the mercy of a few individuals. Free enterprise perished in Italy after Mussolini streamlined his corporative state in 1928. In the U.S.S.R. the same situation developed in industry from 1919 on, and in agriculture, under Stalin, after 1928. The tempo of change in Britain and America was slower; nevertheless, in the former, five banks, together with the Bank of England, became so powerful that no one dreamed of competing with them; in the latter, certain corporations gained monopolistic control, since no one in his senses could hope to compete with General Electric or with the Bell system, to say nothing of the Aluminum Company of America.

Some there were who optimistically maintained that this concentration of management made for world peace and wrote enthusiastically of a Gold International in process of formation, a kind of consortium of economic interests on a world scale. But it did not work out that way. Agreements were reached between business men across national boundaries—cartels they were called; but these proved flimsy and ephemeral. In general, the practice was for entrepreneurs to seek and to obtain state aid in furthering their own expansion. Thus, the American government supported American business in Latin America as the Japanese government did theirs in China, the French in Poland. Even Britain, former champion of the free market, followed this course. Before World War I, the British led the world in exporting cotton textiles. Subsequently Japanese competition raided former British markets so that spindles ceased to turn in many a Lancashire mill. Soon in Afghanistan, Abyssinia, and even in the British West Indies ubiquitous Japanese salesmen were seen, and Hindu women bought fewer and fewer saris made in Britain. There was nothing the British government could do about this except rationalize the cotton industry by further consolidation and more state intervention, and what had hitherto been competition between individuals now began to be competition between states, a fact not conducive to international amity.

This situation diminished the flow of international trade but did not quite dam it up. Despite tariffs, quotas, bounties, cartels and other restrictions on the free market, a revival of world trade was noted from 1923 to 1929, due in large measure, though not exclusively, to American loans. During those years there were tremendous gains in industrial production in the United States. Labor-saving devices, conveyor belts, automatic tools, improved automobiles and a thirsty demand therefor, ditto for radios and electric refrigerators, accounted for it in part; skilful advertising, instalment buying, incessant ballyhoo about our future boosted it higher. We had emerged from World War I, richest of all nations; we had money to burn and money to lend, and we proceeded to lend it. The foreign loans we made and the credits we granted, amounting to billions of dollars, were a reflex of our naïve optimism. The nations to which we loaned money used it to pay interest on debts already incurred, to buy American goods, to modernize their industrial plants. Those nations in turn were given over, for a time, to optimism. British loans to the Continent supplemented American loans; French luxury trades felt the stimulus; German engineers and technical experts found well-paid work in underskilled Russia. For a while all went well.

Then came the panic of 1929 in America and the subsequent great depression. There was more produced but less money to buy it; wages rose but consumer goods increased three times as rapidly, whereupon merchandise bought on credit fell back on manufacturers who curtailed production, and men lost jobs; a land boom in Florida collapsed; loans made to Europe could not be collected; stockbrokers raised their margin rates; and fear succeeded confidence. October 29, 1929, the crash came in Wall Street. And soon "what had so long been called securities became mere paper flying before the wind."

1930, 1931, 1932, and the depression settled like a black fog on all the earth. It spread from America to Europe; the woolen mills of England, the chemical plants of Germany, the silk mills of France and Italy closed their doors. It spread to South America; Argentina could not sell its beef and Brazil burned coffee for fuel. It spread to Asia; Javanese and Malayan rubber and Japanese silk were no longer wanted. Soon the total of the world's unemployed stood at 30 million. There was food enough (never before had there been such a superabundance of wheat); there were machines to manufacture clothing and shoes, and raw materials to feed them. But the unemployed had no money to buy. In our country their necessities were supplied in large measure by the state, and to a less degree this was done in Europe. But in China, Japan and India men lived on a narrower margin, and in those countries the extent to which they had been penetrated by the Industrial Revolution was the index of popular misery. Soon newspapers carried accounts of cholera and starvation in China and Japan. Of the latter, the London *Times* reported in 1932 "that many villages are almost moneyless, that petty trades are done by barter, that people are eating the roughest grains and bracken roots, even beancake being cooked." Thus did the depression cover all the earth.

One country alone excepted—Soviet Russia. No unemployment could be noticed there, no "redundant harvests, rotting goods, rusting machinery." In Russia there was suffering in reverse—too much work, too little food. Stalin's five-year plan, started in 1928, was in full swing. It promised the Russian people that ultimately the living standards of the West would be overtaken and surpassed. But for the time being there must be hardship, coarse, monotonous and insufficient food, and great scarcity of consumer goods. Railroads, power dams, tractors, blast furnaces held high priority in Russia. Hope and confidence in the future, Yes! For the present, physical comfort, No!

The two countries most adversely affected by the depression were Germany and Japan, the one thrown prostrate twice in a single decade; the other, too highly and too hastily industrialized, too utterly dependent for its livelihood on selling manufactured goods abroad.

The Germans had not simply been thrashed in war, 1914-1918; they had gone through an inferno in 1923 when the French occupied the Ruhr, when inflation brought Germany low, and the value of their money dropped to zero. More particularly the German middle class suffered. The rich always exist somehow when times are bad, and for the poor there is unemployment insurance.

But the middling folk in Germany lost all in 1923, savings bank accounts, life insurance policies, homes.

After this currency debacle, help came to the Germans from the Dawes and Young plans. By loans from England and America they started all over again; by hard work, intelligence, scientific acumen, and not a little trickery they were by 1930 on the road to recovery. Their markets were coming back; their ships were seen once more on ocean lanes; their factories and workshops were humming. Politically, Germany was a distraught country, her people still smarting from hurt pride, her politicians, inexperienced in democratic practices, trying to adjust themselves to a constitution impossible for the most sapient to operate. But economically Germany seemed sound; her internal debt was low, her industrial plants rebuilt, modernized, smooth-running, her people competent, disciplined, capable in handling dynamos and dye-vats.

Then came 1930, hard times, and a Reichstag election. In 1928 twelve Nazis secured seats; in 1930, 107 were elected, an increase in their vote in two years of 800 per cent. Anyone scornful of economic determinism may well ponder these statistics: while Germany was relatively prosperous the most adroit propaganda and the world's ablest political mountebank made little headway; reverse the economic order, fill the streets with unemployed, empty the larder, and the ranting of the showman is taken for the voice of Gabriel.

Three years later Hitler was chancellor of Germany, master of the Reich. His final victory was the result of many factors: the senile stupidity, perhaps treachery, of the aged Hindenburg, the conceit and arrogance of Prussian junkers who thought they could make a stooge of the ex-Austrian, the ability of the latter to gain the financial support of Rhine industrialists and munition-makers while promising everything to the enraptured poor, the golden chance offered by the Reichstag fire to eliminate the Communists by blaming them for a fire which the Nazis had started, and a long protracted industrial slump. That the last was decisive cannot be demonstrated, but that it was the backdrop for Hitler's seizure of power cannot be denied.

In Japan, as in Germany, the world depression raised desperate gangsters to high authority. The economic background of the two countries was widely different, but the political consequences of economic blackout were much the same. The First World War, a curse to Germany, was a boon to Japan. Neither during its course nor in the years immediately following did she suffer reverses. Quite the contrary; of all the victors she gained the most. Germany's strategic atolls fell into her lap; prostrate China lay at her mercy; neither in lives nor in treasure did she lose. Her geographic position was superb, an island empire off the coast of Asia analogous to the British Isles off the coast of Europe. Her mineral resources were slight, but those of Manchuria were more than adequate, and there were none capable of denying them to her. For labor she could draw upon a docile and fecund peasantry, and for markets there were the teeming millions of East Asia across the narrow seas and opulent America beyond the further ocean. In consequence, no country, unless it be the United States, prospered during the 1920s as did Japan. From Tokyo to Osaka, across the southern belt of her largest island, factories sprang up, their products carried east, west and south by an excellent mercantile marine, the fastest growing one in all the world.

This prosperity rested on a shaky foundation. Of all countries Japan was the most overcrowded. Her homeland could be dumped into California with space to spare, while that part of her mountainous and volcanic islands suitable for agriculture was only about the area of Iowa. When World War II broke "the population per square mile of arable land in Japan stood at 2,430, in Germany at 578, and in Italy at 500, contrasted with the Russian figure of 68 and that of the United States of 102."[1]

This meant that the Japanese must (a) starve, or (b) migrate, or (c) find markets for expanding industries. They could not live by agriculture; their tiny two- and three-acre farms would not have provided sustenance even for those living on them had it not been for raising silk cocoons, a semi-farming industry, and the steady drain of farmers' daughters to the textile mills.

Then, too, the very rapidity with which industrial Japan had risen put heavy strain upon her resources. A large fraction of her annual income had immediately to be reinvested if new factories were to be constructed, new machinery installed, and rapidly growing cities equipped with the minimum of lighting, sewage, water and transportation facilities. This meant living on the narrowest of margins. Behind an imposing façade of modern grandeur there was of necessity much squalor. Deftly concealed, it was nonetheless extant, a

[1] Brooks Emeny, "Mainsprings of World Politics," Foreign Policy Association, *Headline Series*, (New York, 1943), p. 51.

fact more conducive to nervous strain than to genuine self-confidence.

Possibly this explains the trigger-like insolence of the Japanese military and the hypersensitivity of Japanese diplomats and publicists. No matter how deep and secure might be the human foundations upon which their culture rested, those upon which their material economy were based were new, fragile, and easily shattered should adverse circumstance limit or destroy the foreign trade of Nippon.

That is just what happened. Even in the twenties the success of the Kuomingtang, the Chinese Nationalist party, in bringing partial unity to the Chinese Republic, threatened those monopolistic advantages which Japan had wrung from the helpless Chinese during the First World War. But that was a mere pinprick on the surface of Japan's economy compared with losses sustained as a result of the depression in the United States. Despite the high American tariff the Japanese had won an extensive market in our country for all sorts of commodities. First and foremost there was silk, but later came chinaware, electric light bulbs and endless imitative minor articles which in bulk brought millions in profits. And this lucrative trade was hard hit as the American pocketbook shrank.

The repercussion on Japan as a state was not simply economic but political as well, since it threw greater power to the Fascist-minded military men. The army had long held extensive influence in the Japanese government but had been forced to share it with more liberal groups of semi-democratic principles, who thought the nation better served by keeping armed force in the background.

But now the army got on top. The officers came largely from a class hard hit by the depression, that of the rural landlords, heavily in debt to the banks, frequently compelled either to lower rents because of sheer inability on the part of their tenants to pay or else to farm their own midget holdings. These officers were bitter foes of the big industrialists, the bankers, the factory magnates, the men who believed in conciliating English and American public opinion, and who wanted economy in government even at the expense of the armed forces. Many of these officers belonged to secret revolutionary societies, such as the Black Dragon and the Black Ocean, and plotted the assassination of prominent industrialists, some of whom were forced to hire gangsters for protection and to wear bullet-proof vests while playing tennis. Some Japanese statesmen were murdered, especially those favoring the naval limitation treaty of 1930. Meanwhile the army officers began to prate loudly of the "Showa Restoration," said to have begun in 1926 with the reign of Hirohito, a restoration which would give back to the throne the arbitrary powers falsely presumed to have lapsed owing to Japan's flirtation with parliamentary government and adoption of Western ideas.

In 1932 army officers, members of the League of Blood, murdered the premier of Japan, threw bombs at banks in Tokyo, tried to take over the city. Their creed was: "Against political parties which are concerned only with gaining possession of power and with their own interests; against the capitalists who form a bloc with the political parties in order to oppress their own countrymen; against feeble democracy; against dangerous ideas; for the peasants and workers who are suffering dire need." The authors probably never heard of Hitler in Germany or of Huey Long in America; nevertheless the comparison is of interest.

And again in 1936 came a second try at a military coup. This time the more important sections of Tokyo were occupied by insurgent regiments as fanatic cutthroats murdered a number of the older and more conservative Japanese statesmen. The conspirators claimed that this was done because "The present time is a favorable moment for Japan to bring about a greater expansion of national power and prestige. In recent years, however, there have appeared many persons whose chief aim and purpose have been to amass personal wealth, disregarding the general welfare. ... The imperial work will fail unless we take proper steps to safeguard the Fatherland by killing all those responsible for impeding the Showa Restoration. . . ." This outbreak was suppressed, but not too cruelly. A very few were executed, and the government shortly afterwards granted some of their demands. Two years later one of their nominees for office, Baron Hiranuma, became premier.

These émeutes were evidence of profound economic malaise in the Mikado's empire. They were a protest against finance capitalism which in three or four decades had revolutionized the way of living of the Japanese people. The revolts, however, were indicative of more than that; cloudy references to the Showa revolution meant full steam backward, a repudiation of the West, a retreat into and a reaffirmation of chauvinistic nationalism. And in this Japan was not alone.

INTENSIFIED NATIONALISM

Within a century the railway, steamship, telegraph, cable, radio and airplane drew into closer touch all human societies, groups, races, nations. Space shrank and time, so far as it delayed inter-communication, all but disappeared. The result has not been credit-able to either man's heart or head. Instead of leading to ties of understanding and sympathy, jealousies were augmented, particu-larism sharpened, nationalism intensified.

Particularly noticeable was this after the First World War. The completely independent status of Finland, Esthonia, Latvia, Lithu-ania, Poland, Czechoslovakia, Albania and Eire is proof; and the subsequent course of events in Egypt, Turkey, Syria, Saud Arabia, Iraq, India, Burma and China is further proof. From Scotland and Wales in northwestern Europe to Albania in the southeast, from Palestine in West Asia to Korea on the Sea of Japan waves of na-tionalistic fervor and propaganda inundated the Eastern Hem-isphere. Nor were the Americas exempt. Canadian nationalism more than once stood in the way of a common foreign policy for the British Commonwealth of Nations. An exclusive nationalism in the United States rejected the League of Nations and refused ad-herence to the World Court. In South America jibes and jeers at that "Colossus of the North," the United States, made joint action through the Pan-American Union or any other agency difficult. What seemingly was taking place among men was analogous to that occurring inside the globe on which they lived: a cooling planet suffers from tidal waves, earthquakes, volcanic eruptions; the closer proximity of man to man and nation to nation necessitated a reorien-tation of human relationships and heightened man's suspicion and fear of his neighbor.

Nationalism flourished everywhere on the eve of the Second World War, from the mild unwillingness of the Scandinavian states to join any northern front, however limited, to the chauvinistic will of Italians, Germans and Japanese set on carving out great empires. Generally speaking, those countries with democratic institutions were less affected than those which rejected democracy. American nationalism took the form primarily of isolation, in some ways an ostrich-like policy tinged with idealistic tradition. British national-ism, diluted somewhat by a bad conscience in the matter of the Versailles Treaty and disconcerted by the rising tide of nativism in

Asia, gave evidence of willingness to make compromises—not too extensive. The French, confronted by conflicting ideologies of Fascism and Communism, well-nigh forgot their traditional loyalty to the Tricolor.

The nationalism of Soviet Russia somewhat resembled that of the United States. The defeat of Trotsky and the victory of Stalin was a triumph for Russian isolationism over world-wide proletarian revolt. Stalin's policy, it is true, was less isolationist than that of the United States, for Russia became a member of the League. Nevertheless Stalin's interests lay more in Asia than in Europe, in the economic development of Soviet territory beyond the Urals. Under him, quietly but steadily, the Russian motherland was substituted for the international proletariat as the keynote of the Bolshevik revolution.

Three large countries drank the heady wine of nationalism to the last drop—Italy, Germany, Japan. In each instance this was due not merely to economic dissatisfaction and acute misery but also to inherited tradition in which democracy had no part.

The experience of Italy with constitutional government had been limited, and with democracy even more so. There had only been an Italy since 1861, and the Italian government since that date had not tried to educate the Italian people in democratic ways, or hardly, for that matter, to educate them at all. The country was poor and backward, and illiteracy among peasants was common. Skilled craftsmen in the north and a scattering of intelligentsia without much political experience raised the cultural status of Italy well above that of the Balkan states and possibly above that of Spain. Nonetheless, from 1861 to 1922, the date of Mussolini's march on Rome, the political history of Italy is petty politics, ins versus outs, a country with scant resources pretending to play a major rôle in world affairs.

Then came Fascism to the Italian peninsula, delight and joy in physical violence, at first ideologically defined in terms of negation—anti-liberalism, anti-Communism, anti-internationalism, anti-rationalism. Neither Mussolini nor his followers knew how to define what they hoped to accomplish or cared very much to do so; it was easier to gain adherents by incitation to riot than to formulate a program. The latter of necessity would antagonize either bourgeoisie or proletariat, and the frisking youth of the castor-oil bottle were led by a demagogue who was neither rightest nor leftist, neither republican nor Socialist, neither monarchist nor anti-monarchist, but a reincarnated thug of the Renaissance who saw his chance and took it to establish a dictatorship—his own!

The Duce, unlike Hitler and the Japanese generals, was without faith. There is no evidence that he had any convictions whatsoever concerning government, history or destiny. He considered himself an artist, as Nero did, and was such in all that has to do with pomp and grandeur, sensuality, greed and vanity. Like Robin Hood, he robbed the rich and fed the poor, but unlike Robin he despised both. He specialized in bluff and bluster, low cunning and intimidation, and by such means entrenched himself in power. This he retained for over twenty years by generous awards to faithful gangsters and instant assault on potential rivals, by having the wit to realize that laissez-faire in economics was played out, and above all by beating the drums of empire and deluding his countrymen with dreams of Roman eagles.

Fascism, as it evolved in Italy, tended to gravitate more and more to the central theme of nationalism; Italy, a power-state, first dominating the Adriatic, then the Mediterranean—the mare nostrum of Rome and of Fascist Italy. This was Italy's birthright and Fascism's destiny, to be won by daring, sacrifice and bloodshed. Women must play their part by breeding more intensively; boys must train themselves to hardihood by dangerous exploits; adult Italians, obedient to the Duce's orders and influenced by his example, must win battles for more wheat in Italy, must build larger and faster ships for Italy, must fill the skies with planes, must carry Fascism's flag into Africa, create an empire.

"Fascism is not an article for export," Mussolini warned. It was Italian and Roman. S.P.Q.R. the Duce painted on the street-cars of his capital city, Senatus Populusque Romanorum, the Senate and the People of the Romans. The mantle of heroic Augustus and of conquering Vespasian, it must be understood, was the exclusive inheritance of Italian bambinos; little French, German and British babies had no claim to it. And to do Mussolini justice, he was willing to exemplify in person Roman initiative and energy. Back and forth across Italy he dashed in fast motor cars driven by himself; in the battle of wheat he, sweating heavily, helped gather the harvest (before the camera). In Libya he erected triumphant arches and flew his own plane to dedicate them. The upclenched fist of Mussolini, his steel-helmeted head, his fire-darting eye and threatening gesture served notice on a wondering, perplexed and half-impressed world that Italy at long last was a great power— and that Fascism had made her so.

For years the world took it all too seriously, but the similar and much more dangerous disease in Germany and Japan received far too little attention. As a permanent solution for social and economic problems, nationalistic autarchy really had nothing to offer Germany and Japan: but the vista of a triumphant mastery of all difficulties by a return to the sword of Siegfried or a glance at the mirror of the Sun Goddess proved too great a temptation to sentimental Germans and to mystic Japanese. And because of that, disaster overtook the world!

First, Germany. What took place in that country had more serious repercussions than what happened in Italy. There were twice as many Germans, if we include Austrians, as there were Italians, and in every way much more highly organized. If they chose to run amok, wedged in as they were between French and Slav neighbors, the chances for European peace were indeed slight.

Nationalistic enthusiasm was an old habit of the Germans, particularly those who lived in that central and eastern core known as Prussia. And it must be remembered that both the Second German Reich, which perished in 1919, and the Third, which bit the dust in 1945, drew their fighting energy from this Prussian background.

From time immemorial the flat plains of north central Europe offered free passage to conquering hordes from further east. And always it had been a two-way passage, open also to crusading Teutonic knights, professionally engaged in wresting the South Baltic lands from pagan occupants and no less actively interested in securing those lands for themselves.

The military spirit born of these misty wars had served the Germans well in Frederican and Napoleonic days, and upon it Bismarck relied in making Germany a nation. Hitler had come from Austria, but as a wandering and homeless boy in Vienna it was the spirit of Prussia, fused with that of Wagnerian opera, which had caught his imagination. The platform on which he stood was labeled National Socialism, but when he spoke it was the adjective and not the noun he emphasized.

In 1933, with Hitler's elevation to the chancellorship, German nationalism stood on the threshold of a new day. It was a more dangerous type than any Europe had hitherto encountered. Expressions of Germanic racial madness dropped from the pen of Turnvater Jahn in Napoleon's time, as poisonous as ever dripped from Dr. Goebbels', and just as much bitterness was aroused in German hearts by Napoleonic tyranny as ever resulted from any injustice legalized by the Treaty of Versailles. But there was this difference: between Jahn and Goebbels intervened the Darwinian theory of evolution and the science of anthropology. Deductions drawn from the latter were woven into more nonsensical theories of race than anyone even dreamed in the early nineteenth century. Hypotheses which were regarded by German enthusiasts as plausible in 1914 were made mandatory by Hitler after 1933.

The quintessence of the accepted Nazi doctrine in regard to race, as elaborated in the primer of the Hitler Jugund, is that the white races may be scientifically divided into six easily recognized subraces, the Nordic, the Phalic, the Dinaric, the Eastern, the East Baltic and the Western. Unquestionable superiority in physique, morals and intelligence belongs to the Nordic. Not all Germans are Nordics, but most Nordics are Germans. Fortunately for the latter, the next largest element in their blood stream is the Phalic, closely resembling the Nordic and not very inferior to it; fortunately also, only 2 per cent of the Germans belong to the Western race, which has little steadiness and is not given to reason.

This curious notion, elaborately argued from selected data, helps clarify the first word in the Nazi slogan—"Blut und Boden." Blood, it seems, is something that is peculiarly sacred—that is, German blood. In the blood stream through the ages flow spiritual as well as physical qualities. The German blood stream has been polluted by Jewish blood; that must end. The German blood must be refined, purified. Only thus can it come to pass that the best shall rule, the true Nordic. Hitler, it was explained, had a Nordic soul.

Equally sacred was "Boden," German soil. It seems that all soil upon which Germans have lived in historic times is German soil, holy soil that must be redeemed. Much of it lay in southeastern Europe, in the Ukraine, and concerning this Nazi orators grew eloquent. Whether the land of northern Italy held by the Lombards was German Boden, they did not say, nor land upon which German babies were born in Brazil.

So much for the theoretical basis of Nazi ideology. Its elaboration was left to the party's pundit, Dr. Rosenburg, for Hitler was a busy man. The learned doctor of course did not invent all this. Some of his data was derived from Plato (the submerged continent of Atlantis whence sailed forth his Nordic heroes); some of it came from Gobineau, a Frenchman; some from H. S. Chamberlain, an Englishman and son-in-law of Wagner; and most all of it can be traced back to the days of William II and the Second Reich. But the point is that now it became dogma, held sacred by a political party that in turn was identical with the state. It provided an ideological foundation for a new type of nationalism, not based on geographic propinquity, language, culture, religion, or even traditional unity, but on biology.

England and France had troubles enough of their own in 1933 without worrying about Germany; relations between those two democracies were none too friendly, and leading politicians in both countries were pleased with the Führer's wordy assaults on Communist rascals who threatened Germany. To most Frenchmen and to most Englishmen he was more lunatic than dangerous demagogue, and if he made his own country a dyke to protect them from Moscow's Third International so much the better. By doing so, would he not also protect western Europe? Here and there the impending danger was seen, and even before Hitler became chancellor Winston Churchill warned the House of Commons that "these bands of sturdy Teutonic youth, marching through the streets and roads of Germany with the light of desire in their eyes... are looking for weapons...." But Churchill was regarded as a political firebrand and alarmist.

Lady fortune continued to smile on the Third Reich. For eight years, from 1933 to the invasion of Russia in 1941, unparalleled luck dogged the heels of history's greatest gambler, Adolf Hitler. Only once did the cards fail him. The murder of Dollfuss in the Hofburg in 1934 was his one misplay. Victory followed victory: his rearmament of Germany met no challenge; the Saar was restored to the Fatherland; the wehrmacht crossed the Rhine at Cologne and no hostile shot was fired; it marched into Vienna with flowers on its bayonets; it crashed through the Böhmerwald and the Sudeten mountains to occupy Prague, opposed only by snowballs. Hitler's laurel wreaths before 1939, except for a few technicians lost in Spanish practice, and a handful of Nazi aviators undergoing training, had come without bloodshed.

Little wonder that during these years the clinical thermometer of German nationalism showed a rapid rise in temperature; for Hitler was German nationalism personified, and his victories the yardstick whereby its greatness was measured.

In some respects the giant growth of nationalism in Asia was even more remarkable than in Europe, for aside from Japan (an exception to nearly everything) the roots of nationalism had been so choked with diverse cultural layers as scarcely to exist. That Turks and Persians, for example, after centuries of somnolent indifference, suddenly became not simply enthusiastic devotees of independence but also devout worshipers of half-forgotten or newly devised ancestral traditions was an astonishing and arresting fact.

More astonishing yet was the coming of nationalism to India, for here it really was something new. There had been a Turkey, there had been a Persia, but never known to history had there been an Indian nation. From remotest antiquity to the present there is no record of any single race, state or government that might truly be called Indian. There were cultures, dynasties, confederations, and even for a few centuries a Mogul empire; but none of them ruled more than a part of the peninsula.

The first beginnings of an Indian nationalist movement date only from the late nineteenth century. They were caused by the working out of Macaulay's proposal for university education along Western lines, whereby Indians became first acquainted with Anglo-Saxon traditions of liberty; by a rising Anglophobia, quite as much social as political, perhaps more so; and finally by the revival of interest in indigenous religious faiths, possibly a natural reaction to doctrinal emphasis on the part of Christian missionaries. Not, however, until the Russo-Japanese War of 1904-1905 was it necessary to take serious note of this nationalism. Hitherto it had been largely academic; now an Asiatic nation had defeated in battle a great European power for the first time in the memory of living man, a fact duly noted in Indian bazaars as well as in Chinese cities. Men spoke now of an India, a country which might govern itself; and to this talk the British, not wholly unresponsive, gave heed, as the Morley-Minto reforms suggest.

Came World War I, and wide publicity for Wilson's national self-determination. Once again the British countered by introducing the constitutional changes of 1919. Devolution became the order of the day, and the sanguine looked forward to an India safely ensconced in the British Commonwealth of Nations.

Such hopes were scarcely warranted by the course of events.

Those very qualities of mind and heart and character which enabled the British to win their empire so rapidly made it increasingly difficult for them to retain it. Personal integrity, hard work and courage in confronting danger, these qualities they possessed; but a sympathetic and imaginative sensitivity to how others felt was not common among them. Their education was too unfeminine. The children of their upper classes, trustees of empire in distant lands, were torn from their homes at an early age, compressed and silenced by Spartan custom in preparatory and public schools, a kind of hardening education alien to the give and take, the elasticity needed for meeting on a common level proud and sensitive folk of different background—and of different color.

Perhaps it would have been impossible under any circumstances to have won the permanent coöperation of the unfathomable Gandhi, but that of other Indian leaders like the Nehrus, father and son, might have been secured had a different spirit motivated Anglo-Indians. The latter, possibly, may not in their hearts have felt generically superior to the brown-skinned peoples they ruled and served, but they gave the impression they did.

Economic injustice there surely was in India, but that was true throughout the world. In the long run it is doubtful if it alienated the Indian public as much as did accumulated petty grievances, a cold and distant manner (frequently the result of mere shyness in upper-class Englishmen), an absence of good fellowship, exclusive clubs, the non-commissioning of Indians in the Indian army, the reserved compartment for the white traveler in railway coaches, the inclusion in the Indian budget of a handsome stipend for an Anglican bishop, and many other like matters. Constant pinpricks lead to open sores. The British found it almost impossible to live down the impression made by the Amritsar massacre of 1919, not so much because rioters were killed as because Indians subsequently passing through a certain street had to do so on their hands and knees. Humiliation sometimes cuts deeper than sheer cruelty, and so it came to pass that for these and other reasons a swelling tide of anti-British sentiment rose in India, and reached dangerous proportions when Japan struck at nearby Singapore and Burma.

Chinese nationalism is more important to us than Indian since the Nationalist revolution in China brought that country and Japan into a war which led straight to Pearl Harbor. Whether the Second World War commenced with Japan's invasion of Manchuria in

1931 or not is a moot question, but certainly the Pearl Harbor attack directly resulted from American sympathy and aid for fighting Chinese Nationalists.

From our Western point of view it may seem strange that a strong and gifted people like the Chinese should have been so slow to realize the advantage of national unity. "East is East, and West is West," might possibly be the explanation. It would be plausible if applied to India, but in the case of China, where objective worldliness has long held sway and men have not been primarily concerned with the inner life, we must look elsewhere.

The reluctance of the Chinese to follow Western precedents, one suspects, resulted largely from the fact that there were older and more civilized Chinese precedents. The Chinese were already a cultured people when Druid priests offered human sacrifices in English forests, and they very naturally regarded their own ways as superior to those of upstart societies. Loyalty to the family, to the clan, was part of the Chinese way of life, but loyalty to a mystic entity called the nation was alien to them. The respect paid to warriors was a barbaric custom which they had long outgrown. They were content with what they had; all they asked of the rest of the world was to be let alone.

But instead, Englishmen, Frenchmen, Russians, Germans, Americans and Japanese broke down China's isolation, forced their armed way into her cities, patrolled her rivers, industrialized her economy, scorned her traditions, lorded it over her people.

To this there could be but one answer. It was given by Dr. Sun Yat-sen, prophet of Chinese nationalism, hero and martyr of the new China. The power of the foreigner, wrote Dr. Sun, comes from his nationalism; we shall build one that is stronger. Only by cohesion and unity can we be free, and only by freedom can we find deliverance. We must be proud of our past, our literature, our architecture, our invention of writing paper, gunpowder, the compass; but only as a token of what we are capable of doing in years to come. We will modernize our country, knit it together by railroads, irrigate its deserts, drain its swamps, fertilize its fields, make sanitary its cities, purify its laws: and we shall do this by copying every worth-while principle and gadget the West can offer, whether political or power machinery, whether economic organization or Marxian ideas of social welfare. All these things we can do if we rid ourselves of alien control, concessions, treaty rights, spheres of influence, extra-territorial jurisdictions, all limitations on our sovereignty imposed by the foreigner.

Not all foreigners. The Germans were out of the picture after the Japanese expelled them from Shantung Province in World War I. The Russian Communists were sympathetic, and from them Dr. Sun obtained much needed assistance in drilling his diminutive Nationalist army, and to them he sent his most trusted lieutenant, young Chiang Kai-shek. The wrath of Dr. Sun was directed against those foreigners, to some extent Americans but primarily Britons and Japanese, whose factories were operated by cheap Chinese labor and whose banking and transportation monopolies spread over China like the tentacles of an octopus.

It was not, however, just the foreigner who blocked their path to national unity. Had that been so, Dr. Sun's task would have been easier. He had Chinese to contend with: lethargic Chinese, half-asleep, content with the good old days; wealthy Chinese, emulating the example of Europeans and Japanese, exploiting their own countrymen by the introduction of power machinery; prosperous landlords, well pleased with their inherited right to the soil of whole villages, fattening themselves on the work of tenant farmers; Chinese war lords, crude, rough, pugnacious village bullies who took advantage of the anarchy of the times to form private armies, whereby they gained control over whole provinces, fighting one another like dogs over a bone.

Finally, and unfortunately, the bulk of the Chinese people were illiterate, knowing nothing of the world of men beyond ancestral landmarks, utterly ignorant of government, legislature, constitution, independence, nationalism.

Dr. Sun's propaganda made headway slowly. He did not excel as an administrator, and for a season after the First World War his Kuomintang Nationalist party was confined to southern China. After his death it gained power rapidly. General Chiang Kai-shek, husband of Dr. Sun's sister-in-law, a wily, obdurate and brave commander, marched north, conquered city after city, moved his capital to Nanking and, as president of the Chinese Republic, was congratulated on having completed the unification of his country.

That unity, however, was open to question. Look below the surface of events. Go to Nanking in 1929. Past the ancient walls of China's old and new capital, past stone elephants marking the tombs of Ming emperors, out to the magnificent mausoleum prepared for the hero of the Chinese Republic moves a procession. The body of Dr. Sun Yat-sen is on its way to its last resting place. In attendance is Sun Yat-sen's widow, recently arrived from Moscow. She is asked to comment on China's progress under the auspices of her brother-in-law, Chiang Kai-shek. Surely the new boulevards, the shiny automobiles, the impressive buldings of the Kuomingtang government, the removal of China's capital from reactionary Peiping, and the seeming victory for all her husband stood for deserved commendation.

Madame Sun was not impressed. "I have noticed nothing," she said, "but the killing of tens of thousands of revolutionary youth who might some day have replaced rotten officials; nothing but the hopeless misery of the people; nothing but the selfish struggling of the militarists for power; nothing but extortions laid upon the starving masses; in short, nothing but counter-revolutionary activities."

Here certainly was no unity. If Madame Sun was right, her brother-in-law, the general, had betrayed the very cause for which her husband fought. And many Chinese believed that this was so. They were known to the Kuomingtang as Communists, and were considered such by the outside world and by themselves, a fact which gives a somewhat unfair color to their opinions. But they were without question leftists, whether real Communists or not, and they had been driven out of the Kuomingtang and mercilessly slaughtered by Chiang Kai-shek. Since they were very numerous, the unity thus far achieved in China was superficial.

Whether Chiang Kai-shek's political machine (the Kuomingtang) or the Chinese Communists more closely adhered to the principles of Dr. Sun, one cannot say. His final will and testament, solemnly read each week to the massed troops of Chiang Kai-shek as a religious credo, warned his people that they remain loyal to his teachings as found in his writings. But the latter are contradictory. In them he is both Marxian and anti-Marxian. His widow was partly right in believing that he had been repudiated; so also were his numerous in-laws of the Soong family in asserting that Dr. Sun repudiated Communism. The result was a profound rift, as yet unhealed, in the ranks of Chinese Nationalists. A new capital might shine and deceive the world. But this did not make a united country; not while millions of Chinese Communists bitterly hated the landlords protected by Chiang Kai-shek's government; not while hundreds of young student Communists (also good Nationalists) were being beheaded by his soldiers; not while war lords ravaged interior provinces and paid but lip service to the Republic.

Several of those provinces collectively were called Manchuria, an integral part of China but north of the Great Wall and originally the breeding ground of those stalwart Manchus who centuries earlier had conquered China far to the south and placed their dynasty on the peacock throne. Manchuria, nearly as large as France and Germany combined, had a population of some 30 million, of whom approximately 150,000 were Russians, 230,000 were Japanese, 800,000 were Koreans, the remainder Chinese. It is a rich land, both agriculturally and in minerals, particularly coal and iron. Although politically Chinese, Japan had certain specific economic rights in it, and political rights also, since boundaries between modern economics and politics cannot always be clearly marked. The Southern Manchurian Railway from Mukden south to Port Arthur was a Japanese enterprise which policed its lines for a considerable distance on both sides; the Liaotung Peninsula was leased Japanese territory; and Japanese business men and immigrants had many special privileges in regard to land and railroads under treaties forced earlier from an impotent China. Obviously Manchuria was destined to become a battleground should Japanese nationalism clash there with that of China.

From 1916 to 1928 a restless and ambitious Chinese, Chang Tso-lin, the Old Marshal, ruled Manchuria. In theory he took orders from the Republic; in practice he was his own master, heading several expeditions against Peiping, contesting with other war lords for that city, openly defying orders from Nanking. The Japanese wanted Chang Tso-lin to rule as their puppet and accept their "advice." This he refused, though he did declare his areas independent of China. Homeward bound from Peiping in 1928 he was mysteriously assassinated. The Japanese hoped that his son and successor, Chang Hsueh-liang, would be more compliant. They were to be disappointed.

The Young Marshal proceeded to identify himself and Manchuria with Nanking; he ran up the Chinese flag; he built a large arsenal at Mukden and enlisted what might become a powerful army. He not only made no obeisance to Japanese authority, he defied it. In accordance with treaty rights, no railroad could be constructed in Manchuria if it ran parallel to the Southern Manchurian and diverted traffic from it. Japan claimed this provision was violated. There were disputes concerning police jurisdiction, taxes, land laws. A clash was almost inevitable. The Southern Manchurian with its hotels, warehouses, and armed guards was a semi-autonomous power within a Chinese province. The Japanese had extra-territorial rights in Manchuria and that meant Japanese consular courts. The Chinese, fearful lest their land be bought by Japanese, tried unlawfully to prevent the latter from making purchases. Koreans accepted Chinese citizenship in order to purchase land, but the Japanese vetoed their change in national allegiance. There were innumerable disputes between Korean immigrants and Chinese farmers, with occasional bloodshed. A Japanese captain traveling in mufti was killed by a Chinese soldier while trying to escape as his passports were being examined. The Japanese said the Chinese lied, that the excuse was paltry, that the captain was murdered, that Japan was insulted. Tempers became frayed on both sides, in far distant Chinese seaports there were boycotts of Japanese goods, and in Japan the army circles made ready.

Came then the night of September 18, 1931, and possibly the commencement of World War II. Six Japanese soldiers patrolling the Southern Manchurian Railway south of Mukden heard an explosion and discovered, so they said, thirty-one inches of rail destroyed. They were fired on, so they said, from ambush. Before dawn a Japanese detachment, five hundred strong, attacked the Chinese barracks close to Mukden. Ordered not to fight and taken by surprise, 11,000 Chinese troops fled through the night. One regiment, cut off, resisted. Result, two dead Japanese, 320 dead Chinese. Simultaneously the Japanese army stormed the walled Chinese city of Mukden. Result, seven Japanese wounded, thirty Chinese dead, mostly police. Within six months Manchuria was under the thumb of the Japanese army and Japan launched a new state, Manchukuo, ostensibly free and independent but accepting protection and advice from Japan.

By so doing, the Japanese repudiated the League of Nations, violated the Nine Power Treaty which they signed in Washington in 1922 guaranteeing the independence of China, and snapped their fingers at the Briand-Kellogg Peace Pact to which they also were signatories. Their excuse was a triple one: it was not a war which they had started, only "an incident"; they had not annexed Manchuria, instead they had only enabled the citizens of that bandit-ridden country to declare their independence of China; and finally, the special status of Japan in Manchuria, made sacred by the blood of Japanese troops in the Russian war and legalized by treaties with both Russia and China, warranted their prompt and salutary intervention.

The first two excuses are so flimsy as not to deserve discussion. For the third there was much to be said, as the report of the League of Nations recognized. Japan did have economic rights in Manchuria, and was entitled to them, both on historic grounds and on those of necessity. Their maintenance, however, did not require an act of war. Japan was thus the first country, subsequent to World War I, to set completely at naught solemn agreements, in this instance triple agreements, to settle international disputes by pacific means. It might be argued that the Japanese did no more than Mussolini did when he bombarded Corfu in 1921. But Mussolini withdrew from Corfu; the island remained Grecian territory, and Italy stayed in the League of Nations. The Manchurian incident was different. From then on, from 1931 to 1939, a series of little wars raged with growing intensity in the Far East, in Ethiopia, in Spain, until in 1939 all were merged in one.

The flood-tide of Japanese nationalism was running strong, more potently than any conjured forth in China, or elsewhere in all the world. German racial theories in their ideological form are an invention of the late nineteenth century; those of Japan date from remote antiquity. German cultural and humanistic traditions, aside from military prowess, were numerous and strong; those of Japan were few and weak. Germans had tasted defeat in World War I; Japan enjoyed unending victory from her war with China in 1894. A comic-opera country to us, celebrated principally for cherry blossoms and geisha girls, it had nevertheless become all powerful in East Asia. The time had now come for the Yamata race to entrench itself in Manchuria, not only to secure raw materials for its industry but also to pave the way for future conquest.

We know something concerning the antecedents of the Japanese. Apparently they are racially Mongolian and Malayan, the fusion of immigration from the mainland of Asia meeting that from islands to the south. But that is not the Japanese theory. According to their earliest documents, the *Kojiki* and the *Nihongi*, both dating from the eighth century A.D., their origin is divine. Gods and goddesses appear on the bridge of heaven. The two youngest dip their spear into what is below and lift the spear. From it there drips down Japan. Concerning the descent of the two divinities to the earth, their incestuous behavior, the remarkable fecundity which gave birth both to islands and to divinities, the far from seemly behavior of the Sun Goddess, her present to her grandson of the sacred mirror, the sword and jewel string, and how his descendant became in 660 B.C. Jimmu Tenno, first emperor of Nippon, it is not necessary to write at length. What is of paramount importance is the popular acceptance of this power-legend in Japan. It has no parallel in Germany. No Nazi ever held that Hitler was Thor's distant grandson. But Hirohito is regarded as the 124th male descendant in the royal line from Tenno.

Faith in the divinity of the emperor and by inference in that of all his distant cousins, the Yamata race and all Japanese, is the cult of Shintoism, the cult of Japan. Buddhism blended nicely with it, since "the wantless beatitude" of Buddha did not contradict the Mikado's heavenly origin; Confucianism and Shintoism offer no contradiction, for did not the Chinese sage praise the good ruler and counsel obedience to him? Even Christianity was not banned by Shintoists, nor, for that matter, did Japanese Christians ban Shintoism. But whether it be cult or religion is of slight significance; what is important is the fiery patriotic propaganda which Shintoism energized.

The war with Russia showed its intensity. In that conflict the Russians took very few prisoners, and of one Japanese transport it is recorded that when torpedoed the troops on it jumped to their death rather than disgrace the emperor by surrender. To die for him was not simply a duty, it was an honor. Casualty lists did not bring bereavement in Japan; on the contrary they were the occasion for hanging out Japanese lanterns, for family rejoicing and much honorific drinking of saki.

By adopting with skill and readiness the Western tools of material power (technology in all its branches) Japan had defeated Russia. The secrets she had learned from the West were utilized for national advantage—in plundering Korea, in exploiting Manchuria. Were they the only secrets worth copying? Concerning that she was dubious, and for several decades she stood at the parting of the ways. Constitutional practices on the model of Bismarck's Germany apparently worked well, constitutional guarantees, political parties, even an extended suffrage. The emperor, Meiji, had proclaimed in the nineteenth century that "Old, unworthy ways and customs shall be destroyed. . . ." and again that "Knowledge shall be sought among the nations of the world. . . ." Slowly there had come seeping into Japan all kinds of knowledge, and not merely technological. There was talk of liberalism, individualism, Socialism, and soon of Communism. It was not simply machines, stiff collars and frock coats that were imported from the West; the yeasty fermentation of ideas prevalent there affected Japan as well as China and India.

In all three lands it brought revolution, but in opposed directions. That in Japan was a violent reaction against the Occident, a renewal of faith in antique and half-forgotten folklore, a refurbishing of ancestral shrines, and a hot-house cultivation of imperial grandeur and glory such as the world had not seen since the days of Alexander.

Two reasons explain why: fear lest "dangerous thoughts," once firmly seeded in the minds of the common people, might cloud the mirror of true patriotism and undermine the prestige of the military caste; and American insistence on excluding all Asiatics from her shores. Concerning the first, our evidence is scattered and hard to evaluate, but in regard to the second it is crystal clear. The valiant efforts of the Japanese to write into the Versailles Treaty a guarantee of racial equality and the way in which they were prevented from so doing by Woodrow Wilson is common knowledge. So also is the wave of bitterness that swept all before it in Japan when news of our exclusion act of 1924 reached her. It was not because we excluded foreigners but because we excluded Orientals *as such* that aroused the ire of supersensitive Japanese patriots who suspected the law was aimed primarily, not at Hindus or Chinese, but at Japanese.

The Japanese revolution was nonetheless real because concealed behind a smoke-screen of conventional parliamentarianism. The Japanese did not abolish their legislature; they simply reduced it, as Cromwell had done in England, to a sounding board for whomsoever the ruling caste in the army had selected as its representative. Strictly speaking, they were not Fascists in the Italian and German sense, since they had neither duce nor führer. Nevertheless the spirit of their institutions, recurring to their historic tradition, rapidly became more authoritarian than in either Italy or Germany. Up to 1935 there had been in Japanese schools a widely read textbook on government. In it Professor Minobe had portrayed the throne as an organ of government, somewhat as Burke had written of the British crown in the eighteenth century. Suddenly Minobe's book was pounced upon as seditious, a breeder of "dangerous thoughts." The author had insulted the emperor. The latter's status was God-derived, so far above all government that to consider it an integral part of a constitution was abominable. The book was forbidden, Minobe punished.

This trend in Japan toward authoritarian submission to what supposedly was the emperor's will, steadily gathered momentum from the Manchurian "incident" of 1931 to the outbreak of World War II. From the beginning it had, to our minds, a certain religious tinge. By the Lateran Accord Mussolini compounded certain disputes with the Pope, but the Duce made no pretense of being God's voice. In Germany Hitler was regarded by certain praying zealots as a kind of reincarnated Christ, but this was not true of even a majority of the Nazi party members. In Japan Shintoism grew steadily, the emperor reporting to the sacred shrine of his ancestors at Ise, deifying dead soldiers in solemn ceremonial, his faithful people convinced that the emperor himself fights, invisible, by their side. By the advent of the 1940s religion and patriotism were fused, a potent stimulus to action, a dangerous portent for the future. Autocracy became theocracy; a divine government ruled Japan, destined, so its adherents said, to rule the world.

THE LIBERAL HERITAGE OF THE NINETEENTH CENTURY

What was put to the test through the decade of the thirties was the liberal heritage of the nineteenth century. By 1939 this had been repudiated by four great powers, Italy, Germany, Japan, Russia, and by several smaller ones, among them Poland, Spain, Turkey, Greece. France stood at the parting of the ways. In the United States and the British Commonwealth that heritage was in danger, not so much because of open opposition as because those who proclaimed its validity were not sure in their hearts where they stood.

Superficially the liberal heritage might be expressed by two words, capitalism and democracy; words generally linked in the nineteenth century, not so much because the ideas they represented were necessarily inseparable as because capitalism and democracy advanced along parallel lines; the countries in which democracy staged its greatest successes being the ones where capitalism was most strongly entrenched.

There are many definitions of capitalism, none satisfactory to the historian. Production for profit rather than for use has too socialistic a tinge; the use of money to beget money is too scholastic, also faintly theological; the production and distribution of economic goods controlled by individual ownership, whether inherited or acquired, is one-sided and too favorable to the well-to-do. Capitalism is all these and more. Historically there is this to be said for it: our railroads, steamships and machines, our cities, schools, hospitals, and material well-being in general have come primarily from the surplus savings of many millions of capitalists, great or small. But even in the nineteenth century capitalism did not function smoothly, and in the twentieth it threatened to break up altogether. To write in 1946 that it is doomed is too rash a prophecy; to write of it as badly shattered in both theory and practice is but to tell the truth.

Capitalism and democracy were seen together, that is, if democracy be defined in political terms as the right of a majority of individuals to elect, to direct, and to cashier their rulers. Did that mean that they were interdependent, integral parts of a common whole, the sovereign national state? Mussolini condemned "plutodemocracies," and his attack is suggestive, but its implication is invalid if we widen our definition of democracy to include the right of everyone to participate in all decisions which affect his life. Any such definition carries with it a revolutionary change in, if not a denial of, the very bases of capitalism.

The liberal heritage of the nineteenth century, however, goes back of such concepts as capitalism and democracy, to the spirit which nurtured them, a spirit exulting in the individual, not sinner but sinless, conquering his environment through liberation from past superstition, the man liberated, a happy disciple of life on earth. This, of course, was not the nineteenth century alone. The eighteenth had proclaimed that man was born free. The nineteenth shifted the keynote but kept the tune. See, said this evolution-fascinated century, this glorious creature, man, struggling upward from the slime of the earth-dawn, marching forward through thousands of years to the magnificent present, destined, who knows in what future time, to harness the planets if not the stars. Here is the liberal vision; democracy and capitalism are but its servants.

Such a philosophy of life looked better in 1914 than in 1919. The

First World War undermined its foundations, tarnished its dream. Instead of reaching upward to the stars, men thought rather of the trenches, the mud and filth and horror from which they had recently emerged. A war fought to make the world safe for democracy had been won by the democracies, yet their victory did not fortify their faith. It crumbled and disintegrated steadily through twenty shabby years. The Marx-intoxicated Russians, though promptly discarding capitalism and dismissing democracy, kept faith in the optimism of the nineteenth century better than the Western men. The Soviets had no use for democracy as a form of government, but they did want more food and time to digest it, books, music, electric light for all, a program with democratic overtones.

Since nature abhors a vacuum and the mind cannot be emptied, man listened for a season to every prophet and to every semi-prophet. Followers there were of that massive-mind, Spengler, who in his *Decline of the West* argued that civilizations and culture, like trees, birds and mammals, were born, grew to maturity and died. Our own milieu, the Faustian, was dying and none could prevent its death. Some, preferring personal intimacies to civilization, cast anchor in the happy harbor of Dr. Freud of Vienna, whose researches in the dream-life of neurotics in certain cases did bring relief. Mussolini and others found a reincarnated Machiavelli in Pareto, mathematician, sociologist and economist in one, with his elaboration of the rôle of the élite, the human lions and foxes who fought each other endlessly for supremacy, the common herd participating in the fight but never reaping the rewards of victory. Still others paid dumb homage in Moscow's Red Square before the sepulcher of Lenin, strange combination of Marxian scholar, revolutionary rabble-rouser, and practical politician whose gospel of proletarian revolt made wealthy old dowagers of both sexes shudder from Pittsburgh, Pa. to the Riviera. Many Germans succumbed to mass hysteria, pathologically not dissimilar from the children's crusade in the Middle Ages. *Zusammenmarschieren*, to march together, that they knew how to do: the pied piper of Hamelin town come back to lead his children, now grown men, tough in muscle, with guns and tanks and planes.

Everywhere there was a tendency to follow strange new gods, or no god at all. For the most part men of letters were pessimistic. The one considerable poet of the period, T. S. Eliot, caught its tempo when he wrote *The Waste Land*, a reverie of futility, decay and death in London. Sad young writers dubbed themselves "the lost generation." Novelists like Proust in France portrayed a dying world. "We are always feeling with Proust," wrote Edmund Wilson, "as though we were reading about the end of something." A note of sickly despair pervaded most literature. In Thomas Mann's *Magic Mountain* there is charming and erudite discourse, but all the characters are dying of tuberculosis. The novels of D. H. Lawrence deal not only with sex, but with thwarted sex. The grandson of T. H. Huxley, Darwin's bulldog, Aldous Huxley, wrote brilliantly, but how different in tone from the letters and lectures of his buoyant Victorian grandfather; the theme is still science, but the implication now is disaster. Of Hemingway in America and of James Joyce in Dublin the same may be said. None can deny physical vigor to Hemingway, so much to his credit; nor to Joyce a lively imagination, profound learning, new literary modes artistically perfected; but both writers are without objective, the dynamism of the one, the lethal quality of the other pointing nowhere.

In both art and letters confusion reigned. Let standards be abolished; they were too static for "Brave New Worlds." But for new standards there were no new foundations, let alone superstructure, unless incessant and restless movement, both physical and mental, be considered such. Futurist artists, eager to break with tradition, tried to express speed by horses with twenty-four legs, tried to put dynamism in portraiture by multiplying eyes, ears, noses, or by joining them together. First jazz, then swing in music are indicative of the same surging desire to keep going—somewhere? The same motif is the clue to certain poets like Gertrude Stein and Ezra Pound. Instead of ignoring them as pure exhibitionists, as one is tempted to do, a kindlier judgment would be that they simply represent purposeless energy. Word-explosions certainly occur, if nothing else does. The mountains tremble, but not a mouse comes forth. There is nothing. Yet thousands of undergraduates have been hypnotized by Pound. He seems so bold, so forcible, such a superb rebel. But what would be substitute for the status quo; can it be a hurricane of words?

Did these men truly reflect the spirit of the interval between the wars? In a certain sense they did not; the average man and woman were too busy making a living and bringing up children to think of Gertrude Stein. Also, of course, what has been written is rather a verbal cartoon. Artists did continue to paint pictures which were recognizable as such; concerts of classical music were still attended and won universal hearing on the radio; Mozart did not die; few college professors read Joyce, and still fewer, Pound.

But their students read them; and their students rejoiced in swing bands. A cartoon is not a picture; its only function is to point to one thing and say it is significant. And it is significant that during these years of serpentine diplomacy, swelling armaments, augmenting totalitarianism, the general spirit of the democracies was not sturdy, self-reliant confidence. They did not know where they were headed, and many did not care.

The old liberalism of the nineteenth century lay moribund. Some, like John Dewey, pragmatic philosopher of the machine age, had ideas as to what should be done. He wanted to rebuild on the old foundation a fairer house wherein common folk by rational intelligence could so order their affairs and educate their young by intellectual processes alone that a Brave New World, in no ironic sense, would come to pass. Dewey did not reject liberalism and individualism, but rather sought to deepen and widen what they meant and give them communal values. The troubles of the world did not result from missing the trail for the city of man, but because progress was too slow. Dewey wrote with vigor, skill and acumen, stiffening the will and clarifying the vision of a good many young radicals. Other philosophers, like Jacques Maritain, argued that terrestrial justice and human liberty could only be found by a renewed vision of the city of God. This did not mean an aloofness to bread, butter, rent, clothing—quite the contrary. "If Christians," Maritain wrote, "who live by faith in their private lives, lay aside their faith when they approach the things of political and social life, they must be content to be towed like slaves in the wake of history."[1] Maritain urged action, proclaimed the sword of the civil power an essential adjunct to the Cross Universal, and stiffened the will and clarified the vision of a good many young conservatives.

Most men, however, in the Western democracies paid little heed either to Maritain or Dewey. Unaware of the lateness of the hour, blind to the handwriting on the wall, hardly aware of what was happening in eastern Asia, wistfully dreaming that Hitler and Stalin might destroy one another for our benefit, the democracies remained distrait and impotent until Dunkirk and Pearl Harbor exploded in their ears.

[1] Jacques Maritain, *Freedom in the Modern World* (New York, Charles Scribner's Sons, 1935), p. 152.

2. INCIDENTS INTO WARS: ETHIOPIA, SPAIN, CHINA

BY THE early thirties the restless, seething passions of *genus homo* had burst the thin crust of civilized restraint, brought man closer to world catastrophe. The dark days of 1931 in Manchuria fore-shadowed it; but two combatants are requisite for war, and the Japanese inundation of northeastern China cannot strictly be called war. But from 1935 on, rifles cracked, shells whined, planes dropped their eggs, burst into flame or scuttled off for new death loads, and Mars was crowned "Lord of All."

One hardly would have expected Italy, the least of big Fascist powers, to lead the death parade. The racial nonsense of the Japanese and Germans never gripped the Italian people; they were too cynical. But Mussolini and his gang fed on violence. Unlike the Nazis he could not satisfy their appetite by killing Jews: there were not enough in Italy; he could not satiate it by slopping castor-oil down the throats of his countrymen: none were left openly to oppose him. Draining swamps and reaping wheat meant heavy sweat; his preference was for blood—not too much, for he was crafty. So he bethought himself of Ethiopia, a death trap for Italy in 1896, but perhaps as good a theater as might be found in 1935 to display his Black-Shirt prowess. Since the Duce's will was law in Italy, the high honor of leading Europe all the way back to the beast-man belongs to her.

Ethiopia, to use the original Greek word for what had come to be known as Abyssinia, was not easy to penetrate. Italian Somaliland on the south, Italian Eritrea on the north, outflanked the rugged land where Haile Selassie, Negus Negesti, King of Kings, held sway. But those two colonies, dreary wastes of low-lying sand and desert, were over seven hundred miles apart. Furthermore, neither could be approached from Italy without passing through the Suez Canal and paying big transport charges which Italy must first drop into the purses of hungry French and British stockholders, and that only by permission of his Britannic Majesty's government who might violate international law some day and close the canal.

A railroad, French owned, ran from French Somaliland to Addis Ababa, Ethiopia's capital. Aside from this, transportation depended almost exclusively on camels, horses, and the humble ass. The country measured some 350,000 square miles, but much of this lay low, was completely arid and so torrid that it was shunned by whites and blacks alike; another large part was equally impossible because of rugged mountains and Alpine climate; and upon the remainder, a high plateau good for grazing and certain crops, lived most of the Ethiopians.

They numbered well over 5 million, part Negroid in race, part Semitic, as Herodotus noticed long before the Christian era. At one time Ethiopians had conquered Egypt and had extended their rule across the Red Sea, deep into the Arabian Peninsula. They had a civilization of a sort, a Christian tradition (somewhat faint), a written language in which some books had been printed, a society strictly feudal, the local ras or lord possessing inherited powers of high justice and low, making formal acknowledgment only of the overlordship of the negus or king.

As the First World War raged in Europe, civil war was waged in Ethiopia. From it emerged victorious Ras Tafari, of the royal line of Solomon and the Queen of Sheba. Ras Tafari from regent became king (1928), and soon proclaimed the empire (1930), himself the emperor, named Haile Selassie, Power of the Trinity.

His relations with imperial European neighbors, British, French, and Italian, at first were excellent. The British were only interested in Lake Tana, source of the Blue Nile in northwestern Ethiopia; the Italians wished to link their two colonies by a railroad running north and south to bisect the French railroad, and this proposal won French, British, and Ethiopian blessing. The Italians seemed particularly intent on playing the good neighbor; in 1923 they sponsored Ethiopia's admission to the League of Nations, despite British warnings about anarchy and slavery still extant there; in 1928 they signed a treaty of "perpetual friendship" with the Negus, in whose lands Italian "archaeologists" and "botanists" now abounded.

Seven years later (1935) the frowning Duce ordered his armies to the kill. He proposed to conquer Ethiopia. A frontier dispute near some well in southern Ethiopia, or in northern Somaliland (the frontier between the two had never been accurately delimited) was the pretext; but what was the cause? Haile Selassie was not trouble-some. Quite properly he sought to refer this minor incident to the League of Nations, and recalled to Mussolini's attention the treaty of 1928. But Mussolini refused to arbitrate; he demanded apologies, salutes, commenced military preparations in his two colonies on a minor scale and at home on a larger one.

There were rumors of oil and metals but perhaps all he sought was blackmail. The French already had ceded 450,000 square miles of the Sahara south of Libya to Italy, and Britain had made terri-torial concessions to Italian Somaliland. Perhaps still more might be had from France and Britain? More probably, however, the Duce was intrigued by the easily won victories of the Nazis and Japanese. Japan had defied Geneva in the matter of Manchuria, Germany in that of rearmament. Both countries had resigned membership. The League, always weak, now was weaker. Presumably it would be safe for him to take a fling at northeast Africa.

Throughout the winter and spring of 1935 Italy mobilized; trans-ports heavily loaded passed the Suez, the soldiers on them receiv-ing little portraits of the Duce inscribed, "Better live one day as lions than a hundred years as lambs."

The British advised Haile Selassie to deal directly with Mussolini, not to wait for the League. Pierre Laval, slimy and unwashed French politician, intimated that France had no interest in defend-ing Ethiopian independence. The American public was amused rather than indignant. Haile Selassie's removal for safe-keeping of what he said was Moses' ark had news value in this country; but no one cared what happened to Ethiopia except racially conscious and imaginative American Negroes who saw in this distant black emperor a champion of their people.

Spring gave way to summer; and at Massua in Eritrea while Italian soldiers unloaded endless tons of war matériel, the British made money selling them drinking water, the Ethiopians selling coffee. Anthony Eden, in his capacity as minister to the League of Nations, went to Rome, returned discomfited. The Duce was said to have told him that "Ethiopia is as important to Italy as British imperial conquests were to Britain in the time of Raleigh." In the United States Secretary Cordell Hull voiced what he called "con-cern." The Italian embassy replied that it was "surprised" at the "concern"—both routine moves in the endless diplomatic game. In Rome Mussolini informed American correspondents that "The invasion of sovereign rights has been in process for centuries. . . . Take the United States; how did you push your frontier back?" And all the while in Ethiopia Haile Selassie waited. He did not dare mobilize, a word his tribesmen would not understand. If he gave orders to that effect, the guns would go off of themselves and he would be held responsible for war.

There was nothing for the Negus to do except appeal to the League of Nations, and he did so three times. The League could do nothing without the coöperation of France and Britain, both semi-paralyzed with fright lest Mussolini make overtures to a fast-rearming Germany. Therefore the League stalled for time, appointed a committee. It finally reported that no one was responsible for the frontier incident at Ualal. Whereupon the Ethiopian representative at Geneva said, "Since nobody is to blame then there is no cause for war." But the Italians promptly demanded that the League expel Ethiopia and, to prove the unworthiness of that country for membership, they passed around pictures allegedly taken in Ethiopia, showing Haile Selassie's subjects eating human flesh, drawing blood from babies for ritualistic purposes. One ras, they claimed, was known to have made a living torch out of a prisoner, and lepers haunted the streets of Addis Ababa. There were no pictures of the Fascist outrages in Libya.

In September, 1935, Geneva acted; the League would assist Ethiopia in organizing schools, in supervising public health and the administration of justice; and France and Britain would cede to her a corridor to the sea, provided she in turn made territorial concessions to Italy. The Ethiopians were willing to discuss this proposal; the Italians refused. They were waiting for October and the end of the rainy season which turned the red soil of Ethiopia into soap-like paste. With 200,000 soldiers about to attack they looked for a quick victory.

October came, rains ceased, Italians crossed the border, Haile Selassie's war drums sounded. From mountain to mountain, from valley to valley they reëchoed. In a thousand cow villages chiefs donned their lion-maned collars, warriors grasped rifles, muskets, spears and shields, the women their cooking pots. The Ethiopians advanced en masse to war.

On came the Italians with whippet tanks, trucks, airplanes and poison gas. Within three days they had revenged their defeat of 1896 at Adowa; a week later the holy city of Aksum was in their hands. The tribesmen opposed them as best they might, sniping at their columns from behind crags and rocks. But they had no jungles in which to take refuge, and one cannot fight death from the skies with a rifle.

The dark-skinned warriors had no chance. In all of Ethiopia there were but twenty-four anti-aircraft guns, seven commercial planes, one truck. Apart from the bodyguard of the Negus, his soldiers never had been drilled. They simply took to the field, men, women and children, loyal only to their local rases, who might or might not be loyal to Haile Selassie.

Only one thing stayed the enemy—communications. In ten days the Italians were seventy-five miles inside Ethiopia and had to build roads. Accordingly, "This people of heroes," to quote the Duce, "of poets, saints, navigators, colonizers," became an army of road-builders. And so they continued throughout the remainder of 1935, sweating more at their highways than at killing—except, that is, for air raids in which the Duce's son-in-law, Ciano, vied with the Duce's son, Vittorio Mussolini, in spraying poison gas on villages.

Meanwhile, action of some sort by the League could no longer be delayed. Fifty nations out of fifty-three voted that Italy was the aggressor, that sanctions be taken, Austria, Hungary and Albania alone voting in the negative. But Laval and Hoare, for France and for England, saw to it that these sanctions were purely economic, and that oil was not on the list. To put it there, Mussolini stated, would mean war.

The British public was angry at the Duce but not the British government. There was rumor of intervention. The most powerful of British ironclads were stationed at Gibraltar. The British Mediterranean fleet steamed away from Malta to Alexandria, lest it be caught by Italian bombers at its island base. And much publicity was given to Italian motor-boats, each armed with one torpedo, manned by men so brave that none even thought to return alive from the attack. But these were only gestures for public titillation. The French did not go so far. Irritated, and rightly so, at the Anglo-German naval pact, made earlier in the year without consulting Paris, they gave Mussolini the green light. The Duce had their measure; also that of Prime Minister Baldwin and Sir Samuel Hoare, British foreign secretary, men determined there be no war involving them.

Meanwhile, Mussolini grew impatient, sent Badoglio to command

his troops in northern Ethiopia, ordered the campaign speeded up.
Badoglio struck south. The Ethiopians, weary of guerrilla tactics,
their only hope, fought him boldly at Tembien. Here they were
crushed. As Badoglio wrote, "Against the organized fire of our defending troops their soldiers, many of them armed only with cold
steel, attacked again and again in compact phalanxes, pushing right
up to our wire entanglements which they tried to beat down with
their curved scimitars." [1] By March, 1936, the war was won. Graziani, sweeping north from Somaliland, was well on his way to
Harrar in central Ethiopia; disaffected rases here and there were
throwing in their lot with the Italians; the Gallas, Mohammedan
tribesmen, were lukewarm in their loyalty to the Negus; and the
only obstacle confronting Badoglio now was geography, Addis
Ababa being two hundred miles distant and no roads worth the
name leading to it.

Haile Selassie still had his imperial guard, the tribesmen who
recognized him as their ras, and with it he marched forth in April.
They fought at Lake Ascianghi. From five in the morning until
seven at night his warriors charged the Italian lines. They were
hurled back. A few hundred Italians lost their lives and several
thousand Ethiopians. "The Gallas," the Negus wrote his wife,
"helped us only with shouts."

Soon Italian planes circled over Addis Ababa. The Negus thought
somewhat of retreating to the southwest corner of his empire, then
yielded to advice and escaped by train to French Somaliland. May
4, 1936 he embarked on a British cruiser en route for England via
Palestine. May 5 Badoglio marched into Addis Ababa, and May 8
the Italian army from Somaliland joined that from Eritrea. Aside
from sporadic sharpshooting the war was finished.

So also, to all practical purpose, was the League of Nations. For
a short time it had seemed as though it might be resuscitated. Laval,
the Frenchman, and Hoare, the Englishman, went so far in subservience to Mussolini that they brought on a healthy reaction, particularly in Britain. In December, 1935, they signed a pact whereby
Ethiopia was to acknowledge Italian annexation of most of the good
land in northern Ethiopia and at the same time grant Italy extensive economic rights in southern district—all in return for a corridor to the sea and recognition of sovereign rights over what was

[1] Pietro Badoglio, *The War in Abyssinia* (New York, G. P. Putnam's Sons,
1937), p. 66.

left of their country! This betrayal of the League was too much for the British stomach. Baldwin had to dismiss Hoare and recall Eden, friend of collective security and honest dealing.

In March, 1936, Eden went to Geneva to tighten sanctions. Before he had a chance to do so, Hitler, with Mussolini's tacit approval, tore up the Locarno pacts which Germany voluntarily had signed, invaded the Rhineland. Confronted with this Nazi coup d'état, all thought of black folk was forgotten. A month later, resigned to German garrisons on the Rhine, Britain again became interested in Ethiopia. Before advancing on Addis Ababa the Italians had sent a column toward Lake Tana and that came pretty close to England's imperial backyard. And there were other grievances against Badoglio's soldiers. Eden went to Geneva that they might be aired. This time he informed the League that 250 tons of Italian poison gas had been shipped through the Suez Canal in four months. "The British government," he said, "feels that what is done today in Addis Ababa is likely to happen tomorrow in Paris or London if Italians are allowed to commit atrocities with impunity." The Italians did not deny the gas; they said they used it in just reprisal for dum-dum bullets made in Britain. There was fiery recrimination, but it was now too late to save Ethiopia.

In May, Italy annexed that country and in June, Eden informed the House of Commons that it was useless to continue sanctions. Again there was fierce discussion, this time in London. But to what purpose? Ethiopia no longer lived, and the League of Nations as an instrumentality of world peace lay moribund. In a second great crisis it had failed. It might, perhaps, be argued that it was not feasible to stop Japan in 1931, but that did not hold true of Italy in 1935-1936. All that was necessary then was for Britain to close the Suez to Italian shipping and for France to concentrate troops on the Tunis-Libyan border. Mussolini was no fool. He had no allies anywhere; he was not yet on terms with Hitler; and even if he had been, the Nazis would never have risked a fight in 1936. Rather than lose Eritrea, Libya, and Somaliland, the Duce would have knuckled under. But now he had made laughing-stocks of France, Britain, and the League of Nations, all three.

The League, half-dead, was to suffer one more humiliation. In July, 1936, Haile Selassie betook himself to Geneva. Eden tried to prevent his speaking, but the majority agreed with de Valera of Ireland when he said, "I am unwilling that there should be even a discussion of his undoubted right to speak." The Negus spoke gently but at length. His closing sentence is worth remembering. "God and history," he said, "will remember your judgment."

SPAIN

As war died down in Ethiopia it broke out afresh in Spain. Eighteen days after Haile Selassie's valedictory the garrisons in nearly every Spanish city seized their arms and Spaniards leaped at each other's throats.

They had been doing so rather noticeably since the establishment of the Republic five years earlier. About the only thing they agreed on was that they were Spaniards, and many living in Catalonia in the northeast would not, without qualification, have assented to that, preferring to call themselves Catalans. In all that concerned economics, education, religion, the army and politics this proud, quick-tempered and essentially individualistic people differed. Some wanted Alfonso recalled from exile; others, known as Carlists, longed for a monarchy on the eighteenth-century model, but had no use for the fugitive Alfonso; a few, growing in numbers, pinned their hopes to a Fascist dictatorship somewhat on the Italian model; conservative Republicans were more concerned about law and order than interested in reform; liberal Republicans were alive to grave injustices rampant in Spain; Socialists were numerous, devoted to democracy, both social and political; Anarchist-Syndicalists, more numerous yet, hated church, army, Socialists and all authority. Here and there in the larger cities were a few Communists who, when not fighting one another, vented their spleen quite impartially on church, republic, Socialists and Anarchists alike. Add the intense regionalism of the Basque provinces in the north and of Catalonia in the northeast, and the fact that almost every Spaniard either adored the Roman Catholic Church or despised it and we have Spain.

The problems which confronted the Cortes or parliament were baffling. Wind-swept arid uplands comprised the greater part of the Iberian Peninsula and were agriculturally of little use except for grazing. Choice earth nearer the sea bore good crops, but the peasants there did not own the land. Agrarian unrest was widespread; but could the solution be found in scientific irrigation and drainage, in coöperative farming as in Russia or in peasant proprietorship as the Anarchists demanded? Most thoughtful Spaniards agreed that the Church hierarchy and the monastic orders were too wealthy and too powerful for their own good; but was it desirable to separate church from state, and if so, how? Should the Church retain its property; should the monastic orders control education, should they be forbidden all teaching, should they be driven out of Spain? What of the army, that stronghold of the aristocracy which time and again for over a century had fomented and crushed rebellions? Could army officers be made subservient to a mere republic, to civilian politicians shorn even of such tinsel as clung to the memory of monarchy?

Baffling but not insoluble were these problems for men conditioned to adjustments, compromises, acceptance for the time being of the lesser of two evils. But Spaniards were not thus conditioned: blood-letting with murder rated a trifling offense, was more in line with their tradition than parliamentary debate; unlike Italy they had never had a Cavour; their middle class was neither large nor influential, their aristocracy the most unenlightened in western Europe, their peasantry and their urban proletariat more passionate and trigger-happy than even that which Lenin had charmed in Russia.

It cannot be said the Cortes altogether failed. It passed laws dealing with mass illiteracy, even if it found little money for schools and few teachers to instruct. Something was achieved in lifting the weight of ecclesiastical prerogative from the back of the people, even if many poor parish priests as well as Catholic laymen were needlessly offended by sequestration of property, by removing the crucifix from schools, by exiling the Jesuits on the somewhat specious pretext that in addition to the three monastic vows they prescribed a fourth—loyalty to the Pope, a charge which figured in our presidential campaign of 1928.

But these things were not done peacefully. No sooner was the Republic inaugurated than reactionary army officers led a revolt against it and failed. Then, when the elections of 1934 gave the rightist party a majority, the radicals took their turn with fire and incendiary bombs. A Catalan republic was proclaimed at Barcelona, only to be crushed. The miners of Oviedo stormed police barracks with dynamite and were slaughtered by Moors brought in from Spanish Morocco. In 1936 the elective tables were turned again, this time in favor of the left.

Sobered by the repeal or emasculation of the reform laws, angered by rightist terrorism, the left had formed a Popular Front composed of Anarchist-Syndicalists, Socialists, Communists and middle-class liberals. Syndicalism on the Sorel model and anarchism more reminiscent of the hell-roaring Bakunin than of gentle Prince Kropotkin had taken deep root in Spain, and the red and black flag of the Anarchist-Syndicalists was seen more frequently than the red flag of Socialism. The Anarchist-Syndicalists in some instances were pure idealists, puritanically minded, zealous for the destruction of all government, convinced that all crime and wickedness emanated from authority. Many of them, however, were neither pure nor puritan, but ruffians emerging from the backwash of society, quick at rifle, poniard, bomb. Anarchist-Syndicalists hated Socialism almost as much as they did Christianity. Socialists, strongly entrenched in the unions, carried on a three-front war against rightists, Anarchist-Syndicalists and also Communists, inferior in numbers to the other groups and themselves split by ideological strife, Trotsky Communists denouncing those who upheld Stalin and vice versa. For Communists, Socialists, Anarchist-Syndicalists and white-collared liberals, mostly professional men of the middle class, all to agree upon a common platform, one of mild reform, and to contest an election as one party, was no less than a miracle. Nevertheless they did and they won the election; they obtained a decided majority in the Cortes. Legally and constitutionally the Popular Front was entitled to recognition as the government of Spain.

But the army had no intention of letting it do so. A secret plot of officers came to fruition in July, 1936, with open rebellion both in Spain and Morocco. Two large southern cities, Cadiz and Seville, immediately fell to the rebels, and an important one in the north, Burgos. Simultaneously in Morocco the Foreign Legion declared against the Republic and enlisted heathen Moors. In an incredibly short time these soldiers, assisted by Carlist militia, swept over a large part of western Spain. With approximately 90 per cent of the army favoring their revolution, and with a coalition government of diverse and disparate factions at Madrid, the likelihood of immediate success was excellent.

Three things thwarted it; the loyal navy, the rage and courage of leftist Republicans, utterly indifferent to death, their own or anyone's else, and the inpouring to Spain of volunteers from foreign countries, who saw their war in its true light, one waged as much against Hitler and Mussolini as against the Republic's enemies.

The navy was not of much account, but it did delay transfer of Moors from Morocco, thus granting the Republic a slight breathing spell. Naval officers favored the rebellion, but the crews mutinied, and until one old battleship was put out of commission by Italian planes it was only possible to send the ferocious Moors to Spain by air, and only then because German and Italian planes were available.

The respite was brief, but long enough to incite the proletariat, to arm it after a fashion, and to appeal to the outside world for help. In Barcelona, Madrid and other cities swift vengeance was taken on all suspected of anti-Republican plotting. Many churches were destroyed, many priests and some nuns killed, and scenes reminiscent of France in 1792 were all too common until the government put an end to unauthorized killing. Meanwhile, workmen, miners, trade unionists, peasants, and intellectuals started *de novo* to learn the art of war.

It was learned, after a fashion, in the hardest of schools—actual combat. The rebels under General Mola advanced south from Burgos against the capital and were repulsed in the mountains north of Madrid. Mola, unable to rush the capital and worried about communications, retreated, joined forces with General Franco, marching north with his rebel army from Seville. At Badajoz in western Spain the rebels, or Nationalists, as they preferred to be called, retaliated by summary executions for the bloodshed in Madrid. They now had sealed the Portuguese border and secured for themselves an entry of war matériel through Lisbon from Germany. Recognizing Franco as supreme commander, they were by September within forty miles of Madrid.

Franco might, perhaps, have taken that city then, had he not first relieved his partisans in the Alcazar at Toledo. The Alcazar, a military academy in which about one thousand cadets, soldiers, and rightist sympathizers had taken refuge, was immensely large and strong, the walls several feet thick, the cellars veritable catacombs. For weeks it had been under attack from the not too skilful Republican militia. The defenders had little water and less food, and would speedily have starved had they not had horses and mules to slaughter. Too weak to take the offensive, they watched their fortress gradually crumble around them, pulverized by incessant machine-gun fire, by bombs from the air, by mines sprung from beneath their cellars.

The very chaos, into which the Alcazar had been turned helped the defenders. Their enemy could not charge through it; Republican tanks could not get over the high-piled debris. Meanwhile a tin trunk dropped from the air brought a bit of food and Franco's promise to march to their relief. This he did, lifting a dramatic six-week siege.

Meanwhile there dashed to the rescue of Madrid several thousand volunteers from Catalonia, hotbed of Spanish radicalism. Likewise came foreigners to enroll in the "International Brigade." Consisting at first almost exclusively of French, German and Italian Communists, they felt that in fighting Franco they were fighting Fascism at home. The brigade quickly grew until it numbered over 20,000. One section of Americans was called the Abraham Lincoln Brigade. Another came from Canada, the "Mac-Paps," short for MacKenzie-Papineau; a third came from Belgium. Russians, Hungarians, Poles, Cubans, Yugoslavs, and even Ethiopians joined. The Brigade had originally been organized by the French Communist party, and the volunteers who flocked to it from all over the world did so largely through the agencies of the Third International. But this was not exclusively the case. Men joined for different reasons, some out of hatred for Fascist oppression in their homeland, as in the Thaelman Brigade of Germans and the Garibaldi Brigade of Italians, some because they had the itching foot and wanted excitement, a few aviators because they were well paid and needed the money. Almost all were good fighters and proved it in November and December, 1936, as they fought hand to hand with the Nationalists for University City in the western suburbs of Madrid, where laboratories, libraries and classrooms alternately were captured by Franco's Moors and the International Brigade, without whose assistance it is doubtful if the capital could have been saved.

The civil war by the end of 1936 seemed pretty much a draw. The Republicans, now referred to as Loyalists, still held Madrid, the eastern half of Spain, and a few cities in the northwest. The rest of the country was ruled by the rebel Nationalists, and General Mola, in storming the Basque cities of San Sebastian and Irun, had cut the main gateway to France. The Loyalists had received planes from Russia and much encouragement from the Third International everywhere. On the other hand, Italy and Germany not only recognized the Nationalists as belligerents but as the "legal" (that is, Fascist) government of Spain, and some 14,000 Italians and 10,000 Germans were units of Franco's army.

1937, and the fortunes of the Loyalists sank perceptibly. Madrid held out. Franco tried to capture it from the southeast but the International Brigade was there to thwart him; the Italians tried to capture it from the northeast but close to Guadalajara in the mountains they suffered a great reverse, the worst since Caporetto in the First World War. Thousands of Mussolini's Black Shirts fled in panic leaving behind much booty. Those captured said they had volunteered to go to Spain because they were told that jobs were to be had there; they did not know there was a war! The remnant of this Italian army was rescued by Franco's Moors. Madrid's record was indeed superb. Despite never ending bombardment, falling houses, mangled bodies, that city resisted nearly three years, long after all hope had vanished elsewhere. But Madrid was not Spain. In the south the Nationalists drove eastward to capture Malaga on the seacoast where Italian intervention stayed General Llano's hand in killing Loyalists. In the north they carried the war to the Basques who, while loyal to the Republic, had organized an autonomous local republic with its capital at Bilbao on the Bay of Biscay. Bilbao held out many weeks, its inhabitants living largely on sea gulls. Unable to reduce it, the Nationalists turned their wrath against Guernica, a small town twelve miles distant. Here men, women and children were killed indiscriminately as German planes machine-gunned fugitives, a fact attested to, and protested against, by Catholic priests. In north central Spain the Nationalist tide engulfed Saragossa and then swung south and east, threatening to cut off Madrid and Valencia (new capital of the Loyalists) from the revolutionary volcano ever in eruption in Catalonia. By the end of 1937 a good three-fifths of Spain was in Franco's grip.

Nor was this the worst; the European countries and the United States as well guaranteed Franco's victory. They did this by an embargo, theoretically enforced against both combatants, actually enforced against Loyalists alone. England, supinely confident that British wealth and British investments in Spanish industry would cause Spain to lean their way in the future, irrespective of the war's outcome, did not much care who won it. Upper and middle-class England and France did not favor Fascism but they thought it preferable to Communism; and the Spanish Civil War they officially

and superficially interpreted as simply Whites *vs* Reds. Decidedly
less than a third of the Loyalists were Communists, but it is true
that a Communist color was given to the Loyalist cause, partly
because of help given by Russia, partly because as the war approached its second year the Loyalist government swung further
to the left, supplanting a middle-class premier with Largo Caballero, a leftist Socialist who wore overalls, in whose cabinet Socialists
and Communists combined had a majority. The working class was
more sympathetic toward the Loyalists, particularly in France. The
British Labor party, in which right-wing Socialists predominated,
would have no dealings with Communists. Also it was bitten with
the virus of pacifism. In France cultured Premier Blum was a Socialist and the Popular Front which he headed had been joined
by the Communists. But Blum, gentle pacifist, was an ineffective
lion in domestic reform, a tardy sheep in foreign policy.

Blum, with British approval, proposed a cordon sanitaire be
drawn around Spain, that neither arms nor fighting men be admitted
to that country, a most extraordinary act, since it denied to the
constitutional and legal government of Spain its right to defend
itself by buying arms. A non-intervention committee was then set
up in London. England, France and twenty-five other states joined.
Russia, at first recalcitrant, finally agreed not to help the Loyalists.
Germany and Italy cynically and openly broke their word, continuing to send men and munitions to Franco after they had promised
to desist from so doing. In consequence, Franco got more and
more assistance from without, the Loyalists less and less. Had it
not been for this Italian and German backing he could not have
won.

1938, and the Loyalist cause was lost. Hotly contested battles,
internal strife in both camps, Nationalist as well as Loyalist, and
farcical pretense of "non-intervention" characterized the year. But
by its end the handwriting on the wall was as distinct as any read
by Daniel in Babylon. Italian and German duplicity, French and
British timidity, and American muddle-headedness had done their
work. Weight of metal and swiftness of planes were not to be
denied. The Republic of Spain was to die.

Fierce was the fighting around Teruel and Belchite, apex of the
Nationalist triangle pointing seaward from north central Spain.
Twice the wrecked towns changed hands, only to be lost as Franco's
armies sweeping seaward reached the Mediterranean, cutting all

land communications between Madrid and Valencia on the one hand and Catalonia on the other. The Loyalists, however, had no thought of yielding. Madrid still was joined to Valencia by rail, and could be reinforced with troops if not with arms from without. Barcelona, now the Loyalist capital, was in communication with Valencia by sea and with the rest of Loyalist Spain by air. The Loyalists still thought they had a chance to win, and did secure a stay of execution. Along the banks of the Ebro, which formed the boundary of Catalonia, Franco's lines were strung out thinly. The river was in flood, bridges destroyed; but first in rowboats and then on pontoons the Loyalists crossed, spearheaded by the remnant of the International Brigade. They came in force; they marched inland to high ground at Gandesa; and now for a few weeks it almost seemed as though they might turn the tables on the enemy, drive a wedge between his regiments on the Mediterranean and those in the north and west.

The Loyalists did not, however, have sufficient momentum to go farther, and soon were under attack from swarming Fascist planes. Fighting on open ground and having no planes of their own, they were slowly driven back to the Ebro. In the autumn Franco's men crossed it and soon were in the heart of Catalonia. Barcelona was besieged. Hitler had to try out his bombers, and that doomed city received a strafing from the air even more severe than Madrid suffered. As the year closed Franco was at its gates. He might have been there sooner had his own followers been united. Not only did the Requetes (Monarchists) dislike the Phalange (rightists in favor of a streamlined Fascism) but both disliked Germans and Italians. "Beasts of prey," one of Franco's own generals tersely described them, and here and there in his army there were mutinies forced by dislike of collaboration with the foreigner. Particularly hated were the Germans who insisted that the best hotels and the best bawdy houses be reserved for exclusive Teutonic use.

Unfortunately for the Republic, internal dissensions among Loyalists exceeded those in the enemy's camp. Only in moments of great crisis did the various radical factions work in harmony. In one respect Anarchist-Syndicalists and left-wing Communists saw eye to eye; both objected to centralization of military authority and put their faith in militia. Largo Caballero had to stop in the middle of the war to suppress their excesses in Barcelona. This led to Caballero's resignation. His successor, Negrin, time and again was com-

pelled to follow the official (Stalin) line even though he was no
Communist. He knew it was essential for purposes of morale to
support La Passionaria, famous woman orator, ardent Loyalist—
also ardent Communist. The Communists were well disciplined;
they provided the backbone of resistance. But they did cause
trouble: "To them winning the war meant winning it for the Communist party, and they were always ready to sacrifice military
advantage to prevent a rival party on their own side from strengthening its position." [1] And since this was so, there were even deeper
fissures in the Loyalist ranks than in those of the Nationalists.

1939, and a spark of life still flickered in the Republic. The
government moved while there was time from Barcelona to
Fugueras in the extreme northeast. It could not go farther and
remain in Spain. Barcelona surrendered. Premier Negrin flew to
Madrid. To his horror he discovered that his generals proposed to
follow Barcelona's example. Negrin would not have it, and in
Madrid pro-war Republicans and anti-war Republicans knifed one
another as only Spaniards can. Negrin fled. Franco entered Madrid
March 28. Within twenty-four hours all resistance ended and the
executions began.

The consequences were what the world deserved. Ethiopia
killed any hope of united action by means of the League of Nations.
As a matter of form, the Spaniards made several appeals to the
League, and the assembly of that body always could muster a good
majority in favor of urging Germany and Italy to withdraw their
troops. No move was made to impose sanctions; to have done so
after Ethiopia would have been too ironic. The real decision never
rested at Geneva and everyone knew it. Only England, France,
Russia and the United States could have done anything to prevent
Fascist and Nazi war lords from plunging their sword into the
living corpse of Spain.

Why did those countries not act? As far as the United States is
concerned, the facts are evident: we were so green about Fascism
as really to believe it merely an uncouth way of stemming revolution; we knew little of Communism save from experience with the
utterly unprincipled political behavior of American Communists
which made us unsympathetic to any cause in Spain or elsewhere
which Communists praised; and finally, so righteous was our in-

[1] From Gerald Brenan, *The Spanish Labyrinth* (New York, 1943), p. 326. By
permission of The Macmillan Company, publishers.

dignation at profits pouring into the pockets of munition manufacturers, and so snugly complacent were we in our transatlantic
security, that we considered it the height of morality to refuse to
sell guns to anyone. The Loyalists had four billion gold dollars to
buy with; they were the de jure and de facto government of Spain;
unless there was a state of war proclaimed they had a right to buy
our planes and guns. We were careful not to declare a state of war
in China vis-à-vis Japan, and we sold freely to both sides. But in
Spain we did declare a state of war, embargoed all exports to the
Loyalists.

Russia is not so easy to understand. That country began by helping the Loyalists and ended by withdrawing her support. Stalin may
have argued that a Loyalist victory was not necessarily a Communist one, and since Communism was his meat and drink, why
risk good planes in Spain? The treason trials then being held in
Moscow may have made him cautious. The kow-towing of Britain
and France to the Nazis in Munich may have convinced him that
Britain and France would gladly see him embroiled with Germany.
Whatever the reason his decision was hands off.

As for France and Britain, both countries knew that Spain was a
testing ground for Nazi tanks, field guns and Stuka dive-bombers,
for psychological warfare that would have made Machiavelli wince.
France had fought a war in 1870 at the mere threat of a German
ruler south of the Pyrenees. Now German planes and engineers
were there as well as on the Rhine. The British knew that Italians
boasted of the Mediterranean as their mare nostrum, knew that the
Spanish island of Majorca commanded the western end of the Middle Sea, knew that Gibraltar was easy to assail by land, knew that
Spanish Nationalists would demand its retrocession.

Although well aware that these things were so, the British were
willing to go any length to keep Mussolini outside Hitler's tent.
They seemed to think this could be done by shutting the other eye
as Italian infantry poured into Spain. True, when their own cargo
ships were torpedoed off the Spanish coast one after another by
mysterious submarines, unquestionably of Italian origin, they bared
their own bulldog teeth and called for an international patrol
against piracy. Italy asked to join and did so; no more ships were
sunk by torpedoes; bombing sufficed. The war was about over.
Toward the end, the Italians were quite reasonable. If the Loyalists
would send the International Brigade back home, then the Italians

would withdraw an equal number of Black Shirts. The International Brigade was dissolved, its members shipped over the French border. The Italians were generous and withdrew a large number, some 10,000 men. But from 20,000 to 30,000 Italians still remained with Franco. Still, to Neville Chamberlain, now prime minister of England, this did not appear extraordinary.

The end of March, 1939, and the guns ceased firing in Spain—except for shooting condemned Loyalists. The next month Franco signed an anti-Comintern pact with Fascist Italy, Fascist Germany, Fascist Japan. And Hitler had learned by actual war the strength and weakness of his army's weapons, by actual practice the impact of high explosive bombing on undefended cities.

CHINA

1937, and a third "incident" was in the making. At long last in the Orient the Chinese really began to fight Japan. They were not to let their guns cool for eight years. The Fascist steamroller which crushed Ethiopians in 1936, which creaked to final victory in Madrid in 1939, bogged down in China. The distances were too great, the Chinese people too resilient, too determined.

Simply to exploit Manchukuo did not satisfy Japan. Within a year her hand stretched south and east to Jehol, a Chinese province directly north of the Great Wall, famous for opium. General Tang, war lord, made a show of resistance, but confessed he did not know the whereabouts of his own "army." February, 1933, and Japan's flag flew over Jehol. May, and the Chinese Republic recognized the inevitable, gave up not only Jehol but promised to demilitarize north China directly south of the Wall (the Tangku Truce). Promptly came further nibbling. Five northern provinces of China, including Chihli where Peiping was located, were made autonomous through Japanese pressure (1935) and subsequently Chihli was subdivided, the eastern part, including Peiping and Tientsin its port, placed under a régime still more detached from Nanking, even more subject to Japanese pressure than the rest of the northern provinces. And as this happened, the Japanese continued relentless pressure on eastern Mongolia, early in 1937 declaring Cahar Province the autonomous state of Mongokuo under the protection of Manchukuo.

Japan's ultimate intentions are matter for speculation. But years before the Manchurian incident, one Baron Tanaka drew up a secret memorial to the throne full of suggestions inimical to the world's repose. The gist of it was that the conquest of the United States was vital to Japan; that to conquer the United States, China must first be conquered; to conquer China, Mongolia must be secured; to secure Mongolia, Manchuria must be brought under Japan's sway. The authenticity of the document embodying this program is open to question. What gives it verisimilitude is that Japan proceeded for more than ten years as if according to the Tanaka plan: first Manchuria, then Jehol and eastern Mongolia (they stopped further depredations in that area when Russia showed her teeth), then China, and finally Pearl Harbor. This at least is evident. The Japanese thought north China ripe for the plucking. Into their controlled port of Tientsin they poured their manufactured products, paying no attention whatsoever to the Chinese tariff. Once landed, these commodities, including large quantities of opium, were openly distributed throughout the five northern provinces. China lost revenue and lost "face." The Japanese called the tune; the Chinese puppets danced, paying no attention to their technical superiors in Nanking.

Chiang Kai-shek saw these things with heavy heart; but there was nothing much he could do about it. He did not have behind him a united country. The Chinese revolution which established the republic was both national and social. In its former aspect it meant China for the Chinese, and drive out the invader; in the latter aspect it was a revolution "against the landlord, the tax-collector, the money-lender and the grain merchant." Chiang Kai-shek and his Kuomingtang party were in a quandary. They had a grave agrarian problem on their hands, to make decent the livelihood of the peasants. On the other hand, if their régime was to prosper it seemed to them essential that foreign bankers be not antagonized, that Chinese entrepreneurs be encouraged to increase their capital. None of this could be done, they feared, if the taint of Communism was attached to the Kuomingtang.

Rightly or wrongly, Chiang Kai-shek came to the conclusion that his first task was to crush the social revolution in his own country. That meant leading Kuomingtang armies against Chinese Reds rather than against Japanese. This had been his policy since the death of Sun Yat-sen, but now in 1933 he planned carefully, stepped warily. This time it would not be a raid but extermination.

The center of Red strength lay in the province of Kiang-si in the southeast where the Communists had a régime of their own, supporting their Red army as we did in 1776 by confiscating the property of conservative landlords. That army Chiang Kai-shek proposed to capture, not merely to defeat, by surrounding it with a network of blockhouses.

The plan was about to succeed. The Red army was in desperate plight. There seemed to the Communists to be but one chance of salvation, to abandon Kiang-si altogether, to burst through the iron ring and retreat thousands of miles to the far northwest where they could unite with other Communists on terrain difficult for Chiang Kai-shek to penetrate, and where they would be close to Outer Mongolia, whence help might be had from Soviet Russia.

October 16, 1934, some 90,000 started on this journey, destined in history's annals to surpass the retreat of Xenophon's Ten Thousand. This was no ordinary military campaign. It was a migration of men, women and children seeking security and freedom in distant lands. The Communists loaded everything they had from printing press to machine tools on donkeys, wheelbarrows, and their own shoulders as they forced their way in and through Chiang Kai-shek's blockade.

At first they headed like an arrow, straight northwest, but in so doing ran into the superior forces of the Kuomingtang. They turned sharply south and east and entered Yün-nan Province on the borders of Burma. A diversionary thrust at Kunming, its capital, sent Chiang Kai-shek scurrying to its defense. The Reds then turned almost due north, keeping well to the west of Chungking. They had a few days start or else they never could have crossed the upper Yangtze River. Beyond it lay the Tatu River, flowing through deep gorges. Their destination still lay 2,000 miles ahead. Before it could be reached, seven mountain chains had to be crossed, among them the Snowy Mountains, 16,000 feet in elevation from which Tibet was visible. Their line of march stretched out fifty miles; hardly a day passed without sanguinary encounters either with wild aboriginal tribes or with Kuomingtang soldiers striking at their flank or rear. Their numbers shrank to 45,000, but soon other detachments joined and finally no less than 100,000 were said to be on the march. They had to pass through Lololand, held by Chinese-hating Lolos whom they conciliated by presents of food and speeches. The Great Grasslands came next, low swampy fields covered with slimy weeds.

The Reds approached the borders of Tibet, fought the wild Mant-zus, and finally reached the province of Shensi near the Great Wall. In a year's time they had covered between 5,000 and 6,000 miles.

To Shensi flocked radical sympathizers from all over China. Again these so-called Communists had a régime of their own, an army, newspapers, schools. They were bitterly hostile to the Japanese, now not far away, but they also had no respect for landlords, confiscating surplus grain, driving out money-lenders, dividing the land into small holdings. It was a revolution inside a war and surrounded by clan feuds.

Kuomingtang was much annoyed. The Japanese said they were in China to protect that country against the Red menace, and they offered to help wipe out the Communist pests. That was the last thing that Chiang Kai-shek wanted and so in 1936 he despatched another army against the Reds. It was led by the Young Marshal, Chang Hsueh-liang, who, driven from his capital in Mukden by the Japanese, had become a Kuomingtang general. The Young Marshal not only did not supress the Reds but was accused of fraternizing with them. To investigate these rumors Chiang Kai-shek flew by plane to Sian, Kuomingtang headquarters. Strange events followed. The Young Marshal and his officers kidnapped their own generalissimo that they might persuade him to open a common front with the Red army against Japan. Chiang Kai-shek begged that he be killed; his wife flew by plane to Sian; and then back by plane to Nanking went the Generalissimo, wife and the Young Marshal, who asked most humble pardon for his offense. The tragi-comedy was not without significance. Kuomingtang concealed for the time being its enmity toward Communism and the Red army. The hatchet was not buried but put aside, as China made ready to oppose the aggression of the "black dwarfs" from Japan.

1937 in the Far East, and the "fear of Japan sickness," hitherto so prevalent in Nanking began to evaporate. Chinese officials in Peiping plucked up courage and beheaded many smugglers of Japanese opium. There was an incident at a bridge where a Japanese soldier was said to have been killed (he was reported to have appeared the next day). Japan poured troops into Tientsin. They marched on Peiping. In quite unusual manner Chiang Kai-shek demanded from Japan both apology and indemnity. "If we allow," he said, "one inch more of our territory to be lost we will be guilty of an unpardonable offense against our race." This did not prevent Japan from taking Peiping and driving south against the Chinese forces. But this time the latter fought. And thus, informally, commenced a war which broadened continuously until it merged in 1941 with World War II.

Chiang Kai-shek's troops had been drilled by German officers and by this time knew something of the art of war. On the other hand, they were poorly equipped. Czechoslovakian cannons did not fit German gun carriages, nor could French ammunition be fired from British rifles. The war was no surprise but it came ahead of schedule, and the Chinese were not ready for it. The same could not be said for the enemy. Konoye, premier of Japan, dripped honeyed words to the effect that Japan wanted no Chinese soil, only the co-operation of Nanking in crushing Communism—that world menace. But the quickness of Japanese action belied these soft assurances. The armies of Nippon drove the Chinese south of Peiping and Tientsin, and doubtless would have kept right on in the immediate conquest of north China had it not been for anti-Japanese demonstrations in Shanghai.

That all-important entrepôt of imperial foreign trade was China's greatest seaport. A brief but most bloodthirsty fight took place there in 1932, when the Chinese boycotted Japanese goods in retaliation for the Manchurian attack of the preceding year. A punitive force of Japanese marines was defeated by the Chinese XIX Route Army, and Japan to save "face" had to send heavy reinforcements. Since, however, the XIX Route Army was officered by Communists, it received no support from Chiang Kai-shek and the Chinese were compelled to withdraw. Now, five years later, came more serious fighting. An "incident" in which a Japanese officer was killed by a Chinese sentry brought to Shanghai both the army and the navy of Nippon. Chinese planes bombed most unscientifically, doing more damage to civilians than to Japanese, but Chiang Kai-shek's German-trained soldiers fought stubbornly and well. The slum suburb of Shanghai was wrecked, and what the Japanese planned as a skirmish turned out to be a battle of world-war proportions lasting many weeks.

It took the Japanese three good months to clear the enemy from the interlacing network of canals, ruins and rivers behind Shanghai, and not until well into November were they able to force their way up the Yangtze Valley toward Nanking. Chiang Kai-shek promptly moved his capital up-river to Hankow and against the advice of his German specialists tried to defend Nanking, which by the middle of December was forced to capitulate to massacre.

The Japanese armies in the north found it relatively easy to scatter their enemy on the flat plains of Chihli; but when they struck toward the mountain passes in the west they found themselves stoutly withstood by the VIII Route Army, pride of Red China. General Chu Teh, commander, had had long experience in dodging Kuomingtang; now he was to dodge the Japanese. He fought on the defensive, dividing his soldiers into many small detachments so the element of surprise might make up for lack of matériel. His Reds seldom had more than twenty rifles per hundred men, but they did excel in the manufacture and use of hand grenades. Though by the end of the year the Japanese had dug deep into Red China, it was still possible to carry on partisan war behind the enemy lines, occasionally within gunshot of Peiping.

Japan, meanwhile, having signed an anti-Comintern pact with Germany and Italy, felt fairly safe from European interference, and shortly after was to feel just as safe so far as the United States was concerned. To be sure, our facile sympathies were volubly pro-Chinese. Our markets had been sensitive to cheap Japanese goods. Our many missionaries, educators and doctors in China agreed that the invader sank to the brute level, not simply in his treatment of captured soldiers but in his bestial behavior toward women and young girls. The undeniable case histories of those who sought refuge in our hospitals in China aroused our wrath. "The Spanish Fury" of the sixteenth century was matched again and again in a dozen Chinese cities. But our wrath was one thing; our willingness to do anything about it something else! Here and there women pledged themselves not to buy Japanese silk stockings, and money was subscribed for hungry Chinese orphans. That seemed the upper limit of American aid.

President Roosevelt in a speech in Chicago (October, 1937) tried to wake up his dozing countrymen to the lawlessness sweeping Europe and Asia. But Roosevelt's effort got more brickbats than roses. He drew an analogy between world affairs and infectious diseases, and intimated that a quarantine might be the answer to those countries engaged in breaking world peace. But most Americans thought the word *quarantine*, thus used, rather silly. One year earlier Congress had passed a strict neutrality act whereby we professed to seal ourselves off completely from foreign war.

The President's speech was seen by many as setting aside the spirit of that law. Even American leftists and liberals were displeased. They attacked the President for not doing justice to Loyalist Spain, but when he made a friendly gesture toward Chinese patriots their courage shrank to zero.

The popular reaction in America to Roosevelt's suggested quarantine made pleasant music in the ears of Japan. This might be the opportune moment to take the measure of America, to see if any real danger could threaten Nippon from the transpacific republic. It is difficult to find any other explanation, except private adventure, for the smashing of our gunboat, *Panay*, on December 12, 1937. This little ship in the Yangtze River was clearly marked with the American colors. Yet she was strafed four times by waves of Japanese bombers before she was sent to the bottom, and survivors were machine-gunned as they tried to hide among the reeds on the river bank. The Japanese government apologized, paid indemnity promptly, and it is not fair to assume that the Japanese people, as such, were pleased by this act of war. But the Japanese army found out what it wanted to know: that the Americans were not really enraged by the *Panay* affair; that great numbers of us thought an American warship had no business in Chinese waters accompanying American tankers belonging to private American firms; and that American citizens should stay out of war zones or take the consequences.

Roosevelt was powerless to check the rising power of the Rising Sun. He did refuse to proclaim our neutrality laws applicable to the Far East, and this he could do since the Japanese had refused to admit they were waging war in China. But in all other respects he was at the mercy of an isolationist Congress. Japan had violated the Nine Power Treaty which she signed at Washington in 1922, guaranteeing the status quo in the Orient, and the Kellogg Peace Pact which she signed later, together with almost every country on the globe, outlawing war; but when our State Department made the slightest move to implement these international agreements it was accused of complicity with "the international intriguers of Geneva," that is, the League of Nations. The isolationists even tried to go farther; they almost succeeded in gaining the approval of the House of Representatives for the Ludlow amendment which would have deprived Congress of the right to declare war except in case of actual invasion of the United States. This was an oblique

way of hitting at the President, and was so understood not only in
this country but also in Japan. It was an indirect way of saying to
all and sundry that it would be fairly safe for venturesome countries to defy the warnings of our chief executive. Yet the amendment was only defeated 209-188, and that too within one month
of the sinking of the *Panay*.

The Japanese offensive continued through 1938 and, as far as
concerns strategic places occupied, was eminently successful. The
conquest of rich Shan-tung, already begun, was completed, the
Kuomingtang general in command there being beheaded by Chiang
Kai-shek for cowardice. Canton, far to the south, fell to the victorious Nipponese, thus cutting off one more port through which war
necessities might find their way to China. And finally in October
Hirohito's warriors captured Chiang Kai-shek's second capital,
Hankow, far up the Yangtze from Nanking.

The Chinese, however, gave no sign of yielding. Again they
moved their capital, this time several hundred miles further up the
Yangtze Valley, beyond the Ichang gorges, all the way to Chungking in western China. China had lost most of her railways, most
of her cities, most of her seaports; but not more than a quarter
of her land had been overrun and even this the enemy did not
hold securely. Railways in Japanese hands were always in danger
of being cut by fast-moving guerrilla bands. Some 800,000 Japanese
troops in China were insufficient to control even that part of the
country supposedly subject to their jurisdiction.

In 1939 the Japanese kept advancing, but at slower tempo; they
tightened their blockade of the Chinese coast; they captured
Nan-ning in the southeast, thus severing rail connections between
Yün-nan Province and French Indo-China; they occupied the large
island of Hai-nan in the Gulf of Tonking, a convenient drill ground
for the invasion of the Philippines; and they sent their planes,
swarm after swarm, up the Yangtze Valley to smash and to ter-
rorize Chungking.

Surely the Chinese would now submit, and some few did, among
them a member of the Kuomingtang executive committee who was
appointed a puppet ruler of China. But most Chinese, whether
Kuomingtang or Red, stayed in the fight. Their wealth, their coal,
their iron, their rich delta lands, their factories were to the east,
and more particularly in the valleys of the Yellow River and the
Yangtze—the latter easily navigable for the Japanese navy to Han-

kow and beyond. But why not transfer in one great mass migration both people and the equipment for their livelihood to western China, beyond the reach of the invader; pick up bodily everything which willing hands could lift, machinery, steel rails, looms, forges, printing presses, libraries, laboratories? They could not take everything, but they could and did take much, prepared to trade space for time, prepared for a much harder life, but as resolute for liberty as we were at Valley Forge.

The Japanese having tested the United States in the matter of the *Panay*, thought it just as well to try out Russia. That country had proved amenable when asked to sell her interests in the Chinese-Eastern Railway, and the Russian Bear had not growled when Japan signed the anti-Comintern pact. Confronted as she was by hostile Germany on her western borders, by treason trials at home, the Russians, perhaps, might not feel disposed to defend their land in the far distant East Asia. The Japanese thought it was worth while finding out.

Not far from Vladivostok and at the corner where Korea, Manchukuo and the Russian Maritime provinces meet are certain wild and desolate hills known as the Changkufeng Heights. Soviet forces had fortified them, asserting they were Soviet territory; Japanese troops carried them at the point of the bayonet, asserting that they lay within the boundaries of Manchukuo; then Stalin's soldiers swept back, recovering a part of what they had lost. Action ceased; neither country declared war; both seemingly were content with the status quo. The next year, 1939, the Japanese tested out the Russians in another area, this time on the borders of Outer Mongolia, the greater part of Inner Mongolia by this time having been absorbed by Japanese-controlled Manchukuo. The Russians had a military alliance with Outer Mongolia and the Japanese, apparently, were curious to discover whether the alliance was real or not. So a considerable battle was waged with tanks, artillery, planes. It lasted ten days, and the Japanese retreated licking their wounds. Casualties on both sides exceeded 18,000.

It might seem that this was war, or that war would follow. But this was Asia. Stalin certainly did not want to be caught between wars on two fronts; Japan found Russia stronger than she suspected. It might be just as well, the Japanese thought, to wait for Russia to be softened by European enemies. Japan could then move in on Siberia as she had done in 1918.

Meanwhile The League of Nations, belatedly and timidly moving, appointed the inevitable committee which suggested the inevitable conference. Germany and Japan, no longer members, were invited to attend; both declined, as did Italy. Mussolini had already expressed his opinion. After the quarantine speech of the President, the Italian ambassador called at the Foreign Office in Tokyo to announce "Italy's support in Japan's self-defensive campaign in China," and the Duce himself snorted, "The speeches of spinsters and the sermons of archbishops make me laugh." Chamberlain was more dignified. "It certainly would be premature," he cautiously stated, "at this stage for me to commit this government to any particular course of action." American public opinion, it is true, grew steadily more anti-Japanese. But since deeds count for more than words, Tokyo was more impressed by the refusal of Congress to fortify Guam than it was by expressions of sympathy for China.

In Ethiopia, in Spain, in China three little Fascist wars had won three little Fascist victories. Though far apart in space and fought on different continents, in spirit, method, purpose and significance they were the same. In each instance they stood for the defeat of democracy, the triumph of force, the denial of collective security. So close were they in time and meaning to the demise of Czechoslovakia and Poland in 1939 that they may justly be described as the opening campaigns of the Second World War.

3. WAR SPREADS, AUSTRIA, CZECHOSLOVAKIA, POLAND

As Benito's weary Black Shirts scuffled through the dust of Addis Ababa, goose-stepping German soldiers crossed the Rhine. The war was on in Europe as well as in Africa and Asia, though not recognized by all for what it was. As in the *Iliad* the gods deceived Father Zeus by drowsy slumber, so now they blinded Frenchmen to their government's incredible folly. In Berlin, Schacht, finance minister, Von Neurath, foreign secretary, Von Blomberg, commander of the wehrmacht, all opposed the Führer's rash adventure. The French could have arrested it easily. They needed no help from others. Even after a week the invading Germans numbered only 90,000. Back across the Rhine and fifty kilometers east was where they belonged by the Locarno Treaty (1926), and where they had agreed to stay; it would have been a simple matter to have driven them there. In fact they rather expected this rebuff, their own withdrawal.

Once Hitler had set the Locarno pacts at naught, the way was open down victory's long avenue to Stalingrad on the Volga. Country after country now fell before his armor. When Menelaus led his warriors on the Trojan plain the gods divided, Poseidon aiding the Greeks, Aphrodite rescuing Trojan Paris. But now a different Paris was to get no help from Olympus, the heathen gods backing Nazi Germany for six good years.

AUSTRIA

Hitler's first conquest was Austria—a bloodless winning. The Austrians, he knew, were powerless against him. Russia would not fight to protect a Fascist régime in Vienna, one which had shot down Socialists in cold blood. In France Hitler's Judas, Otto Abetz, had mesmerized the French so completely that many thought Germany their country's friend. The Cagoulards, a secret society, hooded like the Ku-Klux-Klan, secretly was storing ammunition wherewith to strike down the Republic. Ministry succeeded wire-pulling ministry on the banks of the Seine, and parliamentary government reached a new low—even for France. In Britain the Tory party, firmly in the saddle, had a domestic policy which made sense; but its handling of international affairs would have disgusted Pitt or Disraeli. Neville Chamberlain, prime minister, would not have Churchill in his cabinet, and Anthony Eden was forced out of it because he told the truth about Mussolini. Between Germany and Italy a new and beautiful friendship had arisen. Hitler supported the Duce tacitly in Ethiopia and openly in Spain. It was now his turn, and the pay and the prey was Austria.

The tragi-comedy performed there in the spring of 1938 set a political pattern soon followed in Czechoslovakia, Poland, and elsewhere. First from without the border of the Reich come loud cries of anguish from excellent, oppressed, browbeaten Germans. Then from within the Reich the Führer of all Germans responds to the appeal, promises to set his blood-comrades free. Next the chief of state of the oppressor régime is summoned to Berchtesgaden, there to be reproached, intimidated, and third-degreed. Promises are made, promises are broken. Orders to march are given; German soldiers with speed and thorough organization swarm over the offending country; racial comrades fall into one another's arms goose-stepping happily the while, and a new *Gau* (district) is taken to the bosom of *Das Dritte Reich*.

This hijacking procedure worked like oil in Austria and Czechoslovakia, and all but succeeded in Poland. Youthful knights of the backward cross belligerently defied city fathers in Vienna and a dozen other Austrian towns. They were jailed; they asked for mighty Germany's protecting arm; their pleas were heard. Hitler ordered a command reception for the Austrian chancellor at Berchtesgaden and the latter did not dare decline. He came back to Vienna, fulfilled his promise, released his Nazi prisoners, appointed two Nazis to his cabinet. The rest was foreordained, since one of the new ministers controlled the gendarmerie. Anti-Semitic and pro-Nazi riots followed, and within a few days the streets of Vienna were radiant with Nazi tanks, Nazi guns, and a smiling Führer, while the low heavens were luminous with Nazi planes. Hitler's triumph in the land of his fathers was complete. After April, 1938, there was no more Austria.

CZECHOSLOVAKIA

The Czechs had watched with anxious eye, as well they might, the absorption of their southern neighbor into the German Reich. Not only were Nazis to the north of them and Nazis to the south of them, but within their own borders was a clamorous German minority, the redemption of which might be sponsored any day by Adolf Hitler. That minority had received more consideration than any other in the postwar world. It had full parliamentary representation and equal educational opportunities—in fact, there were more German secondary schools in Czechoslovakia in proportion than there were for Czechs. On the other hand, that German minority had cause for complaint: public officials were generally Czechs, and minor officials, such as postmen and ticket agents, were apt to pretend they did not understand German. Many great estates in pre-1914 Czechoslovakia had been owned by German landlords who were dissatisfied with the compensation paid them when after the war the lands were subdivided among the peasants. More important yet, the condition of German workingmen in Czech industrial districts was deplorable. The Czechs were not responsible for the world economic depression of the 1930s, but they might have been more generous in relief to the stricken areas. At one time there were nearly a million unemployed in this little country, and over half were Germans!

Until 1935 most of the Germans in Czechoslovakia coöperated with the Czechs in carrying on parliamentary government, but in that year Konrad Henlein's *Sudetendeutsch Partei,* intransigent and disaffected, captured 60 per cent of the German vote. This party, the SdP, was not originally allied with the German Nazis. It did, however, stress German principles: hatred of democracy, devout obedience to a führer—Henlein—and racial particularism. The SdP's demands now increased, one of them being "full liberty for Germans to proclaim their Germanism and their adhesion to the ideology of Germans," and another a demand that Czechoslovakia should renounce its treaties with France and Russia, the former calling for the military support of the Third Republic should Germany threaten invasion, the latter promising Russian aid, provided France aided the threatened state first. Neither of these demands could safely be granted by the Czech majority; to accede to the first would invite open propaganda against democracy in a democratic state; to accede to the second would make Czechoslovakia defenseless in case of attack.

War was narrowly averted in May, 1938. A frontier incident resulted in the death of two Germans; Hitler promptly cut off negotiations, hastened troops to the border. Czechoslovakia as promptly mobilized and rushed 400,000 men to the German frontier. France affirmed her support of Czechoslovakia and that meant that Russia must follow suit. Britain agreed to support France, and Hitler withdrew his troops.

But he did not change his intentions, nor did the Czechs their resolution to fight for their country. What did take place during the four succeeding months was the betrayal of Czechoslovakia by France, aided and abetted by England.

Czechoslovakia was by no means defenseless in the summer of 1938. She had a good army, a mountainous frontier, defended by a Maginot line reputed stronger than even the famous line of that name in France. Near Prague were the strategic Skoda munitions works, the largest in all Europe, owned by a resolute people, protected not simply by their natural frontiers but by the pledged might of France. In addition, Czechoslovakia was a member of the Little Entente, and both Yugoslavia and Rumania were sworn to aid her. True, Yugoslavia might stand aside for fear of Mussolini, and Rumania was not a dependable ally. But the Rumanians presumably would at least permit the passage of Soviet troops through their territory to aid the Czechs if attacked. With France, England, and Russia behind them it seemed improbable that Mussolini would give any active aid to Hitler in occupying Prague.

Nevertheless, the British and the French between them opened the mountain passes to the Bohemian plain, permitted Nazi troops to pass through unopposed, and thus made sure of a war in which they would not have Czechoslovakia as their ally, and Hitler would have Skoda.

The feeble and inept behavior of Britain and France during these last six months of 1938 is incredible. It began when the British sent Lord Runciman, a pious shipping magnate, to Prague as unofficial adviser to the Czechs. The Czechs did not ask for him; they did not want him, but were afraid that if they did not accept him Britain would wash her hands of them altogether and get France to do likewise. Chamberlain had blown neither hot nor cold. He had refused a definite guarantee of Czechish independence, but at the

same time had intimated that British policy was not to be interpreted as one of non-intervention under all circumstances. Plainly,
they had better dicker with Runciman.

The Czechs, urged by his lordship, offered generous concessions
to the SdP and Henlein. They agreed to a cantonal division of
Czechoslovakia on the Swiss model. "All nationalities should share
proportionately in all state offices and in state enterprises, monopolies, institutions and other organizations." Autonomy in all local
matters was assured the Sudetendeutsch, and a large sum of money
was to be granted for their economic relief.

This was fair enough, but not for the London *Times*. It proposed
that Czechoslovakia cede its border districts to Germany. The
Times flew the Chamberlain kite. Hitler took the cue. A few days
later, September 12, he addressed a huge meeting of Nazis and said
that he intended to come instantly to the relief of his oppressed
racial comrades in Czechoslovakia, and announced that the most
impregnable defenses ever built by man were being rushed to completion on the western frontier of Germany.

On September 13 there were uprisings among the Sudeten Germans (acknowledged later by Runciman to have been stirred up
by Nazi agitators) and the instant reply of Beneš, president of
Czechoslovakia, was to proclaim martial law. One day later Chamberlain announced that he would go by airplane to consult with
Hitler.

This was to be the first of three trips by air to Canossa which
the prime minister of England was to take—successive steps, all of
them, in humiliating subservience to the will of the German dictator. The first flight was to Berchtesgaden, where he was told by
Hitler that Germany insisted on the instant inclusion of the Sudeten
Germans in the Third Reich, even at the cost of a general war. Time
would be given Chamberlain to consult with his ministers; no other
concession was offered.

What was to be done? The British cabinet was divided; so was
the French. The premier of France and his foreign secretary flew
to London and a decision was reached without consulting Prague.
Czechoslovakia was told by England and France that she must
deliver "the districts mainly inhabited by the Sudeten Germans" to
Germany. If this was done there would be guarantees of her future
independence.

This was selling the pass, for the districts to be ceded lay along the frontier where the Czechs had their fortifications. England and France were now offering Hitler all that he demanded. Benes and his cabinet begged for reconsideration. Czechoslovakia had, they said, a treaty of arbitration with Germany. Why, therefore, not invoke it?

Runciman, meanwhile, made his formal report. It proposed not only to give Germany all that Hitler had demanded but more, for he suggested not only that parts of Czechoslovakia be ceded Germany but also that the rump remaining should renounce all treaties of defense, suppress all anti-German agitation, and enter into close economic relations with the Reich, in short, be swallowed quietly.

The Runciman report was followed by sharp insistence at Prague on the part of the French and British ambassadors that Beneš agree to it. Beneš asked that the demands be given him in writing; he was refused. Would the Czechs yield or not? If France fought on their side they had a chance, but even so there were German divisions to the south of them in Austria and their own Maginot line was in the north. They would, in any case, be subject to severe bombardments from the air. But France had now repudiated her word, and without France, Russia was under no obligation. Beneš and his colleagues decided to yield—with the understanding, they said, that Britain and France guaranteed the future independence of what was left of their country, and that the land transferred to Germany would not be occupied by German troops until the new frontiers had been delimited.

Whereupon followed Chamberlain's second flight to Canossa, this time to the little German town of Godesberg. To his surprise he found Hitler in a towering rage. The German army was going to march on October 1, roared the Führer, and nothing could stop it. There might be "subsequent corrections" in the boundaries suggested, and perhaps plebiscites. But Germany was going to take by force what was hers by right and would listen to no one. Hitler presented Chamberlain with a map showing what districts Germany was going to annex immediately, and Chamberlain received it, agreed to present it to the Czechs without recommendation, and flew back to London.

The Czechs indignantly rejected the Godesberg ultimatum, the British mobilized their fleet, the French their army. It looked like war. Trenches were dug in London, tanks and trucks rolled through Berlin on their way south, and gas-masks were distributed in Paris.

The British foreign office gave categorical assurance to France that Britain would come to her assistance if she took military action against Germany in the event of that country's invading Czechoslovakia—a much stronger guarantee than Britain gave France on August 2, 1914. Seemingly, Hitler must give way or the Second World War would break.

The Führer gave no indication of yielding. Within five days his Germans were to march. He had no claims, he said, against Poland or France. "After the Sudeten German question is regulated," he asserted, "we have no further territorial claims to make in Europe." But October 1 was the deadline, and to prove that he meant business, German divisions were concentrated on the Czech frontier, and German workmen labored day and night on the "Westwall." To frighten the democracies he even took another step: "German action" (whatever that meant), he told the British ambassador, would commence the next day at 2 P.M., namely, on September 28, 1938.

The democracies, on the other hand, did give signs of yielding. The French newspapers deliberately minimized as unofficial the British guarantee of standing by France; and Chamberlain, in a most ambiguous speech, showed that he was of two minds—he spoke of Czechoslovakia as a "far-away country" for whom it seemed almost impossible that England would be fighting. Then, just as the last sands were running out of the hour-glass, the Führer, at the request of Mussolini, postponed mobilization twenty-four hours and invited Daladier and Chamberlain to a conference with the Duce and himself at Munich.

Chamberlain accepted, and for the third time journeyed to Canossa. This Munich conference was still another victory for the dictators. Czechoslovakia was an uninvited onlooker as the four statesmen carved up that unhappy country in accordance with the Godesberg ultimatum. Minute concessions of no importance were made by which England and France might save face. Four zones were to be occupied by the Germans "in four rapid bites instead of one." A fifth zone was created in which there were supposed to be plebiscites. "But the final result was worse for the Czechs than Godesberg would have been." The international commission supposedly in control of plebiscites was a farce. The Germans took what they wanted, marched to within forty miles of Prague, and absorbed about 750,000 Czechs in the new Germany. As they did so the Poles invaded Teschen, annexing about 80,000 Poles and 120,000 Czechs. Hungary then advanced on the helpless Czechs from the south, crossed the Danube, took Bratislava, and would have divided Ruthenia and perhaps Slovakia with Poland had she been permitted by the all-powerful Germans. The latter, together with the Italians, decided everything. All French and British guarantees vanished into thin air.

"I return from Germany," said Chamberlain to cheering thousands, "bringing peace with honor." He brought neither.

Great was the peaceful joy in Naziland—two resounding victories won in six months, Austria and the mountain bastions of Bohemia safely now incorporated in the Third Reich, the famous Skoda munition works (largest in the world!) and Prague itself ripe for plucking. Better a führer than an emperor, so many a German must have felt. Emperors win wars but lose men doing so.

Meanwhile what was left of Czechoslovakia was independent in name only; the British and French guarantees meant nothing. The Germans demanded and obtained from the Czechs a German corridor across their country for an auto highway, demanded and obtained anti-Semitic laws, the right to decide upon the destinies of Ruthenia and Slovakia. Hacha, last president of Czechoslovakia, protested against Hitler's high-handed interference. He was summoned promptly to Berchtesgaden. Before he reached that high nest of wisdom German troops were on their way south. Berated, browbeaten, and chased around the table by Hitler, he signed away the remnant independence of his country. Simultaneously the Germans entered Prague, March 15, 1939.

POLAND

Just where the German dictator proposed next to strike none could tell. If he sought more blood-brothers to redeem, they might be spotted in Poland, Alsace-Lorraine, Denmark, or the Ukraine. The inclusion of Slavic Czechs in his domain would seem to indicate that the siren voice of blood comradeship was not the only sound he heard. In Prague he had lauded the First German Reich, the Holy Roman Empire of the German nation, which included not merely Alsace-Lorraine but also Verdun and Toul in France and Lombardy in Italy. To resurrect that phantom greatness, to undo the 1648 treaties of Westphalia was not beyond his scope. One

thing was inevitable; he would not, and could not, rest content with
what he had; he had not been put in power for that.

Until the end of January, 1939, storm signals pointed toward the
Ukraine and the Black Sea. Why otherwise should Hitler after
Munich have insisted on the autonomy of Carpatho-Ukraine, that
narrow splinter of Czechoslovakia jutting far eastward into the
Carpathians, a convenient spring-board for a dive into Kiev and
beyond? In southwest Russia lived some 35 million Ukrainians,
Little Russians. To detach them from Russia and bring them with
their wonderful black soil and rich mines under German sway had
been the eastern dream of the First World War. Here, Hitler had
prophesied, lay his lebensraum. The premier of newly created Carpatho-Ukraine had no doubt of the German war lord's intentions.
Said he, "The creation of a great Ukraine will be realized in a few
months."

To make the Ukraine a Nazi satrapy meant war with Russia, and
therefore, for a while, a conciliatory attitude toward France and
Poland, the former country still having (on paper) a defensive
treaty with Russia, the second a large Ukrainian minority apt for
racial reasons to side with Russia. It proved easier for Hitler to deal
with France than with Poland. The weak and perhaps treacherous
French foreign minister, Bonnet, hinted to Hitler that he should
not take too seriously the treaty of France with the Soviets. Josef
Beck, premier of Poland, was not so easily cajoled by Nazi suggestions of a possible German-Polish front against Bolshevism. Hitler
wisely preferred to take on his enemies one by one. Therefore, for
the first time since his rise to power, Russia ceased miraculously
to be the object of German press attack. Instead, the German newspapers turned their venom spray on Poland. After he had disposed
of that country, quite apparently his next victim, Hitler could throw
his might east or west as opportunity offered, renew his Ukrainian
project or agitate in Alsace-Lorraine and complain of Anglo-French
tyranny in former German colonies administered by the two democracies under the League of Nations.

Poland, like Czechoslovakia, was a child of the Versailles treaties,
a petted and unruly child with a record none too promising. That
the democracies should fight for her, a semi-Fascist state, while
abandoning to black fate the truly democratic Czechoslovakia, is
one of those ironies which perplex the historian.

There was no Masaryk or Beneš in Poland to counsel moderation and strive for justice. Pilsudski, Poland's strong man, had tried to make his country once more a great power. He drove his armies into the heart of the Ukraine; he took Vilna from Lithuania; he pressed far beyond the Curzon line, the eastern boundary suggested by the Versailles peace-makers, and annexed much of White Russia. He did not overthrow the republic, but his contempt for democracy was marked; and to all intent and purpose he was about to become dictator at the time of his death in 1935 when a new constitution was adopted for an "authoritarian democracy."

The democracy was nominal only. The president had a choice in the selection of his successor and many additional powers not customarily granted to the head of a democratic state. Generals and colonels filled many seats in the Polish cabinet. All Communist propaganda was forbidden, and the political pendulum in Poland swung back and forth, not between right and left, but between right and center. Superficially the country seemed strong. A Polish port, Gdynia, was constructed on the sandy wastes of the Baltic and through it flowed considerable commerce; a Polish mercantile marine was in the making; and there were even demands for Polish colonies. Seemingly, the government was in good position financially, with monopolies of alcohol, salt, matches, tobacco, and lotteries to buttress up its treasury. But this was on the surface only; below was a poverty-stricken peasantry, so poor that in eastern Poland matches were divided four ways before being struck.

The Germans, the Ukrainians, and the Jews in Poland kept up an outcry about the discriminations against them. Scattered throughout western Poland, German landlords complained that their leases were illegally defined by Polish law courts, and that, contrary to the Treaty of Versailles, the use of German in schools was frowned upon. The Ukrainians asserted that they were deprived of the cultural autonomy promised, and that even Ukrainian Boy Scouts were disbanded by Polish orders. The Jews, who comprised some 27 per cent of the city population, were humiliated by "ghetto benches," separate seats assigned to Jews in university lecture halls, a practice encouraged by the government, although not ordered by it. The Jews also were subjected to boycotts, again indirectly approved by the government, and when anti-Semitic riots broke out, the authorities apparently encouraged them. The treatment given minorities was far less fair and just than in her sister republic, Czechoslovakia.

Come weal or woe, Hitler had to be stopped or obeyed. If he won on the Vistula, he might win on the Seine, perhaps ultimately cross the Channel. Munich and the march on Prague shocked the Western world as nothing else had. Always until then the Nazi war against the world outside had been carried on so circumspectly that it was possible to argue it was not war at all but strong and vigorous assertion of German rights. Thus had it been in the rearmament of Germany, the reoccupation of the Rhineland, the annexation of Austria, the support of the Sudetendeutsch in Czechoslovakia. The German legions in Spain cannot be so easily expunged from the Nazi record, nor the abominable cruelties within Germany. Nevertheless it had always been possible for Nazi apologists to sneer "tu quoque," pointing to lynchings in our own deep South or to British suppressions of disorder in India. But now Munich and subsequent events in Czechoslovakia persuaded even the more stupid of what clearer heads had long suspected, that world revolution and a new world war were en route, and that soon for most nations the question would simmer down to "we or they?"

Thus was it apparently in England. The day after the German march to Prague the House of Commons buzzed like a hornet's nest and even that reputed Germanophile, Lady Astor, demanded that "the Prime Minister lose no time in letting the German government know with what horror the whole of this country regards Germany's action." Chamberlain did not do this, but he did immediately start negotiations with Poland lest it, too, fall a prey to the insinuating Nazis. So long as conversations to this end were being held, he assured the House, Britain was pledged to come to the armed assistance of the Poles if they said their independence was threatened and if they fought to maintain it, a pledge which France had joined in making.

This definitive alignment of France and Britain with Poland did not even ruffle the dictators. They thought Chamberlain would meet this crisis as he had earlier ones by talk. So Hitler promptly occupied Memel and Memel-land northeast of Poland, the city being German, the hinterland Lithuanian, and two weeks later the oil-seeking Italians stabbed so rapidly across the Adriatic that within eight days Victor Emmanuel found himself crowned "King of Albania." The French, British and American governments, all three, protested, the two former promptly extending the same unilateral pledge to Rumania and Greece that they had given Poland.

Roosevelt might possibly have done likewise had he possessed constitutional authority. As it was, the United States had refused to dismiss the Czechoslovakian ambassador, refused to deliver to German hands Czechoslovakian gold kept here. Now Hull, secretary of state, denounced the Albanian raid, and Roosevelt determined to throw what weight he could against the aggressors. On May 15 he sent Hitler and Mussolini an open letter. In it he said, "Three nations in Europe and one in Asia have seen their independent existence terminated. A vast territory of another nation in the Far East has been occupied by a neighboring state. Reports which we trust are not true insist that further actions of aggression are contemplated against still other independent nations. Plainly the world is moving toward the moment when this situation must end in catastrophe unless a more rational way of guiding events is found." Bluntly the President asked for a guarantee that no other nation should be attacked. His letter encouraged the British and the French, perhaps unduly. It infuriated isolationists in the United States, and Hitler, too, who replied in nasty vein, bitterly sarcastic as to Woodrow Wilson, the Treaty of Versailles, the presence of British troops in Palestine and in India.

Throughout the late spring and early summer of 1939 the Nazis followed the pattern used in 1938. They made relatively moderate demands on Poland which later could be extended if granted; they started a number of anti-Polish demonstrations, little incidents to show the world and their own German people how wicked Poles were tyrannizing over Germans; and they sowed with skill the seeds of discord among the four countries left able to oppose them, Britain, France, Russia, and the United States.

The German demands on Poland were twofold, the return of Danzig to the Reich and the cession of a strip of territory across the Polish Corridor of sufficient width to build a four-track auto highway. For the first there was much to be said, and something for the second. Danzig was German in population, and historically had been so for several hundred years. The Poles did not administer it, since the city was autonomous under the League of Nations, and the city government, freely elected, was controlled by Danzig Nazis. Nonetheless Danzig was not in the Third Reich and could only be reached by sea, or by railroad crossing Polish lands. The trains were German trains; the cars were sealed; there was no Polish inspection of them; but the situation could not be called satisfactory, and the German claim to Danzig could not be called unreasonable. Had it not been for the engorgement of Czechoslovakia by the Nazi boa constrictor in 1938 and 1939, and for Hitler's long record of aggression since 1935, the Danzig matter might have been settled peacefully and Poland forced to make concessions by pressure from all the powers. But Poland knew, and all Europe feared, that Hitler's preliminary demands were never final, that the more one yielded the more one had to yield, until all was lost.

1939 followed the pattern of 1937 and 1938, only this time Poland and not Spain, Austria, Czechoslovakia, was the scene of action. The Nazis sent "visitors," also thugs, into Danzig. Their function was to pick quarrels, start a clamor, stir up riots. Elsewhere in Poland the same game was played; German school children were set upon by Polish mobs, German babies were thrown from windows by drunken Poles, German women were molested by Polish police. All sorts of atrocity stories were aired to prove that German intervention must come soon or else all Germans in Poland would be massacred. Dr. Goebbels was very clever at devising this sort of thing. Perhaps he did convince Hitler and many Germans that these gory tales were true, emotionally true at least.

Meanwhile one stark fact may be discerned above all others in the fatal summer of 1939: the British and the French, pledged to fight for Polish independence if the Poles fought, could not make their promise good without aid from Russia. Poland was a large flat plain without natural boundaries; the German wehrmacht was on the northern frontier, on the eastern frontier, and now, thanks to Chamberlain's Munich and the German occupation of Slovakia, on the southern frontier. Even if we rate the French and British armies as equal to the wehrmacht they could not reach Poland; they could not come in contact with either their ally or their enemy. Russia must fight or Poland must die.

Two years earlier this had been seen by Winston Churchill. Originally a bitter foe of the Soviets, an admirer of Mussolini and a pro-Franco advocate, that hard-bitten British Tory long since had acknowledged his mistake and since Munich had warned, admonished and pleaded with the British government to come to terms quickly with Russia.

But that is just what Chamberlain and his ally Daladier, the French premier, dared not do. They abhorred Bolshevism and scorned Russia at Munich; they rebuffed Russian proposals for a mutual-aid pact after the occupation of Prague; they went ahead on their own, making a unilateral pact with the Poles without consulting Russia; they took this same risky action in making identical pacts guaranteeing Greece and Rumania; they promised to protect Turkey; and then finally they approached Stalin. When they did so their manner was so stiffly superior, their proposals so unauthoritative, so overly guarded that Stalin felt he could not trust them.

There were two major points at issue in this summer of 1939: the extent to which Britain, France and Russia would commit themselves to joint action and the military procedure to be adopted should these three countries find themselves at war with Hitler. What the Russians wanted was a binding treaty of alliance guaranteeing their far-flung boundary against the Reich and then, if war broke, the right to face the Germans, not on the Russo-Polish frontier but on the Polish-German border. The French and British did not see eye to eye with Russia on this. They had already committed themselves to Poland, Rumania, Greece and Turkey, and they did not want to go further, not with Russia at least. But Stalin thought of the North, of Finland, Esthonia, Latvia and Lithuania. Leningrad was within big gun fire of the Finnish frontier and closely adjacent to the other Baltic states. Why not a guarantee of the entire status quo?

The French and the British now shed crocodile tears. Since the four Baltic countries specifically stated that they did not desire any guarantees it would be highly improper for others to insist. Stalin had been explicit; he had asked for guarantees not simply against external agression but internal also. By this he meant that France, Britain and Russia should act as a unit in preventing Goebbels and Hitler from stirring up Fascist revolutions within the four Baltic countries on the pattern followed in Spain, Austria, Czechoslovakia and Poland. Chamberlain and Daladier would not agree. Their highly moral attitude towards Russian intervention contrasted sharply with that taken by them in preceding crises, when Italy and Germany were doing the intervening.

Stalin was suspicious; he could trust neither the Fascist nor the democratic camp. The sudden silence in Germany on anti-Bolshevik propaganda showed that Hitler was prepared to offer neutrality or possibly "friendship." Such offers he knew were synthetic. On the other hand the democracies were not only reluctant to accept any full-fledged alliance; they were also insulting in the offhand way in which they sought Russian aid. Chamberlain had not hesitated to fly to Rome and three times to Germany, and he had sent Halifax, then his secretary for foreign affairs, shuttling back and forth across Europe. But Halifax, apparently, was too important to send to Moscow. Even Vansittart, Foreign Office adviser, was not named for that most important mission. Instead Britain sent a certain minor Mr. Strang, a subordinate official of the Foreign Office, to carry on negotiations involving life and death for Poland, Britain and France. Strang stayed several weeks in Moscow. Details of his sojourn there have not been published. The Russians lost patience. On June 29 *Pravda* editorialized as follows: "Anglo-Russian negotiations ... have been going on for seventy-five days. Of these the Soviet government took sixteen days in preparing an answer to the various British projects and proposals while the remaining fifty-nine days have been consumed by the delays and procrastination on the part of the British and the French."[1] No wonder Stalin thought the democracies only half-honest, half in earnest. His price was definite enough; the Baltic states must be included in any Anglo-Soviet treaty. Said Winston Churchill in May, "I cannot understand these refinements of diplomacy and delay ... we are up to our necks in it already...." That was in May, and now it was the end of June!

Stalin refused to dally indefinitely with the democracies. If they were unwilling to face the facts, he would see what he could get from the Germans. His foreign minister, Litvinoff, friend of the democracies and of the League, resigned, to be succeeded by Molotov, who entered into conversations with the Germans in June and July. But the door was not yet closed completely on the democracies. Molotov suggested that a joint Anglo-French military commission be sent to Moscow and on August 5 it started. By that date very few grains of sand remained in the hour-glass. Nevertheless the commission did not go by air; it did not go by rail; it took a slow steamer, reaching Moscow August 11. There still remained one slight chance for Russian collaboration. Would those touring emissaries guarantee permission for the Red army to fight the Germans on the Polish-German frontier in case Russia joined England and France in a war for the defense of Poland? It seemed only sense to the Russians that they should fight there before Poland was conquered, rather than await a German army later on their own

[1] Frederick Lewis Schuman, *Night Over Europe* (New York, Alfred A. Knopf, 1941), p. 253.

frontier. But the commission would not or could not give the Russians the assurance requested, since the Poles would not allow a Russian army in their country. After this refusal the hour-glass was empty. Von Ribbentrop on August 23 signed in Moscow a non-aggression pact between Germany and Russia, the two contracting powers agreeing that for a period of ten years they would "refrain from any violence, from any aggressive action, and any attack against each other, individually or jointly with other powers."

Inexplicable in this hour of gravest peril was the French, British and Polish nonchalance. With full blare of publicity Italy and Germany had signed in the late spring a hard and fast military alliance; and the one source of friction between them subsequently was removed when Hitler dragged out of the Upper Tyrol thousands of German families settled there since time immemorial, thus surrendering that valley completely to the Duce's domination. Japanese soldiers already had blockaded the British concession at Tientsin, stripped British citizens naked, forced Britain to deliver to Japanese justice various unfortunate Chinese who had sought refuge under the Union Jack. Chamberlain said, "This makes my blood boil." The events which thus heated the Prime Minister's blood took place two months before the Russo-German non-aggression pact!

Hitler, now secure on the east, immediately inflamed and inflated his demands on the Poles, spoke vaguely of further annexations, said he had no quarrel with the democracies, but what took place in eastern Europe was none of their business. The Poles, he said, were killing German citizens, were castrating them, and this he could not endure. The French and British ambassadors tried to calm an excited Führer, promised impartial investigation of all atrocity stories, urged Beck, Polish premier, to negotiate directly with the Germans. Just what were the German demands? Henderson, British ambassador at Berlin, reported that at midnight, August 30, Von Ribbentrop read to him sixteen points so rapidly and so indistinctly that he could only get their general drift. When asked for a printed copy Von Ribbentrop refused, saying the points were already outdated! Lipski, Polish ambassador, never received this ultimatum officially, the Germans insisting that they would not deal with him but only with a Polish plenipotentiary. But Lipski did have a chance to read them in the newspapers, as did everyone else on August 31. They called for not only the surrender of Danzig and for the extra-territorial highway, but also for plebiscites which would reopen the entire Corridor question. All that day, August 31, constant effort was made by the French and British to gain time. Poland neither refused nor accepted the sixteen published points. At 4 A.M., September 1, the German army crossed the border.

As the armed flood swept over the Polish plain Britain and France did nothing. They were delayed by Mussolini who suggested to the French an armistice to be followed by a conference "to examine the clauses of the Treaty of Versailles which are the cause of the present trouble." To this Britain was sleepily agreeable provided Hitler would withdraw his troops to their posts of August 31. The French, seemingly, did not insist on that concession. But the Nazis now had tasted blood. Hitler sent his forces storming ahead and on September 3, 1939, four years late, France and England declared war on the Reich.

4. COUNTRIES FALL LIKE NINEPINS

ONLY Germany was ware and fit for war. "Not butter—guns," had been her slogan for two years. In matériel and morale she stood ready. The three allies, Poland, France, and Britain, were in no condition to fight. The only Polish asset of consequence was battle bravery. The Poles were relatively few in number; they were short of equipment, poor in resources, muddled both as to organization and military intelligence. The terrain helped the invader along and so did the parched weather. Without motorized divisions, with a scant one thousand planes (mostly obsolete) the Poles never had a chance. The French had no stomach for war; their past-minded armies were honeycombed with defeat—generals without love for the Republic, poilus downhearted and suspicious. The waste of French lives in World War I had been worse than in any other country, and Frenchmen felt they could not go through with it again. Not backed by the people the dry-rotted French army went stale. The British despised or patronized Hitler and stupidly underrated him. Being sea animals they thought the new war less onerous than in 1914-1918 because the Germany navy was far less a menace now than then. Despite Churchill's warning blasts they had no clear foreboding of hell hurtling down from the skies. Evacuating children from London, they soon brought them back again, refused to ration anything, thought more or less comfortably of how that earlier war had ended as sea power slowly strangled a Germany hurling her armies against American, French and British trenches, the English countryside unscathed by foreign war, as it had been since 1066 A.D.

Both France and England were in military alliance with Poland, under moral obligation to succor her. Since it was physically impossible to do this directly all that remained possible was some attack on Germany's western flank. On September 5 the French cautiously opened a minor drive on the west bank of the Rhine between that river and the Moselle. It made trifling progress and came to an abrupt halt when the Germans counterattacked ten days later. Air offensive there was none, either by France or Britain. Poland was left to die. Not an Allied plane flew to her relief. Under the circumstances perhaps this was inevitable. The French and British had not asserted they were supermen, nor had they promised Poland that they would strike at Germany the very day and hour she opened fire on her eastern neighbor. Poland's error in relying on their help was her own.

Within little more than a week the Poles were done for, and within five weeks all organized resistance ceased within their borders. The very first day of the war the Germans bombed Warsaw and demolished most of the Polish air force on the ground. Almost before the Poles could mobilize, Nazi tanks and Nazi planes were smashing railroad junctions, viaducts, power plants, bridges, munition depots. The Poles had counted on their swamps and rivers to block the Nazi panzer (armored) divisions; but there was no rain; the sun-baked plains were easily crossed, and the rivers, unusually low, were no impediment. Swift and sure was the advance of the invader; helpless, confused and blind the defense. German infantry set new records for long marches with heavy equipment; German tanks murdered the charges of Polish cavalry; the German espionage worked. By mid-September all important cities except Warsaw were in German hands and the Polish government in flight to the Rumanian frontier.

The Poles fought bravely, and here and there scattered Polish divisions struck hard at the encircling foe. At the Danzig *Westerplatte* and at Warsaw they made last-ditch stands. The civilians of Warsaw turned out en masse to dig trenches, and the Warsaw radio alternated martial music, defiance of the enemy and appeals to the outside world as Nazi bombers droned overhead, reducing that proud city to rubble.

Then, on September 17 the Russians took a hand, thrust their knife deep into the side of the dying country. Molotov, Soviet foreign secretary, announced over the radio that since no one could tell where the government of Poland was located it could be assumed there was neither government nor Poland. It was Russia's duty to protect the millions of Ukrainians and White Russians in what had once been Poland, and for that purpose the Red army was crossing the border. Without opposition it swept over eastern Poland all the way to the Vistula, where it came in contact with the Germans; it fanned out to the south until it reached the

Hungarian frontier. Warsaw, that shell of a city, bombed and burning in a dozen areas, held out until September 27. Sporadic fighting continued a week or two after, for Poland was a large country and her forests were deep. The Polish war, however, was over.

Roughly speaking one-third of Poland, the agricultural east, was incorporated in Russia, and Stalin amiably advised the peasants to pay their landlord's rent with hatchet and pitchfork. The Germans took the rest, annexed to the Reich such districts as fitted their schemes, set up under strict Nazi control a truncated district in the center in which they harshly proceeded to isolate Poles and Jews.

To the democracies of western Europe and to America this butchering of Poland looked like treacherous imperialism on the part of that European Ishmael, Soviet Russia. But one needs to remember that Poland was lost anyhow and that if the Red army had stayed at home the Germans would have gone straight through to the Russian frontier. Furthermore, when it came to carving Poland for keeps the Russians retired east of the Bug River and retained only that part to which they had a reasonably fair claim, the new Russian boundary being approximately on the Curzon line, as close to the ethnological boundary as the Versailles congress had been able to fix it. Within Russia now were the Ukrainians and White Russians who wrongfully had been incorporated in Poland owing to the national megalomania of Pilsudski. To offset all this was the unquestioned fact that Russia had had a non-aggression treaty with Poland, and that had several years to run.

The six months that follow (October, 1939-March, 1940) will puzzle historians many a year. Technically Britain and France were at war with Germany; but fighting there was practically none, except at sea, and not much there. A few bombs were dropped by Germany upon the British naval base at Scapa Flow, and the British retaliated with a few bombs dropped on the German air base on the island of Sylt. British planes also scattered leaflets over Germany. Other air activity could scarcely be noted. Neither France nor Germany, apparently, cared to fight. Paris at first darkened her streets and then lit them again. There were sandbags piled high, art treasures removed to safety, paper strips pasted across plate-glass windows as precautions against enemy planes that never came. The French, manning their Maginot line, supposedly impregnable, now and then shelled the German Westwall, and occasionally a German shell lit in French soil. In general, display posters and aural blasts by radio were substituted for gunfire. The Germans taunted the French with dying for Danzig and asserted with no justification whatever that the British would fight until the last Frenchman was killed. The British landed the bulk of their regular army in France, upwards of 300,000 men, but they did nothing except get as comfortably as possible into winter quarters. Expensive news gatherers found difficulty emptying their fountain pens and in America the sneer, "phoney war," made rapid headway.

At sea there were some sharp skirmishes. During the autumn German submarines sank a number of British merchantmen, one airplane carrier and a battleship, the *Royal Oak*. These victories were offset in December in the South Atlantic when the German pocket-battleship *Graf Spee* crept into Montevideo after an eighteen-hour engagement with three British cruisers, and was later blown up by her own crew rather than let her fall into British hands. Aside, however, from these maritime encounters there was little action on the high seas.

This comparative calm pleased the democracies rather than otherwise. They thought the war would be won by weight of economic blockade and by sheer staying power. Did not the British and French have free access to the world's raw materials, have infinitely more money to spend overseas, infinitely more money to buy up at any price the war-exports of Turkey and the Balkan states? France and Britain were still hypnotized by World War I which they knew had demonstrated that wars of maneuver were outmoded. Even Poland's defeat taught them nothing. The Poles were foolhardy, unscientific! Let the Nazis once try their rough, rush tactics in the west and they soon would discover that a breakthrough was impossible. Defensive war and maritime blockade, there were the keys to victory!

FINLAND

Meanwhile Red Russia bestirred herself. She did not like the Nazi victory march into Poland. Stalin had no more objection to blood drainage in the west than France and Britain had to a Russo-German war of exhaustion, but a triumphant Germany on his doorstep worried him. He well knew that in Lithuania, Latvia, and Esthonia were over 100,000 German Balts and that the three pseudo-republics on the southern side of the Baltic had long been earmarked for German lebensraum. Russia acted quickly. Demands were made and promptly granted which put all three little states under Soviet protection and provided for stationing Russian forces within their borders. The German Balts hastily were withdrawn by Hitler and presented with farms in western Poland, their former owners being dispossessed. The Führer did not relish this Russian intervention but until the west was secure he did not intend to challenge Stalin.

The latter now turned his attention to the fourth small Baltic state, Finland. Leningrad was only twenty miles away from the Finnish frontier, too close for comfort, and Finnish islands and the peninsula of Hango commanded the north shore of the Baltic. The Finns had won their independence through German aid, and the commander of their army, Baron Mannerheim, was a well-known hater of Bolshevism. Russians outnumbered Finns fifty to one, but Stalin determined to take no chances. Germany would have no opportunity to use Finland successfully as her catspaw, not if he could help it.

The Russians pressed the Finns hard. They asked for a rectification of their frontier at Petsamo, a port on the Arctic belonging to Finland, for six islands commanding the approaches to Leningrad, for a naval station at Hango, for that part of the Karelian Isthmus on which was located the strongly fortified Mannerheim line, too close to Leningrad. If the Finns agreed to these cessions of territory, amounting to almost 3,000 square kilometers, then Russia would cede to Finland some 5,500 square kilometers between Lake Ladoga and the Arctic.

All November negotiations continued. The Finns would not give way. Stalin forced the issue. Soviet planes bombed Helsinki. November 30, and a new war, within a war, commenced.

The world expected that Finland speedily would be overrun; but the world was mistaken. From December 1, 1939, to March 12, 1940, the Finns put up an astonishing resistance, only to capitulate when their vastly outnumbered soldiers, without ammunition and without sleep, could fight no more.

History has on record no braver epic than this. The Russians swept into Finland along several different routes. They tried to conquer north Finland near Petsamo; they tried to cut across the narrow central section or waist of that underpopulated country, thus severing the north from the south; and they advanced on both sides of huge Lake Ladoga on the southeast, endeavoring to storm the main Finnish defenses, the Mannerheim line, which stretched across the Karelian Peninsula from Lake Ladoga to the Gulf of Finland.

In every direction the Finns beat them off. There was only a handful of Finns; but their country was two-thirds the size of France and said to contain 65,000 lakes, while the land between was covered for the most part with dense forests where roads were few and poor. The athletic Finns, skilful on their skis and well-nigh invisible in their white clothing against the background of their frozen country-side, mowed down the invaders from endless ambushes; they dug traps for Russian tanks; they placed and set off dynamite under the ice; they broke the Russian lines of communication and captured thousands of the enemy.

Aside from the Karelian Peninsula, immediately in front of Leningrad, the Russians had only one approach to Finland, a railway 800 miles long which stretched from Leningrad all the way north to the Murmansk coast and at no great distance from the Finnish frontier. This railway was easy to raid. The Finnish air force, as might have been expected, was unable to cope with the air armada let loose by the Russians; but on other hand a number of planes were sent to Finland by France, England, Sweden, and even Italy, and the Finns were not helpless in the air. Furthermore, Finland was almost exclusively an agricultural country, and outside of Helsinki and Viborg there were few towns worth bombing.

The Soviet army, meanwhile, proved inefficient, particularly during the early stages of the war. The army purge of 1937 had resulted in the execution of three out of five field-marshals; and all of the eight general officers who court-martialed them had since been shot. It was estimated that no less than 30,000 officers of the Red army had thus been disposed of, and in consequence the morale of the Russian troops was poor. So also was the equipment; the soldiers were clad in flimsy cotton uniforms and thin boots; the fighting was in sub-zero weather; they never had seen skis; their tanks, huge and cumbersome, broke down in swamps, were surrounded, isolated, captured. Not until Russia threw the best of her fighting men into the war in 1940 was she able to make headway.

Then came a final massed assault by the Russians on the Mannerheim line. Throughout February an incessant rain of steel blasted away its concrete fortresses and wave after wave of Russian tanks drove at the defenses. The number of fresh Russian troops was inexhaustible, but for the Finnish regiments no more men were available. Finland, therefore, with inevitable collapse staring her in the face, yielded to all of Russia's demands, made peace in the middle of March, and commenced evacuating the choicest part of what had been Finnish soil, the Karelian Peninsula. From it some 400,000 Finns, more than one-tenth of Finland's population, packed their scanty possessions and moved westward into what was left of their country.

Great was the wrath of Sweden, Denmark, Norway, England, France, Italy, the United States and other countries against Soviet Russia. Only Germany remained impassive, coldly neutral and stiffly correct.

Swedes were particularly indignant. There had been numerous intermarriages between Swedes and Finns, and many of the wealthier Finns were of Swedish extraction. The Swedes feared the Russian Bear and his presence in Finland made him altogether too close a neighbor. Large sums of money were raised for Finland in Sweden and Finnish refugees were welcome there. A good many Swedes resigned from the army to become officers in the Swedish Legion, reported 10,000 strong and informally organized to fight for Finland. Members of it were continually slipping over the border and participating in the war. Danes and Norwegians, as individuals, did likewise. Scandinavians as good skiers were especially welcomed and the three Scandinavian countries would unquestionably have given further aid had it not been for Nazi growls as to what might happen if they did so.

France and Britain also proffered aid. War matériel in bulk was sent to Finland. In London there was open recruiting for the Finnish army and even distant South Africa released British planes that it had ordered that they might be used against the Russian invader. Only by a narrow margin did France and Britain miss waging war on the Soviets. As it was, an Anglo-French expeditionary force of 100,000 men was slowly accrued for that purpose in the winter of 1939-1940 and would have been sent had there been any way of reaching the fighting front. It could do so only by crossing Scandinavia and this Germany vetoed. The Nazis secretly sympathized with the Finns but they had no intention whatsoever of permitting their foes to land in Norway or Sweden. The excellent iron deposits of north Sweden were essential for their war industries and an Anglo-French army in the north would endanger the Reich. Sweden and Norway paid heed to Berlin's warning and refused permission for the transit of troops. Winston Churchill was disgusted. He urged the little countries to throw off their fears. "Each one hopes," he said, "that if he feeds the crocodile enough, the crocodile will eat him last."

Italy, too, was hotly angry at this Russian war. Despite the Italian treaty with Hitler, even the Duce could not prevent (if he had wanted to) pro-Finnish demonstrations in Rome. Italian aviators flew for Finland. The *Observatore Romano*, generally regarded as expressing the papal views, represented pretty well the opinion of most Italians. "This ferocious Ivan," it said of Stalin, "sits in the Kremlin in a worker's smock . . . regiments the wretched moujiks in the Red army and transforms it into a blind instrument for the oppression of the liberty of nations."

Our own country likewise joined in the anti-Russian hue and cry. There were numerous Finns in America and the fact that Finland alone of the countries of Europe paid the annual instalment on its war debt endeared that land of innumerable lakes to thrifty Americans. We raised two large sums for Finland, one for civilian relief, the other under the attractive title of "Fighting Funds for Finland" to buy guns and ammunition. Congressional halls reëchoed with praise of the valiant Finns; the Navy Department surrendered its rights to purchase a number of planes that Finland might receive them; adventurous Canadians and Americans went overseas to drive back the Red army; and for months the only thrilling radio broadcasts Americans heard from Europe came from Helsinki or from the embattled Finnish army.

Red Russia was never so unpopular in western Europe and the United States as during the "phoney war." Russia had been the first country to ratify the Briand-Kellogg peace pacts; she had spoken bravely at Geneva on behalf of Ethiopia, Spain, Czechoslovakia; she had signed a non-aggression pact with Poland; she had signed a non-aggression pact with Finland. And now Russia had copied the Japanese precedents in Manchuria! Nor was this the sum total of her evil record as our democracies saw it. She not only had participated in the partition of Poland, she also heartily and vociferously denounced England and France for continuing the war. Said

Izvestia, Stalin's newspaper mouthpiece, "One may respect or hate Hitlerism just as any other system of political views. This is a matter of taste. But to undertake war for the annihilation of Hitlerism means to commit an act of criminal folly in politics." Said Molotov, Stalin's mouthpiece, "The British and the French have declared something in the nature of an ideological war on Germany, reminiscent of the religious wars of olden times.... Is it back to the Middle Ages, to the days of religious wars, superstition and cultural deterioration that the ruling classes of Britain and France want to drag us? ... The imperialistic character of this war is obvious to anyone who wants to face realities and does not close his eyes to facts."

Meanwhile in Britain, France and the United States the Communists followed this new party line with pedantic care. A short time before they had been eager to join in a common front against Fascism and had denounced Social Democrats for not being willing to do so. Now barefacedly they reversed their stand. It was generally believed then that British, French and American Communists were without loyalty to their country and obedient only to orders from Moscow. Deep was suspicion of the Kremlin. Ostensibly Stalin was neutral but he wore no necktie and his words seemed to favor the Nazis. There were ominous sentences in the declaration of September 28 which accompanied the Russo-German treaty of that date relative to partitioning Poland. If it became apparent that Britain and France were responsible for continuing an unnecessary war, then "the governments of Germany and the U.S.S.R. will consult each other as to necessary measures." Just what did this mean?

So unpopular had Russia become that life even stirred in Geneva, and the League of Nations, what was left of it, expelled Russia. Out of the sixty nations who at one time belonged, there were still forty-two and none voted in the negative on the motion to expel. The Chinese refused to vote, magnanimously refusing to condemn the one country in all the world which had helped China in her war with Japan.

The democracies became so excited about the little Russo-Finnish war that they almost forgot they had a larger one on their hands. In retrospect it is astonishing indeed to note how yawningly France and Britain (apart from sea war) confronted the crisis. Frugally did Germans celebrate Christmas in 1939. As a special concession every German woman was entitled to buy one unrationed pair of

stockings and every man an additional necktie. Food and clothing
was guarded with care and, indeed, for many months before war
broke it was illegal to buy or sell cream in Germany. But in Paris
at Noël time there was said to be an abundance of "oysters, caviar,
pâté de fois gras, turkey, geese, chicken, wines and liqueurs." The
French were more interested in hunting down French Communists,
of whom there were many, than in killing Germans. Why worry?
Did not France have her Maginot line; was there not a little Maginot line in process of construction (there was no hurry to finish
it) along France's northeastern frontier; was there not a capable
Belgian army still further beyond which would absorb the shock of
any German offense; were not the Belgians infinitely better prepared than in 1914; did they not have superb fortifications all the
way south and east from Liége to the Meuse, and north and west
from Liége along the Albert Canal to Antwerp? Why, the Albert
Canal was 250 feet wide and the trees on the north side had all
been leveled. Before the Nazi army could get near that protecting
body of water it would be smashed by Belgian artillery.

In Britain this same somnolence prevailed. Prime Minister Chamberlain assured the House of Commons that the war was going very
favorably because the Germans after their conquest of Poland
made no effort to attack on the west. This presumably meant that
they were unable to do so. Since the Allied blockade of Germany
was more effective than the German blockade of Britain it was
simply a question of time before Germany was brought to heel.
Even British military experts gave way to this easy optimism. In
a widely read book, *The Defense of Britain*, Captain Liddell Hart
eulogized defensive tactics. World War I had been won thus;
history proved that for attack a three-to-one superiority in both
numbers and firing power was the prerequisite to victory. "Defense," wrote Hart, "is the psychological attack," a sharp jab now
and then. Large-scale attack was unintelligent. And so Britain
drowsed on. At the commencement of the war she had enrolled
among her unemployed 1,400,000. After a month of conflict the
number had increased by 100,000. But why worry?

Six months of war and the Nazis apparently were as pacifically
inclined as the democracies; as far as words went, even more so.
After Poland's fall Hitler intimated that he would welcome a peace
conference. "Why should this war in the west be fought?" he said.
The French might destroy a few German towns, the Germans

might do likewise in France. If we keep on, "instead of flourishing towns there will be ruins and graveyards." He had no enmity for the British and the French; he wanted to end his life not as a soldier but as an artist. The premiers of France and Britain did not reply in kind. Their words were quite belligerent; they said they were going to make an end to Hitlerism. But they took few active steps toward it. The British, somewhat disturbed over losses to their mercantile marine, intensified their blockade of Germany; and the French, slightly perturbed by a growing scarcity of foodstuffs, went in for rationing; but both countries thought time on their side. Never, perhaps, in history had there been a major war in which the loss of life had been so slight. If we exclude the Polish and the Finnish campaigns the total casualties after half a year were estimated as 5,500 for the Allies, 4,750 for the Germans.

Thus it was until April, 1940, when the Germans struck with fury. Denmark, Norway, Holland, Belgium, Luxembourg and France went down like ninepins. All in three months. It was "phoney war" no longer. The Nazi victory parade had started, not to be halted until it reached the Volga, not to be transformed into a death retreat for four long years.

GERMANS CONQUER DENMARK, NORWAY, HOLLAND, BELGIUM

Of all small states the one which suffered most from the war was Norway. Ship after ship of the Norwegian merchant fleet had been destroyed by Nazi mines and submarines while plying between British and Norwegian ports. There was nothing the Norwegians could do about it except put their shipping under protection of the British convoy system which the Germans claimed was unneutral. Norway, indeed, had legitimate complaint against both Germans and British. A British destroyer boldly entered Norwegian territorial waters to rescue British seamen from a Nazi prison ship, and the British constantly interfered with German shipping threading its way down the coast of Norway with the much prized iron ore of Sweden which, when the Baltic was frozen in winter, reached Germany via the Norwegian port of Narvik, far north within the Arctic Circle.

Then, on April 8, 1940, the British destroyer *Glowworm,* engaged in mining Norwegian waters, radioed that she had encountered a

German destroyer. There was no more word of the *Glowworm,*
for the German destroyer was the German cruiser, *Admiral Hipper,*
which promptly sank the British warship. Simultaneously on this
very day the Germans occupied Denmark, invaded Norway.

The Danes did not resist. Their country was under Germany's
very shadow, a flat and crowded plain with a quarter of their
people in the city of Copenhagen. With Norway it was different:
a rugged terrain, deep valleys, poor transportation facilities, a
scattered and scant population gave Norway some chance. In Paris
and in London there were even chortles of glee at so silly and
unscientific a venture on the part of Hitler, and even Churchill
claimed that "Hitler committed a grave strategic error in spreading
the war so far to the north...." Not yet did he appreciate the
potentialities of the German army.

The very day the Germans swept the Danish plain, small picked
detachments of the German army seized Oslo, Norway's capital, and
her important ports—Stavanger, Bergen, Trondhjem, and Narvik.
Only a few thousand men proved necessary for this undertaking,
1,500 being sufficient to secure Oslo. By various routes the Germans
came—some by sea, some by transport planes, some disembarking
from German merchant ships anchored innocently alongside Norwegian wharfs, while some were already within the country in
disguise.

The Norwegians, taken by complete surprise, honeycombed by
Nazi propaganda, and ill equipped for war, were not able to put
up much resistance. Here and there, Norwegian detachments
fought bravely, and effectively. A Norwegian mine-sweeper sank a
German cruiser and so did a land battery, and in the mountains
hastily assembled militia (the Norwegian army was scarcely more
than militia) retarded the German advance.

But there was treachery in Norway. Some Norwegian "fifth columnists," welcomed the invaders, and among them were officers in
the army. German plans had been prepared in great detail, long
before the British mine-laying at Narvik, and everything ran like
clockwork. On the very first day all the Norwegian air-fields were
occupied by Germans and the tiny air force of Norway was of no
use at all. So completely taken by surprise were the Norwegians
that their king, pursued by Nazi troopers in four auto-buses, barely
escaped capture.

Nevertheless, for two weeks or so it looked as though the Allies might rescue Norway. It was some seventy miles from Denmark to southern Norway and three times as far from Norway to Britain. With the British, however, in command of the sea it would seem as though they had an equal chance with the Germans to rush soldiers to the fray.

But the facts were that the Germans commanded the air if not the sea, that they did not need many troops, that at the start they had secured all the available ports at which any large number of troops could be disembarked easily. The British navy did sink some German ships in the Skagerrak; but it proved difficult for the British to operate in those nearby waters, with the German submarine beneath and the German airplane overhead, and after all it was not necessary for the Nazis to transport men by water. Speed counted far more than numbers, and needed reinforcements were sent by plane.

It was a difficult task to dislodge the German invader, and one beyond the none too brilliant British War Office. At Narvik the British had their greatest success when their battleship *Warspite*, veteran of Jutland, broke into Narvik fiord, there to sink seven German destroyers. And this most northern port of Norway, far away from German reinforcements was captured by the Allied besieging army, only to be evacuated in early summer, as the German advance in the Low Countries and in France made Britain recall all soldiers available for the defense of their island home. The Allies could not well fight the Germans from Narvik; too many miles of trackless forest intervened between that Arctic port and the more inhabited parts of Norway. Therefore an expedition against Trondhjem was decided upon. This Norwegian port, at the head of a long and winding fiord well to the north of Scotland, could not be approached directly because of German mines, even though there were only a handful of German soldiers within the city. The plan was to assault the port from the land, and for that purpose the British landed a division, approximately 12,000 troops, on either side of Trondhjem, at Namsos to the north, at Andalsnes to the south. By marching on Trondhjem, it was fondly thought, they could speedily take that city by a pincer movement.

Disembarkation, however, proved difficult; men had to be landed in barges; they were most poorly equipped; they had no anti-aircraft guns at all and very little artillery; they did not even have white hoods to match the snow over which they marched. The troops marching south from Namsos were terribly mauled by the Germans who had good air support—the British had practically none. Those advancing from Andalsnes did succeed in joining forces with what was left of the Norwegian army but were out-maneuvered by onrushing Germans advancing over mountain passes and through difficult valleys. There was nothing left except to evacuate Norway, May 1, scarcely two weeks after landing.

This forced retreat was but the first of many which Britain was to make before the war turned her way. It was a bitter pill for her to swallow. But since Britain had no landing fields in Norway and was forced to use frozen lakes, while the Germans held the only available Norwegian airdromes, and since the British had neglected air transport, while the Germans had perfected it, Norway had to be abandoned.

To conquer Poland took five weeks; now within less than a month Denmark and Norway (aside from half-frozen Narvik) followed Austria, Czechoslovakia, and Poland down the Nazi maw. With Denmark gone, the British lost an important source of food; with Norway gone, the British lost not only supplies of fish and timber but were confronted by German airmen within striking distance of northern England and Scotland; and in addition the coastline of Scandinavia, indented with deep fiords, provided ideal lurking places for the submarine. A consolation prize for Britain was the Norwegian mercantile marine, the larger part of which was at sea.

For a few days the Nazis rested. There were ominous troop concentrations on the borders of Holland, Belgium, and Switzerland, but none knew where the next blow would fall. In Parliament there was angry debate. Men asserted that the Norwegian fiasco might have been prevented, that a bold assault on Trondhjem fiord by the navy would have captured the city, that Chamberlain was inept, supine. Some used stronger language. Mr. Amery, a life-long Tory, struck out at the Prime Minister in a burst of rage quoting Oliver Cromwell to the Long Parliament. "You have sat too long here for any good you have been doing. Depart, I say, be done with you. In the name of God, go!"

A motion of censure was defeated, but Chamberlain's majority was cut severely. He hung on for several days. Not until the Low Countries fell beneath the swastika scythe did he resign, to die a few months later. *Time* magazine called him "a Galsworthy Soames Forsyte," an apt but cruel valedictory for an old tired man thrust into high office because he was his father's son and was thought innocuous.

May 10, 1940, and over the borders of Holland, Belgium and Luxembourg swarm the Nazi panzers. The same day in London Winston Churchill, leader of lost causes, firebrand of firebrands, becomes prime minister. Nursling of a Tory family, too stupid for Oxford, a soldier in India, a reporter in Cuba, South Africa, the Sudan, a practitioner of painting and brick-laying, a deserter from the Tory ranks, cabinet minister under the Liberals, a prodigal son returning to the Tory fold, Churchill was long thought unstable. Although he had held many important offices under the Crown, home secretary, first lord of the admiralty, chancellor of the exchequer, the politicians distrusted him. They said he could never be prime minister. But now, if ever, daring and imagination there must be or England would be lost. Worthy successor to Burleigh and the Pitts, he took the helm.

THE LOW COUNTRIES

The Nazi occupation of Norway served notice on all the world that Hitler's dive-bombers soon would fly again. Would they swoop over Switzerland or above Holland and Belgium? Some thought Switzerland, since that approach was unorthodox like the Norwegian gambit, and since also it was closer to the heart of France, closer, too, to Italy if a hint was needed to that country to get in the war. But Holland and Belgium, one or the other or both, would bring the swastika nearer hated England. May 10 Hitler chose that route.

The Belgians and Netherlanders had long feared this. In both countries there were active National Socialist factions, fanatical and traitorous Belgian and Dutch Nazis, "Quislings" they soon came to be called, after Major Quisling of the Norwegian army and head of the Norwegian herdmen, the Nazis of Norway, chosen tool of Hitler. The Dutch and Belgians kept close watch on the leaders of these subversives but there was no way of ferreting out their plots, the sending of Dutch and Belgian uniforms to Germany to be worn later by German spies giving forged orders, agreements as to secret signals flashed at night to approaching planes, a trick played successfully in a year or two by Japanese in the Philippines. Thunderous accusations of non-neutrality pouring in on Brussels and The

Hague from Germany indicated that the coming of the avenging Teutons would not be long delayed. The two countries took such precautions as they could, mobilized their armies; the Netherlands made plans to abandon altogether their eastern districts, to open the dykes, and defend Rotterdam, Amsterdam and The Hague from behind water barriers.

The Dutch had no conception of modern warfare. They had tied dynamite on the trees which lined their roadways and fancied that by exploding it they could create barriers against Nazi tanks; they thought if they wrecked bridges over canals and flooded fields they could hold back the enemy. But Nazi panzer divisions were not stopped by fallen trees, and Nazi soldiers had rubber boats at hand to ferry over flooded land. Within five days the Netherlands were completely conquered. A veritable air armada covered Holland like locusts. Down dropped the parachutists, many in Dutch uniform, speaking excellent Dutch, baffling civilians and soldiers alike. The opulent and crowded Rotterdam was reduced to smoldering ruins by aërial bombardment as precise as that which wiped out Warsaw. The Netherlanders surrendered before The Hague, their capital, was captured, Queen Wilhelmina and others fleeing to England in the nick of time.

Belgium, also invaded May 10, withstood the Germans a few days longer. The first line of Belgian defense went down almost without a fight, but the second line, following the course of the Meuse River and the Albert Canal from the French frontier to Antwerp on the Scheldt, was stoutly defended in hope that the on-coming French and British armies might help the Belgian forces there to repel the Nazis.

On the second day of invasion that hope died, as the Germans captured the bridgeheads of the Albert Canal, stormed the great fortress of Eben Emael which fell so rapidly to parachutists that for weeks it was supposed the Nazis took it by means of some weird secret weapon. The boasted defenses of the Albert Canal were of no avail. Bridges were dynamited, but the Germans slipped into place movable ones, prefabricated to the exact millimeter. On to Brussels went the German host. Within the week the Belgian capital was in their hands, Antwerp one day later. Meanwhile the Germans had broken into France at the hinge between the big and little Maginot lines and French and British divisions which had advanced to succor Belgium retreated, leaving the Belgian army up in the air at the extreme left of the Franco-British-Belgian line. The Belgians were in merely tenuous contact with the British army and momentarily in danger of isolation in the narrowest of pockets by the seacoast. They had little ammunition, less food, and no planes, but the Belgian cabinet in Paris begged the King to keep on with the fight. To do so, however, was useless slaughter and on May 28 the King surrendered unconditionally with his entire army. The Belgian parliament now at Limoges, France, condemned this act, and so with much bitterness did Premier Reynaud of France and the Allied press. It was now May 28. To conquer Belgium took eighteen days.

FRANCE

1806 and Jena. Down went proud Prussia, and in three weeks Napoleon was sitting at Sans Souci in the chair of Frederick the Great. 1940, and in three weeks the swastika flew over the Eiffel Tower.

For convenience's sake the German victories which led to the annihilation of what was rated as the finest army in Europe may be summarized under two battles—the Battle of Flanders and the Battle of France. But such description is purely arbitrary. There was continuous and dispersed fighting all the time. The front was always fluid, changing hour by hour. The German flood inundated France so rapidly that half the time French generals did not know where their own armies were. Stuka dive-bombers, artillery, tanks, planes, fleeing civilians, infantry, both those fleeing and those advancing, ambulances, parachutists, private motor cars, and cattle were so churned up together in one steaming hell broth that only in vague outline was it possible to learn what was happening.

The first of these so-called battles, that of Flanders, began with the German break-through at the little Maginot line and ended on June 2 with the miraculous escape from the beaches of Dunkirk of four-fifths of the British expeditionary force. Sometimes it is spoken of as the Battle of the Pockets, due to the way the onrushing Germans segregated by flanking movements large sections of the Allied forces.

What took place was this: the Germans dashed through the gap they had made at Sedan, pressed forward with all speed, tanks and planes, until they reached Soissons on the Aisne. Then, instead of keeping on toward Paris as in 1914, they wheeled right in the direction of the English Channel, to cut off the Allied armies—French, British and Belgian, upward of a million men, which were retreating slowly down the seacoast in western Belgium—from the French armies to the south.

Seemingly it was impossible to stop this destructive process. At the apex of it was the tank and airplane, and not until they opened the way did artillery and infantry follow. The weather was dry and clear, "Hitler weather"; and so rapidly did the German tanks push forward that frequently they became isolated from supporting columns. But the French artillery was too light to destroy the huge German tanks, few of which fell into French hands and the roads were cluttered with fleeing mobs, Belgian and French, which sadly impeded Allied resistance but aided the German advance, since the German Stukas, low-flying dive-bombing planes, struck mercilessly at civilians and soldiers alike.

Speedily the German scythes swept on down the valley of the Somme toward Peronne, scene of desperate fighting in the First World War, and cut down Amiens, a key railway junction never captured in that conflict; then cut through to Abbeville, only a few miles from the Channel, and sweeping toward the north reached Boulogne. The exultant Germans, not stopping, kept on to Calais and, finding that town stoutly defended, swept around it, almost reaching Dunkirk. A million Allied soldiers apparently had been surrounded.

There were for the latter three possibilities: to cut through the German lines of communication, not as yet very wide or strongly held, along which the German armies were driving in; to surrender; or to escape by sea to England.

On paper the first possibility seemed feasible. In less than a week the German lines had been so distended by the huge arc they formed that a simultaneous thrust by the Allies on the Channel and by the main French armies before Paris might have pierced it, thus creating a pocket or pitfall whereby the German armies, which had passed the point of piercing and which had reached the Channel at Abbeville, would be severed from the main German forces and in turn be in danger of segregation and forced surrender.

Why was this not done? Gamelin had been removed as Allied generalissimo and Weygand, pupil of Foch and hero of World War I, now in command, was expected any moment to commence this counterattack. Instead of doing so, he began hastily to dig trenches and to form a new line of defense. Possibly he considered it essential to protect Paris; possibly, and more likely, owing to the confusion created by the sheer audacity of the German thrust, and by the activity of German fifth columnists in France, he was unable to concentrate his troops. Yet every hour this counterattack failed to materialize saw the German lines of communication strengthened by German artillery and German infantry.

Then, whatever chance the Belgian, French, and British armies at the Channel had of piercing the German lines and joining forces with the French armies to their south went begging when the Belgian king surrendered. King Leopold's men held the north end of the Allied forces, and if they were out of combat apparently there was nothing to prevent the German in Belgium from pushing on until they joined hands with the German army advancing eastward along the Channel. The Belgian lines covered thirty miles which instantly had to be covered by the hard-pressed British. The result was that the latter lost contact for the time being with parts of the French army, several divisions of which were cut off by advancing German columns. What was left of the French joined with the British, and these Allies, closing their ranks, pressed together along the seacoast to Dunkirk, where it seemed improbable that more than a few thousand could be conveyed across the Channel.

Then out of the jaws of death and gates of hell over 335,000 French and British soldiers were rescued. From the end of May to the fourth of June the Royal Navy and the Royal Air Force, aided and abetted by all kinds of miscellaneous sea-faring folk, worked at this task. The skies were darkened by planes as the RAF and German planes engaged in one unceasing duel; German artillery sprayed the beaches; German submarines and motor-launches, equipped with torpedo tubes and rapid-firing guns, swarmed out for the kill; and the German infantry threw itself "on the ever narrowing and contracting appendix within which the British and French armies fought."

The British did not use their battleships in these narrow waters, but every available light cruiser and destroyer was sent in, as well as innumerable other craft. Over 200 naval warships took part, and three times as many other vessels. No one will ever know just how many, since the owners of yachts, tugs, fishing-smacks, motor-boats, river steamers, and barges all aided. Anything afloat that could carry men was used. Only one narrow pier at Dunkirk, constantly bombed by the Germans, was available, and over this poured a steady stream of men. Soldiers by the thousand waded into shallow waters off the beaches and stood up to their armpits waiting for a friendly hand. Old men past sixty and young boys of fifteen worked together in hauling them into boats. Almost everyone in southeastern England connected in any way with boats and shipping took part.

Day and night the work continued; back and forth the impromptu ferries plied; and on one day alone over 60,000 half-starved Soldiers of the King reached home in safety.

The evacuation was unparalleled in military annals, and the total loss to the British army was but 30,000. Nevertheless, the very fact that there had to be evacuation made it a disastrous British defeat. Left in the hands of the Germans were over 1,000 heavy pieces of artillery, vast stores of munitions, food, gasoline. For the time being, Britain's scarcity of war matériel was appalling, and a militant foe, flushed with victory, held Scandinavia, Holland, Belgium, and the Straits of Dover.

Dark as the Allied cause was, it speedily grew darker. The Germans did not hesitate a minute. While the world wondered whether they would instantly "sail for England" or try to destroy France first, the Nazi legions embarked on the latter course. On June 5, the superbly mechanized armies of the Third Reich attacked the French in an offensive that stretched from the northern end of the Maginot line all the way to the mouth of the Somme at Abbeville— the Battle of France.

This time, instead of concentrating on one break-through, the Germans hit at four places; they rushed westward across the Somme into northern Normandy; they hit south from Amiens straight toward Paris; they crossed the Aisne farther east for a drive down the Oise River toward the French capital; and still further east they commenced the encirclement of the Maginot line, and tore it apart with pick and bomb.

Everywhere they met victory. For a brief moment it looked as though they might be foiled by the new tactics of Weygand. That general, copying German precedents in 1918, made no attempt at holding a rigid line but let the German tanks through the first French defenses and tried to lead them into traps. But all that Weygand did was to retard the enemy slightly. The Germans now were using 1,500,000 men, nearly 100 divisions, and the French were outnumbered in the field two to one, since large numbers of their best troops were either isolated in the Maginot line or guarding the Italian frontier. The line of battle extended over 200 miles and so swiftly drove the Germans that the breaking French had no time to gather their forces to counterattack.

In this dark hour of France's agony Italy declared war. Ever since Poland's demise Mussolini's attitude had been peculiarly his own. May 22, 1939 was the date of his military alliance with Germany and since then more than a year had passed. The Duce's delay in implementing that alliance by deeds may have been due to any one or all of three reasons. First, if his son-in-law and foreign secretary, Ciano, told the truth, the Duce was displeased by German policy as to Poland and Russia. He did not want a war over Poland and considered that Danzig might have been secured without one; and he was not consulted apparently about the Russo-German pact until just before it was signed, a fact he found irritating. Secondly, it is possible that Mussolini kept his Black Shirts out of the war at Hitler's behest. As long as he stayed neutral the French had to keep many divisions on the Italian frontier. Once they went to war a belligerent north Italy might suddenly be conquered, and Libya as well, before the Germans could prevent it. Finally, and most probable, Mussolini was playing his own fine Italian hand. If Germany was clearly winning he could enter any time; if England and France showed signs of winning he would be safe as a neutral; if the war deadlocked he could consult "Italy's sacred egoism" (the words of Italy's premier of 1915 who sold his country's services on the auction block) and bargain with both sides. Meanwhile Mussolini was getting huge imports of oil.

There are indications that Britain and France would have paid a high price for Italian neutrality, especially after May 10. The French might have offered Djibuti (French Somaliland) and even have been persuaded to cede Tunisia. The British presumably would have delivered British Somaliland to the Duce, and there were hints that Malta might be demilitarized. Some day we shall probably know to what extent the democracies would have fed the sawdust Caesar. They had not hesitated in 1915 when their backs were at the wall to pay a high price for alliance with Italy. Their need now was infinitely greater.

Meanwhile Mussolini's nuisance value to Hitler was considerable, and he had already blackmailed the democracies into buying and selling extensively in the Italian market. So he contented himself at first with merely cackling at Allied reverses. Then, when the latter foreshadowed disaster, he became more belligerent, his growls more sinister. June 11 Mussolini declared war on Britain and France. "We take the field," he said, "against the plutocratic and reactionary democracies who always have blocked our march and frequently plotted against the Italian people."

The stab of the Italian stiletto drew little blood, scarcely shadowed the course of events. The Italian army won a few square kilometers in mountainous southeastern France and that was all. Paris already had been abandoned by the government, and on June 12 Weygand informed a French cabinet meeting at Tours that the war was lost.

Five days were to intervene before France asked for an armistice. The French and British had solemnly sworn in March that they would "neither negotiate nor conclude an armistice or treaty of peace except by mutual consent." France asked to be released from this agreement. Churchill flew to Tours and proposed that the French and British empires merge, one parliament, one war cabinet, one country. France still had planes, France still had soldiers. A retreat might be made into the rocky peninsula of Brittany (De Gaulle's proposal) defended on both sides by the warships of the Allies—a bridgehead for future invasion. If that was not feasible there was still time to transfer government, navy (as yet unscathed) and a good part of the army and air fleet to Algiers. A large French army already was in North Africa and Syria with 1,800 unused planes. With the French and British navies in command of the Mediterranean the Italians could have been whipped out of Libya and starved out of Ethiopia. There was no need for despair; the war might still be won.

The French cabinet by thirteen to eleven rejected this proposal. Reynaud, who had succeeded Daladier as premier, resigned and Marshal Pétain succeeded him. June 17 an armistice was requested. The Germans were in no hurry and did not grant one until the 25th, not until a similar request had been sent to Rome, not until the German armies were south of the Loire.

Hitler's glory and Hitler's happiness were now at their zenith. In 1941 and in 1942 his armies were to march greater distances, to win greater battles: but for him, the corporal of 1918, this was the substance of things hoped for, this moment, with mighty German

Michael, sword in hand, kicking scornfully at the prostrate body of French Marianne.

Appropriate the stage setting, the forest of Compiegne, the railway coach (dragged from a Paris museum) in which German generals in 1918 had had to meet Foch's harsh question, "Why are you here?" And nearby the monument with bronze tablet inscribed: "Here on November 11, 1918, perished the criminal arrogance of the Imperial German Reich, defeated by the free peoples whom it sought to enslave." A superb stage for Adolph Hitler!

His generals were more interested in the armistice terms. They paralleled in many ways those of the earlier armistice but were harsher. Not only were the French to give up all military supplies and equipment and pay the costs of German occupation until after the war, but also more than half of France was to be occupied including the Atlantic coast from Belgium to Spain. Concerning its disposal nothing was stipulated. All French prisoners of war were to be incarcerated until peace was declared. Any German citizen living in the unoccupied zone and wanted by the gestapo must immediately be surrendered. The French fleet was to be disarmed in French ports. A few minor tidbits were given Italy, very minor.

Just what had happened is clear. At the time of the armistice the Germans had taken all France north of a line drawn from the Swiss border to the mouth of the Garonne on the Atlantic, and the Nazis had rounded into captivity 1,900,000 French soldiers at a total expense of 25,000 Germans killed or missing, 68,000 wounded. Just why it happened is not so obvious. French rightists asserted that the debâcle was due to the Popular Front, to the negligence of Blum and other radicals, to Communist influence. The French left said it was Fascism boring from within that had brought France to her knees, that the country had been betrayed by those who preferred Hitler to the loss of social and financial power for themselves and their group or class.

There is much to be said for both accusations. The Popular Front cannot escape all responsibility for unpreparedness and Communists did hold by the Moscow party line in proclaiming the war an imperialistic venture. There were also many in France, particularly in important political and military posts, fevered by the virus of Fascism, distrustful of Britain, convinced of Hitler's inevitable victory, hating democracy, and so fearful of Communism as to prefer Prussian dragoons to any revolt of the French masses.

Nevertheless, these facts do not wholly explain the fall of France. It is likely that the majority of Frenchmen were lukewarm to the war in 1939, but that does not mean they were unwilling to fight when their country was invaded. It has been argued with some show of reason that Frenchmen have been divided ever since the Revolution of 1789 and that this old schism now was more pronounced than ever. But that schism existed in 1914 and did not then prevent Frenchmen from fighting with élan and valor. Why did they fail to do so in 1940?

Wrote André Maurois, "A great civilization saw itself foredoomed because 5,000 tanks and 10,000 airplanes, which we could have built or bought without trouble, were not constructed in time." This, however, is no true explanation. It was not absence of planes and tanks that lost the war; rather the failure to use those already available. "According to documents furnished by Colonel Rivet (at the Riom trial) the French army had approximately 3,500 tanks." Of these the largest types were not used at all and of the others only 2,000 saw action. The record in regard to planes was worse. Up to the armistice the French lost about 2,000 planes, shot down in the air or on the ground. Yet after the war was over some 4,238 military planes were counted in unoccupied France, to say nothing of a fine pool of first-class planes in North Africa which never dropped a bomb. The same was true of anti-aircraft guns, only 45 per cent of those available being used (discounting altogether those on the Maginot line), true also of radios and other military equipment. Nor was this all: planes and tanks were not ably employed; where they were most needed they were not to be found; and when use was made of them it was never coördinated.

The explanation of this goes back to the organization of the French army. Revelations concerning it are reminiscent of the sham, stupidity and vainglory of 1870. France emerged from World War I with a superb military reputation and two commanders, both beloved by the country, both disliking one another cordially, Marshals Foch and Pétain. Unfortunately for France the former died soon after the war and the latter continued to live. Pétain had been a good general from the routine administrative point of view but the laurels he had won at Verdun had not been awarded for initiative, dash and daring. He had been a pillar of defense then, but in 1940 he was eighty-three years old. Pétain retired in 1934 but he continued to be a member of the committee of national defense and its most important one. Both Blum and Daladier looked up to him as the last word in military wisdom despite his reactionary political sentiments. And as long as this was so it was impossible to shake the army out of its lethargy.

Germany commenced rearming in 1933. Her minister of war was then forty, Marshal Göring. Within a year he had organized armored divisions and had experimented with these in coördination with massed planes, experiments carried on later in Spain in actual combat. Pétain was then minister of war in France, age seventy-seven, his chief of staff, General Weygand, sixty-eight, his successor in command and nominated by him, General Maurin, seventy-two. These old gentlemen were not interested in tanks or planes except for auxiliary purposes. All three suffered from Maginot-line psychosis, a fixed idea that defense would win future wars. Yet even despite this, Pétain opposed and prevented, perhaps on political grounds, the extension of the Maginot line to the North Sea, an act which logically he should have approved. The Ardennes forest, he asserted, afforded quite sufficient protection for France's northeastern frontier. The very place he refused to fortify was the point of German attack in 1940.

In 1934 a certain French colonel of whom history was to hear a great deal, Charles André Joseph Marie De Gaulle, wrote a book entitled *The Army of the Future*. De Gaulle was a specialist in tank warfare, an advocate of a highly trained mobile army in which quality and mechanized equipment counted for more than mere numbers. His ideas were anathema to the French military mandarins. The Germans took his book seriously and profited from it, but French authorities ignored it, except for contemptuous attacks by both Weygand and Pétain. Those two ancients preferred the military lore of a certain General Chauvineau, and Pétain wrote a laudatory introduction to that General's book, *Une Invasion, est-elle possible?* published in 1938. A sentence or two from this is indicative of Pétain's mind. "The command of large mechanized units," wrote Chauvineau, "destined to act in isolation poses insoluble problems because of the dispersion and rapid movement of the participants. Such command would require an intuition and presence of mind that no one possesses." And again, "As mobility is the raison d'être and even the safeguard of the caterpillar engine it is fitting to use it only in defensive manoeuvers ... the tank instead of penetrating the enemy lines and engaging in close fight which may prove fatal to it ... withdraws from all its enemies and is content to fire on the vanguard of the infantry or to counter-attack with limited objectives ... every infantry battalion should include a tank company and an anti-tank company."

Until the outbreak of war De Gaulle was only a colonel but he knew about tanks and he knew what the Germans had done with them in Spain and Poland. His insistent and brilliant arguments forced the French general staff to agree to one armored division and three light mechanized divisions. Now, with the war on their hands, they agreed to divert a certain number of tanks from the scattered infantry units to which they had been attached and to form four armored divisions. Had the French had time to organize these, and had the generals really had faith in them, the conquest of France might not have been so easy. As it was, the French tankmen had little chance to show their prowess. The second armored division, for instance, found its tanks posted on bridges as sentinels and not kept in mass formation. The French tanks remained scattered, in-effective for defense, powerless for offense.

An equally doleful story is that of the air force. One argument used by Pétain to show why he had to surrender was that "French aviation was forced to fight outnumbered one to six." This was a misstatement. It was arrived at by taking the total of all German planes whether in Norway, Poland, France or attached to the German navy and comparing it with the total France actually used. True, the Germans outnumbered the French three to one in combat planes, that is, if British planes are not counted. If British combat planes are counted, the German numerical superiority is reduced to three to two.

This French handicap was serious but not necessarily fatal. In the autumn of 1940 the British were under a greater handicap and when Russia was invaded by Hitler the German superiority was almost as marked. Yet the British and the Russians were not driven from the skies and the French were. Why?

The reason was not treachery, Fascism or Communism boring from within, but sheer stupidity and blindness in regard to the function of the plane. French generals still thought in terms of 1914-1918 when the plane was a supplement to the ground forces, on a par, perhaps, with the engineering corps. Its principal use was for reconnaissance, finding out where the enemy was located, mapping battlefields, a kind of scouting super-cavalry.

The quality of many French planes was good, and so, too, the mental alertness and morale of individual French aviators. Whenever they met Germans in equal combat they gave a good account of themselves. The trouble was they seldom had a chance to do so, since the German airmen did not fight this war solo. The luftwaffe fought en masse, as the British and Americans soon learned to do. But in France, 1939-1940, there was not a single aërial division to fight for dominion of the air. The unit of the French air force was the esquadrille, and these were dispersed and scattered among French divisions in the same way as the tanks. This was the system in vogue in the First World War which France had won. Why change?

Napoleon won his battles by concentrating artillery fire. Planes had become the new artillery of the air. But old men seldom recognize new facts.

War as a science had been revolutionized in twenty years. Germans and Russians, crushed in World War I, stripped of matériel, compelled to improvise, to economize, to study past errors, built new armies from the ground up. German and Russian generals trained parachutists (the French had none); German and Russian generals worked out in minute detail how to coördinate tank and plane and infantry, an irresistible combination when opposed by an old-style army such as that of Poland (French-trained) or that of France. The over-all picture resembles that of Europe (1792-1807) in reverse. Austrian and Prussian armies collapsed before those of Napoleon partly because of deficient ésprit and morale, more largely, one suspects, because of incrusted tradition and dry rot. Napoleonic victories up to Austerlitz and Jena, and perhaps beyond, were due partially, it may be admitted, to the revolutionary enthusiasm of 1789-1793, but even more largely to youthful and fresh leadership, brilliant offensive tactics, organization perfected to meet actual conditions.

Since America became involved in this anti-Fascist war it has been fashionable to put the blame for everything on Fascism, except the weather. Because Pétain and Weygand were reactionaries it does not follow that they were, *ipso facto*, unpatriotic Frenchmen. Given the opportunity, reactionaries will fight like demons to defend their hearthstones; conversely, good democrats will surrender incontinently if caught by surprise, deprived of hope. That French morale in 1939 was low must be granted; but to ascribe

French defeat primarily to that factor is an unwarranted assumption. New weapons, new tactics, new leadership, a sustained and brilliant German offense, as opposed to timidity, privilege, conservatism, and sheer ignorance is the truer explanation. After all, the poilus of 1939-1940 were the sons of those who fought the first and second Marne. Given a fair chance, they would have been the heroes their fathers were in 1914-1918. But the science of war had moved on beyond their historic glories, and the German army was the arbiter of European politics which from now on were but a mode of war.

5. BRITAIN BESIEGED

AND now with Dunkirk came Britain's finest hour. Cold rage and stubborn will fused all hearts as one. Welsh miners, London cockneys, Midland loom-tenders, sheepmen, ploughmen, fishermen half round the earth—all alike fared to their country's instant need. A thousand memories of a thousand years, English bowmen at Agincourt, Scottish pikemen standing to the charge of armored knights, Grenville at Flores in the Azores, all this past belonged to all alike. No class, no clique, no little group could stamp it theirs.

To be the present symbol of what all felt who used the English language, to lift high the battle banner for Home and Commonwealth and Empire—that honor fell to Winston Churchill. "We shall defend our island," said he in the House of Commons, "whatever the cost may be; we shall fight on the beaches, we shall fight on landing grounds, we shall fight in the fields, we shall fight in the streets, and we shall fight on the hills. We shall never surrender, and even if, which I do not for a minute believe, this island or a large part of it were subjugated and starving, then our Empire beyond the seas, armed and guarded by the British fleet, will carry on the struggle until in God's good time the New World with all its power and might sets forth to the liberation of the old."

"Until in God's good time the New World!" Churchill spoke with prophetic fire and confidence. He well knew that on the day before in Washington General Marshall, chief of staff, had certified as unnecessary for the defense of the United States, 500,000 rifles and 130,000,000 rounds of ammunition, 900 field guns, 80,000 machine guns and other war matériel to the value of $37,619,556.60. Sold by the federal government to U.S. Export Company, these crucial weapons were immediately resold, chiefly to the British government and, even before transfer papers were signed, were on the way from assemblage centers to the eastern seaboard.

Churchill's speech was on June 5. "A dozen ships sailed from Gravesend Bay and Baltimore with guns for Britain before the end of June. Another fifteen freighters sailing between July 1st and August 1st took what was left. The first vessel to reach England arrived June 23rd, six days after France fell. Most of the others reached British ports in July. A million eager hands, empty hands, eagerly reached for the rifles as Hitler hesitated across the Channel." [1] Churchill breathed easier. If the Nazis ever got too close those guns from overseas would help a lot. Meanwhile the brunt of the storm was to be borne by Britain alone, for France had caved in.

That somber fact boosted defense morale to new heights, Churchill's as well as that of his countrymen. Quietly, invincibly, the Prime Minister explained to the House of Commons just where England stood, minimizing no dangers, boasting no resources. There was no word of reproach for France, only sympathy. What concerned him was the coming Battle of Britain. "The whole fury and might of the enemy," he said, "must very soon be turned upon us. Hitler knows that he will have to break us in this island or lose the war. If we can stand up to him, all Europe may be free and the life of the world may move forward into broad, sunlit uplands. If we fail, then the whole world, including the United States, including all that we have known and cared for, will sink into the abyss. . . . Let us therefore brace ourselves to our duties, and so bear ourselves that, if the British Empire and its Commonwealth last for a thousand years, men still will say, 'This was their finest hour.'"

And so it was to be, but first a good six weeks had yet to pass before the fury broke. Hitler seemed to hesitate. He addressed the Reichstag, as if in reply to Churchill: "In this hour," he said, "I feel it to be my own duty before my own conscience to appeal once more to reason and common sense in Great Britain as much as elsewhere. I consider myself in a position to make this appeal, since I am not the vanquished begging favors but the victor speaking in the name of reason. . . . Possibly Mr. Churchill will brush aside this statement of mine by saying that it is merely born of fear and doubt in our final victory. In that case I shall have relieved my conscience in regard to things to come." Thus Hitler suggested peace. It was rumored that, indirectly, at that time he was negotiating with Sir Samuel Hoare of Ethiopian chicane and Munich shame, now British minister to Franco in shattered Madrid.

[1] From Edward R. Stettinius, *Lend-Lease, Weapon for Victory* (New York, 1944), p. 25. By permission of The Macmillan Company, publishers.

But Britain refused to listen. Twice before in England's long history she had beaten back a conqueror bent on her destruction. In Elizabeth's time the galleons of Philip's Spain had been dispersed and shattered in one long-drawn-out running fight at sea, the seasoned infantry close packed upon them, reputed Europe's finest soldiers, drowned in the stormy island seas. Again in the days of William Pitt, as Nelson chased the French fleet to the West Indies and back before sinking it at Trafalgar, there was anxiety in Britain and close watch kept from Martello towers on the short stretch of water that lay between her shores and Boulogne where Napoleon's armies were.

Neither Philip of Spain nor Napoleon of France was as perilous a foe as German Hitler. The Spaniards and French could do no harm so long as British ships and seamen ruled Channel water. With the German it was otherwise. He could ship death by air. Let him gain but a scanty bridgehead by planes and gliders, hold it for twenty-four hours while swift motor boats and invasion barges brought reinforcements, tanks and artillery, then fanning inland, Britain would be at his mercy. The Royal Navy was no longer the decisive barrier to invasion that it had been in preceding centuries.

Britain expected that invasion; so did the rest of the world, and the fear of it was trumpeted abroad for all friends to hear and heed. In these days it seemed but all too grimly real. From Norwegian fiords to the north and northeast of Scotland, all the way to Brittany and southwest of Cornwall, none could now dispute Nazi power. It half-ringed Britain in. If Ireland were added to her foes, then she would be almost shut off from the outside world. Future prospects were not encouraging. But make peace with the Nazis Britain would not.

Meanwhile Hitler first sped south to make an end to France. It certainly was the easiest thing to do; he may have thought that Britain was at his mercy and could later be annihilated; he may have worried lest France, still living, recuperate sufficiently to strike at his rear as he invaded Britain from her shores; it is possible the showman in him overcame his judgment and that he could not resist the temptation first to stage his little drama in Marshal Foch's railway carriage; or, more probable, for the time being he just did not have the ships to launch his wehrmacht against England.

Vast shipping facilities, swift motor-boats and landing barges covered by a cosmic canopy of planes were requisite for an invasion. The luftwaffe could supply the planes; whence the vessels? Norwegian fiords, Dutch, Belgian, German and French coasts were combed, and even from the blue Danube barges were dragged overland to the North Sea. To assemble these motley craft took time, and, when obtained, far too many were unsuitable for invasion work. Had Göring had more imagination, if as minister of war he had not given so great priority to tanks, guns, planes and submarines and had built a thousand landing barges, the Germans would have had a better chance to march on London.

Thus Britain gained a little time. She used it to cover open beaches with barbed wire, to sow land mines, to rip up golf courses where planes might land, to dig tank traps, to tear down sign posts, to camouflage her artillery, to equip her Home Guard, men past military age, with something better than shotguns and sporting rifles, to receive reinforcements from the Dominions, to store food supplies, to revolutionize her industry, to double and redouble her armament, toiling night and day until the stubborn workers reeled where they stood at the machines.

Above all, the modern technique of nation-wide, everybody-in-it, last-ditch resistance, was elaborated, explained, enforced and organized. For the first time in her history Britain was using all her brains and all her energy to forge the deadly sword of a nation's war.

Before the Nazi army could try its cross-Channel leap there was another danger to void. By the rather romantic terms of the armistice the French fleet was to assemble at French ports, there to be dismantled until the war was over and not to be used against Britain, a device, obviously, to prevent a French admiral from taking his squadrons to join the British fleet. If this phoney trick worked, the fleet of France added to that of Italy and the Reich might well win control of the Mediterranean, perhaps the Atlantic. In such an eventuality Britain could be starved, the United States kept out of the war, and the British Commonwealth and Empire ended.

The French fleet was divided: some ships were at anchor in British harbors; some lay off Alexandria, Egypt; still more were stationed at Oran off the North African coast; and one battleship, the *Richelieu,* by reputation the world's finest, was at Dakar, West Africa; a few were in the Caribbean. Churchill was determined that none should fall into German hands. Those in British harbors were quickly taken at the cost of one French and one British tar. The French admiral at Alexandria agreed to demilitarize the ships there, but the commander at Oran was not so amenable. Three proposals were made: to join Britain in fighting Germany; to steam to British ports or to the French West Indies, there to intern the ships; to sink them where they were. He refused all three and the British admiral opened fire. A thousand French sailors lost their lives, as most of their vessels were inoperative; the battleship *Strassbourg* alone limping across the Mediterranean to Toulon. Finally, July 8, the famous *Richelieu* was badly damaged by a British torpedo at Dakar. One threat to Britain's safety was thus removed.

Throughout this lull the German luftwaffe battered hard at British convoys weaving a wary way down the long Channel routes to London. British planes were bombing any and all coastal shipping concentrated in French, Belgian and Dutch ports. Elsewhere, apart from the steady attrition of the British high-seas mercantile marine, there was no concentrated action in the war of Britain vis-à-vis Germany. Then on August 8 came *Der Tag*, the opening of the Battle for Britain, a fight that raged on day after day, week after week, month after month, until the spring of 1941 when Adolf Hitler, unable to bring Britain to her knees, hopeful of delaying America, switched his fury from the Channel to the Balkans.

For a week the Nazis attacked all out, on one day, August 15, putting up over a thousand planes. They confined themselves at first largely to southeastern England, coastal towns and airdromes, and met with a hot reception, the British claiming to have shot down 645 planes while only losing 137. The German figures were approximately in reverse. Those given by the RAF were probably the more authentic. Had this not been the case, the blinding terror of the coming autumn would have had a different ending, since the Germans outnumbered the British in the air three to one. The heavy loss of Nazi planes did not imply less skill and daring than that displayed by the RAF. The luftwaffe, it must be remembered, relied chiefly on bombers and not until later did it buttress them with adequate support by fighter planes. The RAF had relatively few bombers. For the defense of Britain it relied on two types of fighter plane, the Hurricane with machine guns only, and the Spitfire with cannon, the latter a superb achievement in aërial engineering, probably superior in speed and maneuverability to any plane then extant. These day-by-day victories wherein four German planes hit the dirt to one from the RAF were not so incredible as they appeared, for the British were burning American-made gasoline of a decidedly higher octane rating than that then made in Germany, and the Stuka dive-bomber was no match for the Spitfire.

August 20 Churchill congratulated his people on the way they had stood the gaff. This war was different from that of 1914. "The fronts," he said, "are everywhere. The trenches are dug in the towns and streets. Every village is fortified. Every road is barred. The front line runs through the factories. The workmen are soldiers, with different weapons but the same courage.... We have rearmed and rebuilt our armies in a degree which would have been deemed impossible a few months ago. We have ferried across the Atlantic in the month of July, thanks to our friends over there, an immense mass of munitions of all kinds.... More than 2,000,000 determined men have rifles and bayonets in their hands tonight.... The gratitude of every home in our island, in our Empire ... goes out to the British airmen who undaunted by odds, unwearied in their constant challenge and mortal danger, are turning the tide of the World War by their prowess and by their devotion. Never in the field of human conflict was so much owed by so many to so few."

This debt to the Empire's airmen, which the Prime Minister acknowledged, was soon to be increased a hundredfold. The German attack which had slowed down was speeded up. Beginning August 24 it went into high gear, and in two weeks the British shot down 586 enemy planes at a loss of 238. The ratio was still heavily against the Germans but instead of being four to one it was now little more than two to one, as the luftwaffe was throwing more fighter planes into the fray.

Then suddenly on September 7 the Germans made their biggest bid for victory. Too much time was being wasted in softening up cities on the Channel, in trying to root out the RAF from landing fields and airdromes. Since London was the British Empire's heart, they would concentrate on its destruction.

The first day was the worst. Up the Thames valley swarmed the German planes, estimated at 1,500, straight through the thinly held lines of defense. For some eight hours they shuttled back and forth from their continental lairs, dropping some 1,280 tons of bombs, well-nigh wiping out the thick-lined docks and warehouses along the river bank, the nearby slum warrens of the poor collapsing into rubble. It seemed as though London might share the fate of Warsaw and Guernica.

This blasting rain of war the Nazis were to keep up steadily a good two months. There were literally hundreds of raids, for the most part centered on the London area and south and southeastern ports. Every device conceivable was put into play by the Germans. They came in solid formations, they came in diamond-shaped figures, sometimes with fighter planes overhead for protection, sometimes in alternating waves of fighters and bombers. Throughout September not a day passed without Germans overhead. They came by day, they came by night, but generally by night since the RAF was less accurate and deadly then. Their main objectives were railway stations, docks, factories, warehouses, power plants. But night bombing was of necessity more or less indiscriminate, and it was inevitable that hospitals, churches, schools and homes were also hit hard. When we remember that some 50,000 high explosive bombs fell on London from September, 1940, to July, 1941, besides the enormous fires started by incendiaries and by Göring's "bread baskets," we may be more surprised by the extent of London left standing than by the destruction wrought.

Fortunately for Britain, the German bombers were too small for the job and their bombs were too light. London was, and is, a sprawling metropolis, in that respect more like Los Angeles than any other American center. That part known as "The City," the commercial and financial center, was extraordinarily congested, a maze of narrow, crooked streets in the neighborhood of St. Paul's and the Bank of England. The great majority of Londoners, however, lived in small incommodious two-story dwellings rather than apartment houses. In consequence, greater London stretched out miles and miles in every direction until it scattered and dwindled into semi-suburbs. London administratively was highly decentralized; there was no single power house, no single fire department, no single telephone exchange. This costly and clumsy decentralization of essential services had long been held anachronistic, but in these days of peril it proved a blessing, for though many gas and water mains burst, and though many generator plants were disabled, never, even when the blitz was at its worst, was London crippled.

Not until after mid-November did Londoners get a respite. Raids continued intermittently throughout autumn and winter but were for the most part of diminishing intensity. Two or three in December resembled the all-out blows of September and October, and one in particular wrought tremendous havoc in the ancient "City," destroying acre after acre of old buildings in the heart of London, including many Christopher Wren churches around St. Paul's, which miraculously escaped. By mid-autumn the luftwaffe switched its attention from the metropolis to the industrial centers of the north and to British seaports. Coventry, Manchester, Sheffield, Bristol, Liverpool, Portsmouth, the German bombers visited them all, time after time, and many other cities also. But as winter turned to spring (1941) the Germans focused their attention on seaports, so much so that during 1941 all but six out of forty night raids not directed at London were aimed at harbors and harbor facilities.

The reason was evident—the United States. We had promised more planes, more guns, and we had begun to deliver in bulk. To stop this inflow the Germans relied on their subs at sea and their planes hovering over British ports. Hence the deadly concentration on Portsmouth, Cardiff, Swansea, Merseyside, Liverpool, Glasgow and even Belfast. The destruction done was large, the loss of civilian life heavy, the disruption and delay in unloading ships most important; but the ports were not deserted, the people did not run away, the ships were somehow unloaded, the German objective was not realized. Air power was much less effective than the experts and soothsayers had prophesied it would be.

The RAF during 1940 and 1941 knocked down and out some 3,000 German planes, losing some 900 of its own. The latter had to be replaced, their number increased whether possible or not, and repairs innumerable had to be made. "For months," we are told, "during England's crisis plane factories barely managed to maintain a survival rate of production." The factories were dispersed, their locations hard to ferret out, different parts being made at different places. But even so it is doubtful if survival production and maintenance could have been kept up if the Nazis had left the big cities alone and had concentrated on those factories which supplied certain all-important parts. One engineering plant in Yorkshire, for instance, manufactured most of the gear used by the Spitfire upon which Britain's life depended, and another plant not far from London made most of the roller bearings. Presumably these facts were known in Germany in 1939. Why the Yorkshire factory escaped all air raids, and the roller bearing plant also until 1941, is one of the mysteries of this war. Even in raiding Coventry, a nest of munition plants, the Nazi bombers dove for the heart of the city, smashing houses and the cathedral but damaging only slightly important factory buildings on the outskirts. It seems in this case as if the very destructiveness of the bombing, by its hell-raised camouflage of smoke and flame, prevented the achievement sought by the military skill which directed the attack.

The results of these air raids, as regards the civilian population, were both astonishing and heartening. Despite some 40,000 killed and twice as many wounded, despite redoubling these figures for those left homeless and for those forced to adopt a caveman's way of life, sleeping in damp cellars and in London subways, the average Britisher stayed on his or her job, worked incredibly long hours, lived on coarse, dull food, paid huge taxes, and did it all with considerable cheerfulness.

There was dynamic leadership, it is true, and the authorities did much to organize relief, to build air-raid shelters, to put steel bunks in subways, to clamp down on profiteers, to ration food and clothing so that there was an approach to equality in commodities necessary for life; but these rules, regulations, ordinances would have been useless had it not been for the spontaneity with which the ordinary man and woman not only obeyed orders but also of their own accord engaged in all sorts of coöperative work, freely and voluntarily, without pay or recognition. The air-raid wardens tramping ceaselessly through the long damp winter nights of England, the women volunteers who drove ambulances, nursed in hospitals, fed war workers, firemen and the homeless, the British of both sexes who dug the heavy clay soil of their island and turned out bumper crops, the volunteer police and fire wardens, the solicitors of every last penny for war loans, the collectors of old paper, scrap iron, all these responded to their country's call, and kept on responding, regardless of what grim fate was doing to them day by day.

Britain was short of everything and factory operatives worked twelve hours a day, seven days a week during the autumn of 1940. It was not compulsory work, but freely offered, gratefully received. The latent energies of men in times of crisis defy ordinary psychological limitations, and throughout Britain in these black months an emotional excitement, deep and profound, steeled nerve and heart and sinew to accomplish the impossible. Particularly true was this of women who washed and cooked and cared for children in addition to what under ordinary circumstances would have proved incredible hours of toil in industry.

"I noticed," wrote Jennie Lee, "a woman of my mother's age working at her sewing machine with desperate speed and concentration. Her home had been struck the night before. This was her way of carrying herself through the shock. And there was another thing sustaining her. Her youngest son was in the army. 'And who,' she said to me, 'is going to make a coat to wrap around him with the cold days drawing in if his own mother is not willing to help him?'"[1]

Before the war was over there were to be strikes in factories and mines, but while the blitz was on class distinctions faded like magic. The bombs struck rich and poor alike, on Mayfair as well as on Thameside, and rich and poor did equal work, shared equal rations and equal danger, felt equal pride defending through this deadly hour their island home "set in a silver sea."

To the surprise of scientists, public health did not deteriorate, it actually improved. Physical breakdowns had been foretold, from nervous psychoses due to noise, shock and sleeplessness, from foul skin diseases the result of undernourishment, lack of sanitation and nights spent in underground shelters without removing clothing. Hospitals were crowded, it is true, but the cases were mostly those of external accident, burns and bruises. While the blitz lasted the average man and woman was healthier than in time of peace, the children more plump and rosy.

Exaltation of spirit had much to do with this, but what in the long run was just as important was the actual and general improvement in British diet. There was less tea, jam and sweets available, less meat. Their place was taken by vegetables. A scientific regimen was prescribed and of necessity rather closely followed.

Lord Woolton, minister of food and "the greatest quartermaster since Moses," earned the praise of all classes for his stern, just and intelligent handling of food supplies. That driving businessman who had risen from humble circumstances to direct a chain of department stores, undertook the task of feeding 47,000,000 people. Most of prewar Britain's butter, bacon and eggs had come from

[1] Jennie Lee, *This Great Journey* (New York, Rinehart and Company, Inc., 1942), p. 220.

Denmark and the Low Countries. This supply was now cut off. The quantity of food imported from Canada, the United States and Argentine was sharply reduced owing to German subs and the necessity of conserving cargo space. The fruit and cheese and choice vegetables of France no longer were to be had. What for a time looked even more serious was the luftwaffe's bombing of warehouses filled with sugar and beef, stored for emergency rations.

Woolton had to meet a dozen famine crises at once. The stores of food on hand had to be scattered in many places for safety's sake, in cinema houses, chapels, empty buildings; he had to provide a decent sustenance for scores of thousands of homeless fellow-countrymen, to see that everyone got his share of an ever diminishing food supply, and what was hardest of all, to change the eating habits of a stubborn people.

The headway he made was phenomenal: he inaugurated rationing by a point system, afterwards copied in America, whereby the number of food points required (and one paid nothing for the ration book containing them) went up or down in accordance with the scarcity or abundance of any particular food; he obtained the backing of the Queen for mobile canteens serving hot food to the homeless; he advertised on billboards and in newspapers and in circulars just what a balanced diet should provide in calories and vitamins. Soon "Potato Pete" and "Clara Carrot" cartoons were being read by a million children. Meat consumption was cut two-thirds, sugar and tea consumption cut in half. Milk was largely restricted to children and expectant mothers, as was the case with eggs. Such jams and syrups as were available were kept for the children. The resultant diet was not interesting but it was healthful, and schools soon reported that boys and girls averaged heavier in weight than those in the same age groups before the war.

The buoyancy reflected by British press and radio at the commencement of 1941 was amazing. The British thought they were winning the war when in fact they were simply staving off defeat. Part of their sanguine enthusiasm was based on their history, part on belief that the RAF was pulverizing German factories to the same extent as their own were destroyed. This was not the case. The bombers of the RAF pounced continuously on German shipping in French harbors and may have prevented an invasion starting, but the bombardment of Germany was a different matter. There were no huge Lancaster and Halifax bombers early in the war; Britain had specialized in fighter planes of limited cruising range. The luftwaffe had only a short round trip to make, from France to England and back; from England to Germany and return meant more gas, a lighter bomb load, less time available for assault once the targets were located. Furthermore, those sought by the RAF were widely scattered. They ranged all the way east and west from the Baltic to Brittany's port of Brest, where it was necessary to keep disabled the great German warships *Gneisenau* and *Scharnhorst,* and all the way north and south from Hamburg and Bremen on the North Sea to Turin in Italy. Occasionally British airmen annoyed Berlin, but for the most part they confined their attention to the Ruhr Valley and to the interlacing network of coal, steel and transportation facilities there. Some real damage was done, but it was far less extensive than that wrought in Britain by the luftwaffe, which dropped four bombs there for every one the RAF dropped on Germany.

Defeat by air had been averted, but how about defeat by sea? It was not so easy to be optimistic about this. By March, 1941, the Battle for Britain was in its latter stages, the Battle for the Atlantic at its peak. The people of Britain could and would sleep underground if need be, and endure great hardships; but they had to be fed; they had to be armed. There were distinct limits to the food they could grow, to the number of planes and guns they could manufacture. Only by imports could they live, and that meant British control of the Atlantic. Victories over the Italians in the Mediterranean and in Libya were heartening and important, but in the last analysis they were subordinate to keeping clear the sea lanes of the western ocean. Only by drawing on the resources of the Western Hemisphere was it possible for Britain to survive. And that depended on three things: the Royal Navy and mercantile marine, and, above all, on American coöperation.

Not since Nelson and Trafalgar had the Royal Navy faced so baffling a task. The home ports of German submarines were not confined to a bottleneck, as during the First World War. They could now be refitted and refueled all the way from Narvik in northern Norway to Bordeaux in southern France. The subs were larger and more numerous than in 1914, they "could get to their stations faster, and stay longer, and cover a more extensive area." German planes operating overhead guided them to the kill, and new electrical devices enabled them to hunt in packs. In surface craft the Germany navy was less a threat than in 1914, but it did possess swift powerful units which once escaping to the open sea could destroy whole convoys. There were now no French, Italian and Japanese allies to help out; a large British fleet had to be stationed in the Mediterranean to handle the Italians; and the journey through that sea was now so dangerous that shipping to and from India and the Far East had to be routed round the Cape. For the protection of her shipping Britain relied mainly on destroyers and of these she had at the commencement of the war 178. By the autumn of 1940, 36 had been sunk by enemy action and many more were so seriously crippled as to require months in dry dock. In huge battlewagons there was a handy margin of security but the need for more destroyers and lighter craft was desperate.

The British mercantile marine was estimated in 1939 at 21,000,000 tons. During the first half of 1940 it was being added to by new construction as fast as it was sunk; but the second half told a different story, and for the last three months the German toll took over 80,000 tons a week. This meant 4 million tons a year. Since British yards could not construct annually more than 1,200,000 tons, there could be but one ending if losses continued at this rate.

There were, to be sure, Dutch and Norwegian ships now carrying British cargoes. Many of them, however, were thus engaged before the war and were not new tonnage. Futhermore, voyages on the average were longer now, the course taken frequently a zigzag and ships sailed in convoys. To assemble these took a long time, and after they sailed the speed was that of the slowest vessel. Many ships had to be turned into auxiliary cruisers because of the scarcity of essential destroyer escorts. As these were sunk, more and more fast merchantmen had to be converted, thus again reducing cargo space. Heavy and bulky instruments of war had to be given priority over food, food had to be condensed to the last pint and the last ounce, squeezed into the last square inch, and much tonnage had to be diverted to reinforce and supply British troops stationed in the Near East, in Egypt and Palestine. In December, 1940, the scanty meat ration had to be cut. The strain on shipping facilities was terrific, and the margin of safety on the high seas grew narrower and narrower as the spring of 1941 came near.

For more destroyers, more shipping, more war matériel, Britain looked to America. There was nowhere else to look. The Canadians had responded superbly to the call of the Motherland; but Canadian shipyards were few and Canadians were already absorbed in training men for the RAF, in manufacturing planes, in growing wheat, in providing equipment for their own expanding expeditionary force. Australia, New Zealand and South Africa at best could not be expected to do more than help in the defense of Singapore, Egypt and Suez; and as far as South Africa was concerned the endemic bitter internal strife between Afrikander isolationism and Empire loyalism made even that difficult.

So Churchill looked to the United States. He had to do so circumspectly since a presidential election was being held in 1940, and the two candidates were sparring with one another for electoral support. American public opinion was overwhelmingly in favor of keeping out of the war while at the same time profoundly concerned lest Germany win it. What Churchill wanted more than anything was destroyers; what we wanted was protection for the United States and aid to Britain without involving ourselves in the fight. The makeshift bargain then struck was this: the British gave us ninety-nine year leases on island bases in Newfoundland and the West Indies, an insurance against invasion. We gave Britain fifty overage United States destroyers, "fourstackers" as they were called. The transfer was kept secret until announced by Roosevelt on September 3, 1940. But it had been previously hinted at by the journalistic Churchill, who dearly loves a "beat," on August 20, though without any mention of destroyers. We "decided spontaneously," he said, "and without being asked or offered any inducement, to inform the government of the United States that we would be glad to place such defensive facilities at their disposal by leasing suitable sites in our transatlantic possessions for their greater security. . . ." Nothing was said about a *quid pro quo.* Churchill was treading delicate ground and his foot, though firm, was light. The negotiations he was carrying on meant that in the future "the British Empire and the United States will have to be somewhat mixed up together in some of their affairs for mutual and general advantage." This did not disturb him. He would not stop the process. "Like the Mississippi," he said, "it just keeps rolling along. Let it roll. Let it roll on full flood, inexorable, irresistible, benignant, to broader lands and better days."

By what might be termed a prearranged coincidence, British crews were at hand to take over the American destroyers, delivered to Newfoundland ports, ready for instant service from spare tor-

pedoes to typewriters fully equipped and lockers packed with
oranges. They were heartily welcomed by the Royal Navy as were,
somewhat later, ten fast U.S. revenue cutters, originally designed to
enforce prohibition laws and therefore of no more use in 1941.

Next on the list of British needs were ships, planes, and other
war matériel. Some 158 Dutch, Belgian, Norwegian, French, German and Italian ships were tied up in American harbors and
Churchill eyed them covetously. But these could not be delivered
to our British friends without breach of international law. Our
shipyards were working day and night, but mainly building ships
for the American navy. Airplane factories were spreading out rapidly all over the United States, but here again our own need of
speedy rearmament blocked deliveries to Britain. Throughout the
autumn of 1940 we sold the British on an average 300 planes a
month for which they paid on the nail. Their wants were limitless,
not so their pocketbook.

Thanks primarily to Roosevelt these problems were effectively
handled. In November, 1940, he ordered American production
shared with the British on a fifty-fifty basis; of every hundred
planes, tanks, engines built they were at liberty to buy half. But
where was the money to come from? The liquid assets overseas of
British citizens at the outset of the war were over $4,000,000,000
and these had been commandeered by the British government. But
Britain was spending nearly $60,000,000 a day on the war and the
sharp decline in British exports brought in sight the end of their
ability to pay cash in this country. They could not float a bond
issue, since to do so was forbidden by statute for all foreign countries in default on First World War debts to us. To change that law
would be difficult and unless we did so we could not lend Britain
money. There is, however, more than one way of skinning a cat
and Roosevelt found it. Why not "lend-and-lease" the matériel of
war to Britain and to other countries opposing the Axis? As Roosevelt put it, in case of fire one lends one's hose instantly to one's
neighbor; the world was on fire; it might spread to our shores; it
would be the height of folly to try first to sell the hose. In accordance with this theory a lend-lease bill was introduced in Congress
in January, 1941. The debate on it was long, as we shall note later,
but on March 11 it became law. From that date forward America
became Britain's arsenal.

The need for matériel in the spring of 1941 was greater than ever. The sinking of ships continued at a lively rate. There had been a lull in January but a sharp upturn came in the next two months, the average for March running to three or four ships a day. The British had been victorious in the African desert and had whipped the Italians through the Mediterranean, but meanwhile Germany took over Rumania and Bulgaria and the wehrmacht got set for the destruction of Yugoslavia and Greece. It seemed certain that the entire Balkan Peninsula would soon be under the German yoke. Franco in Fascist Spain had shown active sympathy for the Nazis, and there might be a chance for a Nazi push through Spain against Gibraltar. Vichy France under Hitler's whip collaborated more and more with Germany. Japan had signed an alliance with Italy and Germany, and even to get temporary security at Hongkong and Singapore, Churchill had had to surrender Chinese refugees seeking shelter under the Union Jack at Tientsin, had had to close the Burma Road. Twenty years after the Versailles Treaty Britain had not a single real ally in the world, and but one friend of influence and power, the United States.

Churchill was fully aware of this; Britain might survive without American aid for some years; she might perhaps compound the war with Germany, save much of her empire by acknowledging Hitler as overlord of Europe: but to defeat the Nazis the United States must be drawn into the war. Churchill was determined to have that come to pass, and he had on his side in this effort, first, the community of interest between England and America, not simply of economics but of common language, common literature, common religious and social tradition; second, the fear, well grounded, that a victorious Germany in alliance with a bellicose Japan would endanger our security; third, the enthusiastic friendship of Roosevelt whose widespread influence and uncanny political skill from the beginning had supported Britain's cause; fourth, and last but not least, a radio voice that stirred the American people, made them boil with anger, willing and eager to help Britain, the consequences (subconsciously) be damned.

Perhaps some day history will put the radio of the twentieth century on a par with the printing press of the fifteenth. Without the latter, democracy would have been impossible; without the former, it might by now have been stifled. Millions who can read either do not do so or else confine their reading to sentimental slush or sporting news. But everyone, except perhaps a handful of the élite, listens to the radio. No invention ever made has so expanded the influence of human personality. More than that, the voice carries overtones that the printed page does not, betrays quickly the senatorial front, the stuffed shirt, quisling querulousness, all bluff and bluster however staged.

Churchill's voice is far from acoustically perfect; very likely he could not get a job as a professional announcer; he cannot pronounce the letter "s": nevertheless the American people heard him gladly since he most convincingly bespoke honesty and courage, humor and anger, confidence, resolution and duty.

"We have therefore a long and arduous road to travel.... We are still toiling up the hill; we have not yet reached the crestline of it; we cannot survey the landscape or even imagine what its condition will be.... This wicked man, the repository and embodiment of many forms of soul-destroying hatred, this monstrous product of former wrongs and shame, has now resolved to try to break our famous Island race by a process of indiscriminate slaughter and destruction. What he has done is to kindle a fire in British hearts, here and all over the world, which will glow long after all traces of the conflagration he has caused in London have been removed. .... He has lighted a fire which will burn in a steady and consuming flame until the last vestiges of Nazi tyranny have been burned out in Europe...." These are typical Churchillian sentences.

And the quintessence of the man is summed up in another: "Every man and woman will therefore prepare himself to do his duty, whatever it may be, with special pride and care."

Something may be told of character by the choice of words. If the word "spirit" is found in St. John's gospel more than elsewhere and the word "grace" has a corresponding emphasis in St. Luke, we have a clue to the character of the two apostles. So likewise with Churchill. Anyone familiar with his speeches will note the constant recurrence of the word "duty."

That is a key which explains much. One does not often associate the Prime Minister with Oliver Cromwell. The descendant of the Marlboroughs and the son of Lord Randolph Churchill, a connoisseur of whiskey and cigars, was far from being a Puritan. Yet if we think of Cromwell at Dunbar, crowded to the sea by Leslie's men, outnumbered three to one, bluntly saying, "Sir, I thank God I am not in the habit of counting my enemies," the words might have been spoken by Winston Churchill. Both he and Cromwell were practical; both, we may be sure, took good care to count the number of their enemies! But having done that, having taken all precautions, having done their *duty,* they were psychically armed, wholly and completely, showing not so much as an Achilles heel to the weapons of the enemy.

This psychic valor, this stability, strength and confidence was Churchill's radio gift to the English-speaking world. It did not put the United States in the war, but it hastened American intervention; it did not transform ordinary folk in Britain into supermen, but it did compel great leadership, revitalize and freshen latent qualities of vigor semi-comatose from the attrition of mechanized industrialism. That, both Americans and British must gratefully acknowledge.

Until well beyond the spring of 1941 this still was Britain's war, and to the men and women of that island go the high honor of stout faith and sturdy fortitude as German bombs rained on them from above, as German U-boats struck from beneath the seas. And Churchill was their spokesman as the skies grew darker yet and the seas rose higher.

6. THROUGH THE BALKANS TO CRETE

The British must be prepared for still bigger events in March and April. Then they will find out whether we slept through the winter.—ADOLF HITLER

We shall start on five fronts at the same time and have the war ended before the autumn harvest.—DR. GOEBBELS

Germany will attempt a radical solution of the Mediterranean problem.—DIENST AUS DEUTSCHLAND

THUS did the major partner of the Axis give word previews in February, 1941 of what the world might soon see happen. Thunder from the Berchtesgaden Valhalla gave no specific clue to the coming storm's direction, but that from Dr. Goebbels was choice copy for radio commentators. Nazi lightning was to strike its victims five ways at once. What were these? Britain, Spain, the Near East and the sea lanes of commerce make four; but where's the fifth? Was it Russia; would it be Japan's stroke against Singapore and the Dutch East Indies or, nearer, Nippon, against French Indo-China and Thailand? The goals thus darkly hinted were anybody's guess. Owing to American conceit and fatuous confidence, no commentator said Manila, much less Pearl Harbor.

The frenetic Goebbels outdid himself with his pentacle prophecy. Sober truth seems more nearly reflected by the forecast of the Nazi news agency, the *Dienst aus Deutschland*. For Germany the Mediterranean problem involved the Balkans and North Africa, Gibraltar, Malta and Suez—a five-pointed star of magic power to adorn the Nazi shield. If Britain for the moment could not be invaded, then the next best thing to do would be to break her hold on the Mediterranean, and to fix Hitler's grip upon that inland sea.

One tempting gambit toward that end was a march through Vichy France and Spain against Gibraltar. The French could not resist and Franco would help. With the swastika flying over the

Rock, with German paratroopers dropping down across the Straits in Spanish Morocco, the western Middle Sea would be sealed effectively against Britain. The way to Gib was long, the supply problem in half-starved Spain difficult, and victory without a long protracted siege by no means certain. Nevertheless, if Britain was all Hitler had to consider, Gibraltar was his logical objective.

The alternative to this Spanish venture was to invade the Balkans. Conquest of that peninsula would not immediately drive the British out of the Mediterranean basin but it certainly would weaken them there. Great Britain had to defend Greece because of Suez, because of Syria and Turkey, because of the Black Sea routes, and above all because she had pledged herself to do so. To make the effort she must rely on troops withdrawn from Egypt, thereby endangering the Suez (troops inevitably to be mauled by the wehrmacht); if she did not try, her prestige throughout all the Near East Arab world of oil and strife would sink to zero.

Other straws also pointed to the Balkans where Italy was involved in serious difficulties. In December, 1940, the Italians stepped gaily into Greece, only to be frigidly scotched there. They were already clamoring for Germany and rescue. Close at hand in the Balkans were the oil of Rumania, the wheat of Bulgaria, the bauxite of Yugoslavia, all well worth having. But perhaps the most important reason, basic to all others, was to forestall Russia. If the swastika moved down through the Balkans, then Stalin's Panslav hammer and sickle might be kept out.

Those lands of crisscross mountains, tumultuous rivers and smiling valleys had been for centuries one of Europe's choicest cockpits. For ages the Turks had ruled and raided there and had murdered their way to the gates of Vienna and Odessa. In the rocky Balkan defiles during the nineteenth and early twentieth centuries a long saturnalia of blood had culminated during 1914-1918 with Serbs, Russians, Rumanians, Germans, Austrians, Frenchmen, Englishmen, Bulgars, Greeks, Anzacs from "Down Under," Turks, and other nationalities and racial elements all bitterly at one another's throats. Now once again Mars' spotlight lit up his favorite picnic ground and slaughter pen as Hitler's wehrmacht rolled, rushed and roared to the Aegean, leaped with seven-league boots on Crete, tore viciously at Malta, let loose in Libyan deserts Rommel's panzer men, grabbed air fields from weak-kneed Syrian Vichyites, stirred up revolt in Iran, aired tall talk of joining hands in Delhi with the swift-marching Japanese, as their flag of the rising sun swung westward from China and Burma.

Of the five Balkan countries, three leaned toward the Allies, one might be said to be at first almost completely neutral, and one leaned somewhat toward the Axis. The Turks were both anti-German and anti-Italian. They were not, however, anti-Russian, and the defense pact which they had signed with the Allies before the war and which they had strengthened after its advent specifically excluded action against Russia. Yugoslavia and Greece also were pro-Ally in sympathy, not so much because of fair liberty as from fear of Hitler. The Yugoslavs had neither forgotten nor forgiven Italian unwillingness to aid Serbia during the First World War, nor Italian determination to control the Adriatic. The same held true of Grecian memories of Mussolini's bombardment of Corfu. To both these Balkan countries the Italian annexation of Albania in 1939 was ominous warning. Rumania was more or less equally poised between the conflicting powers. She asked nothing of her neighbors but she feared them all; feared Hungary (rapidly becoming a satellite of Berlin), for Hungary would demand the return of Transylvania; feared Bulgaria, from whom she had taken the Dobruja after the Second Balkan War (1913); feared Soviet Russia lest that country invade Bessarabia, a czarist possession in 1914. What Rumania wanted was to be left alone, and therefore she played Germany and the Allies against each other, hoping for the best. Bulgaria somewhat favored the Axis, for the status quo displeased her mightily and she held grudges against all her neighbors.

RUMANIA

Rumania was the wealthiest, also the most stagnant of Balkan states. Her foreigner-exploited oil fields were extensive, her farm lands excellent, but her people the most downtrodden in Europe. A junta of vicious and avaricious insiders headed by King Carol II, whose character was as sloppy as his morals, persistently preyed on the populace, who ignorantly hounded Jews, liberals, and other scapegoats. Neon-glittering Bucharest, that depraved little Paris of the Balkans, was notorious throughout Europe for cheap prostitution, rotten government, and financial swindling. Since oil concessions are valuable, bribes were high. So also were taxes.

Rumanian politics, like bacteria, were complicated. There was, on the eve of the war, a Fascist society in opposition to the king. This Legion of the Archangel Michael (the Iron Guard) was organized on semi-Nazi lines with a somewhat similar program, the main difference being that the Iron Guard was mystically pious, its members bearing the crucifix as well as the revolver and wearing green shirts instead of brown. The Iron Guard was forced underground by Carol when he assumed dictatorship in 1938 and its leading members murdered, a fact which led some to think him anti-Nazi, which he was not. Politically Carol never was anything except pro-Carol, supporting any and all gangs and gangsters, first one faction and then another, including finally the Iron Guard, as long as he could cling to power and profits.

The first attack on this flea-bitten country was made in June, 1940 by Stalin who held a sort of old home week in Bessarabia, a province formerly belonging to czarist Russia, and in Bukovina, once Austrian land. Hitler was too busy in France that month to interfere, but almost immediately thereafter the Nazis began to pay more than a little attention to oil-blest Rumania. This time it was Stalin who could not interfere. Carol's prime minister was ordered to Berchtesgaden, commanded to hand over parts of Transylvania to Hungary. He stalled for time on Carol's orders but, like many another tame premier, signed on the dotted line. In Vienna, Von Ribbentrop cut up Transylvania between Hungary and Rumania, in much the manner of Solomon's judgment on the famous baby lawsuit, the unhappy area simply being sliced in two: the northern part going to Hungary, despite the Rumanian majority in it, the southern part left to Rumania, although it contained many thousand Magyars. The boundary drawn between the two countries by the Versailles map-makers of 1919 had been unscientific; that drawn by Von Ribbentrop was fantastic. The presumption is that he wanted to enlarge Hungary, Hitler's satellite, along its Russian frontier, so that in a Soviet-Nazi war the Magyars would be more willing to fight for Hitler. At any rate there was high talk now in Berlin and Budapest of Hungary's historic mission to protect European culture against Asiatic barbarism. Admiral Horthy's Magyar government professed itself highly gratified.

The Rumanians were not quite so happy. Russia had taken part of their country, the Magyars another part, and even the Bulgars had reoccupied the Dobruja, that Slavic province Rumania had stolen from Bulgaria in 1913. All these humiliations took place in the summer and autumn of 1940, and as they did so more and more German tourists seeped into Rumania. Street signs were mysteriously translated into the nobler German, and now and then one saw an occupied German uniform. British, French and other foreign property was soon confiscated on one pretext or none, the protests of the British ambassador pointedly ignored.

Then in September a revolt broke out as planned by the Iron Guard, presumably with Nazi connivance, to rid the land of Carol. The king escaped with his well-advertised red-haired mistress, valuable paintings, and all available collateral, to seek refuge like Trotsky in Mexico. A Rumanian general, Antonescu, "Red Dog," became dictator with the help of the Archangel Michael Legion, ostensibly to do its bidding.

And actually to do that of Dr. Clodius, Nazi economic expert. The Germans got the oil fields; a trade treaty was signed; and soon masses of German cameras, aspirin and fountain pens, and so forth, began to be exchanged for Rumanian wheat, butter, eggs, and, above all, oil. The Rumanians did not need the aspirin, not at first, and they did miss their food. But this was war.

The Germans had what they wanted; it did not suit their purpose to assume responsibility for governing a country like Rumania, not as long as Antonescu, their puppet, responded so nicely to their string-pulling. Grisly and unsavory days followed. The Legion of Michael, the Germans and Antonescu played hand in hand for awhile, and Hitler sent his personal representative to attend the sacrilegious canonization of the Legion's saintly founder, martyred by Carol. The Legion (Iron Guard) murdered so many Jews that even Nazis were annoyed, particularly when useful artisans were slaughtered. Finally the Iron Guard slew a German officer and lost its standing with the Nazis. This gave the green light to Antonescu's urge to murder the green shirts, which he did with right good will. No wonder the occupying German army preferred to stand to one side; it had the food and oil of Rumania; the rest could wait while the undertakers worked.

The lesser Caesar on the Tiber was not wholly pleased meanwhile with his Berlin big brother's strangulation of Rumania. Italy's spoils of war had been minor indeed, British Somaliland, a few unpopulated corners of Kenya Colony and the Sudan, a few mountain valleys in southeastern France. The Italian army in Libya was far from the Nile and had made no progress beyond Sidi Barrani, a short distance within the Egyptian border. The time had come for Mussolini to assert himself.

He did so in October, 1940, in a meeting with the Führer at Brenner Pass, proposing then that Italy conquer Greece. Hitler was generous and consented. He had no confidence in Benito's eight million bayonets but Italy should certainly be able to do a job on Greece, feeblest of all the Balkan states. If the Duce annexed that country and Germany wanted it later, it would be no great matter to take it.

Greece, like her sister Balkan states, was appallingly poor and misgoverned. She had a Fascist dictator, Metaxas, who ruthlessly suppressed all opposition to his one-man rule. Metaxas had no quarrel with the Germans, nor had they with him. With the Italians, however, it was different: Mussolini had bombed the Greek island of Corfu in 1922; he had invaded and annexed Albania; he had continued to occupy the Dodecanese Islands inhabited by Greeks; and he had boasted loudly that in future the Mediterranean would be an Italian sea or lake. Metaxas liked Germans but hated Italians; therefore, when the latter opened war on Greece on October 28, after a three-hour ultimatum, he decided to fight.

Italy had 200,000 troops in Albania and the entire Greek army numbered only 150,000, supported by a few old crates courteously called planes. The campaign would be but practice maneuvers, so the Italians imagined, as they launched a three-pronged drive from Albania.

Through the winding Greek valleys came the joyful sons of Italy, their reinforcements and baggage trains strung out carelessly behind. The Greeks, well acquainted with their own hills, struck grimly at the invader from flank and rear. On November 9 the largest of the Duce's armies fled back in panic to Albania, a prudent precedent soon followed by the rest of his alleged soldiers. Heavy snow and rain came to the Greeks' assistance. The Italians, thinking to be in Athens and Salonika before snowfall, were cheaply clad and suffered severely. It was not too pleasant for the Greeks, but when one is winning frostbite is easier to bear. By New Year, 1941, the Greeks were deep in Albania, the Italians desperately defending their strongholds there, the laughing-stock of the democracies and of Europe.

At first Hitler's only aid to Mussolini was to lend him a few

German transport planes whereby Italian soldiers could more speedily be transported to Albania. Britain, hard pressed though she was, did more than that to aid the Greeks. She had guaranteed their country against aggression, and even if she had not, any man who would fight Mussolini or Hitler, be he Fascist, Democrat, or Communist, was Churchill's trusty ally. The prime minister of England was careful not to promise the Greeks too much; his own hands were all too full that autumn of 1940. "We will," he said, "help the Greeks to the utmost of our capacity, having regard to our other obligations.... We shall do our best."

That cautious "best" proved to be substantial. Reinforcements were sent to Egypt so General Wavell might attack the Italians in Libya; the Royal Navy took the offensive against the Italian fleet, discovered in protective retirement at Taranto Harbor, and damaged it badly by torpedo planes; and on Crete the British established an air base from which a few planes winged their way to Albania, helping, perhaps decisively, the Greek effort there.

Hitler could not afford to let the Greeks win; if they did, so would the British. He therefore came to Mussolini's help, sent Rommel into Africa to drive for the Suez, and prepared German intervention to end this silly little war in the Balkans. It would not be necessary to fight. All he would have to do would be to move an army to the Greek frontier. But how to get it there? He needed his planes for African and other adventures and did not want to ship troops by air to Albania. There remained the Greco-Bulgarian and Greco-Yugoslav frontiers. The wehrmacht stationed on either should be sufficient, but to make assurance doubly sure he decided to use both.

BULGARIA

First, then, Bulgaria. Vocally, the premier of that country was most patriotic: never, he said, would Bulgaria submit to foreign troops upon her soil. The British and Americans were taken in by this kind of talk but not so Hitler. Bulgaria had always been our pet country in the Near East, largely because so many Bulgars had been educated at Robert College, Constantinople, an American institution. We thought them a clean-living, simple, democratic people, and furthermore they were supposedly under Russian influence and would heed Stalin's counsel not to let the Germans in.

Compared with the Rumanians they were, perhaps, clean-living; but democracy was hardly a word to apply, politically, to Bulgaria. A clique of German-strutting colonels, together with King Boris, of German descent and much inclined to dictatorial authority, determined Bulgaria's foreign policy. Boris was a more kingly gangster than Carol; he was courageous if not intelligent, walking the streets of Sofia without a bodyguard despite pot shots taken at him. But in 1941 he backed the Nazi gang, a mistake he paid for later with his life.

The Bulgars listened covetously to the land-based German Lorelei who whispered of territorial rewards for faithful Bulgars at the expense of Greece and Yugoslavia. We sent our Colonel (Wild Bill) Donovan to Sofia to give them good advice, and Britain sent Anthony Eden, who warned that if Bulgaria admitted the German army then Turkey, England's ally (as she was on paper only, and to the slightest degree at that) might take counter-measures. Churchill cogently recalled to Bulgars the history of their unhappy past, of the First World War, when "Bulgaria, against the wishes of her peasant population, against all her interest, fell in at the Kaiser's tail and got sadly cut up and punished when the victory was won." It was all no use. The Germans were on Bulgaria's frontier and the British were not. In February Bulgaria welcomed more thousands of German engineers and tourists, the former repairing roads, both railroads and highways, preparing air-fields, and the termini for pontoon bridges over the Danube; the latter drinking and making merry, ready to slip into their German uniforms when orders came.

March 1, and the German army crossed the Danube. Up went the swastika in Sofia, and on the same day the Bulgarian foreign minister and the Bulgarian premier signed at Vienna in the presence of Hitler the tripartite pact. In this instance it was not even necessary to browbeat the Bulgar Quislings in the eagle's nest at Berchtesgaden to which Boris of Bulgaria soon afterwards was ordered.

YUGOSLAVIA

Two down in the Balkans and three to go! There still remained to be drawn into the Nazi net Yugoslavia, Greece and Turkey. To get at the last two Yugoslavia must first be tamed, for the roundabout journey to the Aegean through Rumania and Bulgaria did not please the practical Germans, not when there was a more direct route and one rich in bauxite.

The Nazis did not look for trouble in Yugoslavia. Rumania and Bulgaria were absorbed as easily as Austria, Czechoslovakia, and Denmark had been. When it was feasible the Nazis preferred to be orderly gangsters: it was less expensive, and in this instance they had every reason to believe they would avoid any such petty fighting as had been their lot in Poland, Norway, Holland, Belgium, and France. They already had Yugoslavia hemmed in on every side except the south. Surrounded as she was by Hungary, Rumania, Italy and Bulgaria, it would be impossible madness for her to resist. She was not even a united country. Within this new victim state, Croats hated Serbs, Serbs hated Croats, and other minorities hated both. The Nazis knew that the prince regent, Paul the Black, was amenable to reason, their reason especially, and all preliminary diplomatic preparations and financing had been carefully made. Two weeks before German regiments lined the Greco-Bulgarian frontier the premier of Yugoslavia and his foreign secretary had received the fatal invitation to Berchtesgaden. All that remained was to deliver Hitler's ultimatum to the administration at Belgrade. Acceptance of it would follow automatically.

The terms were on the Bulgarian model. Yugoslavia was to sign the tripartite pact; she was guaranteed the protection of the Führer; her boundaries were to be sacrosanct (this despite earlier promissory hints to Bulgaria of Yugoslavian territory); and in return all that was asked of her, ostensibly, was permission to move German troops through her valleys to the Greek frontier.

Almost any other country under similar duress would have yielded. But this was Yugoslavia where the majority were Serbs, people with whom love of freedom and the habit of killing their enemies had been traditional for centuries. Paul the Black was in favor of signing; he stood to get more that way, but he feared the army and the people. He wriggled and tried to hedge. He offered to let German supply and hospital trains pass through Yugoslavia, but not troop trains. The Germans put the heat on their Serbian Quisling (he was only partly Serbian by blood); he must sign on the dotted line, or else!

Paul saw reason and signed. Instantly the army saw red and revolted. Paul fled for his life. Captured near the Hungarian frontier he was sent later to the British colony of Kenya for sake-keeping and reëducation as the Serbs made ready for war.

They had no chance. Their army was much smaller and in much worse condition than that of France. Serbian generals were old, incompetent, French-trained; like Petain they had no use for motorized units, preferring oxen; there were no munition factories in the country; the air arm was negligible; there was not a single portable radio in the army. The Serbs had nothing on which to rely except a fiery spirit proved and tested in bloody centuries of war.

The prospect was worse than in 1915. Then at least they had an avenue of escape. When Von Mackensen striking from the north and the Bulgarians hitting from south and east wrested their country from them, they retreated through the mountains to the Adriatic, there to be rescued by their allies. Now, since Italians were fighting on the other side and had garrisoned Albania, that exit was closed.

The Serbs well remembered 1915; the retreat was on, the snow came. "Oxen and horses swayed and sagged to the earth. Soldiers and prisoners tore the raw flesh from the animals before they were dead and swallowed it. Men, women and children, without coats, without shoes, blinded, separated from each other, wandered, stopped, knelt, lay down and disappeared."[1] But at least those who survived found friendly hands and hospitals awaiting them at blue water. These hopes were now denied. Still they were Serbs, esteeming some things higher than life.

Then as now, 1915 and 1941, came cheers from Britain and some help. In 1915 the Anglo-French troops, weary remnant of those who fought the Turks for Gallipoli, made sorties from Salonika, trying to divert the Bulgars from their prey; in 1941 the British expeditionary force in Greece also tried to help the Yugoslavs. Churchill did what he could with encouraging words. Yugoslavia, he said, had "found her soul." Britain would render "all possible aid and succor." He was too honest to say more. None knew better than he what risks Britain had already run in withdrawing troops from her thinly held lines in Egypt. The United States promised lend-lease help, but there was no chance for it to arrive in time. The Yugoslavs would have to fight to the last ditch and fight in vain.

[1] John Clinton Adams, *Flight in Winter* (Princeton, N. J., Princeton University Press, 1942), p. 116.

April 6 came the formal invasion; April 17, and formal resistance ceased. The plan for the defense of Yugoslavia, worked out by French military experts, had been to concentrate the army in the north, lightly to defend the frontier which was but an extension of the Hungarian plain, and then to stand at bay along the northern ends of the deep gashes between mountains made by the Morava and Vardar valleys, the gateway to the south. But the Germans made their main attack from the east. Their advance in the north was deliberate and slow, as planned, their thrust through the mountain passes of Bulgaria a quick triumph of military skill. Almost before Yugoslavia knew what was taking place the Germans were at Skoplje and Nish in central Serbia, thus bisecting the country and turning the flank of the northern Serbian army.

Despite quite different terrain the German conquest of Serbia in many ways was like that of Poland; in both instances the enemy's air arm was crippled the first day, and in both instances nothing was available to withstand the German armor. The Yugoslavs, by no means modern as to motors, hoped the mountains would hinder their use; but the Germans had devised a light tank most suitable for the Balkans, and with it they easily negotiated the Bulgarian passes and had little difficulty in herding the cannonless and scattered detachments of the Yugoslav army well up into the head of innumerable barren valleys.

The Serbs declared Belgrade an open city, but it did not suit the Germans so to regard it, that city receiving far heavier punishment than was meted out to Rotterdam or Warsaw. Sarajevo in Bosnia became for a few days the capital. The wehrmacht gave no respite. Having cut straight across Yugoslavia to join hands with the Italians in Albania, it rolled south to the Grecian border and northwest to Sarajevo, which soon was encircled. Michael, the boy king, together with many of his cabinet, flew to Jerusalem en route to England, another government-in-exile so-called, and what supposedly was left of his armies surrendered.

Yugoslavia seemed lost, a mere paper creation of Versailles statesmen which the Germans could do with as fancy moved them. They made a thorough job in disposing of their new conquest; a part they presented to Hungary, a part to Italy, a part to Bulgaria, and over what was left they appointed a Quisling administrator to extract minerals for German war needs and to foment as much disorder as possible between Croats and Serbs. He had no difficulty in so doing. Serbs upbraided Croats as either lukewarm in defending Yugoslavia or as actively pro-German; the Croats said they never had been fairly treated by the haughty Serbs who had ruled Yugoslavia as if exclusively their own. War bred civil war and both were fought as blood feuds. The Germans organized and armed bands of Croats called "Utaashi," for the purpose of killing Serbs; the Serbs replied in kind. Thousands of Serbs serving in the army never surrendered but slipped away into the deep mountains; many others never had even been mobilized, so swift was the German advance; and of these a goodly number took to the hills, rifle in hand, to continue fighting, either against Germans or Croats. But for the time being, in this spring of 1941, what had been Yugoslavia was German land. It was now three up and two to go! Of the Balkan states only Turkey and Greece were left to deal with the Nazi dragon.

GREECE

The Greeks, already under German attack before the fall of Sarajevo, were ignorantly lighthearted at taking on a new enemy. Was not the British navy visible in their waters? Having thrashed the Italians without the assistance of an Allied land army, they seemed to think that the British expeditionary force of nearly 60,000 troops would balance the arrival of twice as many Germans. Because Athens swarmed with men in Britain's uniform and there were no Germans as yet around, the Greeks actually thought they were going to win the war. The British knew better. But they had given their promise in the fairer days of 1939 and they were determined to make it good; they had to, even at the risk not simply of defeat in Greece but also of giving up hard-won victories in Libya, as we shall read later.

Nothing could have saved Greece this fatal spring of 1941 from Hitler's legions, but her agony might have been staved off for some time had she followed her original plan of defense, drawn up when it seemed inevitable in March that Yugoslavia would yield to Hitler's ultimatum and let the German army use her railroads. That plan called for strengthening the Greek center, against which the German onslaught presumably would be launched, at the expense of the two wings, in Albania and Thrace; it called also for eventual withdrawal from Albania and for abandoning Salonika, the harbor terminus of the railroad through the Vardar Valley. When the Yugoslavs started to fight, the Greeks changed their strategy, weakened their center, which they hopefully thought would be protected by the insurgent Yugoslavs, and reinforced their two wings.

This change brought disaster. The strongly defended Metaxas line which protected Greece from Bulgarian attack held out for a while, but when the Germans poured into southern Yugoslavia from Bulgaria and turned south they outflanked the Greek army in Thrace and easily took Salonika, thus cutting off and capturing several Greek divisions further to the east. This meant the end of the war on the east flank. On the west the change in plan brought on the final collapse. Since the center of the Greek line had been weakened, it was unable even with British reinforcements to hold back the German flood. The Teutons struck at the point of juncture of Greek and British forces, broke through, forced a retirement. This isolated the Greek armies in Albania who now, instead of chasing Italians, as they had no military right to do, retreated before them. The retreat was leisurely, not pressed by Mussolini's warriors. The Germans, however, were in a hurry. They marched promptly west, got in behind the Greeks in Albania. With Italians to the north, the Adriatic to the west, Germans to the south and east, there was nothing left for the Greeks to do but surrender.

Meanwhile, the British, their left flank exposed, had reluctantly abandoned the superb protection of Mount Olympus and had fallen back to a shorter line running from near Thermopylae on the east to the Ionian Sea on the west, less than half the distance they had tried to defend while their allies were in the fighting. Further retreat was necessitated almost immediately. The Germans had landed on the large island of Euboea to the British right, thus outflanking them from that direction, and the Greeks had notified them on April 20 that Greece could do no more. Therefore, as in 480 B.C. when Leonidas held the pass at Thermopylae, the New Zealanders were asked to stand fast at that same narrow strip of land between mountain and sea, this time not for the defense of Athens but to help their comrades escape from Hitler's power.

The handful of Spartans who held this pass against the Persian host for five days had an advantage denied New Zealanders in 1941; the pass in 480 B.C. had been little more than a narrow shelf, now it was a wide mud flat. Nevertheless the men of the South Seas held it for three days against Nazis tanks and Stukas. Spartans and New Zealanders alike were forced to give over for the same reason —a detour made by their enemies through mountain passes to their rear.

With Thermopylae lost another Dunkirk was inevitable, and the British feared a worse one than that of 1940. This time their forces were more scattered, the beaches narrower, the rescue vessels fewer, the island of Crete on which they sought refuge far distant. All during the last week of April the remnants of their expeditionary force huddled on the beaches or about the ruined harbors of Greece. Pounded overhead by German dive-bombers, wounded, half-dead with loss of sleep and lack of food, they jammed and crowded by night on such wretched ships as the navy was able to assemble. By a miracle of hard work and daring more than 44,000 gained the historic habitat of the Englishman, the sea.

The Germans now had all the Grecian mainland. Of actual fighting in the Balkans they had not experienced more than seven weeks. The campaign was an added feather in Deutschland's cap of glory, another notch in Britain's rapidly augmenting roll of glorious disasters. The British had been outgeneraled and outnumbered; they had had too little of everything; and therefore had been outfought.

CRETE

The scene now shifted rapidly to Crete, the mysterious foyer of pre-Hellenic culture when Athens was a fishing village. This island, third largest in the Mediterranean, lay 175 miles south of Athens and 70 miles southeast of Cape Matapan, at the extreme tip of the Peloponnesus. It was therefore difficult for the Germans to reach, but difficult also for the British to reinforce since it was 350 miles from Egypt. In December, 1940 Britain took over the defense of Crete so the Greek garrison there might be free to fight Italy. For this purpose Wavell sent one infantry brigade from Egypt together with a few anti-aircraft guns and still fewer planes. The British Commonwealth was short of everything this spring of 1941 except seagoing battlewagons, and adequate forces for Crete would mean certain loss of the Suez. From that it followed that if once the Germans got a good grip on Crete British loss of it was inevitable.

Many thousand years ago boats from Athens took youths and maidens to Crete to be devoured by the Minotaur; now other vessels, wheezy little steamboats, fishing craft, British destroyers, even rowboats converged on Crete from Greece, bombed heavily the while by the luftwaffe, carrying British soldiers of the Commonwealth, Australians, New Zealanders, lads from Britain to be sacrificed, not to the Minotaur, but to Mars, Thor, and Odin. Most of the fugitives from the furor Teutonicus reached Crete; far too few were to fight again.

The British commander there was General Freyburg, a New Zealander, ex-dentist, ex-stoker, ex-soldier of fortune in Mexico, a hero of the First World War, wearer of the D.S.O. twice won for valor in the field, recipient of the Victoria Cross, and a man to whom history's major laurels were yet to be awarded. Freyburg could not arm all the fugitives, some he sent on to Egypt. He had left 27,000 Imperial troops, of whom 7,100 were New Zealanders, 6,500 Australians. Under him also were 12,000 Greeks picturesquely armed with "five different kinds of rifle, English, Canadian, American, Italian, Greek."

Freyburg had twelve days to prepare for the Germans. Only from Egypt could he receive the needed matériel of war, none of which could very well be landed on the southern shore of this 160-mile long island, since the harbors, airdromes, and towns were on the north and there was no motor transport available to cross the mountainous spine of Crete. The Germans commanded the air. Cargoes had to be unloaded at night without showing lights. Even as it was, many vessels were sunk by German bombs before they could discharge their cargo. Only one comfort remained to Freyburg; the Royal Navy still ruled the surface of the sea; the Germans must come by air or not at all.

May, 1941, and the Germans wrote a new chapter in the manual of the art of war. Their Cretan campaign was on a relatively minor scale but it did demonstrate something new—the feasibility of airborne invasion, the use and decisive value of glider and parachute training. They had taken those Russian ideas seriously and won Crete by so doing.

The luftwaffe's first task was to exterminate British planes based on Crete. To do this took a week. Never in its glorious history did the RAF face greater odds. Its planes were few and battered, no Spitfires among them, only Hurricanes and Blenheims and some antiquated Gladiators. The flyers were "operationally weary," the technical term for nervously exhausted men, most of whom had just escaped from the Hellenic inferno of the month before. Nevertheless they held out until only a half-dozen planes were fit to fly, and until even this pitiful remnant of an air fleet was ordered back to North Africa.

May 20, and not a British plane over Crete. Instead the kaleidoscopic heavens blazed with the yellow, green, black, white, blue, red 'chutes of descending German paratroopers. With excellent precision the Germans dropped, all at once, machine guns, food, medical supplies, munitions, and the élite personnel of an élite army. And the same day came the gliders, air-towed all the way from Greece, each spilling out its complement of fit and seasoned fighting men.

The British, poorly armed though they were, well-nigh won, and might have, had tanks been available. Air-descending Germans made superb targets for the expert riflemen from "Down Under." And, once landed, with cold bayonets and crudely made hand grenades, the Anzacs slew them by hundreds. The Cretans flocked to the slaughtering. "Who are these people coming down from the skies with umbrellas?" they yelled, as with knives, iron bars and strangling cords they flew at isolated parachutists.

At the end of the first day the Germans had failed in three out of four landings; they failed to take the city of Canea; they failed to capture the two airports to the east; but when night came the Maleme airdrome to the west was in their hands. Could they be pried loose from it? For a time it seemed they might. Some few additional British planes had flown all the way from Africa to contest the boiling skies over Crete. That meant a 700-mile round trip for Hurricanes which had to be stripped of armor to carry additional fuel. The Germans only had half the distance to fly, and there were twice as many of them. But any planes at all were an encouraging sight to the British land troops, and soon they had another inspiration. Twice under cover of night the Nazis tried to invade Crete by sea. Only one of their craft reached shore. The Royal Navy sunk the others, drowning some 5,000 Germans. The price paid was heavy, two cruisers, four destroyers, the battleship *Warspite* so damaged that she had to be sent to America for repairs.

The Germans did not take that risk again. They drove off the new British planes without much trouble and stuck forthwith to gliders and parachutes. Within two or three days they landed

35,000 troops and their matériel from the air, thus, incidentally, rehearsing our 1944 invasion of Normandy. The two British garrisons east of Canea still held out, one to be rescued by the death-defying cruise of H.M.S. *Orion*, which under a hail of bombs ventured at night near shore, the other ultimately forced to surrender. Meanwhile the New Zealanders at Maleme airdrome west of Canea fought their way to the mountains, crossed to the north shore, a number to be rescued off the beaches by the Royal Navy. June 1 it was all over. Some 10,000 soldiers of the Commonwealth were either dead in Crete or prisoners. Out of Norway, out of France and Belgium, out of Greece, out of Crete, the British forces had been driven. The Black Sea route to Russia was now closed, and Hitler that much more free to attack the Soviets.

May, 1941 had been one of the most wracking months in British history; and it would have been far worse had not the Royal Navy, though suffering cruel losses off the shores of Crete, won an outstanding victory in the Atlantic and final control of that ocean's surface.

That month Germany's gigantic battleship, the *Bismarck*, emerged from Bergen, Norway, headed north for Iceland, turned south, sinking the *Hood*, "largest fighting ship in all the world." Unless caught the *Bismarck* could sink convoy after convoy, win the war for Germany.

From Britain, from Gibraltar, from convoy duty in the mid-Atlantic steamed the strongest units of the British navy sent to intercept the raider. Thanks to aircraft they spotted her location; thanks to aërial bombardment they were able to close on the stalled and sorely wounded Nazi battleship and send her to the bottom.

Britain still kept her ancient grip upon the seas. As she did so, however, she ran into new dangers in the Near East.

OUTFLANKING TURKEY

Four down in the Balkans and one to go. Rumania, Bulgaria, Yugoslavia and Greece now were obedient at the Nazi chariot wheels. Only Turkey remained at large.

The Turks announced they would fight; fortunately for them they did not have to. Presumably it might not have been too difficult for the wehrmacht to have taken Constantinople (now

Istanbul) but the Nazi High Command rather speculatively fancied encircling Turkey as it had Yugoslavia.

As the Nazis drove the British out of Grecian valleys and pried loose their grip on Crete, they had noted with glee events in Baghdad. Rashid Ali Beg Gailam, former premier of Iraq, a disgruntled Anglophobe and in contact with Von Papen at Ankara, deposed by force the pro-British regent who acted for the six-year-old king. Britain had secured the admission of Iraq in 1930 to the League of Nations, and Britain had recognized the independence of Iraq; by treaty she was authorized to maintain troops in Iraq, to guard communications, and more especially the precious oil fields. And now, as Britain reinforced her scanty garrison at Basra at the head of the Persian Gulf, Rashid Ali besieged a large British airport at Habbaniah, sixty-five miles west of Bagdad, and besought the aid of Germany. Throughout the month of May the British and the pro-German Iraqui engaged in desultory warfare. Habbaniah was unfortified, and to defend it the British had to fly both men and artillery in from Basra. If the Iraqui won, if they once succeeded in cutting the pipe-line to Haifa in Palestine, the plight of the Royal Navy and of the RAF in the eastern Mediterranean would be serious. Fortunately the Germans were so heavily engaged this month in Crete that they were unable to help Rashid Ali except by flying in a few planes from Syria; fortunately, also, many Arabs revolted against Rashid Ali. By the end of the month his revolt was over and the former regent back on the throne.

The planes the Germans sent to Iraq had been flown from French bases in Syria, and the excuses offered by the Vichy governor there were very flimsy. The British felt they could take no chances; a German occupation of Syria was by no means impossible, and once nested there the Nazis could put pressure on Turkey from the south, on Palestine from the north, and on Iraq from the west. Only part of the oil from Mosul went to Haifa; the pipe-line bifurcated and a great part of it flowed to the sea at Tripoli in Syria, an invaluable source for the luftwaffe whose technicians and ground personnel already were said to have taken over the Syrian airdromes. The British decided to strike. Conjointly with the Free French troops of General De Gaulle they crossed from Palestine into Syria on June 8. The Allied columns moved slowly, for there was no desire to fight Frenchmen. The Vichy régime in Syria put up something more than a token resistance, but the French soldiers in Syria were ill equipped, and many of them were De Gaullists at heart. By June 28, Damascus fell to the Allies and immediate danger was over.

Immediate danger, that is, for Palestine, Syria and Turkey. But in northeastern Africa the seesaw game of war of Britons versus Germans and their fluid Italian allies had as yet come to no decision. In the summer of 1941 the swastika side was up, that of the Union Jack down. Who was to win empire over the treasure of Africa?

7. DEATH IN THE DESERT

WHAT will the archaeologists say some thousand years from now, when North African scholars dig the sand off metal monsters with caterpillar treads and rust-riddled turrets? Will they recognize these for what they once were, ships of the desert, heavily armed and manned and navigated by star and compass, steered through shifting wastes and over rocky ridges, sometimes in fleet formation, again on solitary cruises, crunching, grinding, spitting gas and fire, bursting into flames, torn asunder by land mines or searching shells? Will their missing parts be raked up, reconstructed, assembled, so these horrors of Detroit may loom and lower forever in the larger and stuffier museums of latter-day Harvards, while children gaze on them with wonder and are told that these are history's mementos of the barbaric past, the deadlier chariots of more savage Jehus?

From 1940 to 1943 they embodied the living and killing present. Tanks, working with planes, were the chosen tools of twentieth-century war on the desolate lands of Northeast Africa, the magic means whereby armies were rapidly shuttled back and forth across 500 miles of desert landscape, back and forth in odd dramatic ebb and flow from the border of Tripoli on the west almost to Alexandria in the east, the Western world agape with wonder as Italo-Germans and British alternately won and lost; and strange names, Mersa Matruh, Sidi Barrani, Halfaya, Bardia, Tobruk, Derna, Bengazi, El Agheila and El Alamein flashed back and forth on radio and press before the minds' eyes of multitudes who had been taught to hate geography in school.

With the rhythmic irregularity of a drunken pendulum the fortunes of war in Northeast Africa swing forward and back. In the summer of 1940 the Italians get across the frontier of Egypt, only in turn to be driven back 500 miles to Tripolitania; in 1941 Rommel, German strategist extraordinary, and his hardbitten Afrika Corps chase the British Imperials back across the desert and into Egypt; there the soldiers of Empire and Commonwealth rally; equipped

144

with more English and light American tanks they defeat Rommel and, for the second time, carry their battle flag to the Tripolitan frontier; Rommel gets new tanks, as good as the new American General Grants; his leadership is superb, and for a third and last time the Axis plunges east across the desert, all but capturing Alexandria; then back swings the pendulum; Churchill changes generals; Montgomery, Scottish Calvinist and peacock in reverse, heads the British Eighth Army, hardened and seasoned warriors; he has good hunting; he ousts Rommel from Egypt, races him across 500 miles of desert sand; by Christmas, 1942, the British, New Zealand, South African, and Indian troops in the service of the king-emperor, assisted by British and American flyers, have covered that hell-torn route again past Halfaya and Tobruk far beyond El Agheila. It is the end of the beginning of World War II, the beginning of the end of that war in North Africa. Rommel will have one more scalp on his victory string, an American one; but not again will he defeat the British Eighth Army in Libya.

For these astonishing campaigns the British had certain advantages; so too did the Axis. Britain was firmly entrenched in Egypt and along the Nile Valley, where fertile land could supply foodstuffs and where hospitals and living quarters were available. Egypt's location between Libya and Ethiopia cut the Italian possessions in two, thus giving Britain the inside lines of communication. Britain controlled, for the most part, and in ever increasing degree with the deterioration of the Italian navy, the surface of the Mediterranean, and if Italian air power made somewhat difficult and dangerous the reinforcement of British armies in Africa, so too did British sea power make difficult and dangerous the reinforcement of the enemy. Furthermore, so long as the Indian Ocean and the Red Sea were held and patrolled by the Royal Navy it was always possible to send supplies from the United States and from India by way of the Cape. Last but by no means least was Malta, the unsinkable airplane carrier, planted straight in the path of Axis planes, and of Axis shipping en route from Italy to Tripoli.

The Axis also held cards for this sand-blown war, important trumps. Britain was fighting all around the world, whereas Italy, until she foolishly attacked Greece, had nothing to worry about except North Africa. When the war commenced Italian armies in Ethiopia alone far outnumbered those under Wavell in Egypt, who was confronted at the same time with another large Italian army in Libya. The fall of France made his position very shaky; he dare not denude Palestine of troops since the British Mediterranean fleet depended for its oil on its pipe-line there; he no longer could rely on the French stationed in French Somaliland, nor on the French in Tunisia to threaten the Italian forces from the rear. German scientists and industrialists had been maximizing their war matériel output at least since 1933; it was much easier for the Axis to handle problems of supply. For a good two years it had the upper hand in regard to both quantity and quality of war goods, and not until lend-lease became effective while Great Britain was getting her war industry going, was this disparity in a way to be equalized. Britain was overconfident and underarmed in 1939, and most of her guns and tanks had been left in France during the defeats of 1940. To carry her tanks, planes, cannons, munitions to Egypt, Britain must either run the long gauntlet through the Mediterranean, passing the narrow seas between the heavily armed Italian island of Pantellaria off the African and Sicilian coasts, or else use the 12,000-mile route all the way around Africa via the Cape of Good Hope, the Indian Ocean, and the Red Sea; and this, too, in the face of skilled and relentless submarine attack.

FIRST AXIS OFFENSIVE

These were among the problems which confronted General Wavell, British commander in the Middle East, as he watched the well-groomed and highly advertised legions of Mussolini trooping eastward in the early summer of 1940. Wavell had under his command when the war opened only 36,000 British troops, but he did not await the arrival of the Italians. Hacking through the barbed wire entanglements at the frontier of Egypt, ordered by Mussolini to prevent the remaining Libyan natives from fleeing eastward, he crossed the border into Cyrenaica, caught the Italians napping, destroyed a supply column, captured Fort Capuzzo.

The Italians under General Graziani (well and infamously known as "the Butcher") advanced now in majestic masses. Wavell retreated to Mersa Matruh in Egypt, western terminus of the rail line from Alexandria. Graziani did not pursue him thither. It was summer and in theory one did not campaign extensively in the desert after it got too hot. Graziani, therefore, only penetrated

Egypt as far as Sidi Barrani, fifty miles inside the border, came to a halt, lay inert.

The Duke of Aosta, Italy's commander in Ethiopia, however, bestirred himself; he invaded British Somaliland with 25,000 men and conquered that arid but extensive colony with very little trouble or bloodshed; he sent his forces a little way into the Sudan and into Kenya. British opposition, of necessity, was of the slightest. On paper it looked bad for Wavell; on either flank he was confronted with an army twice his own.

FIRST BRITISH COUNTERATTACK

Meanwhile the British had been fairly active; the navy blasted at Italian seaports along the coasts of Cyrenaica; several thousand Anzacs poured into Egypt in 1940 as in 1915, tough and sturdy volunteers from Australia and New Zealand; from the Union of South Africa came a picked detachment; two divisions of Indian troops arrived; Churchill managed to spare a few tanks and some modern planes; too few, but infinitely superior to the old Gladiator biplane they had been using in Africa. Haile Selassie was dusted off, dressed up and ensconced at Khartoum, dispensing hospitality and optimism, inviting all and sundry to visit him after his return to Addis Ababa.

Wavell, husbanding still scanty resources, prepared to strike. The enemy lay smugly encamped along a string of seven forts, strung out in a vast semicircle around Sidi Barrani. Wavell's plan called for a double offensive, his Indian troops driving directly at Sidi Barrani along the coastline; his seventh armored division cutting overland across sixty miles of desert to punch in behind Graziani's western forts.

Wavell's success was instant and overwhelming. In two days the snoozing Italians were put to rout. They had no notion how to make desert war; they had no reconnaissance to detect the British approach; instead of seeing fluidity of movement and concentration of fire power as the essence of desert warfare they dispersed their forces, shut them up in glorified blockhouses, and acted as though they were in Ethiopia, keeping watch and guard over awed and defeated tribesmen. They encumbered themselves with enormous quantities of food, wine and mineral water and their tanks, trucks and artillery were poor in quality, unsuitable for the task ahead;

the tanks tiny two-man go-carts, weak in armor, their trucks so heavy as to be of use only on paved roads.

Of the Nibeiwa fort which surrendered after a half-hour's fighting a British correspondent wrote, "We found there stores of foodstuffs infinitely more varied and succulent than our own; great tins of ham, huge Parmesan cheeses, long blue packages of spaghetti, seven-pound pots of tomato extract, green vegetables and delicious fruits in tins, jams and quince jelly, tongues and tunny fish in olive oil. There were great vats of exceedingly good wines. There were barrels of brandy. Oil and vinegar stood on mess-tent tables in artistic porcelain vases. Crockery and cutlery were of the finest.

"There were sheets on the beds in the private tents of the officers. On their dressing tables were bottles of scent and pomade. Their ceremonial uniforms depended from coat-hangers."[1] It was eighteenth-century parade war in twentieth-century Africa. Braddock over again.

In two days it was all over at Sidi Barrani, the Italians surrendering en masse or fleeing in disorder toward the west. Forty thousand prisoners were taken with all their cumbering equipment. One whole division surrendered intact and without firing a gun, while those who preferred flight to prison camp did not stop at easily defended Halfaya Pass just beyond Egypt but kept on going all the way to Bardia, their nearest fortified seaport. Machiavelli four hundred years before had described his countrymen as too intelligent and too logical to be tough fighters.

Bardia was well protected by a network of outer forts, but the guns in them faced outward only and no precautions had been taken against tanks which might break through this strong outer rim. The British tanks went through it, Bardia fell, and the prison camps got another 40,000.

The next important town on Mussolini's truly magnificent highway across the north of Cyrenaica was Tobruk, sixty miles beyond Bardia to the west, a larger town, a bigger seaport, more heavily defended. Resistance here was stiffer; it took thirty-six hours to capture Tobruk.

Another sixty miles more or less and one came to Derna where the Italians amazed Australian troops by really fighting. Confident, however, that Derna would soon yield, as it did after three days,

[1] Alexander Clifford, *The Conquest of North Africa* (Boston, Little, Brown & Company, 1943), p. 38.

the British divided their forces, sent their tanks 200 miles south-westerly across the desert toward the Gulf of Sidra, thus by-passing Bengazi, the principal town in Cyrenaica. Progress was slow. Lest the enemy escape to Tripolitania, the British had divided their tanks into two columns, one heading straight west below Bengazi, the other, as we have seen, continuing southwest to the Gulf of Sidra. It was a shrewd maneuver, for the Italians in flight were now hemmed in between the two British tank columns. They put up something better than a token resistance, but the tanks cruised up and down and back and forth alongside a ten-mile stretch of road-way, pouring their fire upon the Italian forces. Mussolini's tanks were no good, the men who ran them badly trained. On the second day, February 6, 1941, resistance ceased.

In two months Wavell had taken 133,000 prisoners, virtually the whole Italian army in Cyrenaica, his own casualties being 1,774, of whom 438 were killed. Carrying their spare clothing in paper suitcases and leading little dogs on strings, the by no means displeased Italians trooped like tourists into the British prison areas, later to be sent to India. Among the prisoners were numerous generals, some noted for having survived the Spanish Civil War, among them General Bergonzoli, popularly known as "electric whiskers."

Mechanized war quite evidently was not the Italian dish, nor, for that matter, any kind of war. Mussolini had boasted of his 400,000 bayonets in Libya, and he still had a chance to use them if they were there. But for the time being he was whipped and driven out of Cyrenaica, Libya's eastern province, and Wavell could devote himself elsewhere.

There was not much time if the British were to help the Greeks at all, for the only troops available for that purpose must be drawn from Wavell's command; there were Italians to be driven out of Kenya and the Sudan, and Haile Selassie to be put back upon the Lion Throne; there was also the fascinating chance to run ragged what Italians were left in Libya. Which course was best? Why stop when the Italians were on the run? On the other hand, the further west Wavell went, the harder was the strain on his overextended supply lines. Oil, munitions, food, all had to be transported hundreds of miles. German dive-bombers had appeared in force in the Mediterranean, and the expulsion of the Italians from Bengazi did not mean that the British could now use that port for supply purposes. Fresh Italian troops, constantly reinforced from Sicily, were strongly entrenched at El Agheila at the top of the Gulf of Sidra, and the distance from there to Tripoli was even greater than the distance to Egypt.

Sound reasoning, both political and military, led Wavell to the conclusion that his forces might better be employed elsewhere. In February the Greeks were bogged down in Albania in guerrilla war with Italian forces, and the German absorption of Rumania and that impending of Bulgaria indicated that British help to Greece was imperative from the military standpoint, and its political advisability beyond question since Britain's aid was pledged.

Meanwhile there were East Africa, Kenya Colony, the Sudan, British Somaliland, to recover; Ethiopia to prop up again. Political considerations in all these cases were paramount. Smuts' majority in the parliament of South Africa was slender and he had only secured permission for South African troops to serve in the war at all by a proviso in his bill (afterwards rescinded) that South African troops should not serve out of Africa. To ensure the safety of Kenya and the Sudan, and to conquer Ethiopia would please South Africa and increase British prestige in the Near East. There were also sound military reasons for an offensive in this direction; Italians in Libya could be reinforced, those in Ethiopia could not; the remaining tribesmen of Haile Selassie itched for revenge and once equipped would strike shrewd blows at their new masters in the bush war at which Italians were so awkward.

Even before the sweep through Cyrenaica had been completed the British were moving eastward. After Sidi Barrani an Indian division not needed against the evanescent Italians had been sent to support a motley array of Sudanese, South Africans, Belgians, Free French and Nigerian Negro troops engaged in defense of the Sudan and Kenya. This colonial ensemble had already been successful; it had driven the Italians out of Kenya and the Sudan; it had even pushed the lethargic Italians back some forty miles in Ethiopia before their comrades went to pieces in Cyrenaica.

Now it was to embark on a fabulous campaign, to win back in record time a region larger than Texas and infinitely less valuable, to eliminate Italy from Northeast Africa and to pump up a new and independent Ethiopia (with strings attached).

To make this offensive a success preliminary propaganda among the Ethiopians was highly developed. No sooner had the war started than Haile Selassie's runners had been sent through the Ethiopian valleys, well supplied with money and with messages in cleft sticks promising a day of liberation. Major Wingate, the same General Wingate later to die in Burma, was the brains of this show. He knew how to outfox the Italians, how to please native chiefs, how to communicate in African fashion over long distances by beat of drum, how to decoy the enemy, how to duck, to dodge, to reappear out of nowhere, to fade silently away. When the campaign got under way Wingate commanded some 2,000 Sudanese. With these dark heroes and his "patriots" (Ethiopian tribesmen) he fell upon Benito's outposts, herded some 14,000 sons of Italy into the sun-blasted hills, and by bluff and bluster rather than by bullets forced them to surrender.

The over-all strategy of the British Imperials was to attack Ethiopia from two directions, from the Sudan through Eritrea to the north, from the Somalilands, Italian and British, from the south and southeast and east. Both Somalilands fell to the Union Jack with a minimum of resistance. It was the Cyrenaican campaign all over again, swift-moving thrusts over flat sand-swept plains, assisted by naval bombardments of Italian shore positions. Fabulous distances were covered with extraordinary rapidity, in one instance 220 miles in two days. Mogadiscio, capital of Italian Somaliland, fell February 24. The British found there 350,000 gallons of motor oil. Putting this into their tanks and planes they swung northwest over Mussolini's imperial highway. Dashing forward forty-five miles a day they threatened to cut off before long the Italian garrison in British Somaliland which, becoming nervous, capitulated March 16 as Berbera, capital of British Somaliland, was retaken.

In the interim the Imperials forced their way into western Eritrea, turned north to Ethiopia. The Italians under General Lorenzini, Lion of the Sahara, resisted better here. High tablelands gashed by precipitate gorges, mule tracks instead of highways impeded the British. Bayonets supplemented by planes took the place of tanks, and the Empire's casualty lists were high, particularly among the Indian troops. In consequence the Imperials coming up from the south and east reached Addis Ababa before joining hands with those coming from the north. May 5, and Haile Selassie was back once more on his uneasy thronelet. It was just five years since he had run away. That a dusky victim of European imperialistic intrigue should be the first restored was a propitious omen of Olympian justice.

Mopping up continued for months, and history should record that at least once in World War II Italians fought long, hard and viciously. On the plateau at Gondar some 15,000 Italian troops withstood a siege of seven months. They made their plateau a strong fortress, surrounded by barbed thorns in lieu of barbed wire. From every side the Imperial forces drew in on Gondar and bombed it heavily from the air. Italian ammunition ran low. One Italian battalion charged with the bayonet until almost all were killed. Then on November 17 Gondar surrendered. All Ethiopia was now clear except for a lost patrol of some fifty men rumored to be hiding in caves in the northeastern part of the country and keeping in touch with Italy by radio.[1]

SECOND AXIS OFFENSIVE

Five days before Haile Selassie's return to Addis Ababa the British in headlong flight evacuated Greece, and British conquest of the African wastelands faded into insignificance by comparison with this perilous disaster.

Nor was that all. During March and April Cyrenaica fell to the Germans, who early in May were battering at the defenses of the Egyptian frontier and driving in on a British garrison at Tobruk. Hitler, completely disillusioned with Italian somnolence and inefficiency, had taken charge of Axis fortunes in February, landing in Tripoli during that month one complete German armored division and parts of two others. These Germans were of different breed from their soft allies. All of them had undergone severe and utterly scientific training for what was advertised to be a post of honor, living in huge sweating chambers to accustom themselves to African humidity and to African sun. Commanding them was General Rommel, history's candidate for principal hero of the African wars, General Montgomery, runner-up. Rommel was a rough-neck soldier of fortune, a bull-dozing go-getter, an amateur of war with not a "von" to his name, but a superb natural strategist who delighted in lecturing captured British officers on their military blunders. He snatched El Agheila away from the British March 24.

[1] The greater part of this paragraph is directly quoted from *The Encyclopedia Britannica Yearbook*, 1942.

They thought lightly of this, for El Agheila was only a wretched little outpost. But Rommel kept right on coming—and swiftly. Sometimes he followed the coastline, sometimes he abandoned it. He struck across the desert by-passing Bengazi. The British fled before him; their forces had been stripped; the New Zealanders and Australians had been sent to Greece. Rommel came on faster than they had in their lightning stroke at Graziani, but he got few prisoners. Some were notched off in Bengazi and two British generals were nabbed in the moonlight by German motor cyclists, but the majority escaped. There was a lot more space than Rommel had soldiers.

On reaching Tobruk the British turned at bay. Rommel swept by them, took Bardia, passed Egypt's frontier, captured Sollum on Egyptian soil.

The prospects for the British Empire and Commonwealth were dark and, in the Near East, looked darker even than the year before. As far as space went the British flag flew over more square miles than in the summer of 1940; it even flew over Tobruk, sixty miles west of Egypt. But the intensive and never ending labor to build up strong Imperial forces under the Near East command seemed Love's Labor Lost. Most of Wavell's good fighters were either shut up in Crete or in Tobruk; and this time he faced not Graziani, used to butchering unarmed men, but Rommel, who asked no odds of man or fate.

The position of Britain in the Near East, to no small degree, depended in May, 1941, on the Australian garrison at Tobruk. Rommel's lines were so strung out that he dared not risk an Egyptian campaign without first ridding himself of those warriors from the South Seas who clung so tenaciously to his flank. The Germans were about to take Crete; perhaps they had a chance of including with it Syria, Iran and Egypt. But these and the Suez they could not have securely as long as Tobruk held.

That port on the Libyan shore had on its landward side only an escarpment of moderate height beyond which in a wide semicircle was strung miles of barbed wire; but behind the barbed wire, holed up in the ruins, were fighting men as good as any in the world, and behind them lay the sea over which in dark nights came shiploads of guns, tanks, supplies and replacements.

"The rats of Tobruk" will be exterminated, so blared Lord Haw Haw, German radio announcer, but those rats had teeth and knew how to use them. They steered clear of the Italian error, a hard rim of defense; they were neither surprised nor alarmed when the enemy's tanks crushed through their barbed wire, since they stood ready to meet them with enfilading fire and counter-tank charges; they swiveled their big guns to cover any direction within the defense zone, and as the German tanks charged about the area like enraged elephants they were shot to bits by men who knew the ranges to a yard. Rommel dented the Australian defenses but did not have the big guns to wipe them out. He then built a forty-mile detour around Tobruk so that supplies might move up to his advance posts at Halfaya Pass and Sollum while he tried to bomb out the stubbornly defended port by air. Day after day in the summer of 1941 the Stukas hurled death on the garrison below; they sank ships in the harbor; they repulverized the town; but the Aussies stuck it out in deep shelters and Tobruk did not fall. They were even able to stab here and there at the attacker. Then in August the British were able to slip into Tobruk a fresh team, a new garrison, in large part Poles, taking the place of weary Aussies who had won the right to beer and bed in Cairo.

What Rommel might have done had Hitler given him full support instead of embarking on his Russian venture will always be an interesting conjecture. Unfortunately for the Germans their technical superiority in matters of detail was matched by blindness in regard to the over-all significance of global strategy. As it was, Rommel was limited this fateful summer of 1941 to frontier fighting, forays not campaigns, his jabs and thrusts returned by the British, neither side making headway for months. Africa was a side-show.

SECOND BRITISH COUNTERATTACK

Then, as Hitler's terrific forces drove all out across Russia toward her heart at Moscow, Stalin demanded a second front and he wanted one on the European continent, an impossible request in the eyes of Allied strategists. There were no American forces in Britain, and the British army there was far from being fully armed. In one place only was it possible to fight the wehrmacht on land, namely Libya. The British therefore undertook to drive the Germans, and incidentally the Italians, out of Africa and there defend the Empire's future.

They went about this task in thoroughgoing fashion. Wavell was sent to India to become commander-in-chief, seemingly a demotion, and Auchinleck left the Delhi post for the Near East command at Cairo, a seeming promotion. Everything humanly possible was done to aid the "Auk." Up through the Red Sea and the Suez came the British convoys, packed with men and matériel, bulky tanks and planes, ambulances, machine guns, thousands of tons of munitions and supplies. The old Army of the Nile became the British Eighth Army, more men in it now from Britain, fewer Anzacs since Aussies were needed for the attempted defense of Singapore, but with total strength much greater than Wavell ever had at his disposal. "We sent them everything we had," said Churchill.

The British knew that Rommel had not been idle, that he had received important reinforcements, that he now had three German divisions (two armored) and seven Italian, that he had approximately 100,000 men under his command. Their reconnaissance also told them that he was planning one final and mighty assault on Tobruk. That, they intended to forestall, and in so doing to outflank and isolate their Axis foe.

The new campaign began November 18, 1941, and ended January 17, 1942. For the second time the Axis was driven out of Cyrenaica, but not in any headlong rout as in 1940. Some of the toughest fighting of the entire war took place during these weeks, and for the first two the British only staved off defeat by the narrowest margin.

An analysis in any detail of the maneuvers involved is extraordinarily difficult because of the confused nature of the fighting; hundreds of tanks crashing into one another, captured, recaptured, withdrawing for fresh supplies of fuel, reëntering the fray, isolated action, advance and retreat in columns, encampments reminiscent of Indian attacks on the western plains, ambulances, field hospitals, action during the day resembling sea war as the tanks, like great ships of the line, jockeyed for position over miles of open water. Only this time it was a sand sea, unchartable, wholly unknowable, mirages, visibility low, choking dust, flies, gnats, bugs, insects of every kind, hostile planes whirling in the upper and nether air.

What the "Auk" planned was to pin down Rommel by a local attack at Sollum and Halfaya near the sea and at the same time deploy the British tanks from much further south, shoot them northwest toward Tobruk, the garrison of that port, greatly reinforced to break out, to join the advancing British and cut off Rommel. It was as though, roughly speaking, one considered the terrain a right triangle: the base to the north, the western end Tobruk, the eastern, the Egyptian frontier; the hypotenuse, a line drawn well from the south of the Germans on the frontier across to Tobruk.

There was nothing wrong with the plan but Rommel was not caught by it. His armor cut in behind the British tanks; he severed British lines of communication; he forced the Tobruk garrison back to the sea; and with his panzers drove into Egypt, fell upon the British lorries and supply depots there "like a shark among mackerel."

Instantly the battle became so confused that intelligence officers knew little more than privates. "Convoys of vehicles were scattered over a hundred miles of desert not knowing where to go.... Men who believed they were holding the end of a continuous salient suddenly found the enemy behind them. And north of them and south of them and all around them.... Prisoners became gaolers. Men were captured and escaped three or four times.... Field stations and hospitals were taking in British and German and Italian wounded impartially, and as the battle flowed back and forth the hospitals would sometimes be under British command, sometimes under German."[1]

Defeat stared the British in the face. Auchinleck replaced his field commander, gave a new order. "Get out and behind the enemy. Attack anything you see." It was to be guerrilla warfare for a few days; it was the Spanish Armada all over again, this time with tanks on land instead of ships, the small patrol, the individual landship, cruising at will, grappling the enemy's flank, the tradition of the past put into a new setting, the desert instead of the Spanish Main, the courage and initiative of individuals on their own, of captains and lieutenants who took perilous chances, who enjoyed pitting their own ill-discipline against the better discipline, the more cohesive serried armor of the Germans, more expert in carrying out orders faithfully and effectively than the British, always somewhat at a loss when superiors are absent and when things have to be done *not* according to plan.

The desert, like the sea, was boundless. For centuries the British

[1] Alan Moorhead, *Don't Blame the Generals* (New York, Harper & Brothers, 1943), p. 72.

had been accustomed to open spaces; it was in their blood. Take the LRDG. The British Long Range Desert Group which later had its headquarters in a distant oasis had no tanks, only trucks, scarcely a commissariat. It struck almost exclusively at night; its object: enemy oil and food dumps, enemy air-fields. Emergency rations plus one cup of tea in the morning, one cup of tea at night, one cup of water to wash in, hand grenades, dynamite, a machine gun or two, the mission done, then vanish, reappear. These were the tactics which enabled the British Eighth Army to catch its breath, to reorganize, to try it again and again.

For a week or two the battle remained fluid. The Tobruk garrison established contact with British tanks and the relief of the "rats" was heralded with joy in England; the joy was premature for Rommel disrupted the narrow British corridor; it was reëstablished; but Rommel broke through with most of his armor, leaving garrisons behind at Bardia and Halfaya; Tobruk was now permanently relieved and Rommel vanished westward, planting land mines in his wake.

The Germans kept on going, all the way past the old landmarks, past Derna and Bengazi, back to El Agheila and the borders of Tripoli. The British followed after. The further they went the longer became their lines of supply, the shorter those of General Rommel. The two pockets of resistance he left behind fought fiercely. The garrison at Bardia, 8,000 in number, was forced to surrender at the point of the bayonet; that at Halfaya, 5,500 strong, was only taken by lack of water. It surrendered January 17, 1942. With the collapse of Hongkong the preceding month and that of Singapore impending, even these minor desert conquests tasted sweet to victory-starved Britishers. But it must be remembered they were dearly bought, and this time there were no masses of prisoners as in 1940.

Nor had the British Eighth Army as yet won its major laurels. There was more and still fiercer fighting to take place in this arena during 1942. Both sides began feverishly to prepare for it. Warfare here, as one of the German generals said, was "a paradise for the tactician, a nightmare to the quartermaster." All of the matériel, every single spare part for tanks and planes, every shell, every bullet, every monkey wrench or bit of wire had to be brought from overseas, a distance of nearly 12,000 miles for the British and Americans if they went around Africa, a much shorter route for the Axis but more dangerous, since of the supplies brought to Rommel it is estimated that he lost 50 per cent from submarine and destroyer attack on their convoys or from British planes based in Libya or Malta. The Germans could not for the time being do anything about Libya, but Malta was another story. Stuck out as it was in the middle of the Middle Sea its continuous occupation by the British was a threat to any German enterprise in Africa. The Germans were determined to capture or at least to immobilize Malta. The former they could not do; the latter they came close to accomplishing in 1942.

MALTA

Malta was only a little island, seventeen and a half miles long, eight and a quarter wide. It had an excellent harbor, unlimited cave refuges and potentially excellent air-fields. The Italians had a fair chance to take it early in the war since there were only three battalions of troops in the garrison then, and the air force was three ancient Gladiators. The Italians, however, contented themselves with high altitude bombing and only intermittently at that. The British had all the time there was to reinforce their garrison, to install anti-aircraft guns, to enlarge their three flying fields, to import planes. To hold the island was most highly important; it was a place of call for naval vessels; it had important docking and repair facilities; and above all else planes based on it, if they were numerous enough, could sink ships and tankers bound for Tripoli.

The first German attack on Malta began in January, 1941 and lasted until their spring invasion of the Balkans, but it was by no means as protracted or as savage as the second German try in 1942. The earlier Nazi objective had been to sink the aircraft carrier *Illustrious* and to ruin the harbor for British shipping; to bombard air strips and to intimidate the civil population were of secondary importance. But when the Germans came in 1942 it was a different story; they had taken over the Italian air-fields in Sicily, had enlarged them greatly, had brought thither swarms of their best Junkers and Messerschmitts; and these they kept on the wing a good four months, throwing in wave after wave several times a day and frequently at night at Malta, to give that island a strafing from the air greater than ever London got, to knock Malta out of the war.

Protracted sieges were not new in Malta's history. In the sixteenth century the power of Suleiman the Magnificent was at its zenith; he had swept across Hungarian plains turning Christian churches into Moslem mosques; he ruled undisputed master of North Africa from Morocco to Egypt; he drove the Knights of St. John out of Rhodes and pursued them to their new defense outpost, the Island of Malta. Here in 1565 the defenders of the Cross locked horns for many months with the warriors of the Crescent and the victory of the former marked the end, perhaps for all time, of Turkish aggrandizement in the Mediterranean.

In 1800 Malta was besieged again, a Napoleonic garrison holding out to the last gasp against the British army and navy. This time the attacker won; Britain took over Malta, and her refusal later to surrender it to Napoleon as she had promised was one cause for the renewal of her duel with him.

Now, for the first four months of 1942, the British were the besieged, the Germans the besiegers. The former had few planes to spare and with utmost difficulty flew their fighting Spitfires to the island's exposed air-fields, for they had first to be transported to the Mediterranean to take off from carriers, and carriers were even scarcer than Spitfires.

Nor was it simply air defense that troubled Britain; her island treasure in the Middle Sea was thickly populated, some 280,000 persons living in one of Europe's most congested areas. On their quarter-acre farms they could and did grow luscious vegetables, but one cannot live on tomatoes and lettuce. Breadstuffs had to be brought in, also ammunition and oil, and only by a long sea route could this be done.

Fortunately for the defenders, Malta's water supply was of the best and protection of civilians against air attack the finest in the world. There were great natural caverns underground and to them several times a day men, women and children hastened so that despite the fury of the bombs the loss of life was at a minimum. Fortunately also the Royal Artillery smashed the Italian motor torpedo boats, and the RAF flyers took heavy toll of the luftwaffe, making a parachute landing so perilous that it was never attempted.

The greatest danger was the food supply. Convoys of merchant shipping and oilers from overseas must reach the island, had to run a thousand-mile gauntlet from Gibraltar to Alexandria and return. They did get through, but almost always with losses, sometimes limping into port with half the vessels sunk, the merchant seamen who made this possible taking risks as heavy as the naval ratings, sometimes heavier. As one Canadian flying pilot wrote: "The final act had been played by the navy and the fleet. But the stage had been cleared for their arrival by Yanks from Georgia and Texas, policemen from Wolverhampton, downy-cheeked lads from the Home Counties and hearty lads from Yorkshire, by Aussies and New Zealanders, by French Canadians and 'guys' from the Prairies, by youngsters who'd traveled the seven seas as deckhands on munition ships for the chance to get in there and fight. It had been defended, too, by 250,000 men and women who were hopping mad and never knew the meaning of the verb 'to quit.' " [1]

The price paid for Malta's safety was stiff but it was worth it. And when the German offense slackened late in 1942 the British could take pride that their long and lengthening list of military disasters was offset somewhat by two notable sieges in which they held fast, Tobruk and Malta.

THIRD AXIS OFFENSIVE

But one objective the Germans did win; for a good three months they immobilized Malta, secured a relatively free passage for tankers to Tripoli, for reinforcements to flow to Rommel so that he might be well equipped for his second and last try at the Nile Valley and the Suez.

The race was close. In numbers the British had the superiority: there were some 100,000 Imperials against 90,000 Axis troops among whom 40,000 odd were Italian; the British had more tanks than their enemy although, aside from the General Grant, their tanks were lighter, incapable of meeting on equal terms the famous Mark IV; in field guns they also outnumbered the enemy; and their lines of communication were shorter.

On the other hand, Rommel enjoyed certain advantages of equipment and training which cumulatively helped much toward victory. The scientific Germans had specialized in preparing the minutiae of desert war: their staff cars were speedier, better adapted to the terrain; the tiny green bivouac tents carried by their soldiers were unusually good in quality and design; their soldiers did not get lost as frequently as did the British, for they were

[1] George F. Beurling, and Leslie Roberts, *Malta Spitfire* (New York, Rinehart and Company, Inc., 1943), p. 235.

taught map reading and were constantly aided by road signs planted everywhere; their tank transports, used like ambulances for carrying disabled tanks from battlefield to repair point were of superior design; their portable repair shops were more efficient; their food was more scientifically adapted to the climate; their gasoline containers were better made than the British, they did not leak, they were easier to load and unload; the German road discipline was superior; the Germans used their spades more willingly. These were advantages possessed by Rommel in both his campaigns, and though the British tried to copy them it was just not in their nature to equal Germans in matters of this sort.

The African campaign of 1942 opened in late May when both British and Americans were being thoroughly thrashed by the Japanese, the Germans advancing with seven league boots to the Volga. The United Nations had tasted nothing but defeat for six months and this time it was hoped the story would be different.

They were to be disappointed. Rommel took the initiative, kept it, reconquered Cyrenaica, almost got in sight of Alexandria, his campaign the most daring, the most brilliant waged by any general in this war.

Although relatively stronger than in 1941, he was confronted by a situation more difficult. This time he could not win by simply demoralizing an expeditionary force hundreds of miles away from its base; this time his enemy was strongly entrenched in fortified positions of his own choosing, halfway, roughly speaking, between its railhead in Egypt and the Gulf of Sidra. What the British had done was to bisect the desert by drawing a line of approximately seventy miles southeast from Gazala on the Mediterranean to Bir Hacheim. At the north at Gazala they stationed their South Africans, at Bir Hacheim the Free French, and at a pinpoint in the desert halfway between, known as Knightsbridge, from the London Underground station, a division of English lads. These three points were not exactly fortresses. For some reason they were called "boxes," and strategically might be said to correspond to the old Roman castra, only in this instance the boxes covered a considerable area surrounded with barbed wire, beyond which were land mines, and wire and mines both protected by anti-tank and anti-aircraft guns. Then, between these three boxes the British planted innumerable land mines; behind them they stationed three tank columns prepared to rescue any box threatened, and still further toward

Egypt they had two other boxes, one at Tobruk on the sea, the other held by Indian troops well to the south.

Rommel determined to sweep around this Gazala line and did so. His panzer divisions went deep into the desert beyond Bir Hacheim. Leaving the Free French besieged he kept on, hoping to reach Tobruk, cutting off the British at Gazala and Knightsbridge. Said to have provisions for only a few days, he was in a desperate hurry. His plans miscarried. The Free French isolated in their sandy waste did not surrender as expected but held on with such desperate valor that even after several days they mustered sufficient grit and guts to escape at night. Rommel's tanks meanwhile engaged the General Grants in a long-distance battle, neither side winning. Then Rommel commenced a retreat through the mine fields, the way through having been prepared by his Italian infantry prodding up mines with their bayonet. It looked like a British victory, as Churchill somewhat cautiously announced on June 2. Said the Prime Minister in the House of Commons, "From all the above [Auchinleck's despatches] it is clear that we have every reason to be satisfied, and more than satisfied, with the course which the battle has so far taken...."

A month later to the day the Prime Minister was to address the House again, this time on a motion to censure his government. It seems that Rommel was not defeated. The British if they had a momentary advantage did not follow it up. Rommel returned to the fray, sent his tanks charging again beyond the British boxes, established what might be called a bridgehead east of them, widened it out until his tanks roamed around in a gigantic boxing ring of approximately 100 square miles, not inappropriately termed "the cauldron," and into it decoyed, enticed and tricked the British tanks, Rommel's artillery and tanks wiping out no less than 200, more than two-thirds of those belonging to the Eighth Army. And so Churchill admitted.

Just how this happened is still somewhat obscure. Apparently the British, as under General Braddock in the Pennsylvania wilderness, advanced flushed with coming victory, were ambushed, this time not by Indians but by Mark IV tanks. And now, without armor the British Eighth Army was at Rommel's mercy.

And now, also, with ever accelerated speed Rommel rushed east. Tobruk, which the year before had withstood a siege for months, fell before his armor in one day. The British fugitives streamed toward Egypt. Their transport service, deprived of tank protection, proved a soft morsel for the German tanks. Had it not been for the devoted aid of the RAF the British collapse would have been complete. The RAF was everywhere at once, helping thousands to escape. The British division cut off at Knightsbridge did not surrender but facing west hurled itself at the Italians, swung around to the south into the desert, and by a long circuitous route reached safety as the main body of their countrymen retreated over 125 miles of waterless sand and spiny rock to the railhead somewhat over a hundred miles west of Alexandria. Even the buoyant Churchill could find no words of comfort to say other than "we do not regard the struggle as in any way decided."

Not a moment's rest did Rommel give his enemy, or his own men either. He rushed the British out of Mersa Matruh all the way to El Alamein, sixty miles from Alexandria. Here they tried desperately to check him, throwing in their last reserves. Forty miles south from El Alamein was the Quattara Depression, an immense egg-oval bowl, most of it below sea level, with sand too soft for even Nazi tanks. It was now or never for the British. Again Rommel threw his Germans at the British lines. They penetrated them. And then were driven back.

For this eleventh hour and fifty-ninth minute victory there was one outstanding cause: not the terrain, suitable as it was for defense; not Rommel's widely distended lines of communication; not even the desperate resolve, superb physique and fine fighting quality of a fresh contingent of Aussies and Freyburg's New Zealanders newly arrived from Palestine. What above all else saved the day was sheer physical exhaustion of Germans. They could scarcely stand for lack of sleep; they fell out of their lorries, off their tanks and stumbled as they charged. "Men slept as they stood and walked doggedly to guns beyond caring what happened."

So for the time being Alexandria, Cairo, the Nile Valley, and the Suez were safe from Rommel's raiders. Rommel had overplayed his hand but held his lines in Egypt. Many a weary and perilous month was to pass before the Allies could organize the forces which in October, 1942, were to drive the raider back all the way from El Alamein to final defeat in Tunisia.

8. HITLER BITES ON RUSSIAN IRON

SPRING 1941, and two men look west. Beyond the Atlantic horizon Churchill searches for the keys of victory; across Russian marsh and Polish plain, in nearby Germany, Stalin sees the sons of the Nibelungen hordes forging their twentieth-century thunderbolts to hurl at Soviet Russia. These two will not have long to wait. Manifest destiny, the gravitational pull of world politics, call it what you will, soon will suck America into the whirling war-vortex; even sooner, delusions of grandeur and his mirage of victory will lure the Berchtesgaden Kaiser to tempt fate too often and too far, to sign unseen the death warrant of his finest fighters.

East Europe's annals had dripped with the death duel of Slav and Teuton for seven hundred slaughtering years. Enigmatic and close-mouthed, Georgian Joseph Stalin was well aware that somewhere in the western shadows Adolf Hitler schemed and plotted as the Wagnerian dwarf Alberich does in the opera, eager to steal not the gold of Rhine maidens but the black soil of the Ukraine, to drain Russian oil fields for Nazi tanks and planes, to beat down all Slavs into serfs and slaves. For centuries these Teutons had seen themselves in the rôle of defending Europe against Slavonic barbarism. They really thought their mission was by divine command, and to their minds it was not a Naboth's vineyard they coveted. The Slav, whether out of Warsaw or of Muscovy, did not appreciate the virile civilizing mission of Teutonic knights in East Prussia, of German barons along the Baltic, and in this respect the Russia of Lenin and Stalin differs not from that of Ivan the Terrible or Nicholas I.

Stalin has the peasant's granite memory. He knew from the first that National Socialism was based on anti-Communism and anti-Slavism, as well as anti-Semitism. Had not Hitler's *Mein Kampf* declared "Germany is today the next great battle aim of bolshevism"; had not the Nazis in their slum-brawling linked Jew and

Communist together; had they not convicted Communists of firing the Reichstag building; had not Hitler announced the Ukraine to be Germany's lebensraum; had he not, as late as 1938 on the fifth anniversary of the Third Reich, proclaimed that "With one country alone have we scorned to enter into relations. That state is Soviet Russia"? Hitler knew, and Stalin knew, that the pact of August 1939 between Russia and Germany was of cynic-convenience merely—and that on both sides.

Stalin did not want war in 1941. True, somewhat earlier he had tried to delay the Nazi engorgement of the Balkans, had warned Bulgaria against German intrigue, had advised Hungary to refrain from attacking her Slav neighbor to the south, had concluded a treaty of friendship with Yugoslavia. But these anti-German gestures had been cautious; and all of them had been made before Hitler conquered Crete. That proof of Nazi prowess, and of Allied incompetence, was far from lost on Stalin. He became almost conciliatory; he dismissed from Moscow the ministers of Yugoslavia and Greece; he speeded the delivery of war matériel to Germany; he pulled back his troops from the Rumanian frontier; he soft-pedaled Russian demands for a share in control of the lower Danube; he even extended diplomatic recognition to Ali Rashid in Iraq, a slap at Britain, a subservient bow to Germany—all this a shrewdly unscrupulous play for time.

Late in 1940, to return Von Ribbentrop's visit of the preceding year, Stalin had sent Molotov to Berlin, only to discover that Russia was slated there to join the Axis as had Rumania and Slovakia. There were hints of "compensation" in Iran and Iraq, to balance territorial concessions in the Ukraine, that German World War dreamland, and the appropriate protestations of honest friendship. But these deceived no one, Stalin least of all. He would not ape Mussolini to play a second fiddle in the Axis orchestra. In 1939 he made one mistake and he was not to be caught napping. The war of Germany vis-à-vis England and France had not turned out as he had hoped. It had not been a mutually exhaustive conflict. The Tricolor and the Union Jack had gone down on the run and Hitler's veteran legions stood guard along the Seine. Why not along the Volga, too?

Whether the trip of tourist Rudolf Hess, Hitler's Man Friday, dropping down on Scotland with a parachute in May 1941, meant the Führer was offering German guarantees for the security of the

British Empire in return for a free hand against Moscow, we have no way of telling. But of this we may be certain: years before Nazi Number Three lit on Great Britain, Stalin knew Hitler would march east. He had said so in his muddled way. The British had, too. More than that, nowhere else could German needs be met, Nazi promises fulfilled.

Stalin started to prepare for the inevitable by signing a ten-year peace pact with Japan, thus insuring Russia against war on two fronts; he lengthened the Soviet workday from seven to eight hours and made it a crime against the state for workmen to be over twenty minutes late at the bench; he shunted nearly a million picked boys and girls into trade schools for special training in mechanical pursuits; he speeded the production of tanks and planes, and the reorganization of the Red army to meet inefficiencies apparent in fighting Finland; he gave orders to dismantle war industries at Moscow, Leningrad and elsewhere, the men and machines involved being moved east to the Urals.

These preparations were none too large and hardly soon enough. Hitler, like Napoleon in 1810, had long planned war on Russia. The French emperor, overshadowing Europe like a colossus, was impregnably secure until wantonly he wrecked his power in Russia. How could the German war gambler of 1940 fail to note what befell his imperial predecessor of the nineteenth century, or, for that matter, forget the catastrophic downfall of Sweden's warrior king in deepest Russia the century before?

But Hitler was oblivious to fateful precedents. His overlordship in Europe was far greater in 1941 than Napoleon's in 1808 when his Erfurt Congress of satellite kings and ancillary archdukes marked the beginning of the fatal rift with Tsar Alexander I. In 1812 when Napoleon invaded Russia many of his best troops had been tied up or done up in Spain; but in 1941 there were no British forces whatever in the Iberian Peninsula and the entire continent lay at the Führer's feet like a bird dog. He, the Austrian Hitler, had been more successful than Corsican Napoleon, and the very ease of his victories spurred him on. Hate and fear of Slavic Bolshevism had been the leitmotiv and theme song of *Mein Kampf's* gospel, interwoven inextricably with the ideology of his party faith. The Führer was much annoyed by the Soviet's successful raids into Bessarabia, northern Bukovina, eastern Poland and down along the Baltic states, but he had not been able to challenge all these outrages

while France was still on her feet. Like everyone else, he saw in
Stalin's difficulties while conquering Finland the decisive proofs
of Soviet military weakness. On the other hand, Hitler may have
thought he never could muster sufficient strength to conquer
Britain without exposing the Reich's long eastern frontier to Soviet
attack now that Poland and Czechoslovakia were gone. And possibly he may have reached some agreement with Japan whereby
the swastika flying over the Kremlin would be either the sign and
token of Germany's gratitude for Pearl Harbor or else the signal for
that act of derring-do by the airmen of the Rising Sun.

NAZIS IN FIVE YARDS OF THE GOAL LINE

And so, June 22, 1941, predating the 1812 Napoleon by three
days, Hitler launched the Russo-German phase of World War II;
both attacks highly advertised as the crusade of all loyal western
Europe against Asia's swarming barbarism; this time Germans assisted by Magyars, Spaniards, Rumanians and Italians spearheading
the advance; that time the French in the lead, with Poles, Dutch,
Austrians, Saxons and Prussians trailing them; the final differences
being that Napoleon got to Moscow and that Hitler did not, that
Napoleon lost his army and Hitler did not.

The Germans were methodical in vast preparation; they mobilized satellite Rumanians on the borders of Bessarabia; they despatched artillery and tanks to Finland to help that Fascist régime
renew the Russian war and thus to threaten Leningrad; they reinforced their large army in central Poland with picked troops
from the conquered Balkans; while the luftwaffe, largely withdrawn from the west, was concentrated in the east, its squadrons
diving close to the Russian plain in reconnaissance flights.

Then, in the modern style, without warning or declaration of
war, the Nazi legions jumped the border and there was war with
Russia! The most gigantic duel in recorded history now had opened.
Never before had so many million men been hurled so savagely
at one another; never before had there been a battle line of 1,800
miles across which so many armies lunged. Tanks ripped holes in
opposing lines and siphoned through to widen salients. And then,
the pincer movements; planes droning overhead and dropping
death amid the áck-áck of the anti-aircraft guns; pockets of resistance, now large, now small, contracting, expanding, encircle-

ments, escapes, the trapper sometimes trapped; a constant fluid war of movement; a ruinous scene of hell on earth which Lucifer himself could not surpass. And all this made possible of articulation and control by a new invention of resourceful man, the pocket radio.

At first all went well. The Russians looked for the main attack in the Ukraine but it did not come there. The Germans struck both north and south of the Pripet marshes in eastern Poland but their greater strength they threw to the north toward Brest-Litovsk and Minsk on the old road to Smolensk and Moscow, Napoleon's trail in his death-haunted retreat from Russia. Within a week the Russians lost all the buffer land they had taken since 1939, the Baltic states, eastern Poland, Bessarabia. It looked like a break-through for the Germans, another Sedan. Their rate of progress had been faster than in the raid on western Europe in 1940 and by July 10 they had forged ahead 200 miles. They took 320,000 Russian prisoners, two full armies, cut off, surrounded, forced to surrender by swift-moving German armor driving south and east from northern Poland and joining forces with the wehrmacht driving north and east.

German estimates of captured were in propagandistic contradiction to their own military communiqués, since if the prisoners were as many as stated later on, the Russians must have surrendered without fighting. Yet Germans themselves deprecated the ferocious pugnacity of the Russians whom they claimed to have trapped, the said Russians dying by thousands. Nevertheless, German penetration into Russia in this Battle of the Frontiers was a real victory for the Nazis, only to be discounted by the fact that 200 miles, even on a wide front, did not mean too much in Russia, and no important objective had as yet been won.

But German success continued. In little over three weeks more the luftwaffe destroyed a considerable part of the Russian air force before it even left the ground, and German tanks and German infantry battered into Smolensk with Moscow only 200 miles away. To have covered two-thirds of the trail to the Soviet capital in twenty-six days was great going. Napoleon did not reach Smolensk until August 16; it had taken him nearly twice as long.

The German plan of campaign, brilliant in design, brilliant in execution, suited well their temperament and their superb military skill. The blitzkrieg tactics so successfully applied two years earlier in Flanders were repeated. The Nazis aimed at Moscow, but it was neither this river nor that town that was their main objective. The Russian armies were their quarry, and these they proposed to run down and exterminate before cold weather came, by wide-open maneuvers across wide, level plains. Dive-bombers and tanks, speed and force would encircle the Slav, enfold him in unexpected pockets, and then crush and slay the ponderous red giant. And this the Germans almost did in 1941, but not quite; and once again in 1942, but not quite.

For the Russians, too, had a plan; one suited to their temperament, their tradition, their climate. It was very simple: to keep their armies intact no matter how much ground they yielded. A hundred thousand square miles was less important than their armies. Space, time, winter weather, and the indomitable spirit of her peoples, those ancient allies, could still be counted on. Russian defense was in depth, not ordinary depth but Russian depth. Stalin's tactics were steadily to retreat, to harass his enemy's supply lines, to hammer at his flanks, above all to be tirelessly patient under defeat, conscious that new Russian armies were forming, that still newer Russian armies, given the time, would hurl themselves at the Hitlerites, expel them at last from Sovietland, the holy earth of the Slav.

It was now mid-summer and the Russians had just begun to show their hand. Already they had fired and dynamited bridges, railways, power houses, water mains, dwellings. In Napoleon's day the peasants hated to destroy their crops, but now fired by enthusiasm for Father Stalin and Soviet Russia, they responded utterly, so that scorched earth and ruinous villages, rather than smiling grain fields, met the German eye. And always as it did so the Russians counterattacked all along the line, warily, intermittently, avoiding encirclement. The series of sanguine battles which raged one after another in quick succession throughout central Russia are all known collectively as the Battle of Smolensk, although for the most part they took place east of that strategic rail center and at some distance from it. The spearhead of German advance reached Vyazma northeast of Smolensk and only a hundred miles from Moscow; it knifed through to Bryansk on the southeast, athwart the Moscow-Kiev-Odessa railroad. But Russian lines were elastic; they bent far back but never broke.

Long before this German pressure on the central front had

slowed down it was felt in the Ukraine in southern Russia and at Leningrad in the north. The black earth of the Ukraine, the mineral wealth of the Donetz basin, and the rich oil fields of the Caucasus lured the Nazis on. From early August to late November they kept strongly advancing. By-passing ancient Kiev, they raced for the Black Sea coast and reached it; then they struck back at Kiev from the east and captured that old capital of the Ukraine. All through October Teutonic victory tides rose higher. They swept on to the Sea of Azov; they submerged Stalino on the Don and Kharkov, the Ukraine's second largest city. Then they abated somewhat, finally seeping into Rostov at the mouth of the Don, a good 800 miles from the old Russian frontier. The Ukraine, Russia's granary and main center of heavy industry, was now entirely in German hands. The blow was heavy but the Red armies still were strong.

Almost simultaneously came a dash for Leningrad. That city once captured, the Nazis would touch hands around the eastern shores of the Baltic with the Finns, who had renewed their war with Russia. Victorious to the far north of Moscow as well as to the far south, the Nazis could then initiate a gigantic pincer movement, which closing in on the Soviet capital could choke and end the Bolshevik menace.

"Leningrad became the first position on the Russian front which the Germans failed to take." No matter how hard they tried; no matter how heavy and sustained their air bombardment; no matter how powerful their siege guns, the Russians still withstood them. A great part of the city was pulverized from the air; so close did the Germans come that the noise of battle echoed in the streets. The civilian population which remained, enduring every hardship, worked day and night upon the fortifications which ringed their city. And since the Nazis could not break them, they settled down on November 1 to a long siege, confident that their own troops and the advancing Finns could force surrender by starvation.

Meanwhile the hard-hitting Germans decided to wait no longer in subduing Moscow. On October 2, Hitler told his troops, "Today begins the last great decisive battle of this year"—a true statement, but not in the sense intended. This time the swastika came close to floating over the Kremlin. The German tanks tore gaps in the Russian lines and in less than three weeks Moscow was two-thirds surrounded. German armor drove remorselessly southeast of the capital; it came on with crushing strength from the north; it surged past Mojaisk on the west, and the roar of cannons was audible in Moscow. German engineers wrecked over 12,000 Russian fortified batteries, but 40,000 remained.

Then on December 6 came the Russian counterattack. It took the Germans by surprise. They had underestimated the killing resilience of the enemy. The main Nazi reliance had been on the tank, but now deep snow stalled tanks and cold froze the lubricants without which they were motionless. Napoleon's horses died by thousands, but at least they could move while life remained. The Germans were not so fortunate.

In this year, 1941, the Nazi tide came close to its apogee. "The German High Command demanded from its army tasks that could not be fulfilled, that far exceeded the German army's strength. As on the Marne, the German offense collapsed for lack of reserves five yards from the goal line. . . ." [1] Also, Russians outnumber Germans at least two to one, and organized numbers are power.

The Battle of Moscow had been won. On December 8, one day after Pearl Harbor, the German War Office tersely stated: "On wide areas of the eastern front there were only local operations, and methods of warfare in the east from now on will be conditioned by the arrival of the Russian winter." The words were official acknowledgement of actual defeat. Succeeding years but proved their truth.

Great had been the German victories, but never great enough. Most of European Russia had been overrun, the Ukraine conquered with its coal and iron and other basic resources, yet Moscow and Leningrad stood unsubdued, as did the Crimea, Russia's bastion on the Black Sea. Hitler was to make an end of Russia in three months. Now half a year had passed and the Russian armies still defied him, still grew in numbers and in killing strength.

As early as October, Hitler betrayed anxiety. "We have not," he said, "been wrong in our plans. We have also not been mistaken about the efficiency and the bravery of the German soldiers. . . . We have, however, been mistaken about one thing. We had no idea how gigantic the preparations of the enemy were against Germany and Europe. . . ." A month later, Hitler spoke again. "Never," he boasted, "was a great empire smashed and destroyed in a shorter time than was Soviet Russia." Apparently the war

[1] Max Werner, *The Great Offensive* (New York, The Viking Press, Inc., 1942), p. 95.

was over! But then in this same speech: "The fight has become the fight not only for Germany but for all Europe, a fight for existence or nonexistence." And behind both speeches lurked dark fear, fear lest Germany lose the war.

A month more, December, and the conquering tide receded; the wehrmacht conceded its inability, for the time being, to advance. The fact is it withdrew approximately a hundred miles on the central front and would have withdrawn farther had Hitler permitted. Instead he announced that he in person would assume command of the German army, as Goebbels said, "in obedience to his intuition to influence in the strongest way the operations and the armament of the army and to reserve for himself all significant decisions concerning them." In short, it is not the fault of the Führer that Russia has not surrendered; it is the fault of the German generals, and, more to the point, the Nazi party front or bluff must be kept intact.

The war could not be called a stalemate as long as German forces were deep within Sovietland. But Russians now could and did feel confident. In November, on the twenty-fourth anniversary of the revolution of 1917, Stalin said: "The enemy has seized the greater part of the Ukraine, White Russia, Moldavia, Lithuania, Latvia, Esthonia and a number of other regions. He has penetrated to the Don, hangs like a dark cloud over Leningrad, and our glorious capital, Moscow...." But the price he paid is enormous. The winter is here. There is a common front against Fascism. England and America are a part of it. They will open a second front. "The German invaders wish to have a war of extermination. If this is the German wish they will get it."

WHY HITLER FAILED

The challenge of the Soviet chieftain rang true. Yet it was neither lack of skill nor lack of bravery that enfeebled the German drive. Five reasons account for their failure: the morale and discipline of the Red army, grimly aware that the Volga was their last ditch; the magnificent response of Russian workers to Stalin's unflinching leadership; the Russian winter; new war production in the Urals; and the influx of what later was to become a torrent of vital war weapons from Britain and the United States.

In 1937 Trotsky's *Revolution Betrayed* charged that the Red army had been transformed by Stalin; lamented that it no longer was "the army of the Proletarian dictatorship"; wailed that it was rapidly becoming a class-conscious military machine, highly professionalized, highly disciplined, "with an officer's hierarchy beginning with lieutenant and ending with marshal." Quite true, for Stalin was primarily concerned with Soviet Russia and the defense of Socialism there. And in this, from the very first, he had differed strongly from both Trotsky and Lenin.

Lenin had written in peacetime in praise of "hard work at developing the revolutionary movement and the revolutionary struggle in one's own land, and the support by propaganda, sympathy and material aid of such and only such struggles in every country without exception." No word here of the "Fatherland," nor, in accordance with the original Marxian gospel, was the proletariat supposed to have one. But times had changed, and Stalin changed all this Red gospel. After he took the helm, *Pravda,* official organ of the Communist party, stated: "The defense of the Fatherland is the supreme law of life.... For the Fatherland, for its honor, glory, might and prosperity."

The new-model army which Stalin created was indoctrinated with this new Russian nationalism. And as the war progressed Stalin stressed this nationalist war-cry practically to the exclusion of all else except the total depravity of Hitler and his Nazis. Gone was all talk of the international proletariat. No longer were Marx, Engels, or even Lenin glorified. The Tsar, Ivan the Terrible, hitherto abhorred for insane cruelty, became now Ivan the Great because of his conquests. The Red army was presented by Stalin with a most remarkable and melodious new list of very old heroes to copy and to admire: Nevsky, Dimitry Donsky, Kusma Minim, Dimitry Pozharsky, Suvaroff and Kutusoff.

No man on this list could be said to embody the class struggle, and every man on it was a fierce warrior and Russian patriot. From the dim past history of Russia Stalin dug them out, by picture, film and epic tale; Nevsky, father of the first duke of Moscow, who in the thirteenth century won massacre-victories over Finns and Teutonic knights; Donsky who drove back the fourteenth-century Tartars of the Golden Horde from the banks of the Don; Minim and Pozharsky who rescued their people in the early seventeenth century from Poles and Cossacks; Suvaroff who captured Berlin in the days of Frederick the Great; and Kutusoff, Russia's hero·

general of the Napoleonic War. Here were the men, presented by every art of modern publicity, the Red army was to emulate. Here were the founding fathers of Holy Russia! On to Berlin! And master engineering to do it!

Promotion was no longer based on party membership. Loyalty to Russia and to Stalin was the prerequisite. Political education still continued and during the early stages of the war, political commissars still went with the forces in the field. But that education now had a different slant, Russian nationalism taking the place of proletarian class consciousness, and soon even the political commissars were dismissed. A new emphasis was placed on technical skill, knowledge and discipline. Back came the salute of officers as in the days of the Tsar, the use of epaulets and the insignia of rank. Breaches of military regulations were sharply punished, more severely, the Russians claimed, than in the armies of capitalistic states, the theory being that in the latter the customary subordination of class made it easier to insure prompt obedience to military orders than in a classless society like Russia, where punishment had of necessity to be more sharp and condign. The apt traditions of Asiatic despotism were not cited. The purge of the army in 1937-1938 had brought new and fresh officer material to the fore. For the comfort, health and training of their Red army, the Russians made every useful sacrifice. The soldiers had better food, better clothing, better housing, better educational facilities than the civilians. In fighting quality and in leadership the Red army rose to equal the German wehrmacht and, without question, to surpass Hitler's non-German allies.

The numerous satellite divisions drafted for Russian conquest and to make Europe safe against the Bolshevik menace, did not cover the German cause with glory. Hungarian and Rumanian soldiers had no zest for this eastern fighting and incurred the dislike of Germans and Russians both. "Ersatz Hussars" was the favorite German expression for Hungarians, while the Rumanians were known as "corn eaters" (that is, pigs). The Slovaks, the Germans dubbed "lousy God-worshippers." Since these Slovaks, Magyars and Rumanians were driven to the war like cattle, they did not care who won it as long as they escaped with a whole skin. As for the Italians sent to Russia, their case was succinctly put by a captured sergeant. "Why should we take Russian towns," he said, "when the Germans have already taken all Italy? Why should I go to certain death? For the Germans? They are pigs. They smoke cigarettes all day and would not even give us the butts."

Nor was it different with the Blue Division of Spanish Fascists sent by Franco, or with the French, Dutch, Danish and Norwegian legions, or with the miscellany of Poles, Czechs, Croats and Slovenes enlisted for the anti-Bolshevik crusade. Quite possibly Germany would have been better off without any of this cannon fodder kidnapped into war by fear or desperation, or perhaps to score some gain for family or loved ones. Hitler's proud advertisements of united Europe overlooked the grim fact that no such unity could exist until welded by total victory, nor could it outlast such victory.

"An army of grandfathers and of children." Thus wrote Ilya Ehrenburg, the Russian counterpart of our own revolutionary Thomas Paine, in describing the Russian partisans.

He should have included women; in fact the entire civil population. Never, perhaps, in all history has guerrilla warfare done more to wrest victory from defeat than in Russia, 1941-1944. Scientific mechanized war had neither terror nor meaning for the Russian peasant. He loved his country, he adored Stalin, he detested Germans, and these he killed wherever and whenever possible.

Opportunities were many. Had all the German armies from all the fronts been sent to Russia, they still would have been insufficient to police Hitler's conquests there; the areas "subdued" were just too big.

As it was, German lines of communication stretched hundreds of miles where highways and railways were few; birch forests, swamps, and river valleys, many. In fortified camps or in captured cities, the Germans were safe, but convoys carrying food and ammunition had to reach such places, and woe betide the truck or tank or column that strayed behind or lost its way, or was not alert. Out of the forests would swoop the partisan, a knife thrust here, a torch there, a hand grenade, a Molotov cocktail (gasoline ignited in a bottle) thrust beneath tank or lorry—then—death.

Death on both sides, often under revolting circumstances, for this was Asiatic war and waged to extermination, as was much of our Indian fighting. German behavior was worse in Russia than in western Europe. Hitler's soldiers had been indoctrinated from the cradle with loathing and disgust for Slavs, the European Jim Crow cult. Swiftly and furiously they had swept through the Balkans. A speedy victory in three months' time had been planned and promised as to Russia. This failing, they turned on the partisans with fury. These partisans were degraded Slavs who did not keep the rules of war. Civilians who thus took up arms were not entitled under international law to the protection given surrendering soldiers in uniform. The Dutch, the Belgians, the French, the Norwegians, and so on, had for the most part submitted. The Russian partisans were indeed a different breed. They did not split hairs over legal or chivalric niceties. They neither asked quarter nor gave it. Their one joy and job was to kill Germans. This they did as most they might with furious zeal and iron will.

And their morale rose higher and higher, not only because of success but also because of the fame and praise of their countrymen. The newspapers *Pravda* and *Red Star* magnified every least victory, and Stalin saw to it that by radio and by leaflets rained from planes all Russia rang with such heroic deeds as those of old men dropping from trees upon passing German motor-cyclists, women throwing sacks over the heads of sleepy sentries and killing them with pitchforks, others being slain with hatchets, young girls forming partisan sniper bands, of information conveyed by bird notes, by notches on trees, of young boys mapping with accuracy the location of enemy batteries. "Who are the partisans?" wrote Ehrenburg. "They are the Russian people." It was their war, a war of continental fear and ruin, of empire-wide ambush and stealthy slaughter.

And carried on, so they came to believe, against beasts in human form. Instead of getting on with the war, said they, the Hitlerites raped the young and buried the old alive, while their leisure was given to casual slaughter and impromptu torture. "These invaders are libertines, sodomites, perverts. They grab Russian girls and drag them to brothels, give them to their soldiers, infect them with syphilis." These hoary slogans of the war propagandists stirred Russian hearts and nerved Russian arms to marvelous feats of war.

Diaries and letters found on the bodies of German dead, were properly edited and translated and constantly republished to whip up the scorn and wrath of Russia's civilian population. These served a double purpose, not simply to degrade the German soldier but also to smear his wife or sweetheart or family back in the Fatherland as aflame with greedy lust. The German excursion into France in 1940 had sent silks and perfumes to German housewives as Napoleon's conquests had enriched the arts and pleasures of Paris, and these historic parallels were strongly harped upon and effectively exploited by patriotic Russian propaganda.

And these letters and diaries were re-presented to serve yet another purpose, to show the increasing dread in Germany of British bombs and the increasing war weariness for home of troops in Russia. Many of the latter had been at the front now for two long, hard years; they had fought through from the Polish front to France, from France to Greece, and now deep into Russia. There was abundant evidence that dirt and death, hardship and hope deferred, were beginning to wear their nerves. The full winter's blast was not upon them yet, but Russian nights were long and cold, and Hitler's men began to suffer, and to suffer most of all, one thinks, from the slowly gnawing fact that the greatest and quickest conquests in all Europe's wars were theirs, and made in vain. They won and won, but won no end to war!

"Grey is the country, grey the sky, everything is grey and empty. . . . The road to Moscow resembles one vast soaked sponge along which men, horses and lorries slog painfully and strenuously. Slowly they move, dragging themselves step by step. Time after time they are bogged down. This is Russia." Thus the German radio in November.

Soon winter broke and the Germans, expecting that all would be over before snowfall, were ill equipped for snow and ice. Their boots were made of leather, not of warm thick felt like Russian boots; their uniforms were thin; they had neither fur hats nor woolen mufflers; and when the thermometer dropped far below zero and stayed there week after week, their plight was miserable. Appeals to the civil populace back home brought some relief. Doorbells rang throughout Germany as collections were made of rugs, shawls, overcoats, and even bathing suits; and the radio pleaded with patriotic housewives to make Hans and Otto warm at whatever sacrifice to domestic comfort, Hans and Otto being advised by radio to comfort themselves with the thought that when spring came around they would be warm again.

On January 30, 1942, Hitler blamed everything on the weather. "It was not Russia," he said, "that forced us to the defensive, but only 38 and 40 and 42 and sometimes 45 below zero that did it." But just wait. "In a few weeks in the South the winter is going to break and then the spring will move further north and the ice will melt. . . ." Nothing could stop the German army then. "We have the strongest army in the world. We have the strongest air force in the world." Victory is assured. And Hitler's words were echoed by Göring, commander of the luftwaffe. "The roaring streams," he said, "were covered with ice, the swamps and lakes as well. One single white cover of death extended over the infinite land...." Railroads did not function. Motors and tanks were buried in the snow. "For days the heroic German infantryman has been out there in snow and ice, his fingers numb."

Meanwhile the Russians sang, "Grandad Frost is coming to our help." And soon white-clad warriors on skis skimmed over the frozen wastes pulling white-painted sleds, getting in the rear of the Germans, laughing heartily at those prisoners they captured, frostbitten and miserable, bundled to the ears in whatever they had been able to steal.

Without steel, war cannot be waged, and the Germans had thought to paralyze Russian defense by their conquests in south Russia during the late autumn. With Kharkov, Stalino and Dnepropetrovsk in their hands, how could the Russians manufacture tanks and cannons? The Germans, however, miscalculated as many other militarists had done; they had not dreamed of the speedy transference of whole factories far to the east and they had been kept in entire ignorance of the phenomenal output of new-built Russian steel mills beyond the Urals.

"Day after day," wrote a correspondent of the New York *Herald Tribune*, "I saw trains of one or two engines and thirty to forty cars carrying machine tools, machinery and workers. They roared past minor stations, their whistles blowing, to the Urals area." Throughout the last half of 1941 and the winter of 1941-1942, this factory migration continued. Wherever possible, from Moscow, from Leningrad, from the industrialized south, the machinery of production was snatched from the German shadow and hurried five or six hundred miles beyond the invader's farthest advance.

Take, for instance, the Kaganovitch factory at Moscow which made ball bearings. As told to Eve Curie in her *Journey Among Warriors*, that section of it which was sent to Russia's temporary capital Kuybyshev, ancient Samara, had been operating in Moscow on October 16. By the 24th of that month, it was being put together again at Kuybyshev and was in operation by the beginning of December. Work was on a twenty-four hour basis, two shifts for some workers, three for others. Most of it was done by women working in unheated sheds, wearing woolen kerchiefs on their heads and high felt boots. The women ate their food at the factory. It was not choice. Neither were their sleeping accommodations. They did not seem to mind. They were making it possible for their men to fight. Many plants at Moscow and Leningrad continued whole or partial production during the entire course of the siege. But raw materials were scarce, and fuel at times. At Leningrad when coal was exhausted, peat moss was used, and women frantically dug peat under German fire to keep the factory wheels turning.

It was not, however, so much the factories being moved that saved Russia in her hour of peril. It was rather the working out of Stalin's slogan, Stalin's policy, "Build and defend Socialism in Russia," that bore iron fruit of victory in Stalin's new railroads, new mines, new blast furnaces far to the east. At Magnitogorsk on the eastern slopes of the Urals, 1,500 miles from any European invader and much farther from Japan, were two mountains so rich in iron as to be one of the principal sources of that mineral in all the world. East again from the two mountains, some 1,400 miles farther, were the Kuznetsk coal-deposit reserves with over 400 million tons of coal easily accessible. Here lay the land of Stalin's iron dream—a Russian greatness to be developed by him and his fellows, a greatness above all other greatnesses; and concerning that dream the Germans (as well as the rest of the world) knew nothing.

The far northern part of this region was traversed by the Trans-Siberian Railroad. Stalin double-tracked it, drove a new railroad south to Magnitogorsk, connected that booming steel city with the Kuznetsk coal, built a new north and south railroad to meet the Transcaucasian line, linked together the oases of Turkestan with the vast tundra and endless forests of Siberia, made a great, and secure, inland industrial empire.

The story of Magnitogorsk is the story of a dozen manufacturing cities of mushroom growth in western Siberia during the late 1930s. The coal deposits at Kuznetsk soon proved far in excess of the Magnitogorsk demand, and smelters at Stalinsk in the Kuznetsk area started turning Magnitogorsk ore into finished steel. Stalinsk by 1939 was already a city of 220,000, connected by rail with the Transcaucasian system on the south, with the Trans-Siberian system on the north, with Magnitogorsk to the west.

When war came, instead of one Pittsburgh, Russia now had two, both safe from the enemy.

Take the famous K. V. tank, the "white mammoth," as it was called. When war started the factory was at Leningrad. To move its machinery and workers to the Urals would have been useless had it not been for the steel of Magnitogorsk. As it was, a steady stream of white mammoths began flowing west to the battle lines, 1,300 miles from the place of production. There were not enough of them, but they helped stem the tide until British and American aid became effective.

Despite German destruction of factories in European Russia it still was possible, thanks to Stalin's second five-year plan, to make good part of the damage done and thus keep the front line going. There was no surplus of weapons in Russia in 1941-1942, but Russian soldiers were not armed with clubs, nor did they have to wait in the trenches as they did in 1916 to seize their rifles from slain comrades.

The British and American governments were quick to promise aid to Russia but were not in a position to implement those promises to any considerable degree before 1942 and 1943. The very day that Hitler invaded Russia, Churchill announced in the House of Commons: "Any man or any state that fights on against Nazidom will have our aid. . . . It follows therefore we shall give whatever help we can to Russia and the Russian people." And two days later Roosevelt expressed himself to this same effect.

But Britain had no surplus supplies on which to draw, and the United States had already made such commitments to England and to the British forces in Egypt as put heavy strain on transportation. The British needed everything they had; their army at home was only half-equipped; their forces in Egypt were in dire need of more armament; and in the summer of 1941 a long delayed but desperate attempt was in progress to put Singapore in a state of defense, at least by sea.

Then, too, how to reach Russia? There were three ways: across the Pacific to Vladivostok and by Trans-Sib, almost a prohibitive distance; around South Africa by the Indian Ocean to Basra, and by rail up and across Persia to the Caspian; and, thirdly, via the Arctic Ocean around the North Cape of Norway to the Russian port of Murmansk. The last two were the more feasible and the two put to best use. But the first of these not only involved the good-will of the Persian government, but also building motor roads, transporting railroad locomotives, rail and rolling stock, and building port facilities; the second meant meeting the German killers out of Norway.

At first more use was made of the northern route. It was extremely hazardous, and the loss of life among merchant seamen, high everywhere during the first half of the war, ran highest of all on the convoy route to Murmansk. Nazi subs were reinforced here by Nazi planes based on Norway, and sub and plane between them raised havoc with this all-important life-line to the Soviets. How many ships were sunk on this route in 1942 remained unstated, but it was an open secret that sometimes a third or even a half or more of the heavily laden vessels went down in these icy waters. The best swimmers here had little chance to live. Suits of rubber might keep out water but did not keep out cold. Escorting craft dared not delay for errands of mercy; their duty was to the convoy. The Nazi planes skimmed the water, sank lifeboats, and the convoy steamed ahead. Tanks lashed on decks broke loose and caromed back and forth, clumsy crates of airplane parts did likewise. The air was thick with fog and bombs and geysers, and across the lead-grey sea torpedoes sped. But some ships got through; planes and tanks and food from America and Britain did reach the Red army.

THE SECOND NAZI OFFENSIVE, 1942

Throughout the winter of 1941-1942 the Nazis went defensive in Russia, withdrawing much of their army and depending on strategic fortresses to hold the furious Russians back. Out around these fortresses were fortified villages like the quills of the hedgehog, and to strike through to the center of a hedgehog or to encircle it point by point and compel surrender was costly business. Yet all winter long that was the main Soviet endeavor. It had a certain measure of success and by spring the Nazis had been worried out from some of their "hedgehogs"; neither Leningrad nor Moscow were threatened as seriously as in December. But that was all.

The Red army fought through long winter months with fiery endurance; the Russian inferiority in tanks, noticeable in the summer of 1941, was now ended. New tanks, "white mammoths," huge brutes of fifty tons, the Red tankmen drove at the Germans with ferocious skill through great snowbanks, across frozen lakes and rivers. The ice groaned and bent beneath their weight but the winter-wise Red soldiers put down timbers, covered them with water so they froze and made precarious roadways like frozen pontoons. Time and again they surprised startled Nazis, cut deep behind German lines, and looked forward hopefully to a major German defeat. It never came. "Hedgehogs" might be surrounded, but their garrisons were supplied with food by plane. There were not enough of the white mammoths, not enough of their "little brothers," English tanks sent to Russia and manned by Russians. The Red cavalry performed prodigies of valor; so did the Red ski troops; so did the Red paratroopers. The Nazis suffered horribly, as Hitler acknowledged. But reinforced in February they held most of their hedgehogs. Staraya Russa, Vyazma, Bryansk, Orel, Kursk, Kharkov were still.in their hands by the spring of 1942. The Russians at most had retaken but 20 per cent of the invaded lands and the invaders were in good shape to try again.

This time the Nazis must not fail. They had been at war two years and a half, and now the United States was a foe, the RAF was hampering German production, and, worst of all, the vast Russian strength was being coördinated. It was now or never for the Vaterland.

This time they did not aim at Moscow, but at the lower Volga River valley and the oil of the Caucasus. They needed that oil for their own use, but even more they wanted to deprive the Russians of it. Their own synthetic plants plus the oil of Rumania sufficed the German army, but Russia had no synthetic oil plants and once the Caucasus was in the Axis grip and the swastika flew on the Caspian over Baku then their enemy would be paralyzed; not only paralyzed but cut off from our aid by way of Persia. Nor was this all; if German armor could reach the Volga early in the summer, it could swing north and attack Moscow from the east.

If the rewards were rich, so also were the hazards, for that's how it is in war. It would be necessary to extend the German lines in Russia another thousand miles. Before the Volga could be reached, the Don Valley with the city of Rostov at its mouth must first be taken. And from Rostov to Baku by rail was nine hundred miles! There were no railroads crossing the Caucasus Mountains and Baku lay on the Caspian or eastern flank. Between the Germans and the main Soviet oil wells lay mountains averaging higher than the Alps. The only way to reach their destination would be first to hit the Volga Valley and then follow the course of that river to where it emptied into the Caspian at Astrakan. And before this could be done, Sebastopol in the southwestern Crimea on the Black Sea must first be taken to protect their right flank, and enough of the upper Don Valley wrested from the Red army to insure elbow room for their left flank. These were colossal undertakings, but in 1942 the German armies had no peer on earth.

Late spring and early summer brought German victories. East of Kharkov at the northern end of this drive the Russians delayed the wehrmacht for six weeks, and at the southern end at Sebastopol, 350 miles away, they held out for twenty-five days against odds unparalleled.

Sebastopol was nearly as hard a nut to crack in World War II as in the nineteenth century. Balaklava and Inkerman, names famous in the Crimean War, filled the headlines once again, and over the buried heroes in French and British cemeteries the Russian marines fought hand to hand with German troops. German planes swarmed in the air and German armor lunged on the ground. But there were rugged hills around the port and a few supplies came in by sea. No quarter was given or taken by either side. The city became a smashed shambles and its defenders, driven from their last subterranean holds, were forced to the water's edge. A handful escaped along the coast to Balaklava, where 2,000 years before the Christian era the Greek Jason had soundly thrashed other Black Sea pirates. But the majority were driven to the tip of the Chersonese, where stood a famous lighthouse dedicated to the Virgin Mary and before her time to the goddess Diana. Here "they hurled their rifles away and swam and swam until they sank and drowned," like the Norwegian lemmings but driven by a grimmer fate.

Meanwhile in the eastern Crimea the Kerch Peninsula had already fallen to the Nazis and just beyond the narrow straits lay the Caucasus. The Nazis were not quite ready for adventure there; an army of several hundred thousand needs room in which to operate, and to secure it the German steam roller moved steadily and relentlessly in June across the eastern Ukraine, pushing the Russians back beyond the Donetz River.

Then at the end of June, 1942 came the final rush for oil and glory. Behind the Donetz lay the Don, sweeping in a majestic arc far to the east before flowing into the sea at Rostov. To force a

crossing of the Don, to seep through the rich lands of the Don
basin, to conquer Rostov at the river's mouth, to cross the Kerch
Straits and invade the Caucasus took the greater part of the
summer.

Timoshenko, Russian commander, traded space reluctantly for
time. He was outnumbered, inferior in equipment, and under orders
on no account to risk encirclement; but he did something more
than make a token resistance as the Nazis thrust their "iron fists"
(a new term representing tank infiltrations much more heavily
supported by infantry and artillery than the tank blitzkrieg tactics
of 1940 and 1941) now here, now there. Early in July the Germans
were across the Don; by the middle of the month they had cut the
railroad between Stalingrad and the Donetz, thus severing the
northern from the southern Russian armies; and by the end of
the month they were attacking Rostov at the Don's mouth from
the east. Early in August the Maikop oil fields which produced 7
per cent of Russia's oil fell to the invader, whose rate of advance in
the Caucasus was rapidly accelerated as the Russians withdrew
their tanks and depended for defense on cavalry. Meanwhile by the
middle of August the entire Don bend was in German hands and
by the 31st a Nazi panzer division shoved into the outskirts of
Stalingrad.

Unlike Bataan or Sebastopol, Stalingrad had no natural defenses.
It stretched north and south along the west bank of the Volga for
twenty straggling miles, and between it and the victorious Germans
was open steppe with a few low-lying hills. The Nazis had superiority in numbers, in tanks, and especially in the air, assailing the
city with a thousand planes. They held the west bank of the Volga
both north and south of Stalingrad; they had cut all rail communication, so they thought; no reinforcements could reach the Russians
except by water; and the German planes hovered over the river.

"The fighting for Stalingrad has reached its final stages." Thus
the German radio on September 1, 1942, as Hitler lashed out at
the "Judeo-Anglo-Saxon capitalistic exploitation...the international hyenas and Bolshevik beasts" which he would now destroy.
Nearer and nearer drew the German armor. September 4 Berlin
announced that "the city's fall in the near future is inevitable."

The Russians said this would be a Red Verdun, but the Western
world thought that improbable. The French in 1915 did not contend against dive-bombers and tanks. But now on they came and

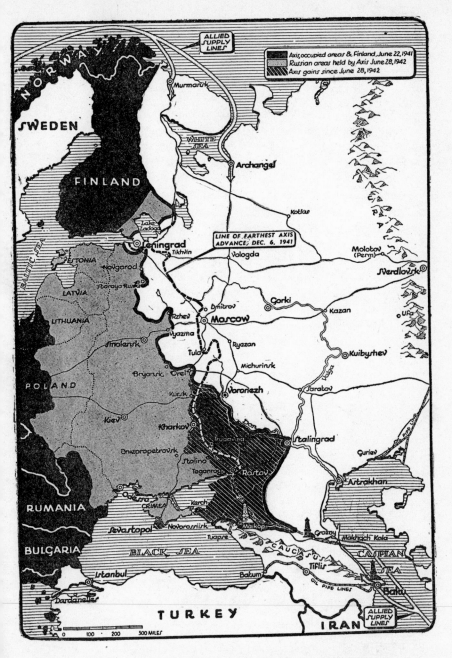

THE RUSSIAN FRONT, SUMMER, 1942

(From Brown and Herlin, *The War in Maps: An Atlas of New York Times Maps* [Oxford University Press], by permission of the publishers)

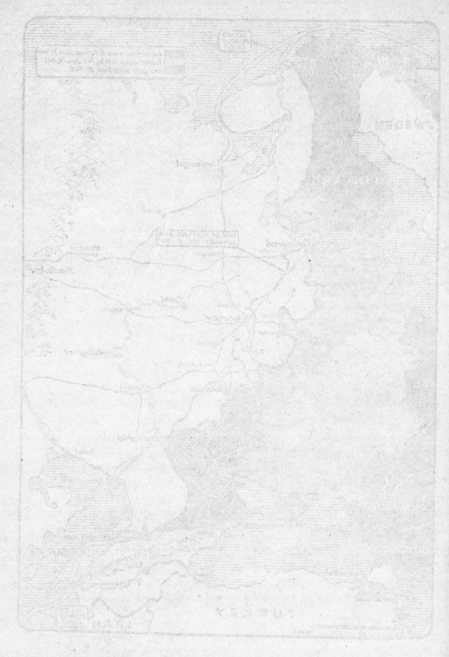

"between them and behind them in dense masses were ranged 40,000 infantrymen, many of them mounted on large armored platforms, each capable of transporting a company of tightly packed men at a speed of fifty miles an hour." So wrote our war correspondents.

In England Churchill evidently feared the worst; and announced that the British Tenth Army, stationed in Iran and Iraq, would defend those lands at all costs; perhaps it might even aid the struggling Russians. Tokyo rejoiced. "Stalingrad is doomed," said the Japanese radio. "An epochal degeneration of Soviet fighting power will follow." And security, of course, for Tokyo's drive against India and Australia.

Slowly the Germans crept ahead. By September 16 the main railroad station was in their hands and now they claimed the city. But the stubborn Russians did not believe a word of it and Ralph Parker wrote in the New York *Times*: "Houses tumble into streets and are swallowed up. The fronts of buildings slide off like fallen shutters. The city ... is a vast cauldron in which two armies with burning hate grapple for the decision."

Throughout September this continued. Nazi armor was handicapped as had been the Spanish Republican tanks in assaulting the military academy of Alcazar in the Spanish Civil War; their caterpillar treads could not surmount the piled rubble of demolished houses. The Nazis claimed the Red army poured boiling oil on German troops, faked retreats and isolated German tanks to wipe them out by concealed artillery. The Germans pressed on, and here and there plunged through the city to the river bank, only to be driven back. Upon the Volga a medley of Russian shipping lurked at night, wood-burning ferryboats, fishing craft, a few cutters, driven desperately to convey reinforcements over from the eastern shore. There was no known railroad reaching Stalingrad from the east, but one existed just the same over which flowed fresh troops and more ammunition. There were no bridges, the German bombers saw to that; but the crafty Russians built bridges two feet under water invisible to German planes, on which soldiers could cross in darkness and in safety.

October came and Hitler pre-reviewed the war. The fight for Stalingrad, he said, was over now and the Germans at last were free to organize their living space, their holy lebensraum. But in fact the fight was far from over. The Germans tried as hard in

October to take Stalingrad as they had done in September. They established themselves in the northern part of the city as well as in the southern; their tanks swarmed for days around the Red October Foundry Works. November came. Time was running out and winter setting in. From the northeast a Russian relief army was approaching. From England 4,000 tanks, 3,000 planes and 830,000 tons of miscellaneous war matériel had come, much of it American. This was not enough, but it helped. And once America got into her stride Russia would not want for guns and tanks and planes.

November 11 and on the Stalingrad front there came "an uncanny lull." Eight days later the Red army exploded into its second great offensive against the German host.

So far in this Russo-German war, honors had been approximately equal, and likewise roughly equal the opposing strengths. The Germans had won the Battle of the Frontiers as well as the Battle of the Crimea, and had occupied Russia's industrial south from whence had come approximately 50 per cent of Russia's steel; the Russians had won the battles of Moscow and Stalingrad. There were heavy losses suffered by the huge armies of both sides. In World War I the Germans had only thrown one-quarter of their men against Russia; in World War II more than twice as many Germans were fighting on the Russian steppes as in western Europe and Africa, perhaps, including satellite troops, as many as 160 divisions. The Germans had more and better tanks than the Russians but their artillery was not as effective. The Germans had more planes but the Russian *Stormovik,* heavily armored for low-altitude flying, was then the best plane of its type in the world. The Germans occupied a large part of the choicest Russian land but their supply lines and their battle fronts stretched for 1,500 miles, and over such distances reserves were weak. The Russian reserves were practically countless, for they were fighting but one war and that on their own home ground.

Throughout 1942 the European-African-Asiatic war expanded until in varying degrees it raged throughout all the world. Japan and America were now combatants, and as the Russians burrowed and battled and died in ruined Stalingrad and beleaguered Leningrad, at Midway in the mid-Pacific and at El Alamein in Egypt events were taking place that boded ill for Adolf Hitler. For now, in the face of all precedent and all past policy, flouting alike their historic fears and dogmas, those great capitalistic and constitutional powers which we call the two democracies, their governments leagued as allies, were rallying their last resources of skill and force to help the peoples of downtrodden China and of resurgent Soviet Russia. These democracies had no other choice and these peoples no other hope. Thus it is eternal justice turns the wrath of man.

9. THE GREAT AMERICAN DEBATE

THE purpose of inscrutable Providence in creating these United States has long been the lively subject of philosophic scrutiny. Orators, editors, clergymen have engaged in protracted and at times acrimonious wrangling as to what was to be our destiny. There has ever been agreement that it would be fair, bright and glorious, worthy of unbounded praise; and so long as their encomiums were confined to the valor, virility and virtue of the American people there were none to dispute their wisdom. But as soon as they wrote of banking, tariffs, slavery and foreign policy, unanimity ceased.

Was America, for instance, destined to hold aloof from European wars in secure isolation from those perpetual conflicts which from time immemorial swept over the original homeland of us all, to be a veritable Beulah land for those who sought our shores to escape tyranny and oppression in the Old World, for those who hoped to found on this happier continent free homes, wherein as by some spirit-magic their memories of ancient grudges and outworn feudal class distinctions might fade away beneath the western sun, be dissipated by the clean fresh air of the American prairie; or, on the other hand, did our duty lie elsewhere, to share the common burden laid upon all nations of good-will, and voluntarily, in accordance with our strength, to accept international responsibilities, to flex our muscles and to draw upon our untapped resources, our reservoirs of manpower and of economic wealth, to strike a blow against tyranny and brutality overseas, to yoke ourselves with other folk in other lands, to build one human future based on equal justice, universal freedom, for all those who on earth do dwell?

From September 3, 1939 until December 7, 1941 this was the great American debate. Around pot-bellied stoves, in country stores and civic clubs, in the press and on the platform, over the radio, in households, in congressional halls and on street corners men argued, each according to his kind, some soberly with good sense, some passionately and without it, but almost all conscious

188

as months dragged on into years that decisions of utmost import to our country's welfare had to be taken. The friction and the turmoil, the clamor and the word-heat of World War I were back again as we drifted into World War II. Old arguments pulled out of the pigeonholes of memory were dusted off and sharpened as propaganda addicts clashed in verbal conflict. Our American democracy, like that of ancient Greece, was of many minds and proclaimed them all, most loudly and emphatically.

"I'll be back in the fall if we don't have war." Thus President Roosevelt to his neighbors as he left Warm Springs, Georgia, April 9, 1939.

War was just around the corner, as the President knew, and he then tried desperately to avert it by means "stronger than words." He thought that perhaps the dictators might be held in check if American aid to the democracies were indicated by repeal of the arms embargo which our neutrality act had imposed. But a request to this effect was turned down by Congress, the Senate Committee on Foreign Relations voting against any present action, twelve to two. The rebuffed President threatened to take his case to the country but wiser counsels prevailed as he heeded Vice-President Garner's report: "Well, Captain, you just haven't got the votes, so there is nothing you can do about it."

Came autumn and the invasion of Poland. Once again the President sought repeal. In January he had stated, "We know what might happen to us of the United States if the new philosophies of force were to encompass other continents and to invade our own." Now in September he denounced the neutrality act as "most vitally dangerous to American neutrality, American security, and the American people." He said, "I regret that Congress ever passed that act. I regret equally that I signed it." He pointed out that the existing law forbade the sale of arms, ammunition and implements of war, but did not forbid the sale of materials out of which and by which they were manufactured. Trucks, machine tools, steel ingots, chemicals, cotton, oil and copper could still be bought in this country, and, what is more, could legally be sent to Europe in American bottoms. "Let no man or group in any walk of life," he solemnly warned, "assume exclusive protectorate over the future well-being of America.... For many years the primary purpose of our foreign policy has been that this nation and this government should strive to the utmost to aid in avoiding war among other nations. But if and when war unhappily comes, the government and the nation must exert every possible effort to avoid being drawn into the war."

Within two hours after delivery of this speech, twenty-four senators met in the office of La Follette of Wisconsin to fight the bill "from hell to breakfast." The great American debate was on.

It was unsatisfactory and inconclusive at this stage because there was no clear-cut issue. Was the purpose of repeal primarily to keep America out of war by lessening the danger of our involvement, or was it primarily to aid the democracies so they might win the war without our fighting in it at all? Ex-President Hoover declaimed against embargo repeal as unnecessary because, he asserted, the democracies did not need our help; they were likely to win anyway, since the French controlled the land, the British the sea; an argument not too convincing after the fall of Warsaw and the Russo-German bifurcation of Poland, all in six weeks. The British had available assets in this country, supposedly of some $4,000,000,000, and the French had perhaps $1,500,000,000. These funds the two Allies wanted to spend for weapons. Their need was not yet desperate but might perhaps become so. To repeal the embargo act would not be a breach of international law, nor of neutrality in the legal sense, but it would be a clear indication of which side we were taking. Could we afford that?

A few men both in Congress and outside it were direct and open in saying yes. President Conant of Harvard announced over the radio that "if France and England are defeated, the hope of free institutions as the basis of modern civilization will be jeopardized." Senator Burke of Nebraska was equally outspoken. According to him, "the bill checks those belligerents I want checked and favors those I want favored." Said Senator Austin of Vermont, "It is to the security and interest of the people of the United States that the Allies win." And those opposed spoke with equal frankness. Said Senator Vandenberg of Michigan, "You cannot become the arsenal of one belligerent without becoming the target for the other," and Senator Borah of Idaho, "Munitions in the end mean men."

Borah's point was prophetically taken, but not necessarily conclusive. After all, the new bill did make us safer by its "cash and carry" clause. If the interventionists were somewhat less than honest in admitting their desire to help the democracies, the isolationists were somewhat less than honest in claiming that the act of

1937 was a better guarantee of peace for America than the new one. A few of them like Senator Taft of Ohio acknowledged that the new law was an improvement, but he was an exception. As for Nye, Wheeler and Borah, so convinced were they that World War II was "just another imperialistic war of power politics" that they were blind to every feature of it except the iniquity of selling guns.

And they were hindered, not helped, by Colonel Lindbergh, the famous aviator, who was so certain of German air superiority that he regarded the war as well-nigh won by Germany and thought it foolish for us to anger Hitler. Lindbergh caused trouble for his own side in this debate, particularly when he took Canada to task for endangering the peace of the Western Hemisphere by sending troops to England's aid. And even greater injury was done by the raucous intervention on the isolationist side of German-American Bundists, Father Coughlin of Detroit, and various neo-Fascist groups whose antics drew more attention than their strength warranted.

Congress debated the bill six weeks, finally passing it in early November, 1939, by a vote in the Senate of 63 to 30 in its favor, that in the House of Representatives being 243 to 181. The significance of the vote in relation to the basic issue was not clear. It was not a mandate to abandon isolation, since many convinced isolationists voted "aye." But it was something more than sympathy for the democracies. We had not yet reached the formula, "All aid short of war." On the other hand, to all intent and purpose we had adopted President Roosevelt's slogan, "Action stronger than words."

"PHONEY WAR" TO DUNKIRK

For six months after embargo repeal American war interest slackened. "The phoney war," we called it, or "the sitzkrieg." Neither the Germans nor the Allies seemed inclined to fight. Militant speeches were made by politicos in London, Paris and elsewhere, but at the front there was only patrol action. Was another Munich brewing? None could be sure but many suspected that Chamberlain and Daladier might recognize the Polish partition as a *fait accompli* and in due time compound their quarrel with Hitler.

Such interest as we had centered more on Finland than western Europe. Radio broadcasts of white-clad Finnish ski-troopers ambushing Russian tanks had greater news value than those retailing the gossip of Parisian boulevards or describing pot shots across the upper Rhine. We knew little of Finland except that she alone of all the countries in the world paid us faithfully the interest on her debt. We had seen many charming photographs of her capital, Helsinki, with its twentieth-century architecture; we admired the prowess of her long-distance athletes and believed her a democratic country, victim of Bolshevik aggression. Had we known more about her actual rôle in European power politics we would not so heartily have praised her fight against the Red militia during the winter of 1939-1940. As it was, enthusiasm for the Finns rose high, "Fighting Funds for Finland Incorporated" collected many an American dollar, and Congress approved (too late to be of any use) a U.S. loan.

Meanwhile there was friction with Britain. Disputes concerning our trade with neutrals overseas and British interference with U.S. mails worried our State Department and augmented isolationist sentiment. We had no use for the Nazis; but also, prior to April-May, 1940, we were sure they would not win. Why, therefore, should America worry? This state of mind was reflected in Roosevelt's message to Congress in January, 1940. "The overwhelming majority of our fellow-countrymen," he said, "do not abandon in the slightest their hope and expectation that the United States will not become involved in military participation. . . ." Possibly the word "military" should be underscored, and the President did say, "There is the greatest difference between keeping out of the war and pretending that the war is none of our business." But no matter how we take it, his address was not a call to arms.

Thus the situation stood until the invasion of Norway, and then in quick succession of Holland and Belgium. American reaction was instant and profound. "We are shocked and angered by the tragic news," said Roosevelt; and going before Congress on May 16 he spoke most alarmingly of the dangers which threatened our country and the immediate necessity of an additional billion dollars for defense. The money was voted at once. Even men hitherto isolationist like Senator Vandenberg approved. A few months earlier he had declaimed, "This war in Europe is none of our business," but now he wanted our country "to give all possible help to the Allies short of going to war or impairing our defense."

The popular weather-vane swung to the interventionist wind. Alternately playing two different tunes, the advocates of intervention met with a favorable response. Some stressed idealism; others preferred more prosaic and materialistic arguments. The former wrote and spoke of justice, humanity, civilization; the latter, priding themselves on their realism, steered clear of such abstract terms and confined their argument to national interest.

Among the idealists Professor Bliss Perry of Harvard; Lewis Mumford, architect and essayist; Dorothy Thompson, columnist; Archibald MacLeish, poet, were prominent. One general motif rang through all their writings. To quote from MacLeish's essay "The Irresponsibles," published in May, 1940, "The truth is, the disorder of our time is in its essence a revolt against the common culture of the West." Civilization itself will be destroyed if the Nazis win. The intellectuals of both Europe and America, the scholars, professors, and miscellaneous literati of two continents, these irresponsibles permitted it to be corroded, undermined by indifference and materialism. They must awaken, raise high the banner of "the invisible power of the ideal." This had been Woodrow Wilson's thesis in 1917.

And then the alternative thesis, the more prosaic and earthly tune of economic security and physical security, safety, the tune of Tolischus of the New York *Times* and of Walter Lippman of the New York *Herald Tribune,* stressing the sinister economics of Nazism whereby nations relying on the gold standard might find their prosperity evaporating; laying emphasis on our protection by the British fleet; statistically demonstrating what plight we would be in if that fleet fell to Nazi hands; vividly protraying how relatively shrunken and impotent in military might our country would become, surrounded on either ocean and to the south by totalitarian nations flushed by easy victories and spitting hate at decadent democracies.

There was dichotomy here. Since war by its very nature is brutal and unidealistic, to urge participation in it in the name of all that is holy seems a contradiction in terms; on the other hand, to ask boys to die for national interest is to rob death of all sacramental significance; for to die for others is divine, even if war is of the Devil.

But such subtle nuances belong to the domain of the philosopher rather than to that of the historian. The truth is, most Americans wanted to do the decent thing. They were disgusted with Nazi brutality and Nazi treachery, and were willing to face death that it should end. They also saw the handwriting on the wall, danger for their way of life, for themselves, their families, their country, if they did not intervene while Britain lived to fight by their side.

The country hummed with agitation which reached a new crescendo after Dunkirk. England now really was in danger, likewise the British fleet. Churchill might speak of moving it to Halifax, but since the wives and children of the sailors must stay in Britain the guarantee of its remaining out of Nazi clutches was none too certain. Prompt despatch to Britain of our surplus guns and ammunition eased the situation. But almost immediately came the capitulation of Paris and jackal Mussolini's joyful leap into the war. All Europe was under Axis power and Britain reeled.

The President gave America's answer at Charlottesville, Virginia on June 10, "We are convinced that military and naval victory for the gods of force and hate would endanger the institutions of democracy in the Western Hemisphere; ... we will extend to the opponents of force the material resources of this nation and at the same time we will harness and speed up the use of those resources in order that we ourselves in the Americas may have equipment and training equal to the task of any emergency and every defense."

Then followed denunciation of Mussolini which raised new hopes in France and England, both criticism and praise in our own country. "On this 10th day of June, 1940," said Roosevelt, "the hand which held the dagger struck it into the back of his neighbor."

The President was a human prism to reflect our public opinion. "Phoney war" was now a bad joke. Once France and Britain were beaten to their knees America knew a change of heart. No longer did war wear the aspect of a Mars-sponsored athletic meet. Now we were angry; now we began to be afraid.

Anger and fear, psychologists assure us, are basic human reflexes to the same phenomenon—danger. It was not just Winston Churchill playing on our sympathies, nor disgust at sadistic Nazi practice as fed to us by Hollywood, that made America war-conscious. Rather it was danger, subconsciously conceived as present rather than logically demonstrated as future, danger of a totalitarian world dominated by Germany and Japan, with help from the Argentine and other ancillary areas.

Psychologically, although we did not realize it, we were close to war. For formal history and legal convention, Pearl Harbor, December 7, 1941, is the occasion. But Hitler's sweep to the English

Channel and the Bay of Biscay eighteen months earlier made that crisis inevitable. Pearl Harbor was incident, not cause. The drive eastward of American GI's toward the Rhine, to kill and to be killed as was the fathers' lot in 1918, the swarming westward of American leathernecks, pig boats, destroyers, battlewagons, multitudinous landing craft and gigantic bombers to wreck the Japanese imperialists resulted directly from Dunkirk and the fall of France.

THE COMMITTEES

When Americans want to do anything they organize a committee, raise money, hire a secretary, publish pamphlets, advertise in newspapers, send telegrams to legislators, hold mass meetings, hire radio time. There were many of these committees during our neutrality but only two were important. Heading the forces which favored aggressive foreign policy, an abandonment of past-minded isolationism, was "The Committee to Defend America by Aiding the Allies," popularly known as the White Committee after its genial chairman, William Allen White. Opposed to it was "The America First Committee," rejoicing in a less cumbersome title and prepared to defend to the last ditch our ironclad aloofness, this the committee of the isolationists or, as some preferred to be called, the non-interveners.

There were advantages which aided and drawbacks which hindered both. That headed by Mr. White had fewer members, possibly less money, but more adroit and influential leaders, outstanding among whom were Henry L. Stimson, not yet secretary of war, Wendell Willkie of Indiana and New York, President Graham of the University of North Carolina, President Conant of Harvard, and White himself, the nationally respected editor of the Emporia *Gazette*, in whose person the folk ways of the Middle West were incarnate.

The White Committee likewise had the backing, both direct and indirect, of the White House. The chairman was a dyed-in-the-wool Republican; he also was an intimate friend of the President, with whom he kept in constant touch, so much so that at times it seemed as though the White Committee and the administration were well-nigh identical.

From the beginning the White Committee labored under one heavy handicap—uncertainty as to procedure. "All aid short of war" was its professed objective, a statement easier to promulgate than to implement. Just what did it mean? Some members interpreted it as everything to help the Allies which did not involve the risk of war for America; to others it signified the green light for anything and everything the situation demanded short of actual shooting, and then, if the Germans declared war, let them do so. The consequence was an official propaganda, sanctioned by the executive committee, at times somewhat obscure; and occasional accusations of insincerity were raised against that body. It is doubtful if these were warranted. The Committee was engaged in a constant internal wrangle as to just how far it ought to go, the New York chapter in particular causing Mr. White many headaches by wanting to take a position more advanced than he was willing to sponsor, it being congenital with White never to stand, as he put it, "too far out in front."

The America First Committee, spearhead of the isolationists, was powerful, well financed by Colonel McCormick of the Chicago *Tribune*, Henry Ford, and other prominent industrialists. Its president was General Robert Wood, chairman of Sears Roebuck; and among its big guns were Colonel Lindbergh, our aviation hero, Philip La Follette, former governor of Wisconsin, and United States Senators B. K. Wheeler of Montana and Gerald Nye of South Dakota.

For the most part, the "America Firsters" were thoroughly patriotic, confident that their country was quite safe behind two ocean bulwarks, positive that only by the strictest neutrality could we avoid war. They were neither Fascist nor pacifist; they abhorred Nazi cruelty and were perfectly willing to defend the Western Hemisphere north of the bulge of Brazil. Beyond that they believed America should assume no responsibilities.

The America Firsters had two great advantages and two great drawbacks. Behind them lay the American tradition. Whatever evidence may be adduced as to the views of the founding fathers, it cannot well be disputed that from 1815 to the end of the nineteenth century the tradition had grown in this land that Europe's quarrels were none of ours, and that the strength, security and well-being of our country were to be found in our hemisphere of isolation. The Spanish-American War modified somewhat this tradition, and for a very short time World War I had shaken it utterly. But the recoil after 1919 had been as pronounced as it was sudden, and from 1920 nearly through 1939 an overwhelming preponderance of American opinion had opposed commitments in either Asiatic or European politics which by any chance might involve us in war with other nations.

Europe seemed far away to most Americans. So thorough-going, indeed, was the reaction in this country against Woodrow Wilson's idealism that many Americans thought on the flimsiest of evidence that our entry into the First World War had been due to hard-boiled munition manufacturers, crafty bankers. Americans were interested in Europe, but at a distance. We were highly critical of the ineptitude of the League of Nations in the Ethiopian crisis and in that of Spain, but we had no intention of doing anything ourselves; we denounced that weak-kneed acquiescence of France and England when confronted by the rape of Austria, but we did not regard that act as our affair; we were indignant at Chamberlain and Bonnet for selling the Czechs down the river, but that America was in any way concerned with Munich never occurred to us. Roosevelt himself had apparently been of the general opinion until his quarantine speech at Chicago in December, 1937; but even his astonishing popularity had not turned the tide. These facts were grist to the mill of the America First Committee. Theirs was the psychological advantage of standing for what seemed to be the old, the approved and the traditional American policy, a policy well seasoned with romantic idealism and grandpa's wisdom.

On the other hand, two serious disadvantages harassed America Firsters. It was their misfortune that various seditious and traitorous elements flocked to their meetings and even joined their Committee. Our country during 1939-1942 was sorely afflicted with such, some Communist, some Fascist. The former were less dangerous, although they aroused more popular indignation. Many of the Communists were foreign-born; their ideology had no roots in the American tradition; and their party was so patently directed from Moscow that patriotic citizens fought shy of it. Conditions were not favorable for Communist propaganda. It was otherwise with Fascism. Hatred of the foreigner, an integral component of Fascism everywhere, unfortunately was nothing new in American history. So, too, was a tradition of violence, in part a characteristic of the frontier, in part due to sudden climatic changes reacting on high-strung nerves, in part because our forefathers were so largely drawn from among the more adventurous and restless folk of the

Old World. Thus it happened that we were not allergic to certain Fascist stimuli.

American Fascism was only part pro-German. The German-American Bund with its Brown Shirts and Bundesführer, Fritz Kuhn, was directly inspired and financed by the Nazi Ausland Institut, and its activities were seditious. But the Bund was only one of many Fascist set-ups. More dangerous to our democracy were the mob disciples of Father Coughlin, who sponsored a gutter sheet called *Social Justice* which poured filth on Communists, Negroes and Jews. Peddled on the street corners of Boston, New York, St. Louis and other cities, it aroused its readers to furious rage. Many of them organized a Christian Front, supposedly Pro Patria et Christi, actually Pro Hell and Hitler. The Christian Front specialized in anti-Semitic demonstrations, and some "Christian Fronters" were said to have armed and drilled for the day when they would crush "the poppycock of democracy." Others, inspired by Coughlin's frothings, called themselves "Christian Mobilizers." Their führer was a certain Joe McWilliams, a handsome man and natural-born orator, part Cherokee, concerning whose followers the less said the better.

Both Christian Fronters and the Christian Mobilizers went unblessed by the Roman Catholic hierarchy. Cardinal Mundelein of Chicago, Father Ryan of the American University at Washington denounced their activities, as did *Commonweal* and *America,* our two leading Catholic periodicals. Nevertheless, despite Pius XI's dictum that "no true Catholic will take part in the persecution of his Jewish compatriots," the howling followers of McWilliams exuded their poison.

In this they were joined by the Ku-Klux-Klan, the Silver Shirts of Dr. Pelley, the Knights of the White Camellia, a rival Fascist organization, and the readers of Senator Reynolds' *American Vindicator,* and the Reverend J. B. Winrod's *Defender,* Fascist and Protestant papers both, and as violently pro-Protestant as Mobilizers and Fronters were pro-Catholic. Yet all in happy unity hated Roosevelt, democracy, the Bill of Rights and the Constitution of the United States. These variegated and assorted ignoramuses were thorns in the flesh of the American First Committee; they attended its meetings, hissed Roosevelt's name, and even booed down "God Bless America" because the song was written by a Jew.

Then, too, if it proved difficult for the America Firsters to disentangle themselves from these leech-like allies it was impossible to combat the fact that technology was making this world one, tending to make it one, socially and politically as well as physically. In a sense the irrepressible conflict of mid-nineteenth century America was reappearing in somewhat different form in the twentieth. As in Lincoln's day, so in Roosevelt's, this conflict between a slave world and a free world loomed on the skyline like the rising sun. What the railroad, steamship and telegraph were to 1860 the airplane and radio were to 1940. Roosevelt put it neatly when he contrasted the rate of speed across the Atlantic of the sailing ship of the eighteenth century, the steamship of the nineteenth and the plane of the twentieth. A universal and integrating human society was a magnet too powerful to be withstood. Granted a little more luck, a less persuasive Churchill, a less politic Roosevelt, and the relative isolation of America from the rest of our planet might have gone on for a while. But it had to end sometime soon and the America First Committee could not prolong it. The stars fought the other way.

DRIFT TOWARD WAR

The second half of 1940 brought us closer to war. Slowly, like an irresistible whirlpool, the European chaos sucked us in. 1940 was election year and both major parties dodged the war question. Both parties were for aiding Britain; both staunchly affirmed their love of peace; and the same held true of both candidates. Willkie in general supported Roosevelt's foreign policy, particularly since 1939, and Roosevelt was always careful to use general terms, rather letting his actions speak for his policy. Yet, despite cautious political sparring, four factors had brought us closer to war by January, 1941. These were: "the destroyer deal," Fascist penetration in the West Indies and in Latin America, Japanese imperialism, and Nazi planes over England.

On the morning of September 3, 1940, many an American was surprised to read in his morning paper that President Roosevelt by a stroke of the pen had delivered to the British admiralty fifty overage destroyers. Some of these were already on their way to Canada to be delivered, so the President said, and in payment Britain was to give us, rent free for ninety-nine years, leases on naval bases in Jamaica, St. Lucia, Trinidad, Antigua, British

Guiana, and in addition a free gift of bases in Bermuda and New-foundland.

This was a splendid bargain for the United States since we had no need of these reconditioned veterans of World War I and the eight bases off our Atlantic coast made it much easier to defend. Some queried Roosevelt's right to dispose of units of the American navy without consulting Congress, despite the opinion of his attorney general approving the validity of the transaction. Yet there was little outcry, partly because of the excellence of the bargain, partly because of the ever increasing need of the British navy for more destroyers if the submarine menace was to be met; and partly because the transaction was a *fait accompli*. There was nothing to be done about it anyhow, except to impeach the President who was then being reëlected.

Since we were in a presidential campaign, Roosevelt's act may have seemed daring. The President, however, was on safe and well-prepared ground. The White Committee, organized as early as the preceding April and greatly enlarged in membership in May, had long prodded him to grant destroyers to Britain, and White, a cautious man well attuned to the variation of political winds, had accused the President of lagging behind public opinion rather than leading it. General Pershing publicly had endorsed the proposal long before it was acted on, and so, too, had several retired admirals. The White Committee was indefatigable in bombarding congressmen and editors, and the Gallup poll had shown a comfortable margin in favor of releasing the destroyers. Wendell Willkie, Republican candidate, could be relied on not to attack. True, he later refused to join the President in a common declaration in favor of what had been done, and grumbled somewhat because Roosevelt did not first consult Congress; but it was nonetheless a foregone conclusion that he would approve "in principle."

There was even less opposition to the President's revolutionary proposal to adopt universal military training in times of peace. The main isolationist argument against further overt aid to Britain was based on the assumption that America was quite competent to defend her own shores no matter what happened in the rest of the world, and the better prepared she was to do so the less need there was to draw closer to the European conflict. In consequence, many of the isolationists were even more in favor of rearmament at home than were the interventionists who insisted that Britain was our first line of defense. Communists in the United States were bitterly opposed to conscription (selective service, it was called) and so, too, were Norman Thomas and the dwindling ranks of Social Democrats who followed him. But Communists, Socialists, and pacifists in both major parties all together compose only a minor fraction of our people. And so Congress passed selective service by a large majority and without protracted debate, stipulating, however, that the troops thus raised should serve only within the boundaries of the United States. War was by now familiar to the American mind.

Meanwhile events in South America and the Caribbean pulled us close to battle. Germans were numerous in South America and strong economically in most of the republics; air routes were largely under German management; and far more South American exports from many countries had gone to Germany than to the United States. There was the usual diplomatic boring from within by German legation attachés, those "termites of alien propaganda" in South American capitals. The President of Uruguay asked for and received a visit from an American warship to ward off a reputed German "putsch," a plot in which officers of the Argentine Republic were said to have been involved. Argentine was none too friendly toward the United States, and of all the countries in Latin America she was the most powerful. There was no democracy in her cities or on her pampas.

In the Caribbean was the Netherlands colony, Dutch Guiana and various islands, likewise the French colonies of Guadeloupe and Martinique. The former were harmless but there was the remnant of a French fleet at Martinique and some $250,000,000 in gold sent across the Atlantic before France fell. At Martinique the ubiquitous "German tourists" put in their appearance and that island, among others, might readily become a refueling depot for German submarines. The French admiral in command of the fleet was also governor and Fascist-minded. The arrogance of his manner was in reverse ratio to his power, but we had to handle him with gloves lest old Marshal Pétain in France take offense and increase collaboration with the Nazis.

There were other headaches to the south. Across the South Atlantic from Brazil it was 1,700 miles to Cape Verde, Africa, and the French colony of Dakar, entrepôt for the Senegal Valley, a well-fortified port with an excellent harbor. In this summer of 1940,

General De Gaulle tried to capture Dakar in the name of the Free French and was repulsed. The British torpedoed the French battleship *Richelieu,* anchored in the harbor. German technicians were reported at Dakar, and the air was full of rumors that the captive government of Pétain might relinquish the colony to Nazi Germany. Dakar was the African air base opposite Brazil, and because of that the State Department kept watchful eyes on Africa as well as on Latin America.

"This is the answer to the destroyer deal," said the spokesman of the German Foreign Office, as Japan signed a treaty on September 27, 1940 with Italy and Nazi Germany. Imperialist Japan was on the march and official America was uneasy.

It would have been intelligent if we had been more so. The pact signed was quite specific. In accordance with it "if one of the three contracting powers is attacked by a power at present not involved in the European war or in the Chinese-Japanese conflict" then the other two powers must assist "with all political, economic and military means."

Ostensibly this pointed to the United States, since that country and Russia were the only powers not in the conflict, and since Article 5 in the treaty expressly stated that its terms "do not in any way affect the political status which exists at present between each of the three contracting parties and Soviet Russia."

Why this treaty? The reasons motivating Japan are easy to fathom. Angered by the Russo-German neutrality pact on the eve of the war, Japan had stood warily one side to see who would win. Now she felt she could wait no longer. The Japanese wanted Indo-China; their mouths also watered at the thought of the Dutch East Indies, so ripe and so rich, prizes almost within their grasp. Victorious Germany would trade Japan the leading part in organizing a "new order in the East" for aid against the United States. If Japan did not accept now and if Germany won the war without her aid, they might not find the Nazis so generous in the future. If, on the other hand, Britain won the war there would be no Indo-China or East Indies for the Japanese Empire, the white man would still rule East Asia, the Japanese would still be colored fellows.

After Japan signed, the administration at Washington enlarged its forces in the Philippines and warned Americans to leave Asiatic ports, but did not change the orientation of our foreign policy and it soft-pedaled the Asiatic danger. Our searchlights still were focused eastward on Europe rather than westward on the Pacific. The majority of Americans did not take Japanese threats seriously; they regarded them as a diversion of the Führer, invented to frighten us. The American public gave as much attention to the antics of French Admiral Robert at Martinique as it did to storm clouds blowing from Tokyo. Nevertheless, the prospect of a two-front war could not now be easily dismissed as idle dreaming.

Through the winter of 1940-1941 we watched with breathless interest the duel in English skies between the Spitfires and the swarms of German bombers. By January, 1941 we were not so sure of British victory, and for the second time in the war we were alarmed for our own safety. First Dunkirk, and now Coventry, Plymouth, London! For a year and a half we had ringside seats on the duel over Britain and cheered lustily our favorite warrior. Between rounds we were vociferous in applause and helped to sponge our contender and to prop him back upon his groggy feet. We still thought the fight not ours, but should we do more than sponge and cheer? The temptation was strong. Suppose our fighter went down, took the count, was finished? How about the victor? Like Atlas, his strength seemed constantly to augment as he used it; he certainly would be in an ugly mood; the better wisdom might be to help Britain floor him lest Britain gasp her last; to take no chances; to place within the reach of our favorite such might and power as could not be withstood by all of banded Europe. If we did not do this while the chance offered, it might soon be too late.

LEND-LEASE

Just where did America stand? The election was over and the formula for both Mr. Willkie and the President was "All aid short of war."

It is always easier to invent a formula than to implement it. Billions of dollars had been voted by Congress in 1940 for national defense; conscription adopted; and a "two-ocean navy," invincible in both Atlantic and Pacific, received congressional approval. Suppose the British called for every available American plane; in what situation would that leave the United States? This was met by the President's assigning 50 per cent of all new government planes to

Britain, thereby presumably inserting "reasonable" between "all" and "aid." But who was to decide on what was "reasonable," the president or Congress; and did such aid involve unlimited credit? The Johnson Act forbade loans to nations defaulting on previous loans, and Britain had defaulted. Would it be necessary to repeal the Johnson Act; was it desirable that more naval vessels be given Britain, with or without a *quid pro quo;* could the United States open its ports to British warships, take German shipping in American ports, release these ships to Britain, and at the same time avoid war with Germany?

In December, 1940, at a press conference, the President suggested a lease-lend program whereby help to Britain could be instantly granted. This he followed up by a radio address in which he suggested that in case of fire one lends one's garden hose to one's neighbor, expecting that it be returned, but not trying to sell the hose first. Then, apparently satisfied with the reaction of public opinion, Roosevelt went further in his annual message to Congress on January 6, 1941: "Let us say to the democracies: 'We Americans are vitally concerned in your defense of freedom. We are putting forth our energies, our resources and our organizing powers to give you the strength to regain and maintain a free world. We shall send you in ever increasing numbers, ships, planes, tanks, guns. That is our purpose and our pledge.'"

Four days later H. R. 1776, the lend-lease bill, was dropped into the hopper of the House of Representatives. March 11 it passed Congress and was signed by the President, thus making a new chapter in the history of the United States.

The bill was revolutionary in giving the President powers such as Lincoln never dreamed. It authorized him to grant on any terms, to any country in the world, whatsoever he deemed necessary for "the defense of the United States." It placed no limit as to time or expense. In accordance with its provisos British ships of war might be repaired in American harbors at American expense; factories might be constructed by presidential fiat, their product placed at the disposal of foreign governments. Shipyards, blast mills, copper mines, the sum total economic strength of this country was to be thrown into the scales against the Axis, and in such ways as the President chose to direct. And the Axis included Japan.

Did the bill mean war; was its passage essential for the safety of our country; could the President be trusted with such extreme power? These major questions were raised in Congress, on the radio, in the press.

"It is a bill," said Charles A. Beard, historian, "for waging undeclared war." The goods we produce, lend and lease, "will be convoyed, and the convoys will be attacked by German planes and submarines."

Beard's logic was hard to dispute. The majority of Americans, however, desperately anxious to stay out of war, preferred not to accept it. That typical American, Wendell Willkie, exuberant and optimistic, would not accept it. His testimony before the Foreign Relations Committee of the Senate was enlightening. "Do you mean to say it is possible to conquer Germany from the air?" he was asked. "Oh yes, Senator," was the reply. The venerable Senator Norris who had voted against our entering World War I, and even against the selective service act, was of the same opinion. "The person most anxious to keep the United States out of the war," he said, "is Hitler. He cannot win if we get in and nobody knows that better than Hitler." Both men stated Hitler's dilemma, which few then saw.

Looking backward from the contemporary scene to February, 1941, we may wonder how two such honest and intelligent Americans as Willkie and Norris could have been so sanguine. Two reasons explain why—the war situation and the American character. Only in the air and on the high seas did Britain seem in desperate plight in February, 1941. Apart from the immediate threat of the luftwaffe and the submarine, the war was going well for her. Those lesser Axis brethren, the Italians, were receiving a thorough drubbing from the Greeks in Albania and from the British in North Africa. The British fleet cruised back and forth through the Middle Sea and British naval guns bombarded Genoa; General Wavell's Army of the Nile, driving five hundred miles west from Egypt, shattered the Italian Tenth Army Corps; and the Ethiopian campaign promised soon the restoration of Haile Selassie. Hitler had not as yet invaded the Balkans, and the Nazi triumph-tide on the Continent, though high, was far from its crest.

The invasion of Britain, however, many considered imminent and to repel it Britain needed immediate succor. The fifty destroyers had helped. Augment that aid a thousandfold, deliver planes to Britain by the tens of thousands, repair the ships of the British navy in our shipyards, take food and guns and tanks to wherever men fought Adolf Hitler, make this country an arsenal for democracy, and the curse of Fascism might be averted from the world. There was some reason to believe that this could be done without our sending men overseas.

Churchill radiated confidence, and his optimism, inherited from his American mother, reflected what America liked to believe. We ever have had unbounded faith in our own energy and competence. If it was simply a matter of food, ships, planes, why, presto, we would produce them. We underrated the Nazis because we liked them less and the British more; we overestimated our own strength because we knew we could multiply it. We were not much disturbed by Japan. Our general attitude was well reflected in the *New Republic* of March 23, 1941, when it stated, "Japan is in essence, bluffing; we, the British and the Dutch are not. That is our strength. Japan has played all her cards; we have aces in the hole." There was nothing the American people could not do once they set their hands to any given task. If it meant supplying Britain with all needed help, we could and would do so.

Americans wanted to keep out of war, but even more than that they wanted to whip Hitler. And the second wish took precedence over the first. If they could not have it both ways, then let war come. The changing percentages in the Gallup poll show this.

	Help England at the Risk of War	Stay Out
May, 1940	36 per cent	64 per cent
June, 1940	36	64
July, 1940	39	61
August, 1940	47	53
September, 1940	52	48
October, 1940	50	50
December, 1940	60	40
January, 1941	68	32

While many argued with Willkie and Norris that we could pass lend-lease and stay out of war, others were more cautious. Secretary of War Stimson testified that he was "Not so much interested in keeping America out of war as in keeping war out of America." "We are next in line for invasion if Britain falls," said Al Smith of New York. "A world enslaved by Hitler is worse than war. It is worse than death. . . ." Thus Senator Austin of Vermont. If war came, let Hitler start the shooting. This was the overwhelming opinion of the majority in favor of the bill. "I guess I am about the only one I know in favor of war," said Senator Glass of Virginia, who earlier had expressed a desire to "blast hell out of Germany." The senior senator from Virginia, however, was a privileged character in American public life. Men did reverence to his age and integrity if they did not always trust his judgment. What he said brought no opprobrium upon him. The same could not be said for Senator Wheeler of Montana, who denounced H. R. 1776 as "The New Deal Triple A foreign policy—plough under every fourth American boy." "The rottenest thing that has been said in public life in a generation." Thus Roosevelt.

"The people have been scared to death." This was the dictum of General Robert Wood of the America First Committee. Crudely put but largely true. Secretaries Stimson and Knox of the War and Navy Departments made it quite clear that Britain would go down without lend-lease. German steel production was twice Britain's and Germany was obtaining from the conquered lands twice the steel that thus far we had shipped to Britain. Birmingham could not match the Ruhr, but Birmingham plus Pittsburgh would be another story. Lend-lease might not save us from war but would save us from unprepared war. It would give us time. The German navy, the Italian navy and the Japanese navy taken together outweighed and outgunned that of the United States. The Royal Navy of Britain, as long as it was afloat and in the war, tipped the maritime balance in our favor. Britain was our first line of defense. The United States, faced on either ocean by a victorious Germany and a victorious Japan, each embittered by the aid we had given a British Empire which they thought lay dying at their feet, would be in grave danger. It might so happen that if we armed to the teeth we could avoid war. Once Britain knuckled under, the Monroe Doctrine would speedily be a joke and our guarantee of the independence of the Philippines not worth the paper it was written on. Thus argued lend-lease advocates.

All this was flatly denied by the opposition. The bitterly Anglophobe Chicago *Tribune* read Wendell Willkie out of the Republican party and Roy Howard of the Scripps-Howard chain newspapers threatened "to break Willkie politically." Lindbergh said he preferred to "see neither side win." According to him, advances in aviation made our military problem of defense much easier, and the corresponding problem for the offense more difficult. He did not believe "a British victory essential to the United States" and he accused the United States of egging on the democracies in a hopeless war. "Even with the full military assistance of the United States," he said, "it would be impossible for Britain successfully to invade Europe"; not, he added, "without an internal revolution in Germany." "The faults and causes of the war," he said, "are evenly divided in Europe." They are no concern of ours.

To quote Lindbergh in extenso would do injustice to the non-interveners. In their ranks, it should be conceded, were many of the ablest men in public life. Such a one was Vandenberg of Michigan, who favored aid to Britain but who opposed the bill since "We cannot assume that Britain won't lose the war. Meanwhile we denude ourselves of what we need to defend America." And yet again he warned, "There is a thrill in magnificent pretensions but there can be cruel disillusionment in their collapse." Taft of Ohio, another man of ability, said many lawyerish things in this debate, such as the following: "The President would order the fleet to Gibraltar, or Singapore, or both, and have it stand by at either place or both. As fast as the crippled British warships put back to either place or both the President would trade a fresh American vessel for it and bring the disabled ship back to the United States for repairs." But he also said this: "We stand today at the cross-roads. So far as is given ordinary mortals to see, both roads which stretch ahead of us are fraught with danger. But if we take one road—the road for which the bill before us is a signpost—what lies ahead is clearly obvious. Down that road lies involvement in Europe's wars, eventual commitments to help bring order out of chaos in all the world, the shouldering of a backbreaking debt for all our people, possibly if not probably, death in some foreign land for the flower of our young men, the end of democracy and civil liberties, certainly, not only for the duration but perhaps for generations until our war-torn economy will be able once again to feed our people."

And so the debate wore on. Would lend-lease be a breach of international law on our part? Yes, said the legally-minded isolationists; no, said lawyer Stimson, quoting chapter and verse from the proceedings of a past meeting of the International Law Association in reporting on what could legally be done against violators of the Kellogg-Briand Pact. Was England now so poor that she could not pay for further war matériel? Yes, said Henry Morgenthau, secretary of the treasury. "I have come to the conclusion that they haven't any dollars left. . . . They can only pay for what is ordered . . . we have searched every possible corner to see if there are any hidden assets and we don't know of any." There were those who challenged Morgenthau's figures. But that Britain was scraping close to the bottom of her economic barrel was evident. What the situation required was unlimited credit, not simply to buy finished goods but to put up factories to make them. Britain did not have this credit and the United States did.

Much more debatable were the arbitrary powers given the President. Short months ago Mr. Willkie, running for the presidency, had made a strong point of Roosevelt's abuse of power, and by this bill that power was doubled, perhaps quadrupled. Willkie, taxed with his old arguments, did not deny them. "The collapse of Britain," he warned, "would end the free way of life in America." There was no other way to save Britain except to grant these powers, much as he disliked conferring them on Roosevelt or anyone else. He recognized that certain limitations as to the amount of money and the time during which it might be spent would have to be written into the bill, but he agreed that the amount should be huge, the limits elastic.

Willkie would concede the point; not so the opposition. They maintained that the bill made the President a dictator, took away the power of the purse from Congress, deprived that body of its constitutional right to declare war. Said Norman Thomas, "I am more afraid of our rushing into our own brand of Hitlerism than I am afraid of anything Hitler can do to us." And, said the Chicago *Tribune*, "This is a bill for the destruction of the American Republic. It is a bill for an unlimited dictatorship with power over the possessions and lives of the American people, with power to make war by alliances for war." Some, indeed, went so far as to prophesy à la Lindbergh that America had witnessed her last free election and if the bill passed democracy was dead.

Whatever the future might do to democracy it was certainly not dead, as slowly but steadily H. R. 1776 made its way through Congress. Demonstrations both pro and con occurred all over the country. Telegrams swamped Congress. A picket line kept in constant motion outside the White House grounds carrying sundry slogans, such as "Benedict Arnold Helped England Too." All kinds of folk were given a hearing before congressional committees. The enemies of H. R. 1776 had several weeks and plenty of radio time and newspaper support with which to rouse the nation.

They made little headway. Finally there seemed nothing to do save concentrate on amendments. Some of these were acceptable to the administration, some not. It was agreed, for instance, that there should be a time limit set for the duration of the act and it was placed at two years, after which it would have to be renewed. It was agreed that not more than $1,300,000,000 of existing war matériel owned by the government could be lent or leased, and that congressional assent would be necessary for further sums. And it was held that nothing in the bill could be considered as authority for American convoys.

On the other hand, the proposal to grant $2,000,000,000 free to Britain to spend as she chose in this country was turned down as not enough and much too slow to meet the emergency. So, too, was a proposal to specify countries to which H. R. 1776 might be applied. An amendment to prohibit convoys was also lost.

Early in the debate, Gillette of Iowa had asked Stimson "Whether it might not soon be considered of paramount import- ance not only to lend defense material to Great Britain but to see it safely delivered as well?" The Secretary of War's answer was, "It might become so." The amendment forbidding convoys was opposed on constitutional grounds. The President was commander- in-chief of the army and navy, and it was not the province of Congress to say what orders he might or might not give his naval commanders. Those who assumed that the British navy had ships enough for convoy duty held that our part was simple to manu- facture war matériel and hustle it to the docks. Perhaps some who took this position were skeptical in their hearts as to British naval sufficiency but did not like to confess it, even to themselves.

The amendments once voted, there was now desperate talk of a filibuster. Nothing came of it. Unfortunately for the America First Committee, its three main orators, Lindbergh, Nye and Wheeler, were all second-rate men. For the aviator there was this to be said: he was young, and his father had been vilely abused during World War I. As for Wheeler and Nye, both were as illogical as they were violent. British imperialism had many oppressive aspects but there was no need for wild exaggeration, nor was it pertinent to the issue of our own security. And the same might be said for that familiar bogyman of the American frontier—Wall Street. The out-pourings of Nye and Wheeler met with tremendous applause just where one might expect it, but from most citizens only a cold response.

And so on March 11 lend-lease became law, the House of Representatives approving, 260-165; the Senate, 60-31, over 96 per cent of both Houses voting. One day later, $7,000,000,000 was appropriated by Congress and placed at the President's disposal. The great American debate was over. The "retreat which began with the rejection of the Treaty of Versailles and the League of Nations had come to an end." The United States had crossed the Rubicon.

THE UNITED STATES CLOSER TO THE BRINK

"Give us the tools and we will finish the job," thus spoke Churchill in 1941 as the American public debated the pros and cons of lend-lease. That was plain talk but did it mean give them to us in America, or deliver them to us in England?

The majority of Americans would avoid "a shooting war," yet that same majority was determined that the Nazis must not win. To find an intermediate way between lend-lease and war was difficult, but the President found it. To order the American navy to convoy transatlantic cargoes meant "shooting"; but how about patrols instead of convoys? There is no difference, cried the isolationists; but in this they erred, somewhat. To use the President's analogy, a patrol on the high seas had the same function as a scout on the western plains: not to fight but warily to watch, and instantly to report the presence of hostile Indians. Warships on patrol would do the same, would look for submarines, and send out the alarm by wireless. If British naval units picked up these warnings and acted thereon, that did not mean war, or did it?

By April 11 our navy was on patrol duty and on April 25 the President said that patrol would be extended, if necessary, to "all the Seven Seas." Two days after, the days the Germans entered Athens, Churchill addressed his faithful House of Commons. "When you come to think of it," he said, "the United States are very closely bound up with us now. . . . When I said ten weeks ago: give us the tools and we will finish the job, I meant, *give* them to us: put them within our reach—and that is what it now seems the

Americans are going to do." The situation in the Near East is perilous but what of it? "Nothing that can happen in the east is comparable with what is happening in the west." And Churchill ended, quoting Clough:

> And not by eastern windows only,
> When daylight comes, comes in the light,
> In front, the sun climbs slow, how slowly,
> But westward, look, the land is bright.

Through the spring we drifted toward war with Nazi Germany; we occupied Greenland to forestall Hitler there; British warships limped into our drydocks to have their war wounds healed, unquestionably an unneutral act on our part; and, May 21, the *Robin Moor*, an American ship far from Germany's prescribed war zone, was sunk in the South Atlantic, unquestionably an act of war on the part of the Reich. Technically we were still at peace, but those isolationists who realized the inevitable were resigning from America First Committees, and more did so when President Roosevelt announced July 7 that our troops had landed in Iceland.

The second week in August the President of the United States and the Prime Minister of England made rendezvous off Newfoundland. While their naval and military staffs took common counsel, the two chief magistrates drew up and signed the Atlantic Charter, a proclamation reminiscent of Wilson's idealism, proposing general principles for future guidance. Both statesmen proclaimed that they opposed "aggression, territorial or otherwise"; that "they desired to see no territorial changes that do not accord with the expressed wishes of the people concerned"; that "they respect the right of all peoples to choose the form of government under which they will live"; that they favored "access on equal terms to the trade and to the raw materials of the word"; that they wished to secure for all nations "improved labor standards, economic advancement and social security"; that "after the destruction of Nazi tyranny" a peace should be established which would guarantee "to all men, in all lands" the chance to live "in freedom from want and fear"; that the high seas be free for all; that the use of force be abandoned; and that "a permanent system of general security is essential."

This charter, of course, was not law; it was not an alliance; it stated a goal toward which both countries promised to strive.

British public opinion would have welcomed an alliance between Britain and America and was disappointed that the Atlantic Charter went no further. But would such a treaty then have been ratified by the United States Senate? As for Roosevelt and Churchill, both were confident that time, tide, and Nazi Germany would soon do more than paper treaties to link their countries in the comradeship of arms.

Even as Roosevelt and Churchill met, a strong current of revived isolationism made itself felt in the United States. The main reason was Hitler's invasion of Russia. Since Stalin was at that time second only to Hitler on our hate-list, many of us thought we had better let our enemies fight it out between themselves. Roosevelt extended lend-lease aid to Russia and this act was not too warmly greeted in his own country. For some months there was difficulty in getting the relevant orders obeyed. At any rate, to most Americans the Russian campaign proved one thing—England was no longer in immediate danger of invasion. Therefore it followed that aid to her could not be as essential as it had been several months earlier. The war theater definitely was moving east rather than west, and farther from our shores.

There were other reasons. The Roosevelt patrols looked to many suspiciously like convoys. Their purpose, ostensibly, was to patrol those waters adjacent to the Western Hemisphere. But who could say where the Eastern Hemisphere left off and the Western one commenced? Twenty-one American republics, including the United States, had proclaimed early in the war a neutral zone 300 miles off shore. But how about Greenland? We had gone in there. An excellent case could be made out for the inclusion of Greenland in the Western Hemisphere, but the same could scarcely be done for Iceland. Yet our troops were landed there because, as President Roosevelt explained, "The United States cannot permit the occupation by Germany of strategic outposts in the Atlantic to be used as air or naval bases for eventual attack against the Western Hemisphere. . . ." British troops were already in Iceland, and when American soldiers superseded them there were grave misgivings in this country. If Iceland was a strategic outpost, why not Ireland, the Azores, Dakar, or even Gibraltar? Many thought the President was stretching his authority too far, and their influence speedily was felt in Congress when the question arose of renewing the selective service act for another eighteen months. It was renewed in the House of Representatives by a majority of one. The President was then on a British battleship to meet Churchill. But the country was not ready for shooting war.

Nevertheless, in two months time we slipped into war, limited in scope and still passionately opposed by a minority of our people, but a "shooting war" just the same as far as action on the high seas went.

On September 4 we were informed that the U.S. destroyer *Greer*, en route to Iceland, had been attacked by a German submarine and had dropped depth bombs. A week later the President told America over the radio, "We have sought no shooting war with Hitler. . . . But when you see a rattlesnake poised to strike, you do not wait until he has struck before you crush him. . . ." The navy, he added, had received orders to protect all merchant ships in our defensive waters, no matter what flag they flew. If German or Italian warships entered these waters they did so at their peril.

The next month, on October 15, the destroyer *Reuben James* sank, struck by a torpedo, and eleven seamen lost their lives. "The shooting war has started," said Roosevelt.

War with Germany! How limited a one? Apparently for the time being limited to naval warfare. The President asked Congress to make further changes in our neutrality legislation but said nothing of any general participation in the war. Congress made the changes; it repealed the ban on arming merchant vessels, that against passing through combat zones, and that forbidding entrance to belligerent ports. "Freedom of the Seas" once more became our slogan. And again the vote was close, in the House of Representatives, 218-194.

This was too close for comfort; it showed a divided Congress, a doubting country. True, the anti-administration minority had been swollen greatly by Roosevelt's refusal to suppress a coal strike. But even allowing for this, the lack of unanimity among us at so late a date was appalling.

The more bellicose members of the old Committee to Defend America by Aiding the Allies now formed a new body, The Fight-for-Freedom Committee, to advocate open and all-out war. The more conservative American Firsters now resigned in their turn, leaving the extremists in control. Among them Lindbergh. At Des Moines, Iowa, he announced that three groups were trying to get the United States into the war, the British, the Jews, the administration. Here was anti-Semitism in the open, and Lindbergh more than ever became the idol of the "Christian Fronters." Praise went to his head. At Fort Wayne, Indiana, he intimated that the Congressional elections due the next year would never be held. Such talk resulted in more resignations.

As for most Americans, they did not know whether we were at war or not!

Meanwhile throughout the autumn the press carried ominous news from the Far East. The Japanese were beating war drums. Their doing so was not new but as usual very few Americans took Nippon's threats at face value, or anything else. Japan might sign a dozen treaties with the Axis, her admirals and generals might foam and sputter, but we knew they wouldn't shoot at us because they were just funny little yellow men. Even historians, aware of Japan's victory in her 1905 war with Russia, were of much the same opinion. In reality, the Far Eastern situation was now serious, whether any of us thought so or not. We might or might not be drawn into war if the Japanese conquered Singapore, Thailand and adjacent areas. But Hawaii was another matter. Our battlewagons and planes at that island outpost were safe enough so long as they did not steam too far west. "No Jap could possibly get within a thousand miles of Hawaii."

Then came December 7, 1941, and all that Sunday afternoon we listened to the radio and knew we were at war, up to the neck in World War II. Japan was on the march, battering down the white man's flimsy Asiatic empires in the swiftest far-flung conquest of history. The outposts of our own homeland, from the Aleutians to Samoa and Panama were at stake. We now must whip the Axis to save ourselves, and in that global enmity we found our national unity at last.

10. THE RED SUN OF JAPAN

DECEMBER 7, 1941, and all mankind was now at war. The conflagration kindled at Marco Polo Bridge four years earlier burned still bright December 7, but that holocaust in ruinous China was no terrestrial combat. "The Government of India" by proclamation had long been at war with Italy and Germany, but of that declaration many millions of Indians knew nothing. Since Siberia was one among all the Soviet Russias, Siberia might technically be written down as in the war; though no bloody battles were being fought on North Asian steppes. It had remained for the war lords of old Japan to crown Mars world sovereign. Their skilful arrogance and lust for racial dominion everywhere enthroned misery, starvation, death—even at last in Tokyo. And now, therefore, ageless Clio has to record one universal war on all continents and throughout every sea, a war of such intensity and horror as though the four horsemen of the Apocalypse had burst reeking out of hell to race and to gallop back and forth over all this trampled planet.

Relations between the United States and Japan had been increasingly worse since 1931. Our refusal to recognize the puppet state of Manchukuo and our steadfast sympathy with China led militarist statesmen of Japan to conclude that they must either abandon East Asia or fight the United States.

The dispute was not primarily economic. Our trade with China was limited and our capital invested there comparatively small. But Americans had educated many Chinese, built missions, schools, universities, hospitals in China, and for a long time had been annoyed, not merely with Japan's outrageous behavior toward China but also with themselves for doing nothing effective to prevent it.

In July, 1939 the United States gave the requisite six months' notice that it intended to denounce its commercial treaty with Japan, due to expire in January, 1940. The Japanese were furious, also somewhat alarmed. The United States was their best customer and from us they imported war goods, particularly scrap iron, airplane engines and high octane gas. Why should America do this? Our ambassador at Tokyo, Joseph Grew, told them the blunt truth. "The people of the United States," he said, "resent the methods which the Japanese armed forces employ in China today and what appears to be their objective."

When the trade treaty expired we did nothing more; Japan continued to buy American oil, scrap iron and other war matériel. They therefore concluded that we cared more for dollars than for China. Just why, indeed, we made this gesture without implementing it is difficult to fathom. Perhaps we wanted to keep Japan from joining the Axis, as she did in 1940; perhaps we did not want her driven toward the conquest of the East Indies; or perhaps we did care more for dollars than for China.

Meanwhile we advanced some loans and credits to the Chinese whereby they might purchase tools of war. But how could these be imported? There were only two feasible routes—one by rail through French Indo-China; the other by the Burma Road, a steep and twisting motor trail from railhead in Burma to Chungking in far western China, a road handmade by Chiang Kai-shek's people with pickax, crowbar and wheelbarrow. The first route the Vichy French sealed, in prompt appeasement, lest Japan seize Indo-China. Britain in 1940 saw little chance to defend Hongkong without aid from America, and very little with it. Therefore she, too, gave way, and that summer closed the Burma Road for three months.

The British held no cards and could not do otherwise, but this was not true for the Americans. We could stop shipping more war matériel to Japan, and this we gingerly began to do by restricting export of scrap iron and gasoline. In September, Japan joined the Axis and shortly after the United States advised her citizens in Japan to return home. Whether this act of ours stayed Japan's hand, or whether the cautious Nipponese were awaiting the results of German air assault on Britain, one cannot say, but the Burma Road was reopened in November without incident.

For some months Japanese policy remained uncertain. Japan might have sailed south to seize the Dutch East Indies, taking French Indo-China, Hongkong, Malaya, Singapore, and the Philippines en route. But Japan was not sure of Russia; and with that traditional foe on friendly terms with Germany, threatening Japan and snugly dug in at Vladivostok, perhaps it was as well to wait, and meanwhile see what diplomacy might win.

And so Matsuoka, secretary for foreign affairs, visited first Berlin, then Moscow, signing a non-aggression pact with Stalin. The absorption of French Indo-China followed, the French, in June, 1941, granting military bases and the right to troop transit. Thereupon soldiers of Japan were rushed to the Thai border, thus putting pressure on Thailand to accept Japanese domination, or else! As Churchill broadcast in August, "They stretch their grasping hand into the southern seas of China. They snatch Indo-China from the wretched Vichy French. They menace by their movements Siam. They menace Singapore, the British link with Australasia, and they menace the Philippine Islands under the protection of the United States. It is certain that this has got to stop."

Who was to stop it, and when? Both Britain and the United States froze Japanese credits this fateful summer of 1941, thus ending trade relations with Nippon; the Dutch East Indies, absorbing courage from the two democracies, grew recalcitrant about selling Tokyo more oil; and there was large talk of the A.B.C.D. powers (America, Britain, China, and the Dutch East Indies) acting in unison. But China was otherwise engaged and so was Britain; only a handful of Netherlanders were in the East Indies; the native peoples were not organized for defense; and that left the United States as a solitary lion in the path of an aggressive Japan.

The American public, engrossed with the European drama, paid little attention to the Far East, and President Roosevelt had been careful since 1939 scarcely to mention Japan in his public addresses. With one war menacing us in the Atlantic we preferred avoiding another in the Pacific, and the State Department did its best to delay an outbreak there. But our government remained pro-Chinese; it extended lend-lease to that country; it permitted an American officer to organize something of a Chinese air service; it despatched a military mission to Chungking; and it continued to protest the conquest of Indo-China.

Few thought the Japanese might attack us. After three years wastage in China and with a million soldiers stationed there, it surely would be folly for Japan to engage America. We little realized the bitter hate and scorn with which we were regarded in Tokyo, or how the war lords had hypnotized their people in regard to their divine ancestry and the equally divine mission of Japan. What we thought was that Tokyo probably intended to absorb

Thailand; and few Americans cared much about Thailand. Once secure there, Japan might invade Burma to close the Burma Road. But why cross that bridge until we came to it; it was not nearly so exciting a topic as the siege of Leningrad or Mr. Roosevelt's Atlantic patrols.

And so when the Konoye cabinet fell in October, 1941, and militarist General Tojo became premier, Americans were not much concerned. Nevertheless, until that month, the Japanese had not decided "whether Japan should reach an agreement with the United States at the cost of considerable concessions, or should pursue her immutable national policies by lining up with Germany under the Axis alliance. The final domestic show-down had now come, and there could be little doubt of the outcome. Konoye was through. . . ."[1] War was close at hand.

On November 5 Tojo announced that he was sending Kurusu as a special envoy to the United States. His "peace mission in effect was but a screen behind which Japan made ready her lightning stroke of December 7, and so Churchill saw it when he warned Tokyo on November 12 that if war came between Japan and the United States, Britain would be at war with Japan "within the hour." Americans did not see their way so clearly in the mazes of power politics. Kurusu doubtless would tempt us to abandon the Chinese, and this we would not do; but possibly he had some compromise to offer; perhaps he came just to hurry Hitler so that he would speed the war on Russia which was not then as decisive as Japan had hoped.

Kurusu did suggest a modus vivendi, with the United States acting as mediator in the Sino-Japanese War. The President agreed under certain conditions to act as "introducer" but not as "mediator"—a subtle distinction to avoid offending China. Kurusu then proposed on November 20 to evacuate southern Indo-China as soon as an agreement was signed with the United States, and all of Indo-China on the conclusion of general peace in the Far East. We were to cease our aid to China and withdraw our economic sanctions against Japan, which meant, if we sold Japan oil and the tools of war she agreed to use them against China and not against us.

We countered with a note withdrawing the President's offer to

[1] Otto Tolischus, *Tokyo Record* (New York, Reynal & Hitchcock, Inc., 1943), p. 269.

act as introducer, reaffirming continued aid to China and proposing that Japan withdraw from China and resign from the Axis. If Japan would do this we would remove all restrictions on exports to Japan and help that country stabilize its currency. In other words, Japan was to drop war and go back to work. The Japanese reply was handed to Mr. Hull on the afternoon of December 7. All this was flummery; torpedo planes and fighter escorts blazoned with the rising sun of Japan were smashing our naval base at Pearl Harbor. Reality had caught up with us at last.

JAPANESE VICTORIES

In December, 1941, the naval forces of the United States were almost evenly divided between the Atlantic and the Pacific oceans. In the Atlantic were eight battleships, four carriers, and somewhat more than half our complement of cruisers and destroyers. In the Pacific were nine battleships, three carriers, and somewhat less than half our cruisers and destroyers. All of the Pacific battleships, with the exception of the *Colorado* at the Bremerton Navy Yard, Washington, were anchored at Pearl Harbor, several thousand miles distant from Japan, snugly protected, so we thought, by ample fortifications and a powerful air fleet.

Then came the attack. Down swooped Japanese planes upon our motionless aircraft, an excellent target, since to prevent sabotage they were lined up in close formation, wing to wing. Having destroyed at one blow most of our planes, the Japanese airmen made for our warships and blasted them at anchor. The crews did what they could with their anti-aircraft batteries, but a battleship at anchor, unsupported by planes, is helpless, and in less than two hours all of our battleships there were either sunk or rendered useless for months to come.

That old battlewagon, the *Oklahoma,* struck by four torpedoes, turned turtle, as near as the shallow water permitted, drowning several hundred men. The *Arizona,* with a Jap bomb dropped through her smokestack and torpedoed as well, sank to the shallow bottom, a mass of hideous twisted wreckage. The *Nevada,* battered and bruised by bomb attack, staggered toward the open sea but sank before she reached it. The *West Virginia* and the *California,* hit and crippled many times by bombs, also sank. The *Maryland* and the *Tennessee,* sheltered somewhat by inside anchorage, escaped torpedoes and, although severely mauled, stayed afloat. The *Pennsylvania* was in dry dock and was damaged least.

For the time being, the United States navy in the Pacific was paralyzed. Fortunately the Japanese got none of our three aircraft carriers, two of them being away from Pearl Harbor with task forces, with cruisers and destroyers so our loss in those categories was comparatively slight. But the battleships were the core of our Pacific naval strength. In the course of time all of them except the *Arizona* and *Oklahoma* were reconditioned, made more powerful than before, able to participate not only in the Pacific war but also to play a strong hand on D-Day in the English Channel. But long and precious months had first to elapse before this could happen.

Meanwhile the enemy had set his grip firm on Wake Island, Guam, the Philippines, the Dutch East Indies, the north coast of New Guinea, and part of the Solomon Islands to the northeast and east of Australia, thus like a giant devil fish reaching out hideous tentacles toward that Commonwealth. And as this took place the Japanese army, spilling like a turbid flood along the southeast coasts of the Asiatic mainland, overran in quick succession Hongkong, Malaya, Singapore, Burma, and surged on to India's frontier, the Mikado's navy darting poisonous tentacles toward Ceylon and distant Madagascar.

Never before in all history had the United States or the British Empire suffered such humiliating defeats as these. Several days before December 7 our commanders at Pearl Harbor had been warned to be on guard against impending trouble. Yet few precautions were taken, not even the elementary one of coördinating naval and military intelligence. The navy took it for granted that the aircraft warning system operated by the army was functioning all the time, and would give adequate advance notice of the approach of enemy planes; but the army only operated this system three hours a day. The army took it for granted that the navy kept constant watch by long-distance reconnaissance flights; but the navy patrolled to the south only, and the Japanese came from the north. The army had one chance to save the day and muffed it; a soldier experimenting after hours with the aircraft detector heard the approaching Japanese planes only to be told by his superior that they were American flying fortresses. A full hour before the attack the navy sank an enemy submarine just off Pearl Harbor but gave no general alarm.

Experts could tell us later and in much more detail how and why we failed; for the time being there were more pressing things: to salvage what we could of matériel and manpower, and to prepare for what every American was certain had ultimately to happen, the utter destruction of Japan.

SPREADING SCOPE OF DISASTER

December 13 "the Navy Department announced that it was unable to communicate with Guam either by radio or cable." The island had already fallen to the Japanese. That rugged outpost on the way to the Philippines never had the slightest chance; there were but 400 navy personnel and 155 marines on Guam; Congress had refused the administration's suggestion to fortify it; and the island was in sight of the Japanese Marianas. Our men fought there one day as best they could.

Roughly halfway from Guam to Pearl Harbor was Wake Island, a coral atoll, a sea-and-land plane base. "Wake had its chin out and its fists ready." The 378 marines stationed there had planes, artillery, anti-aircraft and machine guns. On December 11 twelve Japanese warships tried to cover a landing. It was repulsed. Four Japanese ships were destroyed and several Jap planes. Wake kept up the fight for two whole weeks, in accordance with the best tradition of the United States Marine Corps.

As Churchill promised, and of necessity, Britain was at war with Japan as soon as that country struck. On December 2 two of the very newest and most powerful warships in the Royal Navy, the *Prince of Wales* and the *Repulse*, had reached Singapore. The British, like the Americans, far underestimated an enemy they despised on grounds of race and color. A Japanese troop convoy, lightly protected, was approaching the Malayan coast. Admiral Phillips decided to intercept it with his two battleships and four destroyers, and to do so without waiting for air coverage. On December 10 the storm clouds parted and thirty-six Jap bombers and fifty torpedo planes found their prey. In an hour and a half both the warships and one destroyer were sunk. Nothing but secondary craft confronted naval Japan in all adjacent oceans.

Meanwhile, close to Chinese Canton lay the British island of Hongkong with a superb harbor heavily fortified against attack by sea and a recently reinforced garrison, part British, part Indian, part Canadian, in all 12,000 troops. Within ten days the Japanese had forced a landing from the Asiatic mainland and soon captured or destroyed by bombs all the reservoirs on which the island depended for water. This gone, surrender was inevitable. It came on Christmas Day, 1941.

The Philippines were next. Admiral Hart, commander of our Asiatic squadron, had his headquarters at Manila but very wisely had disposed his vessels so that they could not be trapped in that port. Under his command were the heavy cruiser *Houston,* two light cruisers, the *Marblehead* and the *Boise,* thirteen fourstacker destroyers of First World War vintage, twenty-nine submarines, a few supply ships, motor torpedo boats and thirty naval planes. "From published sources it would appear that for each of the Asiatic fleet's three cruisers the Japanese had four battleships. For each of the thirteen overage destroyers the Japanese had three heavy or light cruisers. And the Japanese had at least nine aircraft carriers, destroyers and submarines by scores...."[1]

General Douglas MacArthur was in command of the Islands' army, in theory a force of 100,000 men. Some 60,000 were Filipino recruits, but yesterday incorporated into our armed forces and whose entire training had been a six-week course; some 12,000 Filipino scouts of excellent quality; some 19,000 United States troops, many of them raw recruits; the Thirty-first Infantry of our regular army and the Fourth Marine Regiment, evacuated from Shanghai in the nick of time, made up the total.

In all the Philippine archipelago there were 316 planes, of which thirty-five were B-17s, "Flying Fortresses." In artillery, anti-aircraft guns and other war matériel we were poorly off. For several months we had been despatching supplies to the Philippines, but much of what we sent did not arrive there. It had to be diverted to Australia.

The first Japanese attack was from the air. It was fast, furious, effective. Straight as a die the Japs thrust at our air-fields from Formosa, 600 miles away, and on the very kick-off eighteen of our big bombers were caught flat on the ground at Clark Field, north of Manila. As an American aviator wrote, "Helpless American bombers, stalled all over the field, hammered defiance from their turrets . . . as courageous crews were shot into eternity, or driven

[1] Walter Karig and Wellbourn Kelly, *Battle Report* (New York, Rinehart & Company, Inc., 1944), p. 137.

into the open by the heat of gasoline-fed flames. The crews had been taking turns at lunch when the attack came. With complete disregard for their lives they had rushed out in a futile attempt to take the big machines off. . . . One after another, these vitally needed, expensive, irreplaceable bombers collapsed in bullet-riddled heaps...." [1] We thought these planes safe; were not our interceptors alert to protect them? But our interceptors were in the wrong place, on patrol west of Manila Bay, and a fortuitous Japanese bomb had severed radio contact with them.

It was very much the same story at Cavite, the naval base, and at Nichols Field close by Manila where the smoke from burning American planes rose high. Our air force, meanwhile, had accomplished something; it had downed some fifty Jap planes and had sunk three transports, seriously damaged a battleship. But this was not sufficient. There was no longer talk of "Japan's bush league air force." We could not replace our losses, and lest they become greater MacArthur ordered on December 17 our remaining fourteen flying fortresses to Australia, later to become the nucleus of a new air fleet there.

On now came the Japanese armies, two of them. The larger one in eighty transports made for the Lingayen Gulf, whither MacArthur was to return three years hence; the lesser force landed well to the south of Manila. By the end of December it was only five miles from the capital of the Philippines which was declared an open city. To defend the city was impossible, and the southern Japanese army occupied it January 2, 1942. There was no fighting and for the time being no disorder. MacArthur was already in retreat to impromptu positions of Bataan, the wild, precipitous peninsula which, jutting down from the north, separated Manila Bay from the Pacific Ocean.

He had to move quickly or else be caught between the large Japanese army moving south from Lingayen Gulf and that already in Manila; MacArthur had to leave behind valuable stores; and it was impossible to concentrate for defense all of our forces in the Philippines, since there were outlying garrisons in Mindanao and other islands. But 40,000 troops, for the most part Filipinos, did dig in on Bataan. They, together with 9,000 stationed on Corregidor

---

[1] Allison Ind, *Bataan the Judgment Seat* (New York, 1944), p. 100. By permission of The Macmillan Company, publishers.

and in Fort Drum, rocky islets at the entrance of Manila Bay, were to keep the flag flying in the Philippines for months to come.

In certain respects the situation which confronted MacArthur was like that which faced Lord Wellington in Portugal in 1809. Both men had to fight a defensive war against tremendous odds; both thought to do so by fortifying a narrow peninsula, the fox holes of Bataan being the twentieth-century equivalent of Wellington's Torres Vedras; and both to a very large extent had to depend on poorly drilled local troops. MacArthur had two advantages—the terrain and Corregidor. Bataan was a natural fortress; its precipitous hills and deep ravines covered by jungle growth and its relatively narrow neck made penetration difficult. The peninsula at the end of which lay the city of Lisbon was hilly, but the mountains of which the French general, Messena, complained did not exist. And four miles from Bataan across the entrance of Manila Bay was Corregidor, The Rock, an island superbly situated for a last-stand fight. It was strongly fortified; it could be approached only by sea or air, and deep within its bowels was a huge tunnel the length of a city block, sufficiently wide to permit two ambulances to pass abreast, and with lateral tunnels on either side. Corregidor seemed a safe refuge from Japanese bombing and artillery fire. So long as our flag flew over it the enemy was not safe in Manila; and so long as our artillery could fire from it we could protect to some extent our troops on Bataan by enfilading fire on Japanese landings on either side of the southern tip of the peninsula. Wellington, on the other hand, not only had nothing to fear from the sea but from it constantly were coming fresh stores and reinforcements. MacArthur faced a hostile ocean, a hostile fleet, and a determined adversary intent not only on forcing his way down through the jungles from the north by land but also constantly assaulting the beaches to the east and west by thousands of small boats and barges protected by large warships, an attack which we could only harass and impede by a few pursuit planes and puny motor torpedo boats.

The defense of Bataan and Corregidor is fully as worthy of commendation as the sieges of Malta, Tobruk, Stalingrad and Leningrad. Our soldiers, marines and Filipino allies showed their mettle. Long after Singapore, Burma, Java and Sumatra had fallen, the flag still flew over Bataan and Corregidor. The fight was hopeless from the start and had to end as soon as the enemy brought up artillery, a fact which gradually seeped into the consciousness of the defenders. But even after realizing that succor could not come, they kept on fighting; their slogan, half in irony, "The Fighting Bastards of Bataan, No Papa, No Mama, No Uncle Sam."

Thus the American-born. And fighting at their side their Filipino allies. The Filipino scouts, hardy, agile, well disciplined, proved themselves as good as any soldiers; and the regular Filipino army, largely without training, acquitted itself with distinction. Even the aboriginal Negritos joined in lustily, capturing Japanese stragglers and bringing them into the American lines in bamboo cages. The wise policy of promising Philippine independence bore good fruit; had it not been for these allies we could have done little to stave off the enemy.

In mid-January, 1942, the Japanese made a major assault on the American lines, and again in early February. And on both occasions they were driven back. None could gainsay their reckless courage: they charged into nests of machine guns without faltering; they hurled themselves on barbed wire, electrically charged, and stuck there, making of themselves a living bridge over which poured their reserves; they dangled like monkeys from tree tops; they fought by night and day. Death had no terrors for the men of Nippon.

After January 1, MacArthur never had more than five military planes, all old models, continuously damaged and repaired with great difficulty. Four antique civilian planes, called "the bamboo fleet," because they were held together by splicing them with bamboo and bits of wire, were his service of supply, and the bamboo fleet could do little to replenish drugs, spare parts, and food, even if Corregidor could have spared them its stores. The defense grew weaker from malnutrition, malaria, dysentery, beri-beri, and hookworm. And as this happened the Japanese changed commanders and resolved to end American resistance no matter what price was paid. Soon our outnumbered men could get no sleep. There was no intermission, no relief, for there were not soldiers enough to spell the half-starved malaria-stricken men in the front-line fox holes. Driven back to the sea some few were evacuated to Corregidor by motor torpedo boats, and some, challenging the sharks, swam four miles to the island where our flag still flew. What remained of the ammunition was destroyed and on April 9, the flag of Nippon flew over the peninsula of Bataan.

General MacArthur, complying with the command of the President, had left by motor-boat and submarine to renew the war as commander-in-chief of the United Nations in Australia. General Wainwright, his successor, continued American resistance on Corregidor until May 6. His men were sick, half-starved, cooped up underground, their island refuge shaken day in and day out by Japanese bombs and shells. Before long the enemy made good a landing. Resistance being futile, Wainwright surrendered.

SINGAPORE

Meanwhile, in February, Singapore had fallen. That populous and wealthy city was a strong bastion of empire, but only as a naval base. Millions had been spent solely to ward off attack by sea. In January, 1942, aside from a cruiser and a few destroyers there was no fleet to defend. The gun emplacements faced seaward, for Singapore was an island as well as a city, and the need of an army base had been ignored. Surely the Malay Peninsula, nine hundred miles long, a grotesque geographical appendix, was a strong wall to landward—and so it would have been with sea and air supremacy.

The British had over 70,000 troops to defend Malaya and Singapore, but their naval strength was puny, their air force utterly inadequate. Even so, if their troops had been trained for jungle fighting (which was not the case) and if the Malays had been given Commonwealth citizenship (or even the promise of it) and trained to fight, the story of Singapore would have been different.

At Singapore there were British regiments famous for tropical warfare of the nineteenth-century variety celebrated by Kipling, the hollow square beating off the Fuzzy Wuzzies. In all the Far East the British had nothing comparable to our Filipino scouts. The Malays were not treacherous, nor had they been ill treated by the British raj, which had left them under their native sultans. But the Malays simply did not consider it their war.

Worst of all was the plane shortage. "In Malaya and Singapore the Japanese command of the air changed gradually from superiority to an almost unchallenged superiority." [4] Then the British were doomed. Reconnaissance in jungle fighting is practically impossible except from the air. As soon as the British tried to establish

[4] George Anthony Weller, *Singapore Is Silent* (New York, Harcourt, Brace and Company, 1943), p. 615.

a base they were photographed from the air and bombarded from it. Week after week the Imperials fought without sighting a friendly plane.

The Japanese fought this brief, incisive, and completely victorious campaign with astonishing skill and foresight. Their shock troops, carefully selected and better paid than the average soldier, were the snipers. Especially trained in tree climbing, in remaining motionless for hours, in camouflaging themselves to look like leaves, the snipers dropped hand grenades on the British by day and, to give the illusion of attack, set off firecrackers by night. Japanese troops were everywhere; they were lightly clad and carried no heavy equipment; they lived on hard rice cake impregnated with meat; they needed no fire; they were prepared for every emergency, with rubber sneakers in place of shoes, with bicycles for jungle paths, with collapsible boats for jungle streams, with chemicals to purify muddy water.

The British army was a land force; that of the Japanese was amphibious, traveling by boat and barge, sometimes by river, sometimes by sea, forcing its way along roads or through rubber plantations, forever getting in the rear of the baffled British and cutting off detachments. The Japanese tanks were light but could cross the rice fields without bogging down and were far superior to the British armored cars, some of which dated from 1918. Excellent, too, were the Japanese paratroopers, skilled in signaling with the radio, adept at ambush. And so the British land army, almost as large as the invading force, later on never had a chance. Defeated in skirmish after skirmish, in foray after foray, it staggered back to the tip of Malaya, crossed the causeway to Singapore, blew up the bridge behind it, and thought to hold Singapore until help came.

The Americans still held Corregidor; the British still held Malta; but Singapore was too big; there were forty miles of coastline and the Straits of Johore were easy to cross, particularly in the west where the water was shallow and where reedy swamps and shallow streams on the Singapore side invited Japanese infiltration. There were no underground caverns as on Malta or man-made tunnels as on Corregidor. Fighting was in the open, and from the pitiless skies poured down the Japanese bombs. The British did their best to send reinforcements, even endangering their Eighth Army in Egypt by so doing. Planes arrived, but too late, for the Japanese had already infiltrated through the marshy shorelands of the west and had repaired the dynamited causeway. With the enemy in command of both sea and air a Dunkirk was impossible. After a thirty-day siege came the surrender (February 15)—the most humiliating in British army annals and, historically speaking, the most significant since Saratoga.

BURMA

Burma in many ways repeated Malaya and Singapore, the soldiers of the rising sun bobbing up where least expected; the Imperials baffled and confused, fighting back blindly, strafed from the air, losing contact with their own detachments, cut off from retreat, poorly led by officers whose ingrained contempt for "natives" was costly.

The Burma campaign synchronized with that of Malaya and Singapore and lasted longer, but only because Burma was of large area and it was impossible to push all the British to the sea. Nevertheless, the outcome was soon a foregone conclusion. At the outset the British, by taking a long chance, might perhaps have made it otherwise. They never had many troops in Burma; but if they had united them in December, 1941, and had pushed boldly into Thailand it is barely possible they could have dammed the Japanese flood until reinforcements came from India and from China, alarmed at the menace to the Burma Road. But instead of this the Imperials remained on the defensive; and during the early campaign the soldiers of Chiang Kai-shek were forbidden to enter Burma.

For a long time that country had been a neglected ward of the Empire, the Burmese complaining that they had no land communication with India, owing to the pull of shipping interests, and that their pleas for self-government were without effect. The Japanese took full advantage of this disaffection; their spy system in Burma was well organized, their promises of independence for Burma loud and emphatic. British propaganda could hardly have been worse; it promised nothing apart from protection; it did not even try to enlist the Burmese to defend their own country. Keep cool and trust us, was the British slogan; and in consequence as fast as the Japanese won victories just so rapidly did the Burmese lose their respect for British arms. Long before the campaign closed the

Burmese were actively aiding the invader by providing food, by acting as guides, and occasionally by fighting at his side.

The main Japanese objective was Rangoon at the mouth of the Irrawaddy where extensive lend-lease cargoes waited transshipment to Mandalay. Once Rangoon fell the Burma Road would be bottled up, the Chinese life-line severed, and the Japanese could attack the oil fields far up the Irrawaddy.

January 15 the invasion started and it took the Japanese over two weeks to cut through the tangled jungles on the Thailand border, to ward off attacks by the RAF and American flyers, to capture Moulmein opposite Rangoon on the Gulf of Martaban. Once there they fanned out, crossed the broad and shallow Salween (three miles wide at its mouth), and circled around to the north of Rangoon. Meanwhile, detachments slipped across the Gulf in small boats to strike at Rangoon from the south and west. The city became impossible to hold and its evacuation in early March was a military necessity.

During the next two months the Japanese swarmed north up the Irrawaddy, the Sittang, and the Salween, driving before them the British and the Chinese, who had finally been welcomed as allies. Numerous and isolated engagements took place between invaders and defenders; the former, wary in frontal attack but swift in movement, appeared with monotonous regularity from nowhere to block roads, to bomb tanks, and to worry and harass the exhausted soldiers of Britain and China; the latter kept on retreating toward the borders of India, the foothills of the Himalayas, and to the far southeastern corner of China, dynamiting oil wells and burning lend-lease matériel as opportunity offered.

The retreat became a rout. The British, burdened with mechanized equipment utterly unsuitable for a terrain of interlaced swamps and forest, abandoned their tanks and scurried on toward India. Most of them made it. The Chinese, under the American General Stilwell, came near being caught. They had stayed, perhaps, too long in central Burma and the Japanese had already cut off their retreat over the Burma Road by penetrating northeast from Thailand. The problem which confronted this fifty-nine-year-old American general was to press north faster than the Japanese could outflank him. Plans laid for so doing were countermanded by the commander-in-chief of the Chinese army. Radio communication with Chungking was interrupted, and the Chinese forces in

Burma widely scattered. Stilwell succeeded in extricating some Chinese and British soldiers and miscellaneous civilians by a march of wild adventure and diversified hardship.

For months to come refugees straggled into India. Fed from the skies by British planes, with swamps under their feet as often as dry land, plunging blindly where trails were not even blazed, many lost their way and perished; how many died will be forever unknown.

NETHERLANDS EAST INDIES

Rich as the Philippines and Malaya might be, not they but the Dutch East Indies was the main objective of Tokyo's empire builders. Here was half of all the tin in the world, much more than half the rubber, almost all the quinine, likewise oil, cotton, sugar, rice, coffee, spices, hemp, lumber in abundance, and native peoples, meek and numerous, choice slave labor for the Yamata race. Ripe for the plucking was this dreamland of the East Asia Co-Prosperity Sphere.

And so the Japanese did not await the fall of Bataan or even that of Singapore before steaming south. Quickly in December, 1941, they won Sarawak, a British-protected state in northern Borneo, and then spreading out took the east coasts of Borneo and the Celebes. Farther south lay a glittering prize, Java, not the largest but the richest island in the East Indies. On it was Batavia, capital of the Dutch empire in Asia, also a not inconsiderable naval base, and what would have been a considerable air force had Britain and the United States had time to deliver to the Dutch the planes they had promised. Since they would have to fight for Java, the Japanese thought first to isolate it, and in so doing pick up booty which might be had for the taking. Therefore their flood-stream was diverted for the time being eastward until it lapped the northern coastline of New Guinea and engulfed New Britain, northeast of Australia, in favorable position to go farther east and south toward the Solomon Islands, the New Hebrides, and New Caledonia, the potential life-line from the United States to Australia.

Then followed action against Java, directed mainly down the Macassar Straits, separating Borneo from Celebes, some 450 miles in length, in breadth from 60 to 250 miles.

The fight for Java was to be decided on the sea. The Dutch had raised their token army of 30,000 men to 100,000; but these were almost exclusively Javanese, poorly trained, poorly equipped. But there was still hope, however slight, that the combined American, Dutch, British and Australian warships in East Indian waters, assisted by our few flying fortresses retrieved from the Philippines and based on Australia, might turn Java into a bulwark sufficiently strong to withstand the enemy until reinforcements of planes, ships and men from the United States and Australia could start the long, long journey, first to the Philippines and thence to Tokyo.

The roster of the entire ABD AFLOAT (the united American, British, Dutch, Australian fleet) was not impressive. At first we had three cruisers, but the *Boise* early was sent limping to India, her keel ripped open by a jagged rock. That reduced us to two. The British had one heavy cruiser, the *Exeter,* which had contended with the German pocket-battleship off Montevideo, also two light cruisers; the Dutch had three light cruisers and the Australians two. These ten cruisers and approximately a dozen destroyers were the ships available for the defense of Java.

They put up a plucky fight and lost, some almost immediately to sink, others simply to disappear as did the American cruiser *Houston* and the British cruiser *Exeter,* presumably sent to the bottom by the Japanese. A few escaped to fight again, as was the lot of the U.S.S. *Marblehead.* This ship was afire and she was sinking; her steering gear was completely out of commission; bombs had struck amidships; bombs had struck aft; and "the hull had been blown inward over an area twenty-seven feet square." But the ship stayed afloat and with very minor repairs her officers and men worked her across the Indian Ocean to a dry dock in South Africa, thence home. Still, there was no doubt but that the Allied fleet took a beating; but before it did so an indefinite number of Japanese cruisers, destroyers and transports were sunk.

There were several engagements in this ferocious little naval war; among them, one in the Straits of Macassar, another off the tiny isle of Bali, close to the eastern tip of Java, and the third and most important, the Battle of the Java Sea, that body of water between Borneo and Java. Accounts vary and accurate knowledge is very skimpy of just what took place in this three-day running fight, but after its conclusion Admiral Helfrich of the Netherlands navy, commander-in-chief of the Allied fleet, dissolved the ABD AFLOAT. The very minor fraction of it left afloat sought refuge in

Australian ports. To carry on the fight there were now only the American submarines. Upon the surface of all Far Eastern seas Japan reigned supreme.

AUSTRALIA

The Commonwealth of Australia lay open to attack. Between it and the Netherlands East Indies was nothing except Portuguese Timor, taken over by a joint Australian-Dutch occupational force which events proved the Japanese would have had no difficulty in pushing aside. Commensurate in size with the United States this smallest of the continents or largest of islands was a big mouthful for Japan to swallow, but those who know their *Swiss Family Robinson* are aware that a boa constrictor's digestive powers are as phenomenal as its appetite. To coil around Australia, to kill or to expel its inhabitants, and make of it an integral part of the East Asia Co-Prosperity Sphere was not beyond the bounds of possibility.

Australia was a young country, and its 7,000,000 people were fresh, vigorous, optimistic. But they had already suffered cruelly in this war. The Aussies had been in the thick of the North African fighting from the beginning and, singing their wild "Waltzing Matilda," had fought their way back and forth across the Libyan desert for many a weary season. Together with their fellow Anzacs, the New Zealanders, they had comprised the bulk of the British army sent to Greece; they had held their own against the Germans on the plains of Thessaly; they had gone through hell on Crete. Sent to Malaya, the weary, mud-stained, blood-stained men from "Down Under" took as heavy a shellacking as any in this war. Australian losses at Singapore were heavier than those of Britain. No less than 18,000 of her volunteer soldiers were behind the barbed wire of Japanese prison camps and 20,000 were to die or be captured in a desperate last chance defense of Rabaul in New Britain. The Australian navy had seen action off Dakar, in the Mediterranean, in the Netherlands East Indies; and for the air defense of the Empire-Commonwealth Australian airmen had vied with those of her sister dominions and the mother country. Australia already had given much to the war.

Fortunately for the Commonwealth, her population was highly concentrated in her southeastern areas, farthest from Japan, and between her and the enemy invaders were two thousand miles of barren desert beyond which were the low-lying jungles of her northern shores, practically uninhabited except at Darwin. The Japanese held Timor, it is true, but that Portuguese island was to the northwest, that section of the Australian continent most inhospitable of all. The northeastern state of Queensland was a different story; but north and northeast of Queensland was New Guinea, one of the world's largest islands with high mountains and dense forests. To reach Queensland and then New South Wales and Victoria farther south, the Japanese had first to secure the northern coastline of New Guinea and then to skirt around it to Port Moresby, the capital of Papua (the eastern part of New Guinea) which had been mandated to Australia by the Versailles Treaty. This the Japanese almost did, but not quite, as we shall later see.

Then, too, the United States came at once and in force to the help of the threatened Commonwealth, the base we had to hold to strike back at Japan. The Aussies had food wholesale with which to supply our armed forces, and we had planes and guns for Aussies. Soon lend-lease was acting in reverse in the South Seas, and Australian and New Zealand beef and mutton made difficulties of supply less onerous. MacArthur was placed in command of the joint Australian-American forces which steadily increased in number during the spring as more and more American transports came. Our aid was strictly limited, due to lend-lease calls from China, Britain and Russia; the voyage to Australia was long and hazardous since it was necessary for our convoys to go well to the south of the Marshall Islands, a Japanese mandate, and even south of the Gilberts, British-owned and seized early in the war by the enterprising enemy; and only a few transports were available. Nevertheless, planes and men were sent in ever increasing numbers, and by May the Americans and the Australians, between them, were able to hold their own against the Japs, even against the swift Zero planes which buzzed over Darwin and Port Moresby.

Both these seaports were wretched little towns, located where the climate was most execrable, difficult of access not only for Japanese but for the Allies. Darwin was strafed time and again from Timor, and presumably the Japanese would have captured it had there been anything to gain by so doing. Port Moresby in Papua could only be reached by water or by plane; but MacArthur was determined to defend it and its adjacent air-fields, since as long as he did so he was in position to flank any Japanese thrust at the populous east coast of the continent. And so, throughout the summer of 1942, Port Moresby was a focal point of Japanese attack and of American-Australian defense, Japanese planes zooming over from Japan-held air-strips at Lae and Salamaua on the northern side of Papua all the way over the Owen Stanley Mountains, engaging in constant dog-fights with Allied airmen flown in from Queensland.

Meanwhile the American navy worked wonders of repair as it made ready to fight again. Fortunately our carriers were undamaged, as were most of our cruisers which had not been caught at anchor in Pearl Harbor. During the late winter and early spring we sent them out in daring raids against the mandated Japanese islands; we even managed a token air raid on Tokyo itself. That was a hit-and-run affair but it was a happy augury of years to come. Part of our depleted Pacific fleet we sent to Australia. It was just in time. The Japanese already were snugly ensconced in the northern Solomons and had begun to build an air-field on Guadalcanal in the southern part of that far-flung archipelago. Early in May they steamed in force down through the Coral Sea off the Australian coast, battleships, cruisers, carriers, destroyers, transports, intent either on an invasion of Australia or else on an attack on French New Caledonia, directly to the east, a French island already occupied by American troops with the blessing of the Free French who had detached it from Vichy.

We drove up fast from the south to meet the oncoming Japs and fought, beginning May 5 through several days, the bitter Battle of the Coral Sea. It was a most peculiar sea fight since surface vessels never came in contact, the fighting being done by planes from carriers. We certainly sank one Japanese carrier and perhaps another, also a cruiser and several destroyers. The Japs on their side sank our carrier *Lexington,* a destroyer and a large tanker. It was not a decisive victory; the Japs continued to hold Guadalcanal. But for once we had struck back hard, and for the time being neither Australia nor New Caledonia were in danger.

Within a few days after Pearl Harbor, Churchill flew to Washington, there to concoct with Roosevelt joint war against Japan. Nor was it to be conducted by Britain and the United States alone. On January 1, 1942, the United Nations, twenty-six in number, signed a military alliance. Britain, China, the United States, the British Dominions, the governments in exile (Luxembourg, Holland, Belgium, Norway, Greece and Yugoslavia), the Central American and Caribbean republics and India made up the list, shortly after to be enlarged by Mexico, Brazil and other countries. Russia for the time being remained at peace with Japan. But the world-wide issue now was joined and global war raged in earnest.

The brunt of the conflict against Japan had to be borne by the United States with some aid from Australia and China. Britain had her hands full in the Near East and Africa, to say nothing of the Atlantic-Mediterranean submarine menace and the ever expanding Allied air attack from Britain on German-dominated western Europe. Britain had to defend India and the Indian Ocean, but aside from that could do little to combat Japan. Australia and China were both relatively weak powers, the one by a scant population and the fact that her troops were still fighting in North Africa, the other by years of exhaustive war, by internal strife, and by a lack of technological skill. The United States alone was relatively free to devise the machines for concentrating tremendous power against the common foe.

We had promised deliveries to Russia and had to make good our pledge, and the same held true of shipments to Britain and Egypt. We also had a war on with Germany, and the toll of losses from the German submarines off the Atlantic coast and in the Caribbean mounted high as the spring of 1942 drew near. For many months the Germans sank Allied ships almost as rapidly as we produced new vessels, and stark necessity compelled us to keep no inconsiderable part of our naval establishment in the Atlantic. First, the battle of production must be fought and won. That kind of battle was no novelty for these United States. Off came our coats and down to it we buckled with hardy grit and genuine efficiency. Cynics might complain that "when the Japs land in San Francisco there will be a real shake up," but most Americans took hold right away. We called William S. Knudsen, a leading industrialist, from his post with General Motors and gave him plenary power in production; we ceased making typewriters, automobiles, electric refrigerators, radios and innumerable machines dear to the American heart; we commenced to build shipyards, and cities for those who were to work in them (Vanport, Oregon, population 45,000, on the Columbia, was built, complete and entirely modern, in eight months); to pour out synthetic rubber; to double, triple and quadruple our plane production. And as we did this we learned, partially at least, to do without. We rationed shoes, gas, food, and so forth. We still lived in luxury according to European standards but not according to our own. And these new activities we undertook with real cheer and coöperative understanding.

The continuous assembly line was an American invention which stood us in good stead in 1942. What hitherto had proved successful for automobiles proved just as feasible for bombers. For an automobile it has been estimated there are 15,000 parts, but for a bomber 101,650 parts and 400,000 rivets. Yet by March, Consolidated Aircraft began rolling out bombers in one continuous assembly line. In Detroit the seventy-eight-year-old Henry Ford, who had tried to stop two world wars, donned overalls to superintend his Willow Run factory, non-existent in January, employing 70,000 men under one roof by summer. "Any factory equipped to do metal work, whether automotive or otherwise, can turn out parts for planes, tanks and other kinds of armament." We had many such factories, and the Battle of Detroit, as it was not inaptly named, was half-won before it started. Meantime from Portland, Oregon, to Portland, Maine, the ships came rolling out. Our total output for 1942 was twenty times that for 1939 and would go higher yet.

The Americans could say with Pericles, "If then we prefer to meet danger with a light heart but without laborious training, and with a courage which is gained from habit and not enforced by law, are we not greatly the gainers?"

SUMMER, 1942

The Japanese war by the summer of 1942 had spread both east and west; east all the way from the Aleutians to the South Pacific, west all the way from the Indian frontier and Ceylon to Madagascar. It was hemmed in, tentatively at any rate, in both directions, eastward by American sailors and airmen, westward by a handful of resolute Britishers.

First, the stopping of the Japanese lunge eastward! In the Far North among the fog-bound Aleutians, of which we had no maps, in the central Pacific at Midway, 1,304 miles west of Hawaii and 1,185 east of Wake, as also at Guadalcanal in the Solomon Islands in the South Pacific, the Americans took the war to their foes.

The most important of these engagements was the Midway

battle. As in that of the Coral Sea, opposing warships never sighted one another and offensive fighting was entirely by plane. Early in June some eighty vessels under the rising-sun ensign—battleships, carriers, cruisers, destroyers, transports—converged on American-held Midway. This was no reconnaissance in force. Clearly the Japanese intended, if victorious here, to attack Hawaii. But the Mikado's soldiers never landed on Midway. Land-based bombers of the army, navy planes from carriers, navy flying boats intercepted the Japanese fleet and it sought safety in flight. Action continued for four days. The loss of American planes was heavy, five out of six in one sortie, eight out of sixteen in another, and fifteen out of fifteen in a third. The Japanese also sank our carrier, the *Yorktown*. But their own losses were far more serious, four carriers being sunk, two heavy cruisers, three destroyers. We also wiped out 275 planes, messed up several battleships, cruisers, and lighter craft. Midway was particularly heartening in the destruction of carriers, a type of craft in which the adversary's navy hitherto had been predominant.

Along with the raid on Midway came a Japanese thrust at Dutch Harbor, our base in the eastern Aleutians, that chain of islands stretching a thousand miles and more across the North Pacific from Alaska well-nigh to Kamchatka in Soviet Siberia. Dutch Harbor, at the eastern end of the chain, was lightly defended, its fortification as yet incomplete. Planes based there could easily raid Alaska, make possible an invasion of continental America.

Again the Japanese came on in force with two carriers, two cruisers, three destroyers. Their fighters and bombers outclassed the few planes we had at Dutch Harbor and probably would have won the day had not the American army surprised them. Sixty miles west of Dutch Harbor lies Umnak Island and upon it two months earlier we had laid steel landing mats for planes. From this secret base in the fog our army Warhawks swooped down upon the foe—and from west of them. Confused by this attack from ambush, the invaders broke and fled. They stopped in retreat to capture Kiska, 672 miles from Dutch Harbor, and Attu, still further distant at the Aleutians' western tip. Hence our North Pacific victory was incomplete. But for the time being Alaska, Canada, and our northwestern states were clear of enemy bombers. Conversely, as long as Kiska and Attu remained in their hands, Nippon was similarly protected.

Two months later there was discouraging news from the South Pacific. Despite the Battle of the Coral Sea the Japanese were still set upon the conquest of Australia. They strove persistently to capture Port Moresby on the southeastern side of New Guinea; their forces fanned out steadily from the northern Solomons southeastward along the thousand-mile length of that archipelago and built an air-field on the large island of Guadalcanal in the southern Solomons. Their objective was evident—cutting the American lifeline to Australia. And this we had to protect by an offensive-defensive at Guadalcanal.

On August 7 our marines, protected by a naval air task force, landed on Guadalcanal and on the nearby islands of Tulagi and Gavutu. They surprised the enemy on Guadalcanal, captured the air-field, renaming it Henderson Field. On Gavutu they ran into a hornet's nest, the Japanese defending with reckless courage and dying to a man. On Guadalcanal the surprised Nipponese rallied to the attack. So did the Japanese navy. Smashing into our task force on August 8, it sank three American heavy cruisers and one Australian. Our transports, however, escaped destruction, and our marines, heavily reinforced, beat off the Japanese on land.

Throughout August and September the enemy did its best to dislodge the marines, strafing from the air and shelling from the sea the narrow and confined area which they had won, only about seven miles along the coast by four or five in depth. On the island there was endless fighting. Japanese troops, continuously reinforced at night by fast destroyers, proved worthy antagonists. Few were captured; many died. So also was it with the marines, who found the hot miasmic air, the malaria, and insect life of Guadalcanal quite as unpleasant as the soldiers of the Mikado. Time after time the latter returned to the fray, supported by naval carriers, destroyers, and battleships; time after time they were repulsed. The flag still flew over Henderson Field, and from it rose American bombers to harry Japanese ships and bomb Japanese installations. The tide of conquest still lapped these shores but it had passed its peak.

It was also anybody's guess this summer of 1942 as to how far Japan might conquer westward. Her fleet had appeared off the coast of Ceylon and had bombarded southern India; her planes had sunk two British cruisers in the Indian Ocean and one old carrier; and there was fear lest Japan's sway be extended not only to India but to Madagascar where her destroyers had prowled.

The troops of Vichy France stationed there said that could never happen, but Vichy France had yielded once without a fight in Indo-China and might do so again. The British would take no chances; they demanded the right to safeguard Madagascar. The French refused to grant it. May 7 the British landed, and by September they assumed control of the entire island, to hold in trust for France and to keep the Japanese out.

Throughout this time the situation in India remained most critical. Supposedly India was one of the United Nations, but the act which made her one was simply a decree of the British-controlled Indian government. Ever since the First World War, India had been sullen and restless under the British yoke. And now the Japs, having humbled the proud British at Hongkong and Singapore, were sliding up Burma rivers toward India's northeast frontier, surely an auspicious occasion for Indians to win freedom.

Presumably a good majority of Indians did not even know a war was going on, but the Indian Congress did. How large a part of India's seething population Congress represented had long been open to question, but that millions of Indians looked to it for leadership was evident. Congress was not pro-Japanese; it even proposed to take an active part in defending India against Japan. The price to be paid for its coöperation, however, was immediate independence.

The British were not ready to pay that price; not even with the Japanese on their doorstep or near it. Gandhi was the most influential man in Congress, and all his life Gandhi had been a pacifist. He had stated that he would not oppose the Japanese by arms if they invaded India. Congress, of course, might repudiate Gandhi and fight, but even so it is difficult to see how this unwieldy and inexperienced body could have organized the country so as to withstand the single-minded invader.

The British, always willing to compromise when they have to, sent Sir Stafford Cripps, an able left-wing lawyer, with a promise of Dominion status after the war, and for the time being further Indian representation in the Viceroy's cabinet. The Indians might even have a minister of defense in the cabinet and take an active share in the war; a share, that is, in preparing and mobilizing for it. The war itself would have to be waged by a British commander-in-chief, untrammeled by political control. Congress refused the olive branch, supposedly by a vote of seven to five, three not voting. So also did the Moslem League. Cripps went home; Congress waited; Congress in August summoned all Indian patriots to revolt. The world looked on, expecting civil war, a Japanese invasion, perhaps both.

These forebodings were premature. The British promptly threw all leading congressmen into jail, suppressed the revolt. The latter was not a call to arms; it was a summons to mass civil disobedience, something more than a sit-down strike, something less than war. "Rails were torn up and cables cut; police stations and other government buildings were set on fire; strikes broke out in the chief centers of industry" but there was no general uprising. There were only a few thousand British troops in India, but they had machine guns and planes, and they used both. With them they restored order.

The Japanese did not interfere except by long-distance radio; they were busy elsewhere. In nine months they had swept over the Philippines, Borneo, Java, Sumatra, Celebes, many other islands, Hongkong, Malaya, Burma; and now were fighting viciously against Australian-Americans and Chinese assisted by a handful of American aviators. For the time being, the Indians could shift for themselves. Surely the spanking which the Japanese had administered so lavishly to the white overlords of India, and elsewhere in Asia, should be sufficient encouragement for all Asiatics to revolt. If the Indians must have help, Japan would give it later. She would teach the Indians how to fight, and toward that end she encouraged Indian rebels to visit Tokyo and in Burma began drilling Indian Nationals for war. In another year or so, after Japan had finished with the Americans in East Asia she would expel the white race from India.

11. THE NOT SO SOFT UNDERBELLY

AGAINST which foe should the United Nations throw their joint strength? Most Americans, as was quite natural, said Japan. Pearl Harbor and Bataan should be avenged as soon as possible; Japan must not be given time to entrench herself in her new empire, time to cajole and to deceive the millions of Asiatics she had conquered by suave talk of co-prosperity spheres and liberation à la Tokyo. There were five Chinese and more for every Japanese. Equip and train the former, and they could drive Japan out of continental Asia as we delivered counter-blows in the Pacific.

But how could help be given China? If could not come by sea; the lower stretches of the Burma Road now swarmed with the Mikado's soldiers; to fly over the shoulders of the Himalayas was possible, but the way was long and not many transport planes available. To eject the Japanese from their island nests in the Pacific called for ships the keels of which were not yet laid. How could America get within punching distance of Japan? The route over the Aleutians looked fascinating on the map, but that island chain was wrapped in fogs and chilly mists, lashed by sudden and terrific storms. No major offensive could be staged there.

The Russians called for all-out attack on Germany. The war was swinging into its fourth year and the Nazis were pressing hard. They had one foot on the Volga River at Stalingrad and were bent on sweeping up that valley to roll on Moscow from the east. They were already deep within the Caucasus; Maikop oil fields had been won; Nazi advance units were grinding steadily on along the western shoreline of the Black Sea toward Batum. On the east, Axis chances of forcing though Daghestan were slight, but the Nazis might slip around the snow-clad mountains of that wild and sparsely settled province and follow the shoreline of the Caspian to Baku, there to quench the thirst of their war machine with endless Soviet oil. Over the Caspian, then, would flaunt the

Nazi banners, and our southern supply line from the United States to Russia would be severed. If necessary, northern Persia could be taken, and Turkestan. Perhaps a junction could be effected with Japan in Afghanistan or in the Pamirs. The prospects were alarming. From the Soviet point of view the second front in Europe was imperative. Stalin coldly demanded it. He said, and in all truth, that Russia had suffered more than any of the United Nations, that an Allied army in France would relieve pressure on the eastern front, that costly as a landing might prove one would have to be made some time: better do this, he warned, while Russia was still in the ring and before the Germans could complete their preparations to receive us on the French coast.

The difficulties of such a project did not impress Stalin but they did Churchill. Where was the shipping which could transport an army to France capable of coping with the Germans? How was it to be supplied? And where was the army to come from? Britain simply did not have manpower available for such an army, and America was across the Atlantic. In August, 1942, an Allied reconnaissance in force met with bloody rebuff at Dieppe on the French coast. The participants were mainly Canadian, and more than half were killed or wounded. After this, it seemed obvious that no second front could be established in 1942, not without too frightful a loss of life. Yet Stalin kept insisting that there must be one. Churchill flew to Moscow to pacify him. The British are sea animals, he explained, the Russians land animals. The latter must be patient. But still the Russian chieftain was dissatisfied; he did not think the British and Americans were doing their fair share to win the war. The hard fact was that in 1942 they were not able to do so.

What Churchill wanted was an attack on North Africa and then Italy. A German force was near the Nile. Once rout Rommel there with American help and Balkan sabotage, and the Axis might be thrown clean out of North Africa and the Mediterranean set wholly free. Such an offensive, though difficult, was feasible and need not require too many long months of preparation. Success in Africa would encourage the Allies' French partisans; it would also lay Italy, the "soft underbelly of the Axis," open to invasion. The Germans would fight for Italy; they could not well let her go by default, have Allied planes launched at Germany from Italian soil, permit a landing on the Continent by Anglo-American troops.

Russian needs could not be met by so limited a second front, nor fatal defeat inflicted on Germany thereby; but it would be a real offensive insofar as German divisions were involved.

Churchill's point was well taken. To try in 1942 for a second front in France would cost the lives of hundreds of thousands; its success would be problematical; a failure would be disastrous; and even if a landing was made good the inevitable result would be that aid to Russia in tanks and planes certainly would be lessened, for a new front in France would strain the resources of Britain and America to the limit.

Roosevelt agreed with Churchill. The President was aware that for the time being no mortal blow could be struck against Japan. He was not anti-Russian and had given Russian aid top priority, at times in disagreement with his own military men. But he had sent General Marshall twice to England, and the latter had decided in conference with British militarists that a second front in France in 1942 was inadvisable. Any offense that year had to be on a limited scale. To expunge the Axis from Africa and possibly to invade Italy was a sufficiently daring enterprise for 1942.

THE BATTLE OF EGYPT

Anglo-American preparations for this African offensive were well under way by summer. The more immediate task was to reëquip, rearm and reinforce the British Eighth Army which had saved Egypt from Rommel in June at El Alamein. This took considerable time. Rommel's tanks, artillery and air force had to be bested before they could be beaten. The convoy route from Britain and America was long and hazardous. Our new General Sherman tanks were just rolling off the assembly lines. By presidential order they were taken from the troops to whom they had been assigned and shipped to Egypt. Welcomed reinforcements and improved field guns reached the Eighth Army from Britain, and the RAF was joined by American bombers and fighters operated by our men. Churchill visited Cairo, made General Alexander commander-in-chief, put General Montgomery at the head of the famous Eighth, now revamped, enlarged, and composed of British, Australian, New Zealand, South African and Indian divisions.

By October all was ready—new army, new commanders, new methods. Rommel's forces were as large numerically but now were inferior in matériel. It was impossible to outflank him since his troops lay between the Quattara Depression and the sea. But it did prove possible to battle through the German lines. The artillery barrage laid down by Montgomery was heavier than any known to World War I. Then with the coming of the night of October 23 the infantry advanced. "General Alexander compared the process to that of a man breaking down a wall with a crowbar. First the point was driven in, then leverage was exerted to make a small hole, and this was gradually widened until enough pressure could be applied to force a breach." [1] This was the infantry's job, always the hardest in any war. The going was slow. It succeeded. But it took a week of hard slugging. The tanks, kept pretty much in reserve, then broke through, fanned out, cut in behind Rommel's lines of communication. The German general now abandoned his infantry (mostly Italian) to their fate and retreated west, saving what he could of his panzer divisions.

Rommel was not routed, but he was badly defeated. His casualties were near the 60,000 mark; his loss in tanks approximately 500, in planes 600, in artillery 1,000 guns. It was a major victory and the church bells rang out over Britain.

The first action of the grand campaign had been carried out successfully. Rommel kept on in retreat at full speed. Ever a clever and wary fighter, he broke into the clear and by the end of November was 400 miles west of Egypt, back at El Agheila, strongly entrenched for the time being behind salt marshes. But the Allies could and did get both gas and oil from America, and Rommel could not.

NORTHWEST AFRICA

Meanwhile on November 8, while Montgomery's artillery still barked at El Alamein, Anglo-American forces landed close by Oran and Algiers, and an American army trained in our own old-time Great American Desert of the Southwest forced its way ashore at Casablanca on the Atlantic in French Morocco. The second chapter of the joint campaign had opened.

The timing had been perfect; not so the diplomatic preparation. There were French troops in Morocco and Algeria, and they did

[1] Edgar Wardwell McInnis, *The War, Fourth Year* (New York, Oxford University Press, 1944), p. 29.

not welcome the Anglo-American liberators. Instead they put up here and there a stout resistance, and good soldiers died.

The situation in French Africa roughly was as follows. In Equatorial Africa the French governor had declared for De Gaulle after the fall of France, and the handful of French troops there were fighting under the Cross of Lorraine superimposed on the Tricolor, the standard of the Free French. De Gaulle, however, had failed at Dakar, and Morocco, and Algeria and Tunis had from the first acknowledged the authority of Marshal Pétain and his Vichy régime. The British would have nothing to do with Vichy, but not so the Americans; and ever since the armistice we had been in constant negotiation with Pétain's government.

Concerning those negotiations stories differ widely, and contemporary historians might as well suspend judgment. The main point in the controversy is this: was the United States State Department wise in conciliating Vichy, thus keeping the Germans from occupying Morocco and Algeria until we were ready to send an army there; or, on the other hand, were there reactionary influences in our State Department which strengthened pro-Axis defeatism and tended to favor pro-Axis régimes, thus imperiling the cause of democracy throughout the world as well as leading to bloodshed in North Africa—bloodshed which might have been averted by more fearless and more honest diplomacy?

The fact is, we were careful not to offend Pétain and Vichy until long after our troops landed in Africa. We treated Admiral Robert at Martinique with courteous restraint when an American occupation of that island, instantly and with few casualties or none, could have solved all problems relative to its use by Axis agencies; we carefully avoided any recognition of De Gaulle; we even compelled the Free French to withdraw from Saint Pierre and Miquelon, the tiny French fishing islands close to Newfoundland; and we permitted shipment of oil and foodstuffs to Algeria at a time when Vichy supposedly was letting Tunis be used as a supply port for Rommel.

These facts infuriated the liberal and radical press in the United States, which from the beginning regarded with chronic suspicion the activities of our ambassador at Vichy, Admiral Leahy, and of his subordinate there, Robert Murphy, later our consul in Algeria. Pétain's appointees to office in Northwest Africa, it was said, were covertly in favor of the Axis, and the United States, instead of supporting De Gaulle outright, was allowing these Fascist-minded French renegades to import good American food and oil, some of which very likely fell into German hands.

There was, however, another side to this picture. To assume that all Vichymen were traitors to their country was unwarranted. Some of them certainly were willing to fight for Northwest Africa rather than have the Nazi flag hoisted over it, as for instance, General Weygand. A well-staffed German mission was in Algiers to supervise the carrying out of the armistice, and as long as Murphy was permitted to live in Algiers he was in a good position to keep tab on German activities and at the same time secretly to promise aid to those Frenchmen who were willing to resist not simply the Germans but also Pétain. It was plot and counter-plot, feud and counter-feud, as the deep, devious Mr. Hull at Washington was well and adequately aware. If the Germans could push through Spain to North Africa, we would be severely handicapped when and if we tried setting foot in the French African areas. If a strictly limited supply of foodstuffs and oils to North Africa would help hold the Germans back, then it was worth the price, even if said Germans got half of what we sent.

The British, owing to their destructive attack on the French fleet in 1940, were even more *persona non grata* at Vichy than we were, and wisely they left preliminary negotiations in our hands. We were in part successful. General Mark Clark of the U.S. army, taken secretly to North Africa in a British submarine, conferred with various French officials friendly to invasion, and consequently French resistance was not as formidable as it might have been. It was hoped that the French garrisons, upwards of 100,000 men, would welcome our arrival. For the most part they did so. As we landed at Algiers only a few shots were fired. At Oran, 130 miles west, there was more serious resistance. And at Casablanca on the Atlantic coast of Morocco there was, for a time, stiff fighting. It was necessary for us to land tanks both east and west of that city and begin siege operations. Meanwhile off the harbor the French battleship *Jean Bart* opened fire on our fleet and had to be destroyed before the French gave over. Fortunately the equivocal Admiral Darlan in Algiers, North African representative of Marshal Pétain, decided to join with us and gave orders to end resistance.

General Eisenhower, commander-in-chief of the expeditionary force, immediately recognized Darlan as head of the civil administration and for this was violently criticized. Darlan's previous career had been that of a bitter Anglophobe, and since he had yielded from time to time to Nazi pressure most Englishmen and many Americans considered it undesirable that we have any dealings with him. But Darlan, as our enemy, could cause us no end of trouble; and as our friend more or less he could, and did, render possible our occupation of great areas in record-making time.

His collaboration with us forced Hitler to occupy all France and to attempt seizing the French ships at Toulon. The French army did not resist but Hitler failed to get the fleet. As the Nazis reached Toulon, their planes filling the skies, the French blew up their vessels and naval base. Meanwhile the British First Army, along with American detachments, raced for Bizerte and Tunis. These two seaports in the French protectorate of Tunisia were five hundred miles from Algiers and less than a hundred from Sicily, too great a handicap. The Germans got there first by air and sea, and in superior numbers. The Allies, within twelve miles of their goal, were driven back.

This bitter disappointment clouded a brilliant achievement. The Allies had landed several hundred thousand men in an amphibious operation unique in history. Over 500 transports and supply vessels and 350 naval craft participated, not to mention airplane transports, yet the loss was less than 5 per cent of the tonnage involved, even if we accept exaggerated German estimates. In less than a month the Allies had swept some four hundred miles from the Atlantic almost to the gates of Tunis and the site of ancient Carthage ten miles beyond. In all the hectic history of a thousand years from Dido to Augustine, North Africa had never witnessed so swift and victorious a conquest.

AXIS OUT OF AFRICA

We turn now to General Montgomery and his Eighth Army converging toward the scene of action from far to the east. Early in the winter it was at El Agheila, still in pursuit of Italians and Germans. The closer the latter got to their main base at Tripoli the shorter became their lines of communication; conversely the further the British shoved ahead the more difficult became theirs. Nevertheless, the British were not held up long at El Agheila. By the time their artillery was ready to clear a passage, and their engineers had exploded mines and booby traps, the Afrika Korps was in full withdrawal. Montgomery pushed on. Beyond lay Tripoli, capital of Libya, a good seaport, well defended by encircling hills. But the Germans did not choose to hold it, and Italians could not. A brief skirmish and Italy's African empire had fallen. In thirteen weeks the Eighth Army had chased the enemy 1,300 miles, the longest drive in history. On went Montgomery. The retreating Germans panted after the security of the Mareth line in French Tunisia, and Montgomery followed them there. To breach these strong fortifications was a first-class military action as Montgomery well knew, and the Eighth Army halted.

Elsewhere in North Africa the situation was more complicated. There was the problem of logistics, how to supply an army of approximately 200,000 with food and guns, tanks and planes, from bases as far distant as England and the United States, with submarines lurking in the ocean pathways; how after matériel once reached Africa to distribute it to fighting men often hundreds of miles from the port of debarkation. The U-boat war was at its height and tankers were sunk, even if troop ships arrived safely; yet without gasoline there was no campaigning. Railways in North Africa were few and in disrepair; in some instances they had to be rebuilt and locomotives and freight cars imported from America.

Then, too, there was the political problem; who was to govern the restless, seething population, part French, part Arab? It had been solved temporarily by putting Darlan in authority; but Darlan was promptly assassinated. The men under him had been of Vichy and in consequence bitterly anti-British. Though not pro-German they were undemocratic, loyal to Pétain alone. They hated De Gaulle and his "Free French" who had done so much to keep alive the fires of French resistance; and the Free French replied in kind.

The only common denominator available seemed to be General Giraud, an officer reputed as patriotic as De Gaulle himself. Giraud had not been a party to the fall of France. Imprisoned by the Germans in 1940, he had escaped from Germany and been taken to North Africa by a British submarine. Giraud succeeded Darlan as the head of French administration in North Africa; but the Free French would not acknowledge his leadership and bitter feud continued.

Another problem was what use to make of the North African French army. That force was ready to fight, but its equipment was far outdated and to supply it with modern weapons was not easy. Units had opposed our landing and many officers were regarded as still under Vichy influence. The French should prove useful in driving the Axis out of Tunisia. But just how far could these new allies be trusted and what particular rôle should be given them in campaigns to come?

And finally there was the problem of strategy. Germans and Italians had entrenched at Bizerte and Tunis and behind those two cities were fortifying a range of hills from which it would be difficult to oust them. They had already forced back the British First Army, and American and French contingents, inexperienced in war. If we were not careful we might be caught between Axis troops striking down from Tunis and the Afrika Korps driving up from the Mareth line. Our lines of communication were far extended, stretching all the way from Casablanca in Morocco to Tunisia. The railway from Casablanca ran closely parallel along the borders of Spanish Morocco. It would not do to leave that vital link unprotected.

To solve these and other problems of United Nations strategy, Roosevelt and Churchill conferred in mid-January 1943 at Casablanca. They declared conjointly that there would be no terms given any Axis nation except the grim dose of unconditional surrender; they agreed on certain measures toward that end; and De Gaulle and Giraud shook hands before the camera, a reconciliation formal rather than genuine.

Meanwhile Hitler insisted that his bridgehead in Africa be held, and Axis reinforcements flowed into Tunis and Bizerte. All over Tunisia the weather was atrociously bad and for a large part of the winter the war was reduced to patrol action. Then it flared up suddenly and with startling reverses for the Americans.

On February 11 the Nazi army poured through Faid Pass at the eastern end of the American sector. Tanks and dive-bombers seemed to come from everywhere, and all at once. We took quite a beating, retreating to Kasserine Pass, surrendering some 4,000 square miles of territory. We were even driven out of the Kasserine, and that was serious, for if the Germans gained the plateau beyond, they might encircle the British First Army to the north and drive the United Nations back into Algeria. This was our baptism of fire, and we were caught with equipment too light, with poor air support, and inferior tactics. We tried to rescue detachments which

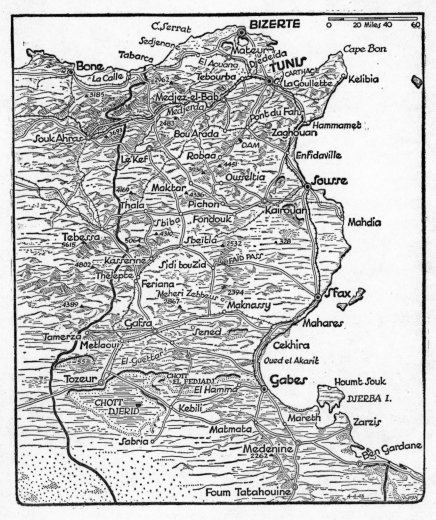

TUNISIA

(Courtesy of the New York *Times*)

could not be rescued; we fell into traps and got what was coming to us. We had to take it.

And then the very next week we held and defeated the wehrmacht. Our army functioned like a well-oiled machine. Stuka bombers were all in the day's work, our artillery fire was excellent; and the Nazis retreated through Kasserine Pass, Eisenhower saying "Our boys will fight better now they are mad."

Autumn victories over the Axis had cautiously been hailed by Churchill as "the end of the beginning." And now as winter turned to spring one could somewhat confidently write of "the beginning of the end." The tide had been slow in turning but by the middle of May it had run out a good six months, and there was rejoicing in the camp of the United Nations.

A second front clearly was impossible until Tunisia was won, and as winter ended that task seemed formidable. In northern Tunisia the Germans and Italians were safe behind a range of jagged hills and in the south they held the Mareth line against Montgomery. Their weakest point was the elongated corridor which led to the Mareth line, but it was protected by the sea on one side and by deep gorges and ravines on the other. Both French and Americans had tried to break through here in the neighborhood of Faid Pass and had been rolled back. Could they have done so they would have split the Axis forces in two. Conversely, so long as Montgomery's Eighth Army was on the other side of the Mareth line the United Nations' armies remained split.

Montgomery tried to crack the Mareth line, failed, then deployed his New Zealanders and the Free French who had crossed the Sahara to join him, into the desert at his left. These sturdy warriors circled far around the Mareth line way to the north thus compelling the outflanked Afrika Korps to abandon their fortifications and follow the coastal plain toward Tunis. Montgomery lunged after them as fast as his engineers could dig up land mines left by the capable Germans, who now had steadily retreated some 1,600 miles from El Alamein.

By these maneuvers the Axis armies were forced back into northern Tunisia in an area somewhat smaller than Connecticut. They could not adopt defense in depth, for they were held too close to the Mediterranean; yet they had a long line to defend, well over one hundred miles. Their front wound like a snake around mountainous crags which their artillery commanded, and it was thought they might hold out many weeks, perhaps longer, if reinforcements could be gotten in from Sicily.

In less than a fortnight, however, the Italians and Germans were surrendering in tens of thousands. What took place was roughly as follows. As Montgomery swept north along the seacoast the British First Army and the French closed in on the now shrinking Axis lines, leaving the Americans apparently far to the rear. For several days there was no report of their whereabouts as they were being shifted rapidly behind the lines of communication of the British First Army and at right angles to it to a critical sector opposite Bizerte. As formed now in late April, the Allied line ran from northwest to southeast thus: French Moroccan troops faced Bizerte on the Mediterranean, then came the Americans, the British First Army, the main body of the French, and the British Eighth Army.

The American assignment was crucial; it was to pry open the mountain gateway at Mateur, leading to Bizerte. To do this it was necessary to storm three hills, the key one, Hill 609, defended by as good troops as Germany had, and in a region so rough that mules took the place of trucks. In the face of heavy machine-gun fire the Americans stormed this hill with hand grenades and bayonets. Beyond they could see Mateur, now defenseless, and farther beyond, shimmering in the sunshine, the white buildings of Bizerte and the blue Mediterranean Sea.

Our men streamed down toward Bizerte, cut the road to Tunis, captured Bizerte without further fighting. An hour or two later the British First Army was in Tunis, likewise meeting no resistance. In almost every direction German and Italian detachments threw down their arms. Some took refuge on Cape Bon but soon surrendered. Part of the famous Afrika Korps, by-passed by the quick dash of the Allies, fought for a few days in the hills. By May 8 victory was assured; by May 13 the African resistance ended everywhere.

This Tunisian campaign cost the Axis dear. It lost over 300,000 men, among whom were 266,000 prisoners; it also lost Africa. More than that, the defeat proved that the morale of some Axis soldiers was impaired; since the men who surrendered were well fed, well armed, not half-starved and hopelessly beaten like the Germans who held so long at Stalingrad. It proved that the U-boat campaign, however successful, had not prevented their enemy's conveying and supplying large armies overseas; it proved that air supremacy had at last shifted from the luftwaffe to the United Nations; that Axis naval supremacy in the Mediterranean was a dream.

Italians went jittery and talked alternately of peace and of fighting to the bitter end. The Nazis belittled what had occurred and explained to their people that they had fought in Tunisia merely to gain time to make invincible their European fortress. The Maginot-line psychology of defensive warfare which bedeviled the French in 1940 had here in turn infected the Nazis, an augury of good fortune for our side.

Was our victorious battle for Bizerte and Tunis to be a turning point, perhaps even *the* turning point of the Second World War? Churchill at once flew to Washington, where final plans were in process for empowering and for speeding the campaigns to follow. The Prime Minister's address in Congress late in May compared Bizerte-Tunis of 1943 to Gettysburg of 1863 but warned that though the grey tide of the Confederacy never rose so high again, two years passed and many thousands died before the victors came to Appomattox.

SICILY

It was late spring, 1943, and for the third time Roosevelt and Churchill were in conference. Both spoke warmly of the absent Stalin, of the magnificent valor of the Red army; but the fact that Russia was not represented at Washington spoke volumes. Rightly or wrongly, Stalin felt that he had been led to expect a second front in France in 1942, and though pleased with the equipment and munitions now reaching Russia he could not help contrasting the colossal battles waged by the men of the Soviets with the campaign recently concluded by his allies in Africa. The Red armies were at death grips with 190 German divisions, plus twenty-eight satellite divisions, Italian, Hungarian, Rumanian and others. The Anglo-Americans had opposing them in Tunisia only fifteen German divisions. From Stalin's point of view the British and the Americans were having a comparatively easy time.

As far as the season went, it was not too early to try for a second front in France. In the air the British and Americans were already able to contest on equal terms with the luftwaffe; on the sea the submarine menace was being coped with, if not exterminated; American troops and American flyers were landing in Britain in ever augmenting numbers. Perhaps it might be possible to smash out a foothold in France.

But there were counter-arguments. Granted this hold established, how could it be extended and, if not extended, could it relieve pressure on the Russians? The United States could not possibly stay on the defensive in the Pacific; Midway, Guadalcanal, the Aleutians and New Guinea must be solidly won and strongly held. American and British convoys loaded to the gunwales with tanks and planes were sifting through the narrow sullen seas around the northern tip of Norway. Other convoys in the red-hot Persian Gulf were discharging precious cargoes to be forced across Persia by truck and over a single-track railway to the Caspian. Preparations were already far advanced for the Alsib Ferry, whereby planes were to fly straight to Russia from Montana by way of Alaska, Bering Sea and Siberia, a 6,000-mile flight over frozen tundra, a ferry in operation by the end of August. Strong Allied forces had to stay in French North Africa, because who could say whether the unpredictable Hitler might or might not unleash a new African campaign. French colonials were in no condition to defend North Africa, torn by dissension between the partisans of De Gaulle (Free French) and those who followed General Giraud. Meanwhile from the Arctic to the South Atlantic, from Gibraltar east to Calcutta, the Royal Navy was on watch and guard against the submarines, and the RAF in almost nightly combat with the luftwaffe over France, Belgium and western Germany.

It was regrettable that Russia had to wait; but so Roosevelt and Churchill, themselves no mean military experts, decided after long consultation with their joint staffs. They would continue the common enterprise laid down at Casablanca in January, and first drive Italy out of the war. And so Churchill darkly hinted when on his return to London he said, "It is evident that amphibious operations of peculiar complexity and hazard on a large scale are approaching."

This meant Sicily, where incessant bombardment of Sicilian airfields and Italian ports like Naples supplying Sicily, foretold an Anglo-American invasion. But first Pantelleria, a rocky islet heavily fortified and lying directly between Tunisia and Sicily had to be captured. To compel surrender took only one day after severe naval and air bombardment. Then, July 9, 1943, came the assault in force.

In 1860 Garibaldi and his Red Shirts fought their way ashore at

Marsala, a west-coast port; and since that part of Sicily lay closest to Tunis an Allied landing had been expected somewhere in that neighborhood. But for this twentieth-century invasion the southeastern tip of Sicily was chosen, since the beaches there were more extensive and Malta was close at hand where Allied planes clustered like hawks.

Simultaneously two Allied armies hit the beaches, the American Seventh well to the west of the tip, Montgomery's Eighth, in which was a new Canadian division, well to the east and not far south of famed Syracuse where the almost empire of Athens had slowly bled to death. The two armies were approximately equal in size as they had been in North Africa, although in the final Tunisian campaign the British troops had considerably outnumbered the Americans who guarded long lines of communication from Tunis to the Atlantic. All told, the Allies at last had under arms some thirteen divisions, the Axis twelve divisions plus really tough paratroopers.

The American Seventh ran into a nasty snag. High winds scattered our paratroopers who landed several hours before the infantry, and an American transport plane was shot down by our own guns. The sea was rough, the coördination of our forces difficult. German tanks came close to driving our men into the sea and, had it not been for unexcelled, tenacious courage, would have done so. The British had less difficulty getting ashore, but their subsequent experiences were even more harrowing than ours since they had rougher terrain, more Germans, fewer Italians to fight.

To conquer Sicily took thirty-nine days. The fighting, comparatively light in the earlier stages, became heavy and bitter, Allied casualties in dead and wounded going over the 20,000 mark, the Axis somewhat more.

Quickly the Americans and the British were in contact, the southeastern tip of Sicily won. The Americans then swung west along the seacoast and into the interior as the British headed north along the east coast, straight toward the Straits of Messina where only two miles of water separated Sicily from the mainland.

The American Seventh Army met slight resistance for the first ten days. It encircled the western shore; its tanks rolled overland to Palermo, capital of Sicily on the Tyrrhenian Sea; the greater part of the island's 9,000-odd square miles was overrun; Italian garrisons surrendered after token resistance; and villagers with smiling faces offered fruit and flowers. Had it not been for a murrain of flies, intolerable heat, omnipresent dirt, the GI's might almost have found this part of the campaign pleasant.

The British Eighth Army had a harder task. The eastern shore up which it slowly pried its way was precipitous, and close to the sea in the northeast towered Mount Etna, 10,000 feet in elevation. To its protecting security the Germans withdrew their three and one-half divisions; their temper was excellent; their courage beyond question; their defense position superb. It was impossible to skirt Mount Etna to the east; it came too close to the Mediterranean. And to circle around its foothills to the north took days of sanguinary fighting.

A great part of this fell to the Canadians on the British left flank. The terrain was so rugged and the ravines cut by swift streams so deep that any break-through by tanks was impossible. Tanks were used for brief snorting charges but the battles, or rather the incessant series of little local battles, were for the artillery and infantry. Slowly the British and Canadians won through the foothills to the west of Mount Etna, where they linked up with the Americans. From one strategic height after another the united Allies pressed hard upon the foe. Ferociously fighting and with great skill, the Germans withdrew by August 16. Almost all their troops were ferried over the narrow straits by plane or in small craft. There was no big bag of German prisoners as in Tunis; this time the booty consisted of Italians and German tanks. The underbelly of the Axis thus far was not so soft.

For the next two weeks Allied air power was turned loose and ran wild in southern Italy, strafing railways and bridges. Then on September 3 the British Eighth crossed the Straits to romp over the toe and heel of Italy, Italian garrisons surrendering with abandon, Germans retreating in good order and as rapidly as they could lay mines.

ITALIANS QUIT THE WAR

The Germans suspected, as well they might, that precious little dependence could be placed on the Italians. As early as April, Mussolini had run to Hitler to beseech further aid, only to be sharply reprimanded for not sending more divisions to the Russian front. In desperation he had again gone on the same errand in July. Results were similar. Whereupon, even before completion of the Sicilian conquest, a revolution of a cloudily political kind took place in Italy. The more forehanded and more treacherous of the Fascist leaders, among whom Dino Grandi, the obsolete Marshal Badoglio, and Count Ciano, the Duce's infamous son-in-law, were notorious, having determined that the ship of state was sinking, decided to desert it. At a ten-hour session of the Fascist Grand Council at which Mussolini presided they somewhat disclosed their hand. A motion was made and carried calling upon the king to take the leadership of the nation. Mussolini sped to Victor Emmanuel, was arrested and sneaked away to prison, and Badoglio was asked by the king to form a "new" government in name at least. Fascism was abolished by fiat and liberty was liberally promised for some future date. But Italy, it was stated, was still a loyal ally of Germany and would stay in the war. For the nonce there were to be no public meetings and the press censorship must of necessity be continued.

The Allies advertised these events joyously, the Germans made light of them. These domestic changes, the German press said, had no bearing on the war. Mussolini simply had retired because of illness.

Ruin came over Italy like some great pestilential fog; Italian armies were in full retreat; the civil population was semi-starved; the lynx-eyed gestapo watched Badoglio; and the German forces in Italy were enlarged, energized.

The crafty, unscrupulous Victor Emmanuel and Badoglio played their cards with treacherous cunning. They were between three fires, the jittery mobs in Italian cities, the coldly suspicious Germans, and the overwhelming Allies. Crookedly willing to double-cross anyone or everybody, they played possum. The Allies gave Badoglio a brief thinking spell, suspected that he still fancied the Hitlerites, then enforced on him a rough reminder of their power by renewed air raids. The effect was instant and salutary. Through devious channels Badoglio intimated that he wished to join the Allies.

The terms offered were harsh, or would have been had Italy had anything to lose, unconditional surrender, demobilization of the Italian forces, surrender of the fleet—what was left of it. Badoglio agreed, begging that negotiations be kept secret lest his German friends and masters get wind of his spoor. No such promises were given, but the news of Italy's surrender was not published until our preparations were complete for the great attack on Salerno's beaches September 9, 1942.

Whether it was wiser thus to negotiate with Badoglio rather than to unleash social revolution in Italy by appealing to factory workers and to all other liberal and leftist sympathizers to clean the land of Fascist poison is an open question. To have done so might, or might not, have smoothed the course of our war. In London the accusation was made, somewhat unfairly, that these parleys with the untouchable Badoglio had delayed the attack. This Churchill denied, pointing out the inevitable necessity of repairing landing barges, planes and tanks, asserting that the original date of September 15, as planned for the grand assault, had actually been preponed, not postponed. However that may be, it is still evident that the democracies were handling pitch in dealing with the likes of Victor Emmanuel and his minister. Both had been hand in glove with Mussolini since the latter's rise in 1921. Badoglio had commanded the Italian army in Ethiopia where his dauntless warriors sprayed poison gas on helpless villagers. And when OWI (the U.S. Office of War Information) casually mentioned Victor Emmanuel as "that moronic little king," it blurted out what every man knew to be the truth.

Left-wing opinion in both Britain and America was vastly annoyed by this coddling of ex-Facsists, asserting that by so doing those liberal and labor groups in Italy which might have risen against the Germans were discouraged. If we had only trusted the Italian people, it was stated, and had dropped parachutists in Rome we might have had that city for the asking and saved the lives of thousands. Plans, indeed, had been laid for a parachutist landing, but had been given up on the advice of Badoglio who said it was too late, since the Germans had already seized airports adjacent to the Eternal City.

The announcement of Italy's surrender precipitated immediate occupation of Rome by the Germans; and by special order of Hitler his dear friend and faithful ally, Benito Mussolini, was rescued by a daring Nazi air raid on his secluded prison. Badoglio and the king, declaring war on Germany, fled to the Allied lines, asking for recognition as belligerents. This was not granted. But the legality of Badoglio's government was microscopically recognized, and former members of the Fascist party were recapped and whitewashed to stay in office under Allied supervision.

THE BEACHES OF SALERNO

With one tremendous military stroke the Allies now planned to bring the fighting in southern Italy to a quick conclusion. Their strategy called for a landing in force on the beaches of Salerno just south of the Bay of Naples and Mount Vesuvius; for the withholding of the news of Italy's surrender until just before disembarking; for a rapid and more or less unimpeded march inland to join forces with British troops advancing north from the heel of Italy. They would then be in position to strike for Naples and Rome.

But the Germans were not caught napping, either by Badoglio or by the Allies. Two days before General Clark led his men ashore on September 9, approximately half from the British Eighth Army and half from the American Fifth, the Germans had cleared the beaches of Italians, armed the hills with Germans, and were at the ready. The Battle of the Beaches swung first this way, then that for several days. The Germans held high ground north, south and east of the dried mud flats and pebbly shores on which the landing barges grated. They strafed the barges, the beaches and the thin line of soldiers in their fox holes, by artillery and from the air; they came so close to driving them into the sea that the German radio blared "another Dunkirk."

It almost was one. What saved the day was Allied fire power. Salerno was the outside limit for land-based planes operating from captured Sicilian air-fields. Fighter aircraft, as it was, could not stay more than fifteen minutes over the front without running short of gas. But there were thousands of them and frequently they made two trips a day. In addition, British and American warships stood close offshore, taking a long chance on German bombers. It was no longer necessary to give any thought to Italian warships, for they had surrendered, and the British brought up their largest battlewagons to pour withering fire on German batteries. Meanwhile on the beaches the LCTs (landing craft tanks) were close-packed together like monster whales. And out of them, full panoplied for war, came tanks to crash incessantly into the choicest armor that German skill had yet devised.

The British Eighth Army was 150 miles to the south when Clark landed at Salerno, but it came on with astonishing speed, leapfrogging forward by the use of planes and parachutists. Within ten days the Allied forces joined, and the Germans, in danger of being outflanked, retired to Naples.

That Italian seaport they most thoroughly wrecked to disable our work of supply, sinking all ships in the harbor. Out of what seems pure malice, and aimless vengeance they burned libraries, plundered art treasures, dynamited the water system as well as gas and electrical services, and set time bombs in hotels and post offices which exploded later and brought death to civilians. After this joint work of coverage and sadism they retired north to strong entrenchments beyond the Volturno River.

From Naples two historic highways led north toward Rome, the Via Appia, across Pontine marshes near the sea, and the Via Latina, often known as the Via Casalina, which wound its way around craggy little mountains on one of which, at Cassino, St. Benedict had founded his famous monastery. By this route the Allies hoped to force their way into Rome before 1943 came to an end.

They were doomed to disappointment. The Germans held savagely all along the Volturno, scene of Garibaldi's victory over the Neapolitans in 1860, and when driven back entrenched themselves anew on the Liri River flowing by Cassino. As the year ended the British Eighth Army on the Adriatic was still short of reaching Pescara, east of Rome and the terminal of the only decent route from the Adriatic to that city. And the American Fifth Army under Clark, to which were attached British, New Zealand, French and Indian troops, had only begun to claw its way through the tangled mountain heights around Cassino.

At this rate, if the war was to be fought out in Italy, it would last for years. Rome was not yet taken, and beyond Rome lay even more inaccessible mountains, and still further to the north beyond Lombardy and the Po, the Brenner Pass and the Alps! If it were only one mountain, or two or three or four; but to the doughboys and the Tommies and our other allies the mountains seemed innumerable.

Perhaps, as the Russians had insisted all along, the more direct approach to the Nazis across the English Channel in the end would pay the highest dividends. One thing was evident: the

Germans held the Italians in the hollow of their hand; and the Germans intended to fight for Italy. It was *not* to be any soft underbelly of the Axis. Hitler had to keep his hold on industrial north Italy and on the resources and fortress-areas that lay north of the upper Adriatic.

12. FESTUNG EUROPA

OF the various works of art attributed to William II, artist-Kaiser and last of the Hohenzollerns, none was more celebrated than his Germania defending Europe from the yellow peril. European civilization could scarcely be said to have been in danger of extinction in 1900, as the international army commanded by a German general rescued the Peking legations from the fury of the Boxers. But that was not the way the Kaiser saw it; to him the Allied conquest and the looting of Peking was a crusade, Europe against Asia, light against darkness. Germania, omnipotent, holy, in shining armor clad, headed the European vanguard, John Bull and French Marianne rejoicing in the might of her protecting sword.

Meanwhile, as our own Mr. Dooley (F.P. Dunne) records it, the Kaiser sat in his ancestral palace of Potsdam "writing a book to take the place of the Bible." No doubt his friend Mr. Hinessey believed that, also some Germans.

Hitler and Goebbels gave their Germany the same historic rôle: again Europe's savior and knight, champion of law, order, decency and justice against world-wide Jewish Bolshevism, an ancient Asiatic menace in new and more evil guise. But now two more sprawling enemies, England and America, rotted through by democratic anarchy, deeply infected by poisonous Jewish cunning, along with bestial Bolshevism itself, beleaguered the Holy Fortress, the Nazi *Festung Europa,* eager to betray it to infamous Asia!

That sacred stronghold, "Ein feste Burg" as Luther sang, could never be taken. It shored up the whole continent for civilization. The central keep was Germany's invincibility; the outer bulwarks, Norway, Denmark, the Channel and Biscayan coasts, Spain, Italy, and on down to Crimea and Crete. Its impassable moats were the North Sea, the Atlantic and Mediterranean. The fortress was one, the command was one. *Ein Reich, Ein Volk, Ein Führer* guaranteed Europa's happiness and safety.

Within the ramparts order reigned; without, with the exception

THE FORTRESS OF EUROPE

(Courtesy of the New York Times)

of Japan, chaos. The war against Nazidom was counter-revolution, the desperate, reactionary plot of cowards to sweep back the wave of the future, to tear down the Nazi "New Order," the "Greater East Asia Co-Prosperity Sphere" of Japan.

The new structure of society must be totalitarian; the divine agents to redeem our lost humanity (Germany and Japan) came not as conquerors but as liberators. This did not mean that direct annexations were forsworn. Alsace-Lorraine, the greater part of Poland, the Baltic states and the Ukraine were incorporated into the Reich; so, too, most of Czechoslovakia. France, Finland, Hungary and other satellite states were to make themselves useful on occasion, always to look to Germanny for advice, discipline, instruction and orders. Folk of Teutonic origin, Netherlanders, Scandinavians, Flemings, German Swiss were to be favored and honored by a sort of dual citizenship; they, too, might share somewhat the rights and privileges of the German burgher.

Politically, the New Order was a complicated hierarchy of multilateral administrative entities on the Napoleonic model, a sort of feudalism of applied social science within which the vassals, loyal, true and effective, were free to do their full duty for the glory of the entity. From different points of view we can see it as a beehive, as a hornet's nest, a shoal of sharks, a horde of wolves. For Americans it has an odd resemblance to some of our more complex holding company systems. Instead of economic autarchy for Germany, all Europe was to be one—economic autarchy for the entire continent. The dynamo, heart and brain was to be Germany, and within that perfect realm most manufacturing was to be centered. Other areas would supply raw materials, wheat from France as well as articles of luxury; iron ore, timber and fish from Norway and Sweden; butter, eggs and bacon from Denmark; fruits, copper, minerals from Spain and Italy; cereals, bauxite, meat and oil from the Balkans. By controls both of finance and of imports, by pegged exchange rates for various currencies, by quota systems for production and trade, by bank credits, cartels, blocked marks and other financial wizardries a single vast European economic system was to be built, somewhat as in the days of the great Napoleon, the principal difference being that the new continental system was worked out in minute detail and put in practice to a degree far greater than was ever blueprinted by St. Helena's exile.

FRANCE IN THE NEW ORDER

The basic outpost area, the key bastion of Fortress Europe, was France. Her Channel ports, closely adjacent to the enemy, called for heavy fortifications and large garrisons; her harbors on the Atlantic, Brest, Cherbourg, Nantes and Lorient screened German submarines that were to sweep the seas; her factories could be geared into German war industry, the more easily since some of the largest had long since been meshed into international peace-time cartels.

The Nazi régime in France fluctuated with the fortunes of war, varied from time to time as pressure alternately was applied to and taken off Pétain's Vichy government. On the whole, it was more lenient than in Poland and southeastern Europe, but harsher than in Denmark, Holland, Belgium and Norway.

For decades Germans had specialized in abstract and applied science; but science in regard to things, not in regard to humanity. Engines of production and engines of destruction, the science of the laboratory the Germans indeed did comprehend; but how to make friends with non-Germans was beyond their ken. It certainly was to Germany's interest to ingratiate the torn, lacerated and humbled France of 1940, and to some extent that was her intention.

The French hated Germans, it is true; but many million Frenchmen disliked Britain, despised Italy, and so on; a far greater degree of coöperation of France with the Reich should have been possible than was actually achieved.

Yet in their own way the Germans thought they behaved decently in Paris. At first they did not loot and they did maintain military discipline; they ordered their soldiers to surrender subway seats to French women; and to show how graciously he could act Hitler visited Napoleon's tomb and ceremoniously offered to return the body of his young son, the Eaglet, to Paris. The Germans hoped that Paris might remain, under the aegis of the New Order, a kind of historic-artistic Mecca, a glorified vacation rendezvous where champagne flowed freely and one bought souvenirs.

But greed mastered good intentions and the fist was felt beneath that velvet glove. To Paris rushed a horde of German sight-seers, their pockets bulging with paper marks exchangeable for French francs at rates favorable to the visitors. Like locusts the German soldiers and officials bought up everything in sight from jewelry and gowns to silk stockings. The stores emptied by magic as Corporal Hans and Private Fritz vied with General Göring and Herr Goebbels in getting whatever pleased their fancy.

The Germans paid for what they took. But the French paid the occupational costs of the German army, the expense of fortifying their coast, and for food supplied to French prisoners of war in the Reich. The total which they paid was only about half what the Germans spent and there was left a surplus for purchase of what seemed desirable in France from factories to fine horses and champagne. Owners might refuse to sell, but this was only a technicality. All that was necessary was to stop raw materials or to divert transportation into different channels. And thus it came about that German and pseudo-German capitalists and bankers were soon the legal owners of large-scale French industry, the former magnates thereof becoming sub-managers, if anything. The Tricolor still flew in southern France, a shadow army and navy took shadow orders from Marshal Pétain. But the Marshal himself received the invaders' veiled commands and open hints which he might not disobey, for the Germans held that part of France in economic stranglehold, and every time they twisted the economic screws Vichy hurried to respond.

So it was in the Riom trials. Hitler's idea was to fasten on the French formal and proved responsibility for World War II, and Pétain had to fetch Blum, Daladier, Reynaud, ex-French premiers, along with Weygand and other militarists, to trial as war plotters. The trials, long postponed, were held with results highly unsatisfactory to Hitler. What he wanted was a public confession of French guilt, equivalent to the extorted German confession of 1919; what he got was abundant evidence of stupidity and corruption, and that was all. As Hitler himself stated in March, 1942, "proceedings are taking place in France which are characterized by the fact that those responsible are not mentioned in a single word. The proceedings merely deal with insufficient preparations for war." This seems quite true, but how could Hitler try his "friend" Laval and others of that sort?

The Germans had ordered the trial; now they ordered it to end. So did Pétain. But the judges refused to obey; they said the accused were entitled to their trial. Pétain adjourned the proceedings, placed the defendants in strict confinement, promised a renewal of the trial at a future date.

The serfdom and subservience of Vichy to Berlin was plain in many ways. Contrary to the armistice the gestapo overran southern France, ostensibly to help Vichy police hunt down refugees, and many such of non-German nationality were handed over to the Germans, a violation of the armistice. Food and coal controls empowered the Germans to do much as they wished in both occupied and unoccupied France. Their agents everywhere bought with depreciated francs, cattle, wheat and potatoes which they shipped to Germany, not simply because in 1941 they had need of these but because they considered it wise to keep the French undernourished. Occasionally the Germans would release some food reserves as proof of good-will. They even bought carloads of food in Vichy France, plastered the cars with posters, "For the relief of the poor of Paris," and then shunted off the train to Germany. So it was with coal. Before the war France imported coal from the Saar. That importation was ended, and since many French coal miners were prisoners of war in Germany French coal production fell off alarmingly. Therefore it was easy for the Germans to half-freeze as well as to half-starve the French.

To a certain degree the regimented and desperate French toed the mark in both zones; they built fortifications along the Channel; their press advertised the proclaimed beauties of civilization's crusade against Russian Bolshevism and the high desirability of joining it; they deprived Jews of civil rights: but certain things they would not do; most of them would not fight for fair Europe on barren Russian steppes; they would not volunteer to work in German factories. And as time went on more and more slipped away to join the Free French of De Gaulle, whose double Cross of old Lorraine flew in odd corners of the earth, the symbol that a newer and better France was in the war, this time to see it through until the very end.

The invaders did not show their full hand until April, 1942, keeping their tame arch-traitor Laval in the background. They even permitted Pétain to dismiss that wretch, thinking it wise not to coerce Vichy too far. What the Germans wanted were French mechanics in German factories, the use of the French fleet, and, if possible, a French declaration of war against England. To demand, however, was no guarantee of delivery. If pressed too hard, the French army in North Africa, Syria and Indo-China might decide to fight against the Axis and not for it. Furthermore, the major forces of the wehrmacht were deployed over Russian plains, and it did not care to take chances on a rebellion in the west.

Thus the Marshal nursed his nervous neutrality until the spring of 1942. By then the Germans began to feel war pressure in grim earnest; they had to finish off their victory in Russia; they must end the war everywhere before American production swamped them; immediate French assistance was crucial; ultimate French coöperation only desirable. Pétain had yielded often, looking the other way when French goods and French ships helped to reinforce Rommel, recalling Weygand from North Africa on German insistence, and on a hint from Germany ordering French merchant shipping in Indo-China surrendered to Japan. There was much more Pétain must do, the Germans thought, and they demanded 300,000 Frenchmen to work in Germany, 52,000 horses for the Russian campaign, French warships to protect French merchantmen en route with food and supplies for Rommel. Pétain balked; he said he was doing everything possible. Whereupon the Germans made him appoint Laval premier.

Laval "promised full coöperation," not only 300,000 workers by July 15, 1942, but eventually a million. He even pledged the French army in the unoccupied zone to oppose any Anglo-American invasion, and asked German help in revamping it for that purpose. The Germans would not trust any French army, even with Laval as premier, but they had to have workingmen and Laval signed a paper whereby one French prisoner of war would be released for every six French workers "volunteering" to work in the Reich.

The plan did not work. Some 20,000 French volunteered and a few prisoners of war were repatriated, most of them about to die anyway and of no use to anybody. Laval discovered that the only way he could keep his word to the Germans was to handcuff workers and drag them off to the Reich. By 1943 he found himself in as unenviable a position as Pétain a year earlier; he could not comply with Nazi orders even if he tried, and he was in danger of being fired or shot by the cutthroats who had backed him. To discharge men from factories, deprive them of unemployment insurance and ration cards did not mean they would leave France for German factories. They could go underground. Sabotage saturated all France under the very eyes of the gestapo, despite the tortures and killings staged by their bestial inquisitors.

THE LOW COUNTRIES, SCANDANAVIA
AND HITLER

Of all the occupied regions on the periphery of the Reich, the Netherlands and Denmark were especially favored. They had offered little more than token resistance, if any; both lands were mainly Teutonic in basic racial origin; and in both local brands of National Socialist agitation had met with partial success before 1939.

At first the Nazis insisted that the Netherlands and Denmark, freely and of their own accord, would seek close unity with the conqueror. Not until two years had passed did they come too late to the verdict that "harmful delusions of racial equality" were so prevalent that they must classify Dutch and Danes as "Under-Germans." Even so, to be an "Under-German" was definitely superior to having Polish or French ancestry.

The Nazis never could quite make up their minds whether to rule the Netherlands through their nativist Quisling, Mussert, or to use sterner methods and trust that veteran Nordic, Seyss-Inquart, the Vienna Gauleiter whom they put over Holland. No matter how kind they were, the Dutch never seemed to have any interest in transferring themselves from "Under-Germans" into true Germans. When thousands of square miles in Lithuania were offered for settlement, only six hundred would emigrate; when Wilhelmina's treachery in ending the House of Orange, by deserting her country was made clear to everyone, Dutchmen continued obstinately to cheer the Queen's name and to wear the royal colors symbolic of their nation; and when one old cabinet member was lured from London to visit his wife he was so obdurate as to announce that it would be wise for his countrymen to stay neutral, as they did in 1914-1918. There certainly was a war being fought against "Asiatic Bolshevism," so the Nazis shouted; but in all the Netherlands not over a thousand men signed up for it. The Dutch were more loyal than that to their alien conqueror called Napoleon!

The Netherlanders were quiet folk and their country was unsuitable for guerrilla war. Therefore their hate of the Nazis was shown by wearing the Jewish Star of David when Jews were maltreated, by refusing to implement Nazi ordinances in regard to schools and churches, by jests and jokes at Nazi gaucheries, by hiding refugee British aviators, by derailing troop trains, and occasionally by bumping careless Germans into innumerable Dutch canals. Dutch intellectuals were brutally mishandled, but there was no wholesale maltreatment of the Dutch before 1943. Blue eyes and blonde hair indicated the right blood, and the Netherlandic agriculture fitted in nicely with Nazi plans for the new economic Europe.

In 1943 the change came. Should there be an invasion of the Continent, it would not do to have 400,000 ex-soldiers of Queen Wilhelmina's exiled government loose in Holland. The Germans felt they had been overkind to these five-day veterans; they had let them shed their uniforms and go home. In 1943 the occupying forces started a man-hunt for those between 18 and 35 whom they might put to work in Germany. One year later the martyrdom of Holland began in earnest.

Denmark was favored even over Holland; the Danes did not resist invasion nor did their king leave his country. The Danes could still govern themselves, and not until 1942 were "occupational marks" (money given Nazi troops to spend in occupied countries) made legal tender in Denmark. Local Danes in Danish Nazi uniforms were roughly handled in Copenhagen streets, the German army not interfering; Danish courts upheld the rights of Jewish students; and even under the eyes of the Nazi overlords the courts penalized newspapers for anti-Semitism, an offense under Danish law.

In one major respect only during the early days did the Germans behave badly; they drained the country of its agricultural wealth by the occupational costs device. Danish banks had to provide the money, and in two years pigs were 50 per cent fewer, and the hen census showed only six million hens in 1942, whereas in 1940 thirty-five million had been reported. Perhaps, however, some hens escaped the 1942 census.

What forced friction in Denmark was the Russo-German war. Some Danes volunteered but not enough; Danes were asked to give blankets for German soldiers defending civilization in the East and they did not comply; when Hitler sent formal and effusive congratulations to Denmark's king on his birthday, the brief reply, "Thank you. Christian, Rex," did not please the Führer.

Still, there was no Gauleiter in Denmark, and Danes could enjoy the incessant quarrels for supremacy between the Nazi ambassador at Copenhagen and the commander of the occupational troops.

These officials issued so many contradictory orders that neither Danes nor Germans knew who was in authority. The Nazis wobbled between severity and leniency; they forbade importing coal into Denmark, hoping thus to increase Danish workers in Germany; on the other hand, they permitted free elections to the Danish parliament, hoping to increase coöperation. No results: 90 to 95 per cent of the electorate voting for a continuance of democracy.

The Danish picture was not one of sweet acquiescence; there was much grumbling, occasional brawls and one nasty street riot in which several civilians were killed. But even there the killing was by pro-Nazi Danes who had fought in Russia.

Since she was a manufacturing country, Belgium caused the Nazis more headaches than Denmark and the Netherlands. The Germans wanted her industrial output, yet would not let Belgian big business compete with the Ruhr; they also needed skilled Belgian workers in Germany; and having had a taste of Belgian resistance (1914-1918) they determined, this time, to eradicate it.

Nazi gestures to win Belgian coöperation did not last long. When King Leopold did not help them, they kept him closely guarded and turned to Degrelle, founder of Fascism in Belgium, the so-called Rexist movement. Degrelle was in such ill repute in his own country that this maneuver to make him a sub-führer had to be abandoned. Next, a racial and linguistic boundary to split Belgium was drawn between Flemings, a supposedly Nordic folk, and Walloons, inferiors speaking French. When neither program proved lucrative the iron fist was clenched.

Pressure on Belgium rose steadily; occupation costs of 15,000,-000,000 francs a year were jacked up to 22,500,000,000; any new building was forbidden and construction firms were sent to the Ruhr to repair air damage; Belgian oil refineries were torn down and rebuilt in Germany; and finally labor conscription to serve the Reich was decreed.

The Belgians retorted as best they might; they went underground; they circulated forbidden newspapers; they engaged in sabotage, and died for it all too often.

Of all these countries Norway was the most intransigent. Much of her area was relatively inaccessible to Germany and relatively accessible to British airmen and commando raids. Her seafaring people, owing to their long coastline, could slip across the North Sea to Scotland; and since most Norwegian merchant shipping escaped capture there was a Norway afloat which armies could not conquer.

Strategically, the German occupation was of great advantage; Norway's fiords flanked the British Isles on the east, and her far northern stretches lay athwart the shipping route to Russia. To win the war Norway had to be held and used to the full. Therefore, the German grip on Norway steadily tightened.

As usual, the Germans said they came as liberators. Britain and France had planned to overrun Norway to fight the Russians, and Germany as Norway's friend had intervened. The king of Norway, constitutionally, had forfeited his throne by leaving the country, but all the Norwegians had to do to keep their independence was to summon their parliament and formally depose the king.

But Norwegians cheered for their nationally symbolic king, would not depose him even in absentia. Then Germany installed a Gauleiter, abolished the Norwegian law forbidding capital punishment, began to use firing squads.

This severity not succeeding, German policy veered. Hitler stuck to his stooge, one Vidkun Quisling, major in the Norwegian army, a native Fascist who hopped the Hitler bandwagon and in obvious ways imitated the German Führer. Major Quisling had been the Norwegian Moseley before 1940, with a uniform of bright red and gold and a bodyguard of young thugs called "Hirdmen." Hitler made him premier of Norway. As such, the name Quisling became a term of scorn, contumely and contempt, ill fame and ridicule throughout the anti-Nazi world.

Backed by German bayonets, this absurd Quisling ordered trade unions to disband, schools to teach Fascism, the press to pump up the new cause, and the National Church to preach its doctrine. Nowhere was he obeyed. Workmen went to jail rather than work on German fortifications, and the Germans had to import more docile Danes to build the concrete pens for their submarines in Norwegian fiords. Teachers resigned, many froze to death in concentration camps rather than teach Quislingism, and it proved impossible to fill their places with the Hirdmen whose ability did not exceed strutting around Quisling's castle.

The National Church was firm and bold in opposition. For many decades observers had commented on the decay of formal religion among the Norwegians. But now in many a fishing village the church lived again. Driven from their pulpits, the pastors preached

in huts, in open fields, amid pine forests, fed and clothed by patriotic fishermen and villagers.

Quisling tried to play James II with the seven bishops of Norway.
They resisted him as stoutly as did the seven English bishops of
the seventeenth century, whose historic stand against Stuart tyranny
has been recorded by Macaulay in words so eloquent that the
memory of their fortitude still lives. Quisling, too, did not dare
hang seven bishops, but he put them under house arrest, took away
their books, put in a bastard bishop of his own making. The Norwegians, however, boycotted Quisling churches, and when the
Hirdmen were ordered to go, there were not enough for a con-
gregation.

Quisling, like Hitler, pulled fits of psychopathic rage, probably
synthetic. This did not help much in cold-blooded Norway. He
built a Berchtesgadenette for himself costing, it was rumored,
$60,000,000, surrounded it with anti-aircraft and machine guns,
and quaked within. This was too much for his Nazi friends who
turned at last against their puppet to enforce strict German overlordship, that is, Norwegian semi-starvation on skimmed milk, a
few potatoes, and a herring or two.

LIBERATION INTO GENOCIDE

For Slav and Jew and Greek the Master Race had no mercy.
Toward them the pattern of Nazi behavior differed sharply from
that for other folk. It best can be expressed by the word "genocide," the destruction of a nation, of its people. "Germanization" is
too weak a term to describe Nazi policy toward those unfortunate
Poles, Jews and, to some extent, Czechs, Slovenes, Serbs and
Greeks who found themselves "protected" within the walls of
Europe's Fortress. The Nazis willed to do more than impose language, customs, legal practices and economic system upon inferior
breeds. Such a program, ignoring biology and the blood stream,
would not enforce the liquidation of a people, their ultimate extinction, but would instead corrupt, betray and at last destroy their
conquerors. As Hitler told Rauschning: "Natural instincts bid all
living beings not merely conquer their enemies but also destroy
them. In former days it was the victor's prerogative to destroy
entire tribes, entire peoples. By doing this gradually and without
bloodshed we demonstrate our humanity."

For the most part genocide was gradual. The Germans did not shoot down every Pole on sight. Instead they dispossessed the Poles in that part of Poland annexed to the Reich and turned over their land to German settlers from the Baltic states; they confiscated their savings; they deported large numbers to Germany, being careful to separate man from wife; they forbade all Polish marriages without permission; they took away children born out of wedlock; and they systematically undernourished all Poles.

There were other devices such as concentration camps to which Poles were sent on indeterminate sentence for smuggling food or falsifying the yield of crops. Poles died there by the thousands from overwork and physical punishment, more often from cold and starvation. To save burial they were discharged when dying, a courtesy not shown to Jews.

The Poles fought back with skill, trickery and nerve. The great area of Poland, its many swamps and forests, made this possible as it was not in the congested urban west. The Polish underground was the best organized in Europe; it tried agents of the Gestapo in absentia, and executed many in person; it frightened German civilians so that they had to carry arms; and forest forays on railways crossing Poland to Russia became so menacing that 40,000 gestapo agents were assigned to protect German troop trains.

When caught there was first torture, then death. But the underground guarded its membership well, and since the Poles who belonged changed names and occupations frequently the gestapo never caught many. It was cunning against cunning, murder at retail on both sides. The Poles had no chance to inflict mass slaughter, nor did the Germans use it. The Reich needed Polish labor and Hitler had proclaimed that by permitting Poles to live at all "we demonstrate our humanity." No doubt it seemed necessary.

Humanity did not include Jews. The principles of genocide had happily been established before war commenced. After it came there was more vigor. Jews were more numerous and more obnoxious to the Nazis in Poland than elsewhere, and the Nazis herded them into cattle cars in the dead of winter and threw out those still alive upon the frozen plains of eastern Poland. New methods were invented by scientific sadists to end once and for all the Jewish menace. These ranged from poison-gas chambers in concentration camps to starvation in ghettos.

The most infamous ghetto was a squalid district of Warsaw, a number of city blocks heavily walled in, where Jews were packed like cattle in a killing pen. Into this mammoth corral fresh arrivals from western Europe were huddled on their way to death; out of its gates went German army trucks draining off for execution the old and useless, no longer worth their keep as workers. At its peak the Warsaw ghetto was said to have 600,000 Jews packed so close as even to cover the gravestones in an old cemetery. Numbers decreased by starvation, disease, and the cessation of newcomers until there were but few Jews left.

When only 35,000 remained, desperate fury seized them. The underground had smuggled some rifles and machine guns into the ghetto. With these the dead men there surprised the Nazis in April, 1942, and electrified the world by a withering fire on storm troopers sent in for more victims.

A lesser parallel to the ruinous seige of Stalingrad that same year, and to the smashing of Berlin in 1945, now took place. For a full months the lost Jews held out; they fought for every room, for every cellar and corner. To end resistance the Germans had to use tanks and artillery, and incendiary bombs from planes. A thousand Germans died, and all the Jews. There was no Josephus present to record the bravery of his co-religionists, but that was hardly necessary. The Jews of Poland and of Europe, the world knew, could and did fight Germans with the courage of their ancestors who fell before the spears of Rome.

In Nazi theory the extermination of all Slavs was desirable; in practice, discrimination was profitable. In theory Czechs were no better than Poles, and Hitler had screamed repeatedly for their degenerate blood; in practice it was soon seen that Czechs had higher value to the German overlord than Poles could possibly have. Bohemia and Moravia, that part of Czechoslovakia which the Nazis chose to term "The Protectorate," was closely knit into the economic core of *Festung Europa*. Millions of Czechs were skilled in crafts and industries. The Skoda Munition Works were vital to the Reich, and that meant also the men and women employed therein. Genocide, therefore, in Bohemia and Moldavia was confined at first to getting rid of poets, teachers, writers and university students who might perpetuate the pattern of Czech culture. The universities were suspended, protesting professors and very young students were shot in cold blood, Czech nationalism earmarked for extermination.

Reinhard Heydrich, "The Hangman," gestapo agent extraordinary and personal associate of Hitler, was appointed protector. He set up a gestapo death-house reminiscent of the Revolutionary Tribunals in the French Reign of Terror. For a long time this killing court averaged seventy cases a day; no defense pleas were heard, no appeal permitted. Between March, 1939, and May, 1943, the gestapo was said to have executed 50,000 Czechs, some of them "pushed into a corner by two SS men who then shot the victim," others hanged by gestapo apprentices in training for liberation work.

When Heydrich himself fell before the bullets of two unknown avengers, Hitler ordered an example made. In the hills near Prague was the village of Lidice, from which certain residents, rumor had it, aided the escape of Heydrich's judges. Contrary to Herod's formula all males in Lidice over seventeen years old were lined up and shot, the children sent to Germany, the women to concentration camps, the cattle to German colonists, all houses razed to the ground. Lidice, officially, no longer existed, gone without trace.

After Heydrich came a lesser and more practical thug who was to keep factories in full blast and railroads in operation. The Czech patriots helped him achieve a stupendous failure, their will to do so strengthened by the ever more active underground, and by the geographic location of their country in greater Germany's industrial heart.

THE CENTRAL KEEP

Only in broadest outline is it possible to tell what occurred within the central keep of *Festung Europa*. The world heard what the radios broadcasted; what was written in news reports smuggled into or out of Switzerland and Sweden; what odd or official travelers might be allowed to see. But what went on in people's minds, their hopes and fears, their loyalty or disloyalty—all this was hidden. Here, as everywhere in wartime, the censor ruled. The shadow of the gestapo was over the land.

1939-1941, and joy and jubilation kept pace with the onrush of the conquering wehrmacht. There were still Germans in the Fatherland's concentration camps, but until June 22, 1941, and the crossing of the Soviet frontier, there was little if any overt evidence of anti-Hitler sentiment. Some trouble in German factories may be inferred from the radio denouncements of "plutocratic Bolshevik individuals" in Stalin's pay impeding war production; but speedily protests were snuffed out. Germans were disappointed that the war had not ended when promised; they were surprised at Hitler's stab into Russia which they did not understand; and the fact that Moscow had not fallen was alarming. Nevertheless, Germans knew well and believed most utterly in discipline, order, hierarchy as the best state of man, and knew also what happened to those infringing thereon; furthermore, as yet there had been nothing but victory. Victory from Narvik to Tobruk, from Vichy to the heart of Russia!

1942 told a different tale; the booty reservoirs of conquered Europe began to dry up and go barren; America was in the war and many Germans have long memories; over the North Sea and Baltic ports, the Rhineland and the Ruhr, Allied planes now fought it out with German fighters on equal terms; and on the Eastern front the death roll lengthened, lengthened month by month. It was a crisis year. This we may judge from speeches by Hitler and Goebbels, from such copies of the *Völkischer Beobachter,* official Nazi newspaper, and *Das Schwarze Korps,* organ of the SS (*Schutzstaffel*), as are here and now available.

The morale of both soldiers and civilians was not what it had been. Said the *Völkischer Beobachter:* "The soldiers are inclined to believe bad news rather than good news." Very likely true. It usually is in all armies. The German army in 1941 had been soaked with a type of propaganda which Hitler derided in *Mein Kampf* as a major cause of German defeat in the First World War. Its theme and leitmotiv was that Russians were putty, could not fight, that glorious victory was sure before the snows of winter. *Das Schwarze Korps* of the SS, a jealous rival group and highly critical of the wehrmacht, deftly insinuated that though German soldiers did not fear death they were "afraid of civil life which they must rejoin some day, affliction, the struggle for existence, the duty to provide for their families, and the necessity to make up for lost years." A left-handed critique of the attack on the U.S.S.R., and no inspiration to tired men whose favorite jest was, "If we were fed like Englishmen, equipped like Russians, and had only the Italians to fight, the war might be bearable." [1]

Meanwhile, soldiers returning from the Russian front spread

[1] M. Seydewitz, *Civil Life in War Time Germany* (The Viking Press, Inc., 1945), p. 87.

gloom at home. The Soviet lands were endless, the innumerable foe elusive, there was no way to stabilize victory. The government did its best by little presents and by little homilies, also by stopping or curtailing leaves of absence, standard devices of all militarism which added nothing to the will to fight. How many Germans died in the Russian lands that winter of 1941-1942 is yet unverified. Official statistics obviously were false—405,109 dead or missing thus far in the war. The people knew better; that was only about 2 per cent of war-able German manhood. Village after village and factory after factory counted their own proportionate loss and came to a different conclusion. So, too, did the Swiss who counted death notices in German papers and compared them with those in the same towns and in the same newspapers during World War I. Many of them were evidently written by convinced Nazis. Often they read, "For Führer and Fatherland, in proud eagerness to defend the New Great German Reich from its Bolshevik foes, our beloved, promising and courageous son was killed in action on the eastern front, believing firmly in final victory." But other notices had a different tone. "God in his inscrutable wisdom," they read, "has seen fit to call away from this earth our beloved, promising, warm-hearted son, who responded to the call of duty and gave his young life for the Fatherland." Reverence for God, Hitler omitted, a fact not without significance.[1]

Hitler sensed something wrong and tried to deflect such implied criticism by magnifying Russian backwardness and poverty under "twenty-five years of Jewish rule," and by ordering an official museum of Soviet horrors, attendance compulsory for certain German groups. The exhibit as a morale builder was not altogether successful; too many things were obviously wrong in Germany. Forebodings of disaster multiplied and were neatly broadcast this summer of 1942 by *Das Schwarze Korps*. "The German war effort," it stated, "of today is governed by three interdependent poles: wehrmacht, armament and provisioning. Whatever is attracted by one of the poles is pulled away by the others...." Germany, like all combatants, had to have more soldiers, more war matériel, more food. Three years of war were beginning to tell. Older men do not make good fighters, but Hitler was forced to draft them. It is difficult for factories to increase output without dependable transporta-

---

[1] Stewart Winfield Herman, *It's Your Souls We Want* (New York, Harper & Brothers, 1943), p. 44.

tion and competent workers; but German railways were in a miserable state of repair before the war, and now there was insufficient oil to use for trucks to take the place of locomotives, and workingmen were tired, undernourished. Then, too, German farms could not produce bumper crops without fertilizers and farm laborers, but if fertilizer importations ceased and fertilizer factories turned to war production, and if laborers were drafted into the army, then less food was inevitable.

Conditions such as these were not found in Germany alone; her adversaries were all suffering the same wear and tear and resorting to the same palliatives. They were not altogether absent in the United States. But Germany was outnumbered, and had to try to make up war's deficit by getting productive skilled labor out of sullenly obstinate enemy aliens.

AIR BLITZ FROM THE WEST

1943 followed, when Germany lost the offensive, never to regain it, except locally, in this war. The siege of *Festung Europa* was now enlarged and intensified. For almost two and a half years it raged and ruined, an incredibly dreary and beastly time. Surging against southern outposts of the Fortress drove the British Eighth and American Fifth Armies, New Zealanders, Poles, Sikhs, Gurkhas, Scots and Englishmen, Frenchmen, Moors, Brazilians, Americans: some units all Negro, some of Japanese origin, others with such racial strains and nationalistic backgrounds as we, above all others the melting pot of the world, can boast. Zooming across the North Sea and English Channel, Anglo-American air fleets destroyed the cities and industries of western Europe. Flying Fortresses with "precision bombing" by day, swift Lancasters with prodigious bomb loads by night, British mosquito bombers stabbing at Berlin itself. It was now the Allies' turn at wholesale devastation, "revenge" for Coventry and Plymouth, the air blitz of 1940-1941 in reverse. And meanwhile in the Donetz basin, in the Ukraine, and in White Russia the eastern ramparts of the Reich armies were stormed and broken, one after another. Colossally the Red army swept westward, killing and being killed in numbers beyond belief, and under battle conditions beyond imagining.

Said Stalin on February 22, 1943, "In view of the absence of a second front, the Red army alone is bearing the whole weight of the war." Stalin knew better. There was now not simply the Italian front on the south; there was also an air front from out of the west carrying the fight to the heart of the Reich itself every day. Throughout 1943 it disrupted German war production, weakened German morale, drew off the luftwaffe from the east, eased the way for Soviet triumph.

British and American planes did much more smashing and killing in western Germany in 1943 than Germans did over Britain in 1940-1941. Bombers were larger; in 1940 the Germans had nothing to compare with the British Lancasters and the American Fortresses. There were many more, carrying vastly heavier bomb loads. Raids were more numerous, more concentrated, more lethal, and they were only beginning.

Versatile German air defense threatened for a time to offset Allied air production; anti-aircraft guns were made more effective, radar location instruments more delicately precise, and numerous gadgets also, to lighten the sky at night above the enemy so as to make his bombers visible, to mount cannons on the wings of fighter planes so as to outrange the machine guns of Fortresses in their daylight raids. But in the long run these could not sufficiently protect Germany. Production in the United States was swelling into incredible torrents of matériel. The Americans and Britons lost 335 heavy bombers in June alone, but meanwhile British plane production had quadrupled and that of the United States had doubled, and redoubled and redoubled again. The new type planes carried four-ton bombs, later to be six- and even eight-ton "block busters." Over Coventry the Germans had strewed 450 tons of small stuff; by summer, 1943, many a German city was being plastered four times that heavily in a single raid.

Some Allied experts were certain of knocking out Germany from the air alone, but Churchill was as ever conservative. "The experiment," he prudently told Congress in May, "is well worth trying so long as other methods are not excluded." The plane did not knock out Germany, but it did severely weaken military power there. The RAF, numerically stronger in 1943 than the American air arm in Europe, concentrated on the Ruhr, pounding congested areas in that industrial valley over and over again, blowing up houses, railroads and dams, flooding towns, pulverizing factories, killing unknown numbers of persons, reducing German steel production perhaps 30 per cent.

Hamburg in particular took heavy punishment, more severe than that inflicted on London. Night after night British bombers blasted docks, shipping, and factories. Their raids were costly, the defense desperate; but there was precious little left of Hamburg, second city of the Reich.

Far and wide through occupied France and Belgium scoured the Allied planes, ripping up air-fields, smashing railroad trains, destroying coastal installations, and focusing on German submarine bases at Lorient and St. Nazaire. The damage done the submarine pens, those cement caverns reinforced with steel of which one at Lorient was spacious enough to stable thirty U-boats, was disappointing; but the ruin inflicted on shipyards, repair depots, and transportation facilities which the U-boats used, was held worth the sacrifice of Allied planes and airmen.

The Allied giant air raids were unpredictable, incessant. Over half the strength of the luftwaffe, it was estimated, was tied up this year in raid-defense work. The bombers ranged as far as Berlin and by the end of the year the Berliners got more samples of what had been done to London. North to Copenhagen and its shipyards, south to Wiener Neustadt and beyond Vienna—the raids ran round the clock, American by day and British by night. The air was thick with planes, dull with their droning, as they sped to their targets, dropped quickly their bomb loads, swung rapidly homeward.

For this harassing from the west the Germans had but small answers—the U-boat and the luftwaffe. In 1943 the Reich navy concentrated exclusively on the U-boat, and Admiral Doenitz predicted as more and more submarines took to the ocean pathways: now they will not only hunt in packs but in "echelons of packs." For awhile it seemed as though the admiral might make good, for sinkings rose rapidly. But there were Allied answers for the new U-boats. One of them was the "frigate," easily constructed in great numbers, somewhat smaller than a destroyer, but capable of convoy duty; another smaller ship was the destroyer escort, and finally there was the patrol plane, weighed down with gas rather than with armament, good for long-distance aërial convoy work. There were ups and downs this year in the U-boat war but gradually its menace faded, particularly in the North Atlantic where the Canadian navy specialized in convoy duty, with some five hundred ships flying the Canadian flag by 1944.

The luftwaffe also failed as signally as did the U-boat. It was not that German science fell behind; it was German production and German manpower that failed to keep pace. The Germans simply did not have the trained pilots, the trained mechanics, factory facilities, aluminum and oil necessary in 1943 to meet what was thrown at the Reich by Allied air raiders. Top priorities went to fighter planes so that German bombing of Britain dwindled. Retreating German armies in Italy and Russia had to have air coverage, and did not get enough of it. Göring's organization for air mastery had planned too small and could not catch up. The relentless process, accelerated in 1944 and 1945, had already begun. The air fleets of the Reich were being kept out of the air, destroyed on the ground.

STALINGRAD TO PRIPET MARSHES

From every side the storm clouds of 1943 converged on Fortress Europe. From the south, so far distant were their thunders echoing in the Apennines that they scarce were heard north of the Alps. Block busters on German cities were devastating proof of very present foul weather; but, after all, such bomb smashes were intermittent, and though black nimbus clouds in westward Britain piled higher with every convoy and transport from America, the Continent still seemed immune from invasion out of the west. Not so on the east! There through all this ghastly year raged the mortal and final war storm, more widespread, more violent than any on record in German history.

It bore some resemblance to that of 1941 and 1942, but this time the all-conquering Germans were not plunging east to circle Leningrad and sight the longed-for Volga; instead they were in retreat. From river to river, from city to city they were crushed back toward their Fatherland. The gains of two superhuman years were erased, the brags of Hitler and Goebbels now proved a mockery by German dead, the flower of the wehrmacht scorched beneath the smoldering ruins of a dozen Russian cities, drowned in swamps, strewn carelessly by indifferent death in forests or on wind-swept steppes. This was the nightmare pressing down in 1943, impossible to dispel by radio or printed word, no matter how martial, how persuasive.

Churchill in May was to compare the Anglo-Saxon victory at Bizerte and Tunis with Gettysburg, to intimate that North Africa was the turning point of World War II. In doing so, he showed predilections natural, if not too sensible, in an average Englishman or American. If this war, however, had a Gettysburg it was in the blood-soaked ruins of Stalingrad, where on January 31, 1943, Field Marshal Von Paulus surrendered with fifteen other generals, and the tattered débris of an army which at the start of that year had numbered 330,000 men.

Six months before, the Russians were nailed down in Stalingrad. By November, 1942, besiegers had become besieged. By December the Russians had cut up and cut off opposing forces, driving them into pockets north, west and south of the city. Before Christmas, 1942, German military experts had advised withdrawal, only to be scolded by the ex-corporal at Berchtesgaden.

From the Berlin government came no explanation; how could there be one? Military disasters in 1941-1942 could be discounted by weather severity, but winter in 1942-1943 had been unusually mild. Hitler had not only promised victory at Stalingrad; he announced it. The Reich's veterans had driven through (some of them) to Volga bank. But 330,000 soldiers do not disappear overnight; they were gone, according to Nazi propaganda dying with their boots on for Fatherland and Führer; gone also was the dream of lebensraum, with hateful Slavs expelled and land overflowing with milk and honey for deserving Germans.

The day before Von Paulus laid down his arms was the tenth anniversary of the National Socialist régime. Hitherto it had always occasioned a Hitler speech. In 1943 the Führer was silent. Two months later he explained: "The winter crisis had only just been overcome"; "undeserved fate" had defrauded the Germans of the fruits of valor.

His words then were no more convincing than his previous silence had been. During the first three months of 1943 the Red armies won back, with the exception of the Crimea, almost all Russian soil occupied by Germans in 1942. At the end of 1942 the latter controlled much of the Caucasus and had forces there aggregating 300,000. By the spring of 1943, about all that was left the Germans was the Tasman Peninsula, bridgehead opposite the Crimea, and a short coastal strip south of it. The Russians had hoped to bag another German army in the Caucasus by cutting the Rostov-Baku railway but in this they were disappointed. Rostov, on the Sea of Azov, was in Soviet hands however, by February 14, and German threats to Soviet oil ended. Equal success crowned Red army campaigns in the Donetz and the Ukraine, and all the way north to Leningrad. Kharkov was taken and the Russians pressed beyond it toward Poltava, where Charles XII of Sweden had had his greatness crushed in the eighteenth century; the massive Nazi noose around Leningrad was somewhat relaxed; and a number of fortified hedgehogs with the rail connections between them were wrested from the German foe.

Then came spring thaws, this time aid and comfort to the retreating wehrmacht, discouragement to advancing Russians. The battle line in three months had been pushed four hundred miles west of Stalingrad, German lines of communication shortened, Russian lines extended. There was a lull in the fighting which encouraged Hitler who, for the third time and for the third year, ordered his army to the attack.

But it was a weakened wehrmacht that marched east that summer of 1943. The men were older, the boys younger than in 1941. This time their offense was strictly localized; no longer was it possible to engage the foe all the way from Black Sea to Baltic. For two weeks German panzer divisions forged ahead in the southern Ukraine, pushing back the Russians on a front some thirty-eight miles wide. Then the offense bogged down, and by the end of July a retreat was ordered.

German propaganda made that seem like victory; the Russians, it was said, had lost so many thousand tanks that they were impotent for the rest of the summer; the Russians were staging "a famine offense," because the Soviets were in danger of starvation without the food of the Ukraine; and even when Russians captured Orel, Stalino, Bryansk and Smolensk in the autumn, the explanation given in Berlin was one of wise Fabian tactics, a kind of strategic victory for clever German generals who voluntarily withdrew from such heavily fortified points of vantage.

Das Schwartze Korps generously chimed in on the army line: "With the surrendered territory we have lost economic war potential and political prestige." But, on the other hand, see what we have gained! "By shortening the front, reducing military reserves for securing territories, by shortening supply lines, we have, in the same breath of war, as it were, won capacity, material strength and hitting force."

Even thus did Germany win the war on paper. But the German

people are not fools; they had maps; they knew the war was going badly, a fact indirectly and naïvely acknowledged by Goebbels when he urged his countrymen to emulate the courage of the British and the Russians in defeat.

As shadows deepened over the Reich, Hitler spoke less frequently and in different strain. No longer did he boast of coming conquests but dwelt rather on how long Germany could withstand her enemies. All that was necessary was for her to hold out staunchly and her foes would tire. Had this not happened in the Seven Years War? Was it not obvious that the great Frederick had emerged triumphant even after the Russians had stormed Berlin? That, too, was Goebbels' theme. But he had others; bombed out civilians would have no chance to get their property restored if the Allies won the war; an American book had urged that Germans be made eunuchs; the "grey wolves" (U-boats) were being steadily improved and would yet starve England; new secret weapons in the blue-print stage would revolutionize the art of war. At times rumors of disaster were faked by Dr. Goebbels so that he could later prove them false, thus demonstrating the absurdity of listening to rumors.

The approaching fourth winter of the war found Germany jittery. There was plenty of money but nothing much to buy with it. Shops were closing all over the Reich and general trade was reduced to barter, a baby carriage for a frying pan, shoes for furniture. Everything was scarce in Germany. In May, 1943, some 30,000,000 persons were employed in field, factory and workshop, a larger number than in time of peace; but of these 12,000,000 were foreigners and of the Germans more than half were women and children. The output of the foreigners was estimated at only 65 per cent by prewar standards and that of the German workers at only 80 per cent, facts which indicated a lowered war potential at a time when the demand for war matériel was at its peak.

Without setting enemies and foreigners to work, outnumbered Germany could not survive; on the other hand, their presence caused uneasiness. A few came more or less willingly to the Reich and relative freedom of movement was granted them. But the great majority were either prisoners of war or deportees from the conquered areas. These had to be watched, confined in barracks. Armed guards and machine guns could and did prevent their rioting, but sloppy work is not easily proved, prevented or punished.

On the surface, discipline in the Reich was excellent. The only approach to disorder was at the University of Munich where some students were executed for advocating Hitler's overthrow. But there was much grumbling and latent fear, as was shown by party members ducking for safety, discarding Nazi insignia, acts against which ordinances were passed.

What kept all this rebelliousness from organizing and breaking out into the open was the appointment of Heinrich Himmler, on August 25, as home secretary. Most criminal in act and in nature of all the Nazis was this gestapo chieftain, a specialist in low cunning and sadistic cruelty, as well as in devilish insight and mastery of police work. His elevation to dictatorial authority over civilians, and the favors showered on his instrument, the SS forces, was proof that Hitler would stop at nothing to hold Germany to the war. If love of Führer and Fatherland could not do it, then fear and tyranny would. The SS, originally Hitler's Praetorian guard, numbered in the summer of 1943 some 1,000,000 men. Himmler enlarged it. Its functions were military and political; it had its own uniform and its own officers, answerable not to German generals but to Himmler; its purpose was terrorism; its political agencies the headsman's axe, the torture chamber and the concentration camp. The SS received higher pay than the wehrmacht; promotion was more rapid; its picked divisions fought to the last man, stiffening resistance on every front; and to its sponsor, Heinrich Himmler, now master of German destiny, it gave unswerving obedience.

And so approached the fifth winter of the war. From Narvik in Norway to Bordeaux, France; from Finland to Odessa still flew the Nazi flag. There was as yet no second front, and the Atlantic Wall, reinforced by heavy guns dragged from the Maginot line, seemed an insuperable obstacle to Anglo-American armies beyond the Channel moat; German armies held Rome and the war-worthy part of Italy. Except for a few guerrilla partisans in Yugoslavia, the entire Balkan Peninsula was under German domination, as well as Crete and the islands of the Aegean Sea.

Seen from without, the *Festung Europa* was impressive in its massive strength. The weaknesses within, which had commenced to sap and to corrode the capacity of its defenders to wage protracted war, were still insufficient to level it to the ground.

13. NIPPON'S EBBING TIDE

NINE months along, and the victorious typhoon of Hirohito's all-Asian team was slowing down. They were to fight hard and tenaciously throughout the Pacific, battling to retain what they had conquered; they were to win control over a corridor across Central China from Peiping on the north past Canton on the south, and with intermittent success to operate the railroads along it; they were to invade Manipur in India, an up-ended province northeast of Bengal, an eruption more spectacular than decisive; but elsewhere they were to be thrown back and held back. They had been surfeited on success; to digest what they had swallowed was now task enough, and perhaps too much, even for the children of a Sun Goddess.

Pessimists were certain that even after Germany had unconditionally surrendered several weary years of exhaustive, tough fighting would be necessary to smash Japan. They pointed to the unique geographical isolation of Nippon and its empire, to the well-guarded inland sea beyond which and at easy distance lay the mineral wealth of Manchukuo; they stressed the far-flung shield of the Ryukyu Islands south and southeast of the adversary's homeland, the Bonin and Volcano Islands to the southeast, the Kurils in curving line from north to east well-nigh to Kamchatka, island wardens along the innermoat of Hirohito's hidden country. And out beyond the Ryukyus was Taiwan (Formosa) and far beyond Taiwan were Hainan, the Philippines, Borneo, Sumatra, Java, the Malay states and French Indo-China, to enclose the whole China Sea with the arrayed imperial outposts of Japan. And still farther, barrier beyond barrier, the once mandated islands in the Marianas, the Carolines, the Marshalls. Here were stationary aircraft carriers past which, if unconquered, it would not be safe for us to venture. Nor was this all. South and east of the Marshalls our foe's talons clutched the once British-owned Gilberts, a threat to Fiji and to the Australian-American life-line, clutched also at the northern coastline of New Guinea, New Britain, and all the Solomons except

286

for one airstrip on Guadalcanal fiercely held by too few American marines.

There seemed no way to get effectively at Japan. Fog and tempest forbade a northern route along the endless Aleutians; island-hopping straight across the world's greatest ocean was possible but precarious; so also was an invasion of the Philippines from Australian bases, even if first New Guinea be conquered, or neutralized. Either way, Tokyo held the trumps. As for rooting those foes out of China: how get to China; and once there, whence would come oil for planes, shells for cannons, food for hungry men? These pessimists were sure that Uncle Sam did not sufficiently know how, and would not spend the money and men, the time and materials that must be paid to win Pacific peace.

Optimists, however, though not ignoring too many outstanding facts, held others equally important. Once Germany went under, they said, Japan would front the hostile world. The United States, Britain, China, a revitalized France and Netherlands would be assured enemies; Russia might not forget Port Arthur, nor how one time the Bear dipped its claws in the Gulf of Pechili, nor the ever ominous threat of Tokyo's bombers over Vladivostok. The air power which had laid German factories in rubbish would be twice as potent against Nippon. Her industries, more highly centralized than those of Germany and far more inflammably housed, would be blasted and burned by such superforts as never had visited Hamburg or Berlin. Iron and coal might yet be had from Manchukuo, but oil only in driblets or not at all. Darting about over and under the South China Sea, our planes and submarines based on the rewon Philippines would destroy Japanese shipping along that all-vital oil route, and without oil no war nation lives. We already had air-fields in China; soon we would have more. Some island bases would have to be wrested from Japan the hard way, but others could be by-passed and starved out. Furthermore, there were our new carriers, larger and larger carriers, more and more of them, not only American but also British. Russia most likely would help toward the end, and Britain would keep her pledged word at once. Then, too, in modern war it is not primarily morale, numbers or geography—all of which the great powers have—that determines the issue, but technological skill. The Japanese possessed a great deal, but we possessed much more. Americans were not necessarily superior to Britons, Japanese or Germans in inventing and in operating machines, but where technology involved wholesale training, production and distribution, then, owing to our resources, security, and our irreverence for tradition, we rated first of all the nations. Upon this technological superiority-in-fact we could build to shorten the Allies' Pacific war against Tokyo.

TUG OF WAR

Meanwhile, during the second half of 1942, the British and Americans in the Pacific were on the defensive; the former engaged in regrouping and renewing their badly mangled Anglo-Indian forces after the Burma fiasco, the latter in trying to make safe their foothold on Guadalcanal, the Australians, powered by American flyers, doing likewise in Papua.

For several months the fortunes of war had swayed back and forth in the South Pacific, the Japanese abandoning their hit-and-run tactics at Guadalcanal for new and desperate efforts to evict the American marines there and to take Port Moresby in Papua.

"Down the slot," the inland waterway between the Solomon Islands, plied the Tokyo Express (regularly scheduled air attack), and night after night reinforcements were slipped into Guadalcanal to strengthen the hostile forces hemming in our marines. Then in late October, 1942, came the first of the Japanese major assaults. It struck hard by land and by sea. On October 25 five waves of infantry supported by tanks were hurled against the western perimeter of the American lines and barely were repulsed. Next day on the south those lines of ours were penetrated. Could this added attack have come simultaneously, as planned, with those on the western flank, we probably would have lost Guadalcanal. Fortunately the enemy columns circling to the south were held up all day by difficult terrain, and on October 27 were forced back into the jungle. The attackers were also defeated by sea. We lost the carrier *Hornet* and a destroyer; how many hostile ships were sunk is still a matter for conjecture. At any rate, a good many of them were hit by our bombs and all withdrew.

Next month the Mikado's men tried again, this time with augmented force both naval and military. But meanwhile, despite essential priorities given the expeditionary force in North Africa, our garrison on Henderson Field had been strengthened, so also our fleet in adjacent waters. It was just as well. For two days and

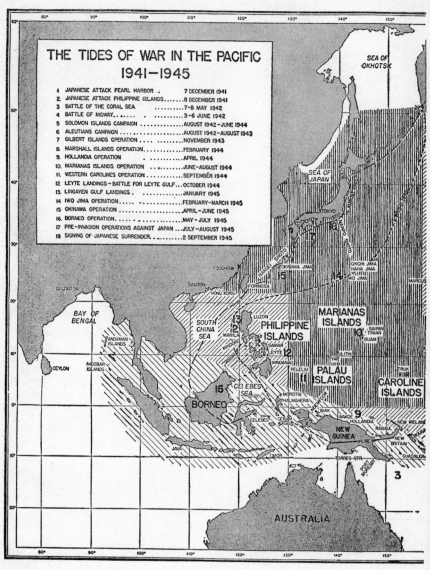

THE TIDES OF WAR IN THE PACIFIC
1941–1945

1   JAPANESE ATTACK PEARL HARBOR .   7 DECEMBER 1941
2   JAPANESE ATTACK PHILIPPINE ISLANDS......8 DECEMBER 1941
3   BATTLE OF THE CORAL SEA   ....7-8 MAY 1942
4   BATTLE OF MIDWAY....... .   ...3-6 JUNE 1942
5   SOLOMON ISLANDS CAMPAIGN ....AUGUST 1942-JUNE 1944
6   ALEUTIANS CAMPAIGN ....AUGUST 1942-AUGUST 1943
7   GILBERT ISLANDS OPERATION ....NOVEMBER 1943
8   MARSHALL ISLANDS OPERATION............FEBRUARY 1944
9   HOLLANDIA OPERATION   . ...APRIL 1944
10 MARIANAS ISLANDS OPERATION .. ..JUNE-AUGUST 1944
11 WESTERN CAROLINES OPERATION ....SEPTEMBER 1944
12 LEYTE LANDINGS - BATTLE FOR LEYTE GULF...OCTOBER 1944
13 LINGAYEN GULF LANDINGS . ...JANUARY 1945
14 IWO JIMA OPERATION.... ....FEBRUARY-MARCH 1945
15 OKINAWA OPERATION ....APRIL-JUNE 1945
16 BORNEO OPERATION....................MAY-JULY 1945
17 PRE-INVASION OPERATIONS AGAINST JAPAN ...JULY-AUGUST 1945
18 SIGNING OF JAPANESE SURRENDER. ....2 SEPTEMBER 1945

THE TIDES OF WAR

(Official U. S.

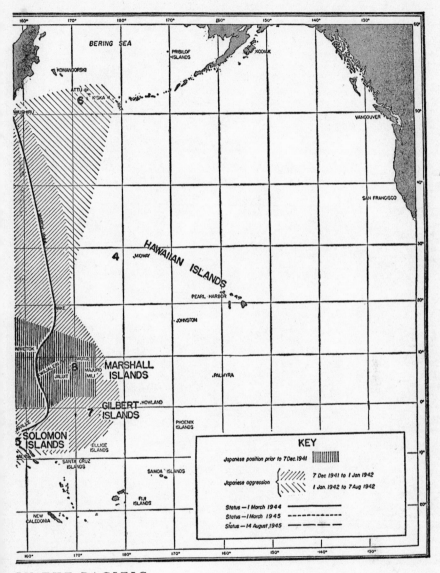

IN THE PACIFIC

Navy Photograph)

two nights, November 13-15, an intermittent and highly complicated naval engagement raged on, with battleships and heavy cruisers thrown in by both sides. We had somewhat the better of it, for one hostile battlewagon was sunk, none of ours, and no less than eight troopships packed with enemy soldiers were sent down to death. The Japanese fleet withdrew, never again to try for a knockout blow in the southern Solomons; but we did not pursue, indication enough that we had not escaped unscathed.

December, January, February, fighting still continued; this time the Japanese on the defensive, the Americans on the warpath. We reinforced our troops; the army took over from the marines; and we surrounded the Japanese encampments, only to find on February 8, 1943, that Guadalcanal had been evacuated.

ISLANDS NOBODY LOVES

So, too, was it to be a fortnight earlier with Papua, Australian New Guinea, where hostile resistance ceased January 22, 1943. Across that dripping Papuan rain forest from east to west ran the tangled masses and ranges of the Owen Stanley Mountains. North of these on the Bismarck Sea lay the Japanese-held village of Buna; on the southern side was Port Moresby, only slightly more populous. It was Australia's strategic outpost upon the Coral Sea and held by Aussies. A jungle trail, difficult to find, more difficult to traverse, wound snakelike through the humid mountains over a 7,000-foot pass. The ambitious invaders, defeated in an effort to skirt the coastline, forced their way thither, and by September, 1942, were well out on the coastal plain where Port Moresby lay.

Then the Aussies and the Americans struck, the infantry at first all Australian, the airmen largely American. MacArthur had twenty less planes than three months earlier but he threw them all in at the adversary, and the Australian veterans of Libya compelled the withdrawal to the pass of the Japanese veterans of Nanking and Singapore. Here they stood at bay and not until November were they to be forced back to the coast. December, 1942, and January, 1943, and the Papuan campaign rose to as bloody a climax as any fought in this or in any other war. Nature proved a more vicious enemy than any armed soldiers could be. "Men slept for weeks in foot-deep mud, drenched to the skin by the cold, sweeping rains of the tropical mountain passes; slept while the giant jungle rats nibbled clumps out of their hair." But the attackers were trouble enough; they neither gave nor expected quarter; they built bunkers of palmetto logs and reinforced these with concrete and steel; they concealed their entrenchments with deft camouflage in dense vegetation and behind swampy estuaries. To destroy such positions by shell fire was all but impossible; one by one they had to be taken by hand grenade, knife and tommy gun, a beastly and a bloody business. Its nastiness was relieved by one fact only—the gentle care given to wounded whites by coal-black Papuans, a tribute both to Australian policy and American generosity in Papua and to Christian missions.

Against the Japanese bunkers MacArthur threw the national guard divisions from Michigan and Oregon, likewise the Aussies, more numerous in this campaign than the Americans. That the Yanks and Aussies won was due not simply to skill, weapons and dogged courage, but also to the U. S. Fifth Air Corps which transported men, food, munitions, and even tanks over the mountains. That air corps had multiple tasks daily; there was Rabaul, the main base on New Britain, to bomb; there was the Bismarck Sea to watch, over which convoys from New Britain skimmed with reinforcements for the hostile garrisons not only at Buna in Papua but also for those at Lae and Salamaua, farther up the coast in New Guinea; and there was the joint Australian-American army to supply. The force was shorthanded. The Japanese sometimes flew as many as one hundred planes in a sortie, but the biggest Allied raid over Rabaul had only thirty-seven planes and could only carry sixty tons of bombs, at a time when two hundred tons were dropped in a single raid on Germany. The Papuan offense could not have been carried on at all without this air force, since the lighter Australian planes could not be transformed into transports and the way overland through the mountains was too long and difficult for anything more pretentious than commando raiding.

With the coming of the spring in 1943 the tempo of the South Pacific campaign rose rapidly. Tokyo's strategists concentrated troops and shipping at their great base of Truk in the Carolines, so far north of Rabaul that it could not be reached effectively. From there they could and did add constantly to their garrisons in New Guinea and the Solomons. The Yanks and Aussies, however, under command of MacArthur were not to be denied. They took the offensive and were not to lose it again in this war; they skirted along the coast of New Guinea to lay siege to Lae and Salamaua; they repeated all over again their experiences in the swamps of Papua; and as this happened the Americans made it their particular business to rout enemy elements out of the central Solomon from whence annoying air raids were still attacking Guadalcanal.

It was mid-September before Lae and Salamaua fell. The Japanese there strove desperately to hang on to their air-fields, to reinforce their garrisons. They had the manpower to do so, but not the transportation. The Battle of the Bismarck Sea in March had ended their hopes. It was an extraordinary sea fight, since on our side not a single vessel was involved. Twelve enemy transports, heavily protected by cruisers and destroyers, were spotted by our planes, which rained death on the ships below, sent 90,000 tons to the bottom, drowned 15,000 of their soldiers. Meanwhile, by landing craft and by parachute the Allies drove in for the kill. With Aussies pressing from one side and Yanks from another, the Japanese garrisons were caught. A few escaped to the jungle, the rest died. A part of northeastern New Guinea, an Australian mandate, was added to Allied Papua and a goodly slice cut from one tentacle of Tokyo threatening Australia. Nevertheless the Aussies kept right on. In October they took Finschhafen, in November, Satelburg, and were advancing overland toward Madang on the north coast. By the end of 1943 the slow and sanguinary process of digging out the Japanese from their close armored nests in New Guinea was well under way.

Simultaneously another arm was torn from the Japanese octopus where it gripped the Solomons. At Munda in New Georgia the enemy had an air base much closer to Guadalcanal than Rabaul in New Britain, and Munda we decided to take. The operation proved long and costly. Before New Georgia could be invaded outlying islands must first be occupied, the Russells, Rendova, and Woodlark. Even after we landed on New Georgia, the advance was yard by yard. Despite bulldozers, tanks and flame throwers, the defenders stuck to their posts until late in August, large numbers escaping then by air. We were now halfway "up the ladder" from the southern Solomons. Still further north lay Bougainville, bigger than New Georgia. Our marines rolled ashore at Empress Augusta Bay in November but the Japanese took to the hills and we did not follow them; instead we isolated their air-fields by the seizure of key islands farther north. By the end of 1943 the Solomons were no longer a menace to our march ahead.

THE ALEUTIANS

By the second half of that year the foe were being hit all over the Pacific. American submarines were ranging far and wide across hostile communication lines; in the Aleutians our infantry was slugging it out hand to hand with the enemy; and the United States Marine Corps was adding Tarawa to the list of its distinguished actions.

One year earlier the Japanese without a blow had captured the island of Kiska, halfway down the Aleutian chain to Alaska. On it they worked with fierce determination to construct and equip an air-field. Some sixty miles to the east was Amchitka. On this we built an air-field of our own from whence to attack Kiska. Weather permitting (it generally didn't) we kept this hostile air-field under bombardment. As soon as our flyers left it useless, the enemy restored it again. The American command therefore decided to crack down on fog-shrouded Kiska by encirclement. Some 170 miles west of Kiska was Attu, upon which we landed in force during mid-May.

For eighteen days our GIs scarcely knew whether the weather or the Japanese was the worst enemy. Our landings, both to the north and to the south were unopposed; but when it came to pushing inland through the deep ravines and being ambushed by snipers hidden on the mountain slopes, then death took a hand. Five days passed before the two American expeditions met, only to find their hardest work still ahead. The soldiers of Nippon were most excellently screened in their base at Chichagov Harbor. Between them and the Americans were mountains 2,000 feet high, swept by snowstorms and thick fogs, and between the mountains were precipitous winding passes of over 800 feet elevation. The Japanese had dug in skilfully; their final defenses could only be reached along a ridge so narrow that two men could not walk abreast thereon, a ridge treacherous half the time from fog and with a sheer drop 200 feet down on both sides. Manpower lugged up the ammunition in this campaign; soldiers fought, ate, and slept in wet snow, or on stones, or on soggy, treacherous tundra; Japs and Yanks stumbled into each other's mist-hidden fox holes; and a hundred miniature mêlées between half-seen combatants scattered by fog and wind made up the summary of the Attu adventure. May 30, and that island, not good for much but still American terrain, had been gripped and firmly held by our forces.

The wind-up of the Aleutian campaign came quickly. The Attu conquest had enabled us to dig in well to the west of the chief enemy base at Kiska; we had that island at our mercy; all that remained necessary was to soften it by intense bombardment from the air and from the sea, and then move in on foot as before. But to our surprise and even to our annoyance, Kiska proved to be quite empty. Some 10,000 Mikado soldiers had slipped through our fog-bedeviled blockade and had betaken themselves far elsewhere. It was a victory of a sort for the United States, or was it? Anyhow, we got Kiska.

TARAWA

The American occupation of Kiska sealed off Alaska from any would-be conquerors but accomplished little else. The Aleutians gave us a spring-board from whence to bomb the Kurils and we did so (intermittently); but the game was scarcely worth the candle. Distances, even for our new planes, were phenomenally long; williwaws, terrific and sudden storms characteristic of the North Pacific, were frequent; and the Kurils were far distant from Hokkaido, northernmost of the Japanese home islands, mountainous, underpopulated, far from the heart of the enemy's empire. Not by attack from the north could the foe's life blood be drained.

The major American offensive therefore continued in the second half of 1943 to be directed against the Solomons and the great enemy base at Rabaul on New Britain to the north. But the way thither was long, some 7,200 miles of circuitous steaming from Hawaii to Port Moresby. The route lay almost due south from Honolulu to Samoa, then curved westward to Fiji and New Caledonia, then north by west to the Solomons. The Japanese-held Carolines, Marshalls and Gilberts lay athwart any direct approach to Australia and the Central Pacific, and until they were either taken or neutralized the recovery of the Philippines was just as impossible as any direct major assault on Hirohito's tensely guarded mainland.

The task of wresting the Gilberts, the nearest of all those islands to our life-line, fell mainly to the navy and marines. Sixteen island groupings comprised that archipelago, about equal in area to one-half of New York City. None were as mountainous as the Carolines, and granted East Pacific naval supremacy, which was ours by November, 1943, their conquest seemingly should have been easier than that of Attu.

But it did not prove so, our four-day fight for Tarawa, keystone of the Gilbert area, being the most costly thus far experienced in the war against Japan. Tarawa was a typical atoll, a cluster of some twenty-five islands grouped in a ragged circle around a lagoon, the islands only a few feet in elevation, most of them joined together at low water by a coral barrier reef. On one, Betio, less than one square mile of land, the garrison had built an air-field and had here stationed some 4,000 of their best fighters. This was the American objective.

As the U. S. marines set out in their landing barges it seemed as though most of the island's defenders must be dead, for hour after hour our battlewagons, cruisers and destroyers had been lobbing shells on Betio; hour after hour American planes had filled the sky, dropping thousands of their smashing eggs on this narrowly constricted target; hour after hour dense smoke had risen from Betio. But our landing barges could not get near shore. A reef far from land obstructed the way and the marines had to be transferred from barges to amphtracks, amphibious contrivances capable of carrying a few men on either land or water. This led to much confusion; the defending garrison, far from dead, strafed both barges and amphtracks; of the latter there were an insufficient number, and our men got ashore as best they could, many of them wading two or three hundred yards waist-high in water, carrying full equipment, many of them dying without touching land.

After one day of fighting they held only a few yards of narrow beach-head. On Betio the enemy had constructed some 500 pill boxes, most of them made of a double section of palmetto logs, filled with sand, covered with sand, almost impossible to destroy by shell fire, impossible to locate with precision from the air or the sea. Here, dug in and armed to the teeth, the Imperial Japanese marines fought to the last man, taking their own lives by hugging exploding hand grenades to their chests rather than surrender. Of our first men ashore almost all died, and in many of the pill boxes were found later two or three dead marines, six or seven dead Japanese. The American dead had given a good account of themselves; they had to die so that their comrades might conquer, for we were in haste to take Tarawa.

Betio once won, and Abemama and Makin, also atolls, the two former by marines, the latter by the army, and the Gilberts by the end of November were ours. The long process of leap-frogging across the far Pacific waters had really begun. And the annals of the United States Marine Corps had another name, Tarawa, as illustrious in their annals as Tripoli in North Africa, Fisher's Island, North Carolina, or Chateau Thierry in 1918, or Guadalcanal of the Solomons.

CHINA—BURMA—INDIA, 1943

1943 was about to close and almost imperceptibly the long, slow tide of this far-flung war was turning. In what became later known as the CBI theater (China, Burma, India) the change was least noticeable, but even here one glimpsed indications that the co-prosperity sphere would ultimately be eased out of all suddenly taken conquests on the Asiatic mainland.

In China the "Flying Tigers" (American airmen employed by the Chinese Republic before Pearl Harbor) had been transformed into the United States Fourteenth Air Force, reinforced, disciplined. The "ships" it used were mostly old, but a few big Liberators had been flown in; and many new air-fields were in course of construction. There were no bulldozers to level them out overnight, only Chinese coolies dragging rollers by hand; but the Japanese no longer hogged the air, and their terrible bomber raids dwindled to a few hit-and-run affairs. Now the Fourteenth Air Force could hit back, bombing enemy railway trains, the shipping on the Yangtze River; destroying hostile installations opposite Hongkong. A trickle of American supplies rode in over "The Hump" (air route from India) and steadily grew larger. Then, too, there was the fiercely hopeful prospect of opening the Ledo Road, a back-door entrance from India to take the place of the Burma Road, two-thirds of which was in the foeman's hands. Monsoons and malaria, jumbled mountains and jungles made progress slow, but yard by yard the bulldozers tore away the festering forests, and Negro troops from America withstood vile hardships in an enterprise which some day would link China to her Allies, whether or not the Japanese were driven from Burma.

In India, meanwhile, the utter inability of the British to imagine their own incompetence and danger tided them over both, as so many times in their past history. As things stood, all but the northern tip of Burma was lost; Japanese planes skimmed over the Bay of Bengal, disaffection was rife, the India congress had proclaimed rebellion. But this did not ruffle Wavell, sent from Egypt to be India's viceroy. He kept Gandhi, Nehru and all leading congressmen in gaol, reorganized the Anglo-Indian army as best he might, prepared to invade Burma, and probably kept up his reading in Browning.

Early in 1943 the British had made a counter-thrust here against the invaders. It was on a most limited scale but won its objectives, largely because of the ability and courage of Major Charles Wingate, an outstanding hero of this war.

Wingate's career paralleled in many ways that of Chinese Gordon, England's erratic roving soldier of the later nineteenth century. Both were masters of the unexpected, devoted to military science, scornful of brass hats, distinguished for exploits in frontier warfare, famous for winning the friendship of rough tribesmen, and assiduous in their study of the Old Testament. As a young officer in Palestine, Wingate had won his spurs by capturing Arab guerrillas; as a major in the British army his exploits in Ethiopia with a rickety plane, camels and native warriors had become legendary; and now Wavell gave him a free hand in Burma.

He introduced something new in warfare. The long protracted hardening of average raw recruits into tough, resilient units was not new, nor was the painstakingly minute drill in geographic lore upon which Wingate insisted: what he did that was novel was to plan a campaign in all its details and involving several thousand men, in which commissariat and munitions were to be transported entirely by plane. Food had been dropped from the air to succor the fleeing remnants of British troops in Burma. Now Wingate proposed to articulate the plane so closely to his projected offense that it would replace railroads, motor trucks, bullock trains, and make possible a victorious rapidity of movement despite rain, forest and jungle.

Early in February, 1943, Major, now General Wingate, led his troops over the Indian border. He called them "Chindits," a name derived from the curious carvings, part lion, part griffin, which protected Burmese temples from the devil. For over two months the Chindits were to emulate on Asiatic land what Elizabeth's sea dogs did to Spain on oceanic waters, to harass and wear down an enemy too potent for them to challenge face to face.

The immediate task was to sever hostile communication lines. These ran north and south following the valley of the Chindwin, the Irrawaddy and the Salween rivers. Most important of all was the north-south railway line from Mandalay to Myitkyina. To get there, the Chindits must drive east-west, over high mountains, chain after chain of jumbled ranges, down through deep valleys, roughing it over bridle paths or no paths at all. For this sort of frontiering they had been especially trained; Wingate's men were a new type of British soldier, guerrillas par excellence, copying Asiatic tactics, going the foeman one better.

Wingate divided his men into three columns. They demolished the Mandalay railway in seventy-five places and blew up three steel bridges as well; they ambushed ammunition trains and captured supply dumps. Scattering to right and left they evaded capture. They were fed and supplied throughout by aërial transport, the RAF flying 50,000 plane miles in their support. With each column went an RAF officer in radio contact with his planes. Smoke signals by day, flares by night, and from the skies rained gasoline, munitions, food, rum, clothes, even false teeth and spectacles, whatever the portable radio ordered.

By the time Wingate's roughies won back to India they had raided on foot over 1,000 miles, penetrated to the east of the Irrawaddy River, disrupted communications over a strategic area of 10,000 square miles in North Burma, killed several thouand foemen, proved that a small army could be fed, clothed and armed, even in the tropics, by air.

Britain, however, had mighty little to spare for such costly fighting in Burma. General Lord Louis Mountbatten was sent out and by agreement with President Roosevelt was to head the South East Asia command for the United Nations. Mountbatten flew to Chungking to confer with Chiang Kai-shek and our generals Stilwell and Somervell. But all this was preparatory merely. Until new air-fields in great number were built and equipped in India, both for the RAF and the United States Tenth Air Force, no large-scale offense could be launched against our implacable enemy in that humid-hot malarial jungle of a dysentery-ridden land.

TOWARD THE PHILIPPINES

Two years had run since Pearl Harbor and as yet the combined Anglo-Saxon-Americanos had only scratched the periphery of Nippon's empire. Viewed around a globe or along the map its new imperial façade seemed almost as imposing now as in the early summer of 1942—just a single dent here and there like Tarawa and Kiska, only minutely visible in terms of mileage and acreage. But there was a more hopeful way of looking at it, and that from the perspective of shipyards rather than of maps. Battlewagons, plane carriers, baby flat-tops, cruisers, destroyers, submarines were laid down, launched, completed to flow out over the oceans in such ever increasing volume that within these two years after Pearl Harbor our fleet topped all others combined, dwarfed that of Britain and stood far superior in tonnage and weight of metal to that of Tokyo. Despite onerous losses, the number of our naval vessels in commission had nearly quadrupled, and the total of our naval planes had been augmented some 1,000 per cent. "The personnel required to man these ships and planes, with their shore stations, expanded, in the two years between Pearl Harbor and 1944, from less than half a million officers and men, including the marine corps and the coast guard, to three million." [1]

It was obvious that the war against Japan could not be won by the navy alone: nevertheless our sailors would have to clear the battle areas for the soldiers, provide the means whereby our fighters on foot might land. That meant landing barges, a device of long ago for landing horses via ramps upon a hostile beach, now a new type of power-propelled vessel developed by British and American ingenuity without which the coming victories of 1944 in both Europe and in the Pacific would have been impossible.

By 1944 we had floated some 80,000 of these craft carrying the American flag. They ranged from the LCRS (landing craft, rubber, small), which held at most seven men, to the LSD (landing ship dock), a dry dock over 450 feet in length crammed with power vehicles and manned by a crew of more than two hundred. In between was every conceivable type the ingenuity of man could devise. There was the "buffalo," an amphibious tank mounting several guns. There was the LCVP (landing craft, vehicles and personnel); the LCM (landing craft medium), to take either sixty

[1] *The World at War* (Washington, D. C., The Infantry Journal), p. 232.

soldiers or thirty tons of supplies; the LCT (landing craft, tanks); the LST (landing ship, tanks) with a complement of 132 men and officers, a cavernous vessel so large that it tucked away in its bowels several smaller type of landing craft filled with still other devices; and the LCIL (landing craft, infantry, large), each capable of putting on shore more than two hundred troops and equipped with machinery to pull itself from a beach back to the open sea. These were the principal American types. The British had still others, as for instance, the LBK (landing barge, kitchen) and the LBF (landing barge, flak). These ships, if they may be called such, were to play as important a rôle in the war as even the submarine or the destroyer. Thanks to our resources, our workers and our vast experience in mass production of machinery, autos, and so forth, the American navy really had the tools to do the job.

By February, 1944, our sea power, in this ultra-modern guise, had grown to such colossal proportions that it was ready to clear the ocean paths all across the Pacific. Never in all history could there possibly have been any enterprise remotely resembling this, a giant-size transoceanic offense over waterways three times any Atlantic distances, involving conquest en route of desperately defended enemy islands; and all the complexities of it concurrent with an even vaster amphibious task in conjunction with Britain, off Normandy beaches, at the opposite end of the world.

The Abemama, Makin and Tarawa battles had won for us a firm hold on the Gilberts two months earlier, precious time put to good use by the indefatigable Seabees (naval construction engineers) who worked day and night subduing conquered fields to our new uses. But northwest of the Gilberts were the Marshalls, another and even larger archipelago, Japanese mandated-island areas, terra incognita and forbidden to foreigners for many years. There were thirty-two islands in the Marshalls, spaced out over hundreds of ocean miles, most of them enclosing spacious lagoons each with its chain of islets. The Marshalls lay across the direct line between the Gilberts and Japan, and were much closer to the all-important Carolines, northeast of New Guinea, than the Gilberts. Quite evidently the Americans had to nail down a few of the Marshalls before proceeding to do anything further.

We did so. Kwajalein atoll was our chosen objective. Not so close to us as the strongly defended Wotje or Jaluit, administrative capital, Kwajalein's thirty-two islets encircled the largest lagoon in the world, and planes based on its air-fields could sweep 600 miles around through all the Marshalls. This time preparations were rather more thorough than at Tarawa. Our naval force was larger, including the very newest battleships and flat-tops we had, a far stronger fleet than any heretofore assembled in the Pacific. The bombardment was heavier and more prolonged. And our planes made so many feints in so many directions that at last we caught the enemy by surprise.

Plans called for a simultaneous landing both to the north and south. On the north were two islands connected by a causeway, Roi and Namur, dominating the entrance to the lagoon and sufficiently large for an excellent air-strip. Similarly situated on the southern end of the atoll was Kwajalein, commanding a second entrance to the lagoon, also having an air-strip and a seaplane base. Our marines made good at the north; so, too, the United States army on the south. More men were engaged than at Tarawa but losses were proportionately much less. There was no difficulty with the landing craft, no trouble with the tide, and enemy installations had been much more thoroughly demolished before we threw our men ashore. This time our preliminary firepower was more effective because it came from three directions instead of two. At either end of the atoll we seized nearby islets before the grand assault on the whole fortress began. Landing artillery on these minor objectives, we were able to fire on Roi and Kwajalein not only from the air and sea but likewise from land batteries. The capture of Kwajalein atoll was the first of our February victories.

Others were to follow. Our fleet swept on westward, by-passed the eastern Carolines, and by the middle of the month was close enough to Truk, the vaunted secret Gibraltar of Japan in the mandated South Pacific, to attack it and the Japanese ships there from American plane carriers. Our planes sank twenty-three hostile vessels and wiped out 201 planes. We had hoped for more, since Truk was reputed to be the rendezvous of Tokyo's main fleet. But the cruisers, destroyers and auxiliary craft we did sink made up in part for Pearl Harbor and gave a sad shock to Japan's pride, as shown by the immediate dismissal of her naval chief of staff. To Japan this fortress Truk was no ordinary atoll. Within its spacious lagoon were several volcanic islands and many air-fields, and from its supposedly impregnable isolation the Japanese had sent their ships and reinforcements to New Britain, New Guinea and the Solomons.

The American navy had the men and the vessels to be seemingly everywhere at once in this vast Central Pacific. One day after Truk our ships hove to off Eniwetok, a Marshall atoll 340 miles beyond Kwajalein, and in three days more the flag flew over Engebi Island there and its air-strip. Two days later, February 21, our fleet was in the Marianas making reconnaissance close to Saipan, 3,000 miles west of Hawaii.

And as this came to pass, MacArthur's men kept right on moving forward in New Guinea, the Aussies and the Americans between them clearing the Huon Peninsula of Japanese, our marines doing likewise in the Green Islands between New Ireland and Bougainville, thus leaving the northern Solomons in complete isolation. February 24, and American leathernecks and doughboys, fighting across rugged country in New Britain, joined forces, thus wresting the western half of that island from the foe. And then on the very last day of the month the First Cavalry of the old U. S. army (jungle experts now) drove ashore and inland on the Admiralty Islands north of New Britain, isolating still further the enemy forces at Rabaul and coördinating MacArthur's pressure against Nippon from the southeast with the onslaught of our Navy throughout the Central Pacific. An encouraging February indeed.

All over the world America was now in the thick of it. In Italy, we were hacking our way heavily toward Rome; our troops were crowding into Britain by the hundred thousands, preparatory for D-Day; and in the Pacific, first doughboys, then sailors and marines, now here, now there, struck resounding blows at the wide-open Empire of Japan.

The tempo and the tension of the Pacific war tended to heighten. Before summer, MacArthur's campaign in New Guinea slogged out a glorious conclusion. Seven enemy-held air-fields were strewn out at irregular intervals along the malarial lowlands of that infernal island, and to have taken them one by one would have involved incommensurate sacrifice. Better to smash steadily at the air-fields until the Japanese air force was thoroughly pulverized there and then leap-frog westward along the coast. For that purpose the American general had at his command sixteen divisions, eight U. S. army, two U. S. marines, five Australian, one New Zealand; and all sixteen were to see action this decisive spring and summer of 1944. By the end of April, MacArthur had jumped 500 miles to the west to Hollandia in Dutch New Guinea. Two landings here, a pincer-closing movement, a march inland through crocodile-infested swamps, U. S. Hellcats, Avengers, Douglas dive-bombers in the air; buffalos, half-tracks, jeeps, bulldozers vomited out of a U. S. LSD (landing ship dock) on land, and very shortly Hollandia was ours, this time the foe preferring flight to the hills rather than to face such tremendous odds; June 20, and Biak Island off the northwestern tip of New Guinea was taken; another month and we had gone one hundred miles farther to the west. Within three hours, thanks to our paratroopers, Numfor Island was occupied, and the Philippines were now but 800 miles away.

As far as the United States was concerned, the South Pacific War, as such, might be said to be concluded. There were still some 60,000 Japanese troops marooned in New Britain, 10,000 in New Ireland, and 20,000 in Bougainville. But there was now no time or cause to hunt them down; they had neither the supplies, serviceable planes, nor ammunition to put up much of a fight. And so we left them to the Aussies, somewhat to the consternation of the latter, who suspected these war-imported sons of Nippon might inter-breed with native women and bring forth within a generation or so a swarming host of hostile young warriors.

SAIPAN AND GUAM

Our Navy, meanwhile, roamed the East Pacific, apparently at will, seeking a battered foe not any too anxious to do battle, launch-ing attacks from carrier planes at Palau in the western Carolines, less than 600 miles from the Philippines and over 2,200 miles from the Marshalls, paying reconnaissance calls in force on the Mari-anas, Guam, Tinian, and Saipan. Whether we were headed straight west via Palau to the Philippines, or northwest from New Guinea to the same goal, or straight toward Tokyo by the Marianas route, was anybody's guess.

The last proved the choice of our strategists, and of the three largest islands in the Marianas they selected the most northern, Saipan. It was the right move; it meant invasion of Japan's inter-mediate defense waters; it skipped any possibility of attack from the other Carolines in our rear, or from the Bonins, or from the Philippines; it involved much more difficult terrain than any thus far encountered, and a stronger enemy garrison; and we had the stuff to do it all. Saipan had three air-fields and a seaplane base, and in distance was 3,800 miles west of Pearl Harbor, about 1,500 miles from either the Philippines or Japan, 110 miles north of Guam, still in hostile hands.

American strategy was on the scale of our strength. Simultaneously it planned to feint south from the Aleutians with bombers and cruisers against the Kurils, to assail the Japanese homeland with the new B-29 superforts now based on Chinese air-fields, to strike north from New Guinea at Yap, Palau and the Philippines, to bomb Truk, Nauru and Ponape in the Carolines, as well as to land on Saipan. Coördination was not perfect but it was pretty good, and though the Japanese got wind of our main objective before our marines were ashore another great victory was won, both by land and by sea.

Land fighting, involving the conquest of Saipan, and Tinian to the south of it, took from June 15 to August 1. As our doughboys were grimly fighting field by field across and along Normandy and forcing their way north through the Apennines, the marines on Saipan with flame throwers, bazookas and rifles were exterminating Japanese warriors in their island caves or mowing them down wholesale as they charged out headlong against American gunfire.

The fight for Saipan was more deadly than that at Tarawa, far more protracted than that at Kwajalein, for the island was long and tapering with a curving mountainous spine well suited for defense. In, under and behind every possible barrier the hostile snipers were located and their fire was deadly. The center of the battle line was reported as safe as anywhere else. First a hundred yards here and a hundred yards there, until finally the foe were forced back into a narrow pocket at the north. Here they re-formed and at last drove out in their frenetic banzai charge. All that were left of the hostile garrison threw themselves recklessly against the Americans and by sheer force of numbers well-nigh broke our ranks. Among their dead, and there were more than 22,000 counted, were high naval officers, including the admiral who smashed Pearl Harbor. Still other Japanese soldiers committed suicide rather than surrender, and the menace of the invader seemed so terrible that numbers of civilians threw themselves from cliffs, together with their children, rather than submit to such destruction as ours.

Where, meanwhile, was the adversary's fleet? This time it did appear at a distance, but only to hurry back to security in the Philippines after being badly mauled once more.

Thanks, probably, to an American submarine which chanced to slip a torpedo over on the *Shokaku*, one of the largest Japanese carriers, we learned in time that a large hostile fleet was rounding the northern Philippines on a course headed for Saipan. The admiral in command was not to come too close. He sent his planes ahead to fly to Saipan, to engage the Americans, to continue to Guam, to refuel there and to return. The Americans were ready for the attack and met it well out to sea. Everything went wrong for the foe. The field they tried for in Guam was so pitted by our bombs as to be utterly useless. They had no place to land; they had no fuel; they were shot down like so many ducks. In one day, June 19, 1944, 404 were lost at the cost to us of 27.

Nor was that all. Admiral Mitscher, with his Task Force 58, scouring the seas west of Saipan, had sent his planes ahead on a scouting party. It was well toward evening next day when they left our flat-tops; but they found their quarry as the day grew dim, sank one of the enemy's best carriers, damaged others, flew back, their fuel spent, to land in the dark as best they might. Some found their own flat-tops; others were lucky enough to get home on the decks belonging to other planes; some fell into the sea; a few were never heard of again. But the navy of Nippon received in this first battle in eastern Asiatic waters a crippling blow.

Shortly after came the reconquest of Guam, in its way as formidable a military obstacle as Saipan. Once more there was a stiff work-out against mountain terrain, resistance to the death. Early in August it was all over and the Marianas, all three, were added to the American string of Pacific islands. In Tokyo the loss of Saipan had forced the resignation of Premier Tojo. In his own oblique way he stated the facts of disaster. "Japan," he said, "has come to face an unprecedentedly great national crisis.... The situation now approaches when the opportunity will occur to crack the enemy and to win the victory." Alarm in Tokyo was well founded. Between that city and our men lay only the Bonin and Volcanic Islands; between them and the Chinese coast but one island, Formosa; and between them and the Philippines only the Palau Islands in the western Carolines, and Halmahara and Morotai northwest of New Guinea.

LEYTE

September, 1944, and the American onsweep in Pacific waters continued. From Iwo Jima in the Volcanic Islands to Celebes in the East Indies our planes were circling, and the MacArthur campaign for the Philippines gathered more momentum. It was skilfully coördinated. As the marines hacked away at the enemy in the Palaus, MacArthur boldly by-passed Halmahara and took Morotai. He was now but 250 miles from the nearest of the Philippines, his new island bagged with relative ease. The Palaus were harder to crack. Peleliu Island proved worse than Guadalcanal. "Bloody Nose Ridge" was terrain so rough that merely to lose one's footing caused serious injuries. The island was hollow with caves, the caves replete with foemen, many with their machine guns chained to them. To clear these dens was a sanguinary and lethal job. Nevertheless, by the end of the month it was so far accomplished as to make Peleliu's air-field available, the Philippines being 600 miles distant.

The war with Japan was still two months short of three years and American planes were soaring again over the Philippines, knocking out of the skies in one day more enemy aircraft than we lost in the Bataan fighting, and sinking in Manila Bay no less than forty Japanese ships. We were coming back.

The Yanks arrived October 20 in the central Philippines and, somewhat to the surprise of military commentators, on the eastern side of Leyte Island. It had been generally assumed that MacArthur would first invade Mindanao in the south, since to by-pass that large island with its excellent air-strips would be risky, and not a few prognosticators had claimed that the Sulu archipelago still farther south was the logical objective. But the American armed forces had long since proved that leap-frogging was the best of tactics; and so we jumped clear to the heart of the Philippines, 600 ships convoying and transporting some 250,000 men, a sea invasion of tremendous magnitude, more dangerous than the Anglo-American invasion of North Africa nearly two years earlier.

Tokyo determined now to put in a lot more blue chips. Their total forces in the Philippines were about equal to our own but widely scattered, ours were concentrated. On the other hand, their navy, though somewhat too much battered and particularly deficient in light craft and carriers, had nevertheless a major advantage.

It could menace our fleet of transports by any one of three different routes: across the Sulu Sea, south of Leyte, from the direction of Singapore; across the China Sea through the San Bernardino Straits north of Leyte; and from farther north, skirting the eastern shores of Luzon and Samar, to hit our transports from the east. It was now or never for Japan, and she must strike quickly before our shore footing was secure. She did her best to do so, and from all three directions. Those were anxious days late in October as we divided our naval strength to face this triple threat, for none could tell which one of the three enemy task forces packed the greater punch. We met all three and drove them back. At one time our defenseless transports were stripped of naval coverage and severe, even catastrophic damage might have overtaken them had it not been for the audacity, courage and skill of our motor torpedo boats, destroyers, light craft and airmen. But the final results were more than satisfactory. In three crucial engagements the enemy naval power was crippled, three of their battleships and six heavy cruisers being sunk, also one large carrier and several small ones, to say nothing of lighter craft and not far short of 700 planes. Out of a total of some sixty hostile ships, only a few destroyers escaped undamaged. Thus by "Navy Day," T. R.'s birthday, October 27, 1944, the sea power of Tokyo was, as Admiral Halsey reported, "beaten, routed and broken." It was our own American Trafalgar.

The American navy reported the loss of the carrier *Princeton* and that of a few destroyers and escort carriers. "Other damage" was said to be light. It may have been heavier than we wished the Japanese to know. The latter announced a smashing victory. "The ghastly annihilation of Allied naval units," said the Tokyo radio, "resulted in forty-five ships sunk"—a cryptic statement in view of the fact that there were left only remnants of their three fleets, and that these were never again to trouble us in Philippine waters during this war.

The Mikado's army, however, could dig in on land and so put up much more of a fight; it constantly brought fresh forces into Leyte from the neighboring islands; it slipped them in by night as on Guadalcanal; it contested every swamp and hilltop. Incessant rain, knee-deep mud, last ditch warriors in multitudinous caves— it was the old, hard story of a dozen islands. An invasion of Leyte's west coast, paralleling the main attack on the east, finally did the trick, cut the Japanese forces into segments as our planes time and time again flattened down their dwindling air strength throughout all the Philippines. On the third anniversary of Pearl Harbor the red and white flag of the Sun Goddess still waved over a corner of Leyte, but with the United States navy master of the sea and our planes darkening the skies, our ultimate recapture of the Philippines was assured. Had the course of the war in Asia only been as favorable as that in the Pacific, the doom of Hirohito's empire would have been closer at hand.

CHINA IN 1944

As Japan's grip was pried loose on sundry Pacific atolls and loosened on various of the Philippines, it tightened on the far-flung misery of China. No longer were the invaders content with hit-and-run air raids on Chungking or ground forays into China's rice bowl followed by retreats. Now they sought instead to cut China in two by a constantly widening corridor north and south from Peiping and on down to the border of French Indo-China. And, what was even more serious, they drove us away from one air-field after another, hitherto used by our Twentieth Air Command in bombarding Tokyo, and by our Fourteenth Air Force, which under General Chennault had long and successfully smashed at Japanese installations all over China.

After endless years of anarchy and grueling war, China was played out and bogged down. Financial inflation was rampant over the prostrate country; lend-lease aid came dribbling in but slowly, all of it borne by air from India; a dubiously pro-Japanese government, presided over by a Chinese carpet-bagger, functioned after the fashion of such rascals at Nanking; in North China so-called Communists had their own régime, bitterly oppressed by and opposed to the landlords and loan sharks of the Kuomingtang party who ruled what it could reach of China from air-battered Chungking; and Chiang Kai-shek, the generalissimo, rapidly aging, always supersensitive, surrounded by politicians of Asiatic craft and greed, did not take kindly to relentless pressure applied by our own high-octane general, Joseph Stilwell (Vinegar Joe), chief of staff for the Burma theater.

In China there were wars within wars, in particular that between the Chinese Communists and the Kuomingtang, occasionally breaking out in open strife, soldier against soldier, gun against gun, more often smouldering under cover, a feud of factions contending for the loyalty of starving men and for the lordship of wasted lands.

This internecine strife had long been far from new, and the quarrels it engendered dated back to the twenties. In 1937 the breach was partially healed; but old sores festered, to break out with renewed fury by the forties, and in 1944 there were two distinct régimes in China, united only by hatred of Tokyo, in all other ways mutually distrustful and hostile.

The Chinese Communists, said to number around 80,000,000, were located mainly in the northwest provinces with their capital at Yenan. Here they had a government of their own, with separate currency, separate taxes, and a separate army which they said existed to fight Japan, which the Kuomingtang said was for the purpose of spreading Communism. Several of Chiang Kai-shek's advisers, if not the Generalissimo himself, were so inclined to this view that many of his Chinese troops, which should have been used against invading Japan, were deployed north to ride herd on the Communists and to keep their power from spreading further, troops which rumor had it (shrilly denied by Chiang Kai-shek) were armed through lend-lease aid from America.

Whether it was necessary thus to act; whether the Communists aimed first at social revolution and only secondarily at clearing China of Japan's power; whether Communism or Kuomingtang were the more loyal to the democratic principles supposedly involved in this war, are questions open to debate. The evidence is so conflicting, so confused, so scanty, so colored with emotion and prejudice that it is hazardous to write thereon without constant qualification. This much is evident. The Chinese government recognized by the United Nations was that of the Kuomingtang at Chungking. We did supply Chiang Kai-shek with some weapons; we gave none to the Communists. This did not necessarily mean that we were opposed to the Communists; there was no way to reach them except through Chiang Kai-shek's territory.

Although both Communists and Kuomingtang protested that they and they only represented true democracy, too much credence cannot be given either side. The Kuomingtang minister of education saw to it that in the schools there was no deviation from the strict party line, as laid down by himself, and he even tried to control the reading of Chinese students sent overseas, much to the displeasure of Harvard. According to Sun Fo, son of Sun Yat-sen, the Kuomingtang represented less than 1 per cent of the Chinese people and by no means could be considered democratic. On the other hand, we may well be sceptical of the highly advertised "one-to-three ratio system" of the Chinese Communists, which forbids the Kungchantang, the Communist equivalent of the Kuomingtang, to elect more than one-third of the elective posts in Communist China. It would be just as well first to have some proof as to how many posts were elective.

The fact that Chiang Kai-shek prevented American correspondents from entering Red China before the summer of 1941 makes it difficult to assess the relative values of the war as waged against Japan by Kuomingtang and Kungchantang, respectively. According to the latter, their "Eighth Route and new Fourth Armies together represent something less than one-fifth of the total Chinese forces racing the Japanese. These Communists troops, however, engaged 49.5 per cent of all the Japanese forces in China. . . . In the seven years of war the Communists have fought over 92,000 battles. They have killed or wounded 1,100,000 Japanese or puppets and captured over 150,000 of the enemy."[1] But according to a Kuomingtang spokesman, "the Communists have not fought a single battle in the past six years." Where lies the truth?

The answer depends upon one's definition of the word "battle." Very likely the Communists did not fight a single battle in our ordinary and modern sense of that large-scale word. Since they were without planes, tanks, almost without artillery and had far too few rifles, it would have been foolish to do so. Their military contribution to the defeat of Japan had to be in the form of guerrilla war and sabotage, road blocks, concealed bombs, and the hand grenade. The figure 92,000 seems extravagant, but that Chinese Communists constantly snipped and sniped at Japanese garrisons strung out all up and down eastern China is a plain and well-established fact. The Communists could urge, at any rate, that if they did not fight battles they did not lose them, as was the constant experience of Chiang Kai-shek's armies in 1944.

In broad outline the question of Kungchantang vs. Kuomingtang resolves itself into whether the Sino-Japanese War was for economic and social justice predicated upon the expulsion of Japan from continental Asia, or primarily a military conflict during which re-

[1] Harrison Forman, *Report from Red China* (New York, Henry Holt and Company, Inc., 1945), p. 125.

form was to be kept in abeyance. In the former instance, the balance inclines toward the Kungchantang, in the latter it swings toward the Kuomingtang. But in either case incalculable harm came out of this snarling schism which gave little indication of ending in 1944.

Meanwhile, the military situation had worsened rapidly. Beginning in the spring of 1944 and continuing at rapid and accelerating tempo through the summer and autumn, the Japanese made good their project to cut and to control a wide swathe through all China from Peiping in the north to Canton and Nan-ning in the south, thus bringing their conquests in overland contact with French Indo-China, a *fait accompli* which made it possible not simply to sever the coastal plans of East China from Chungking but also to reinforce Japanese troops in Thailand and Burma by land alone, now highly necessary in view of American air and submarine raids on Nippon's shipping.

Week by week and month by month the somber news of Chinese defeat monotonously kept leaking out. The foe long since had controlled the Yangtze Valley beyond Hankow. They now pressed north from Hankow and south from Peiping across the wheat belt of Hanoi to capture Chengchow and Loyang farther west; they drove south from Hankow and north from Canton, taking en route the important city of Chang-sha, making good their rail connections from Korea to Canton; they forced the hasty abandonment of many of the Fourteenth American Air Force bases such as Linchow, Kwei-lin, Nan-ning; and as this happened they occupied one after another Chinese coastal ports between Canton and Shanghai, thus sealing off potential landing sites for an American army invading China by sea.

BURMA AND INDIA IN 1944

Farther to the west in Burma and in one small pocket of northeastern India, the Japanese were defeated. In this remote and pestilential corner, Chinese, Americans, Britons, East Africans and Indians, together with sundry local hill tribes, reconquered about one-fifth of all Burma and made possible the linking up of the Ledo Road with the Burma Road in order to reopen a back door into China. This was a truly international achievement but credit primarily should go to the Chinese and to the Indians, the former

serving under General Stilwell, the latter under British high command. Aside from American aviators, engineers and a handful of
picked raiders and machine gunners, few Americans took part in
the obscure campaign which by the end of 1944 had carried Allied
arms as far south as Bhamo, eighty miles beyond Myitkyina; and
while more British than American units participated, the bulk of
the fighting under the Union Jack was done by Indian soldiers
who outnumbered the total of all other Allied soldiers in the Burma-
India theater.

Divergencies of viewpoint, logistical problems, the truly infernal
terrain and the down-streaming monsoon combined to complicate
military problems in Burma-India. The Allied commander-in-chief
in Southeast Asia, Lieutenant General Mountbatten, was more
interested in Central and Southern Burma than in various inaccessible upper valleys; he was more concerned about the recovery of
Rangoon, Mandalay and ultimately Singapore for the British
Empire than about what many considered so hair-brained a scheme
as building an impossible highway across impassable mountains.
As deputy commander under Mountbatten was our own Vinegar
Joe, whose pet project was the Ledo Road. Stilwell did not get on
well with either Mountbatten or with Chiang Kai-shek, upon whom
he had to depend for 90 per cent or more of his soldiers. But what
Stilwell lacked in tact he much more than made up in brains and
energy. Furthermore, and until the end of the year, he had the
backing of Washington.

Many thought Ledo a fantastic idea. It would be necessary to
start from scratch, to transport bulldozers, trucks, workmen and
all their impedimenta hundreds of miles from Calcutta over a
twisting narrow gauge railway way to the extreme upper corner
of Northeast India before even a yard of such road could be constructed. After that, one was confronted with engineering problems
more difficult by far than those encountered in the Alaska highway,
dense forests to be felled, zigzagging corkscrew curves to be constructed down precipitous mountain slopes and up steep ridges,
and this in the face of determined enemy resistance and the worst
climate in the world, with a monsoon arriving in May to terminate
operations if not to wash out with torrential floods everything thus
far accomplished. But Stilwell clung to his plans; he had the money,
the equipment, the engineers, the manpower, and the soldiers to
clear the path; and he was going to do just that.

The Sino-British-American objective (for Mountbatten did finally and generously assist his hard-bitten American deputy) was Myitkyina, railhead of Japanese communications in north Burma. That town and its air-field once occupied, hostile detachments on the north could be cut off and the Ledo enterprise once reaching Myitkyina could be continued eastward, despite very bad terrain, so as ultimately to link up with the Burma Road in the Chinese province of Yün-nan. The British said it would be "impossible" to take Myitkyina before 1945; Stilwell arrived there, aided greatly by the British, and did so by converging attacks on the eve of the 1944 monsoon season. His Chinese troops, whom he had trained and equipped, and whom he considered second to none, headed for Myitkyina from northeast and southeast, an offense which meant among other heartbreaking obstacles the crossing of the Salween River in the teeth of enemy fire. From the southwest came Wingate's raiders, soon to have over them another commander, owing to the untimely death of General Wingate who was killed before he could know how well Americans could carry out and even better the methods he improved and often originated. And from the northwest, like scouts searching out the ways for the Ledo engineers, came Merrill's marauders, the Yankee counterpart to Wingate's men. And now for the first time in Asiatic jungle war gliders were used to convey troops. The commando fighters of Merrill were joined by Indian troops, coming in glider transports, towed off the ground by planes and landing in the jungle. British and American airplane power was making victory possible in North Burma even as it was doing in western Europe and at Saipan.

The Japanese this spring of 1944 meanwhile launched an offense of their own, and in two directions; one, the lesser, in the Arakan region of the Burma-Indian frontier east of the Bay of Bengal, aimed at the conquest of Chittagong, an important seaport and British air base; the other, more important, directed at Imphal, capital of the little Indian state of Manipur, tucked away amid the Naga Hills on the borders of North Burma and India. North of Imphal for some 174 miles a highway led to Dimapur on the Calcutta-Ledo railway. Once the Rising Sun reached Dimapur, Stilwell's way to China would revert to the jungle and the Sino-American-British forces in North Burma would be isolated. All that would be necessary then would be a holding action while Japanese troops, assisted, it was hoped, by revolting Indians, swung down the

Brahmaputra Valley into Bengal, perhaps to stage another Singapore at Calcutta.

This was the Japanese plan. Thanks to General Slim and his Fourteenth British Army, whose exploits can stand comparison with those of Monty's Eighth Army of Alamein fame, it was thwarted, the Japanese soundly thrashed, all that they gained lost and more besides, and by the third anniversary of Pearl Harbor the foundations laid for the reconquest of Burma in 1945.

"The march on Delhi has begun, the Fourteenth British Army is destroyed," thus the Tokyo radio in the first week of February, 1944, as General Tenashi trapped the Fifteenth Corps of that army in the Arakan area. The general's plans were excellent but he had forgotten that Britain, not Japan, had air supremacy over Burma and that the British now were operating on Wingate's advice, "Have no lines of communication on the jungle floor. Bring the goods like Father Christmas down the chimney." The airmen came to the rescue, flew 400 sorties, fed food and munitions to the trapped Imperials, even brought them beer and mail. The foe had rations for ten days only. They stayed too long. Counterattacks sent them reeling eastward into Burma, leaving in the jungle an estimated 7,000 dead.

The real march on Delhi, however, was by way of Imphal. Against that fourth-rate Indian town the Japanese hurled 80,000 picked troops, besieged it for over two months, surged on north, surrounded for eighteen days another British force at Kohima which if they had only by-passed might have brought them to the strategic railroad. But the Jap orders were: "First take Kohima, then the railroad"; and Japanese soldiers always obey orders, which is not always the way to win.

Time now pressed; the monsoon was not far distant; the Japanese made one final try for Manipur. "You will take Manipur," said their commander, "but the division will be annihilated." The second part of his statement time verified. It was now Slim's turn. Like thistledown before the wind the Imperials drove the adversary south, counting more than 50,000 Japanese dead. How many more of the original 80,000 perished in the jungle of sickness or by knives of irate hillmen there is no record.

The Fourteenth Army, too, had suffered heavily; but Slim was back at Kalewa on the frontier where he had buried his guns on his retreat in 1942. Now he could, and did, dig them up again.

From now on it was the British Empire, not Japan, that took the offensive in Burma.

It was not, however, so much what had happened in 1944 as what presumably would happen in 1945 that gave warrant for Allied optimism; the dotting of northeastern India with new air-fields constructed in record time by Indian men and women with the generous and unofficial coöperation of the Indian Tea Growers' Association; the despatch to Ceylon of powerful units of the Royal Navy, as these were no longer needed in Europe; the rapid multiplication of munition factories in India; the mounting numbers of the Indian army and its increasing mechanization. Here were hopeful omens. Even more hopeful the global picture of this war against Japan, as seen in outline of December 7, 1944. In three years her Aladdin's Empire had been shrunk by half; the B-29s, 50 per cent bigger than any flying fortress and several times more powerful, were blasting at her homeland; and all this when Tokyo well knew that Germany was hard down to the very end of her tether. Soon it would be Japan against an Allied world.

14. GERMANY OVERWHELMED

JANUARY, 1944, and most of Europe still in the Nazi clutch. *Festung Europa*, shrunken somewhat, still was spaciously enclosed by frontiers an evil 6,000 miles.

The Russians in little over a year's time had won back 328,000 square miles of scorched and sacred Soviet soil. But none of it was part of Fortress Europe proper, and German troops still besieged Leningrad, held much of White Russia, most of the Ukraine, Odessa, Sebastopol and the Crimea. Those bordering 6,000 miles were not safeguarded throughout by a ring of solid steel, but the most vital length of all came very close to being thus impregnable: the four hundred miles or more of French coast, Brest to Calais, standing over against England. For three years the world's best military engineers had ample time and abundant forced labor wherewith to build Hitler's Atlantic Wall, a world of sunken concrete pill boxes, of barbed wire, machine-gun nests, heavy artillery, some of it from the Maginot fortresses, and land mines innumerable, a deadly maze five to ten miles deep. There was little likelihood of major invasion from the Bay of Biscay or the Mediterranean; logistics forbade. The approach to Deutschland's Alpine passes through spiny Italy was not promising. The plains of White Russia and Poland lay open to Red armies, although the farther west they rolled, the farther they were from food and ammunition. Meanwhile, German scientists were perfecting their new rocket gun with which to blot out London ninety miles away. German strength was slowly ebbing but it might thus be suddenly restored. To any comprehensive view, the war was far from won.

Yet, as it drew fast to its European climax, the United Nations had good reason to feel relatively confident. It was well to know that at long last the big three (Roosevelt, Stalin, Churchill) had met in Teheran, Persia (November, 1943) and had pledged themselves to strike the adversary in one huge three-pronged assault from east, south and west. Hitherto Stalin had been rather plainly and sensibly skeptical of Anglo-American willingness to hurl its whole weight against the Germans; he had not gone to Casablanca; he had refused to join the Cairo conference; in Moscow he had met Churchill but not Roosevelt, and Uncle Joe was shrewdly wary of military commitments. Now at long last the Russians, the British and the Americans had the allied force, the men, the weapons, the will and the skill, to blast Germany back into the homeland and to crush her there. Now coördinated strategy toward that end could be and was perfected. This meant the Second Front, attack from the west and south, for which Stalin had long clamored; it meant threefold hammer blows upon the German anvil for the first time in this war; it meant grimly crashing through to victory. Most of all, it meant that for the first time in history the superlative technology and exhaustless resources of the twentieth-century United States, now (for better or worse) the greatest power mankind had ever known, were to be hurled against the newest of Empire imperialisms until it was literally erased from the earth. Few had dreamed that possible or probable. Now it was happening.

The United States had close to 4,000,000 men overseas, so that Britain was rapidly turning into our armed camp against Hitler, soon to have more GIs than British Tommies stationed there. There was less and less to fear from U-boats. The last German battleship available to threaten sea lanes, the *Scharnhorst,* had been sunk by the Royal Navy the day after Christmas. That great battlewagon, *Tirpitz,* sister ship of the *Bismarck,* lay bottled up, disabled in a Norwegian fiord. The Red armies, driving hard on a winter offensive, were already west of Kiev and in January had planted the hammer and sickle flag within ten miles of the Polish-Latvian border. In Yugoslavia, Marshal Tito and his slashing partisans had tied up several more divisions which the Germans needed in Italy. Rome was only seventy miles distant from the American Fifth and the British Eighth Armies. Few Italians had any notion of fighting further. Finland, Rumania and even Hungary showed no interest in anti-Bolshevism but a great deal in their own safety. German civilians and German industry were being smashed and destroyed by the merciless downpouring of bombs, a blasting flood which constantly augmented. The conquest of the Hitler lands might be delayed but it could not be stopped. General Eisenhower, promoted to command the forthcoming joint invasion, proclaimed 1944 the year of Germany's downfall.

EASTERN FRONT BEFORE D-DAY

For months to come, transchannel attack on the French coast was impossible. January and February are notorious there for fog and storm, March is but little better. High tides and moonlight must coincide for successful landing on the bristling Norman beaches. March 10 there would be full moon and high tides, but bad weather and too early. April 11 moon and tide should be serviceable. Not before then, it was plain to the informed, could D-Day come. And so the Russians had to wait some more for that second front, while crowded England squeezed in still more Yanks and masses of impedimenta of such as Caesar never dreamed. Meanwhile the American Eighth Air Force and the RAF staged bigger and hotter raids on northern France and Germany, smashing to liberate and smashing also to destroy.

But there was no delay in the east. Here from dead of winter until past apple blossoming, Russian and German armies fought to death's finish; the former driving against their adversary with force, craft and vigor so overwhelming as not to be withstood, the latter, with skilled tenacity, exacting a bloody price for every mile of Soviet land pried loose from their hostile hands.

By the first week in January the Red army had crossed the Polish border of 1939 and was threatening Sarny on the main north-south route from the Baltic states to southern Poland. The Russian steam-roller was grinding westward on the road to conquest, hoisting a red warning to the Polish "government" in London, acutely conscious as these exiles were that Stalin's announcement spoke of "Poland" as still 200 miles to the west, and therefore that much west of the 1939 line between Poles and Russians!

That same month Red armies hit the German forces quick blows elsewhere; north of Sarny across the frozen Pripet marshes toward Pinsk in what had once been eastern Poland; south and southeast of Kiev in the Ukraine, thus continuing the vast encircling movement earlier begun to cut off Hitler's divisions in the deep bend of the Dnieper north and east of Odessa; and again in the far north where more triphammer Red offensives brought the Russian army back to Novgorod, threatened relief of Leningrad, boded ill for German garrisons in the Baltic area.

Almost daily Moscow guns roared salute as in successive orders of the day Commander-in-Chief and Marshal Stalin announced new victories. Nor was the Soviet march forward simply military; in politics as well as war the Red army scored gains for Russia. On February 1 Premier Molotov notified the Supreme Soviet's 10th Congress that henceforth the U.S.S.R. would consist of sixteen republics, each having a high degree of autonomy, permitted to raise and to maintain armies, to have separate diplomatic relations with the outside world.

World observers and statesmen were sadly puzzled. Why should, how could, totalitarian Bolshevism proclaim such a contradiction in terms; what was the significance of this declaration? The key, perhaps, may be found in the number "sixteen." In 1939 the U.S.S.R. embraced *eleven* republics. Now five more had been added, Esthonia, Latvia, Lithuania, Moldavia, and the Karelo-Finnish Republic. Here was oblique notice to all and sundry that Stalin would, on conquest, post these contiguous and once Hitler lands as Soviet areas. The Baltic states, still held by German troops, were to be sovietized, so likewise part of prewar Finland. As for the matter of autonomy, possibly that was bait for the Poles and other east Europeans as well to cast their east European lot more fully with Moscow.

Meanwhile the eastern battles raged with mounting fury. Whenever, it was noted, the Nazis suffered reverses anywhere, whether the *Scharnhorst* was sunk or a defeat inflicted in the Ukraine, they speeded up shelling Leningrad, under siege now two and one-half years. That city was not in as dire peril as formerly, for rail connection of a kind had been opened with Moscow. It was no longer necessary to fend off scurvy with a brew of pine needles, nor for women and young girls to shovel earth into their aprons and carry it to desperately driven earthworks. Yet Germans pumped shells into the city, and some thirty German divisions were still involved in what looked like a lunar landscape but was called the Leningrad front.

They could not retreat, partly because it would isolate their ally Finland, partly because of pride in their huge, ingenious "Leningrad Padlock," an inferno of mine fields, booby traps and underground pill boxes or "wells" strung on deep trenches. But the Russians whanged away at the Germans with artillery and dropped hand grenades down into the German wells. By the end of January the padlock was broken; "by February 14th practically the whole of Leningrad Province had been cleared of the Germans—

except for possibly 60,000 or 75,000 new German corpses left behind in the last month." [1]

It was in the milder Ukraine, however, not in the bleak far north, that the startling victory march was staged, where some 500,000 enemy troops were stationed between the Dnieper River and the Rumanian frontier to defend rail communications between south Poland and Odessa, to exploit Krivoi Rog's iron, Nikopol's manganese, to stand off any Soviet drive against Rumanian oil and the southeastern Carpathian passes into the Reich itself.

Here in mid-winter (January 24 - February 3, 1944) the First and Second Red Ukrainian Armies encircled and all but annihilated some ten German divisions, perhaps half the wehrmacht total in far away Italy. Action took place in the Upper Dnieper Bend southeast of Kiev where the Eighth German Army held a front of fifty miles. The Russians threw round their motorized divisions in two great sweeping arcs, forming the aptly named "Russian rat trap." The area, at first broad and spacious, was soon squeezed tight as Don Cossacks and Russian tankmen pared it down into small and smaller pockets, until the last was but a few kilometers across.

The cornered Germans, told by radio that help was near, and fed by parachutes, milled round in these battle pens, stacking their dead like cordwood, as they fought off Russian blows. A few escaped, more were taken prisoner, most died, and ten divisions were thus lost to the Reich. It was Stalingrad in little.

Wiped out on the Upper Dnieper, the Germans soon were hard pressed near its estuary. The Third Ukrainian Army, unable to duplicate the feats of the First and Second, smashed through to Nikopol (February 8) and through Krivoi Rog (February 27). The Germans backed up steadily westward all through March. To the west of the Dnieper and somewhat parallel with it flows the Bug River, a strong defensive barrier. The Russians forced passage March 15. Another and a greater river, the Dniester, was sixty miles farther west. In four days the Red army was on the east bank and Stalin's men surged over to invade Bessarabia, from 1919 to 1939 a province of Rumania but not by any means Russia's frontier as now seen by Stalin. Not until the Red flag waved along the east bank of the Pruth, some seventy miles farther west on March 26, had Soviet forces reached what the Kremlin promptly called "The Soviet State frontier." The Germans were back where they started from in 1941.

[1] Alexander Werth, *Leningrad* (New York, Alfred A. Knopf, 1944), p. 184.

In 1,009 days, to be exact, they had made the round trip of 1,700 miles from the Pruth to the Volga and return—tidal waves of war unique in history.

Then on to Odessa. That city, Russia's largest port on the Black Sea and the only bit of Ukraine left in the Nazi grip, fell on April 10. The Russians declared huge totals of dead and captured Germans, the Germans triumphantly announced their evacuation of Odessa with slight loss.

Five days later Red soldiers overran the Crimea to rebesiege Sebastopol. Nature had made that town of more strength than Gibraltar, as French and British found in 1854 and Germans in 1942, when they were kept at bay a good six months. The fighting ended this time in four weeks, as the garrison was mainly Rumanian, and surrendered May 15. The Black Sea was once more a Soviet lake.

All southern Russia and more, too, had been "redeemed." April 2 the last invaders had been rooted out of the northern Ukraine, and before Odessa fell rail communication between German Poland and that city was severed. Russian armies then marched into Bukovina, another long disputed and lately Rumanian province northeast of the Carpathians. Here they were within rifle shot of the old Mongol conquerors' Tatar Pass leading into Czechoslovakia. They could turn at will north to Poland or south to the Balkans, and the Germans could only reinforce their Balkan forces through Hungary.

The satellite countries now faced disaster. The Finns asked for peace and received terms, might even have accepted had it not been for some six German divisions on watch in Finland. The Germans would not evacuate that country; the Russians would not end the Finnish war unless that was done. Far to the south the Rumanians did not dare ask for peace; the German grip was too tight on their throat. But it was obviously not there for long. As in World War I, so in World War II, the little allies and great conquests of the German Reich were all falling away.

ITALY BEFORE D-DAY

Thus far, of all the United Nations the Russians had done the heavier fighting, scored the greater victories, killed the more Germans, suffered the worst losses. The United States and Britain had sent them huge matériels of war, the United States supplying by January, 1944, 7,200 planes, 170,000 trucks, 2,250,000 tons of food; the British by March, 1944, over 5,000 tanks, ammunition to scale, and much else besides. American and British air raids on the Reich were a very genuine help to the Red armies, but except in Italy and to some extent in the Balkans the Russians were doing all the fighting on the European continent.

The Italian campaign of 1944 is far easier to visualize than those titanic war-torrents inundating the flats of eastern Europe from out of Soviet Russia. For the most part it was only one campaign instead of several, and those kaleidoscoping incessantly in diverse areas; it was on a small scale and easier to follow, for the forces there involved were roughly speaking only one-tenth of those in the east; and then, too, while censorship was reasonably restrictive in Italy, correspondents really did go along with the Allied armies, whereas in Russia there were none anywhere near the front.

1944 opened in Italy with a congeries of French, Polish, Brazilian, Indian, Dominion, British and American troops slowly hacking and edging their way to Rome. From Ortona on the Adriatic to just south of Gaeta on the Mediterranean, the Gustav line wound its way in and out among the mountains, and behind it was the pick of the German Army, SS troops and paratroopers amply supplied with the best of artillery and commanded by Von Kesselring, an able strategist. The advantages of terrain and communications lay with the Germans. From the end of the peninsula to the Po Valley and the Lombardy plains, Italy bristles with precipitous hills and mountains, and is interlaced by narrow twisting valleys through which the now flooded rivers raced to the sea; these for the most part flowed at right angles to the Allied advance. In Lombardy as well as in northwestern Piedmont were great munition plants and war factories with forced labor to operate them. The distance to the German forces was short, while the United Nations had to convey and convoy everything by sea, and this at a time when shipping space was scraped and absorbed to the limit by the Pacific war and by American troops landing in England for D-Day. Far superior air power was with the Allies in Italy, so it was relatively easy for them to sustain their harassing attack on rail lines, roads, bridges and tunnels. They likewise had complete mastery in, over, and under the inland sea. These counter-vailing factors proved insufficient to overcome the natural advantages of mountain defense, so that the fight to drive the Germans out of Italy was long, painful and sanguine, protracted to the very end of the European war.

To reach Rome one must either breach the Gustav line at the town of Cassino through which ran Route VI, the Via Casalina, the only adequate highway leading north to the goal, or else make amphibious landings on the seacoast nearer the Eternal City, thus outflanking the Germans behind the Gustav line and compelling their withdrawal. Ultimately the Allies were successful in doing both, but it took all they had, and nearly five months hard hand fighting.

The Liri Valley, in which Cassino once nestled, was flanked by commanding hills on either side, and through the town ran not only the Via Casalina but also the Rapido River, in winter a raging torrent. On one of the hills east of the town perched the Benedictine monastery of Cassino, from whence in early times there sprang the monasticism which did so much to save civilization in the Dark Ages. During the first stages of the fighting the monastery was kept immune from bombardment.

That immunity proved too costly to the Americans who wormed their way across the Rapido only to be driven back by crossfire from the hills. We claimed the fire either came from or was controlled in the monastery; the Germans said, No. It is possible that they only used the building as an observation post from which to direct their defense against us, but we took no chances. The American Air Force destroyed the monastery. But the ruins still held Germans, and neither airmen nor infantry could drive them from it. We next tried to wipe out Cassino from the air and apparently did so, as far as reconnaissance photographs showed. But the more the ruins, the harder the fighting, as Spanish Alcazar and Russian Stalingrad had proved. New Zealanders did pry open doors with bayonets, killed Germans, and in turn were killed by them; Indian Gurkhas did gain the summit of Hangman's Hill; and Germans did surrender in what had once been the Hotel Continental. But fresh waves of German paratroopers recovered much the New Zealanders had won; the Gurkhas on their hill were isolated and had to be fed by parachute; the hotel filled up again with German warriors as though by magic, and German tanks dashed in and out the ruined lobby. By April, after three months' attack, Cassino was only cellar holes and roofless houses, but in them with machine

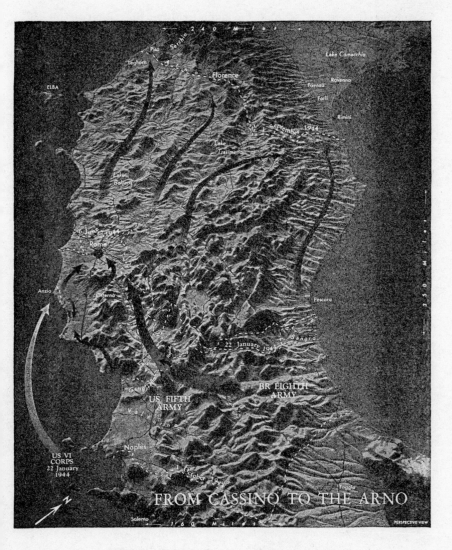

FROM CASSINO TO THE ARNO

(From General Marshall's Report, *The Winning of the War in Europe and the Pacific.*

Courtesy of the U. S. War Department)

guns the Germans held fast, and their artillery on nearby hills still commanded the Via Casalina.

If the Gustav line could not be breached, why not outflank it? This, the Fifth Army, under our General Mark Clark, tried to do in January by a surprise landing above and below the shore village of Anzio on the Mediterranean, some thirty miles south of Rome. Curiously, also ominously, there was at first no opposition. Six divisions got ashore. It seemed too easy and proved far worse than that.

The beachhead was relatively long, fourteen miles, and much too shallow, only eight miles. The land Clark's men squatted on was low and marshy, cut up by numerous drainage ditches in many of which our infantry stood waist-deep. Down from the high ground of the hinterland the enemy soon poured a murderous fire on Anglo-Americans thus packed close, the British to the north, the Americans to the south. Ten days later the rosy prospects of a quick break-through had faded into lurking fear lest another Dunkirk loom ahead. Our staff work and reconnoitering had been none too good.

Meanwhile, sixty miles to the south lay Cassino. A break-through there would save the beachhead; conversely a successfully widened beachhead would disrupt the enemy's communications, cut the Via Casalina north of Cassino, compel its evacuation. But could the Yanks and Tommies do either?

From January 22, through the whole infernal winter until well into spring, day followed day and week followed week at Anzio, a few yards gained, a few yards lost. The Anglo-Americans by day were hammered by German tanks, at night bombed by German planes, soaked at all times by blinding rain and stuck fast in bogs and mud. Only by the narrowest margin did the Fifth Army stick it out. After a month it was stalemate both at Anzio and at Cassino, In London Churchill sounded his usual cheery note, and American war correspondents praised the grim humorous staying quality of the Yanks. But facts are facts: the casualty lists were much too long, and "half a year had gone by since the Salerno landing and the Allies had pushed forward less than a hundred miles."

April wore by, and then with May our air-blasting of the Reich began to tell on their war power, so that a strong thrust forward opened the road to Rome. Although formally under overall command of a British general, it truly was an international fracas in which rôles were played by Free French under General Juin and even by Poles fighting under their own flag. The French contingent opened the attack by storming Mt. Faito to the south of Cassino; the Poles followed and captured the abbey; the British, Canadians and Indians swept forward across the Rapido River and circled toward a junction with the Polish detachment; the Americans, posted between the French and the sea, scored the largest gains in mileage but over easier terrain; on the Adriatic the Eighth Army made good headway, while at Anzio both British and Americans at last secured needed headroom, pressed close on German communications between Rome and Cassino.

May 11 the Allied offensive began and within a week the Germans were in retreat, neatly and quickly abandoning also the Hitler line which lay behind the Gustav barrier. There was talk of cutting off Von Kesselring, bagging his army. He was too alert for that. The wehrmacht was too well trained; it knew how to fight and how to retreat while fighting, and the bulk of the German forces got back to Rome. June 4, 1944, and Rome fell. Barring slight skirmishes in the suburbs, the Allied occupation of their first Axis capital was bloodless. Very probably there were political reasons. There was no sack of Rome. The German army, if not the German rulers of the twentieth century, was after all more civilized than in the days of Alaric or the later soldiery of Emperor Charles V. Taking such small loot as they had a fancy to, the invaders made their way north to the hills surrounding Florence, leaving in war's littered wake mines and booby traps galore.

D-DAY

"One up and two to go," said Roosevelt in announcing the liberation of the Holy City. "The year of invasion," said the Nazi radio, ignoring Rome's capture, "will bring Germany's enemies annihilating defeat." D-Day was near at hand. The Allied war gods were about to stage their mightiest drama somewhere on the coast of France. Some might rejoice in Rome's "redemption," others might make light of it, but both sides knew that what was about to happen would transcend all that had taken or could take place in Italy.

Centuries before the Christian era, Herodotus, history's reputed father, records how Xerxes, the great Persian king, sent out his

summons over eastern Asia, assembled on the shores of the Helles-
pont the Asian world's most famous warriors, and with his magnificent, awe-inspiring force set out to conquer Hellas. Between
Xerxes' day and D-Day history finds no parallel. Philip of Spain did
his best to outfit his Armada, and Napoleon's invasion camp at
Boulogne was the result of careful planning, but the preparations of
all past conquerors together were dwarfed by those of Britain and
America in 1944. It had to be that way to win.

Those preparations had been in train two years or more, the
piling up of reserve supplies innumerable from blood banks and
spare plane parts, to tanks and Bailey bridges; the detailed and
endless rehearsal of invasion tactics, how to get ashore and storm
the enemy beaches, how to use parachutes to best advantage; the
assembling of invasion barges by thousands at Channel ports, naval
rehearsals for their protection, for dealing with hostile submarines
and armored motor-boats, for mapping invasion areas, for con-
structing artificial harbors to speed disembarking troops; widely
scattered air attacks on northern France to confuse the German defenders; the precise choice of H-hour itself, this, that and the other
operations planned to the exact minute prior to it; this, that and
the other to the very minute subsequent. Only D-Day remained
the inscrutable secret.

In 1915 a younger Churchill had fathered an impromptu and
risky invasion of the Dardanelles; it failed and stunted his career
for twenty years. Now an older Churchill was prime minister of
England, a Churchill stubbornly refusing to take chances. It might
have been possible to gain a beachhead on the French coast in
1943 but the cost seemed too frightful, and the question then would
have arisen, how to enlarge it. The Russians had been indignant
because the hazard was not put to the test, also some Americans.
But Churchill preferred the slow and sure, an African landing and
flank attack on Fortress Europe from the south. He had to wait
while Germany was softened up as much as possible from the air
before making the grand attack through France, a truly Allied
enterprise, though one in fact in which the Americans, as much the
greater power, must play the larger rôle.

The Americans had certainly been speeded fast to the battle
lines. June 1, 1944, Secretary Stimson stated that there were
5,223,000 Americans in our armed forces overseas, 3,300,000 of
them soldiers, the great bulk in Britain. Many had only recently

been inducted and these reserves must undergo severe training before action or else incur ghastly losses. In the initial stages it was planned to deploy in approximately equal numbers Americans and British Imperial troops.

And behind all these fighting men, both Yanks and Tommies, were the factories, workshops, shipyards and spacious farmlands of the entire Allied world. There were in Britain 33,000,000 men and women between fourteen and sixty-four, and of these no less than 23,000,000 were in war work of all sorts. To Britain fell the major task of conveying and convoying the Yanks to Europe. The British had to house them, to a considerable degree to feed them, and build new port facilities for their landings in England. All this in addition to piling up munitions and to expanding the tonnage of bombs dropped on Germany (48,200 tons, for instance, for the first quarter of 1944 as opposed to 34,075 for the entire year 1943). And as they did this, it must be remembered that during the one month of May, 1944, British and American ships moved almost 4,000,000 tons of cargo from American ports to Britain.

There was little time to squabble now as to who did what; the crisis was too serious. Into one gigantic pool the industrial products of the whole English-speaking world and their allies were poured to feed the flaming maw of war. A magnificent testimony to the loyal sweat of men and women in overalls making possible the deeds of those obedient in khaki.

June came, an anxious time for all alike. Behind their Atlantic Wall the Germans prepared more sites for the rocket bomb from which war-scarred London was soon to suffer crucifixion anew. Shabby and half-starved French of all ages and both sexes sharpened bayonets and drilled in secret for guerrilla war. And in millions of homes all over the earth there were high-strung nerves and anxious worry, for all knew D-Day was near.

Monday, June 5, was the day set as best for moon and tide. Some 4,000 Allied vessels of one sort or another swarmed in Channel ports, were patrolling Channel waters, marking buoys for invasion barges, searching for elusive submarines. Armed men of all the services were packed in barges ready for the kick-off, but indifferent nature threw her negative in Germany's favor, ferocious gales and huge waves such as the Channel had not seen in forty years tearing wildly through the narrow seas. The appalling responsibility that rested on Eisenhower and his counselors was met at once and

D-Day postponed twenty-four hours to Tuesday, June 6. The weather abated somewhat then and our commander gave the word to go.

From six minutes past midnight paratroopers in long trains of gliders hopped the Channel to drop down in Normandy well before daybreak behind the German lines. And as they did so, landing craft drew near the hostile shore, the larger barges towing behind them pontoons, gigantic life preservers, should the barges fall foul of mines or torpedoes, and behind each pontoon a small craft with outside motors called a "rhino." All night they had worked twisting passage through the choppy seas, keeping lookout for the well-marked buoys, close-convoyed by destroyer watchdogs and corvettes, the GIs and the Bors (British other ranks, the British equivalent for GI) channel-sick, half-frozen, conscious that for many life was a matter of hours or minutes.

Planes by the thousand jammed the skies. The Allied planes had far more than mastery of the air; they filled it. The biggest battle-wagons of the Royal Navy joined with a number of ours, among them a survivor of Pearl Harbor, and threw tons of bombs on the German gun emplacements, while squirming destroyers like sinuous hounds clinging close to some wild beast steamed boldly toward shore.

The landing was hard. Barely beneath the surface of the water the Germans had scientifically driven down six-pronged iron spikes upon which many a landing craft was impaled, and in the same deadly fashion anchored logs lay hidden to which mines were attached. Simply to drop the ramp of a landing barge in shallow water close to shore was a difficult task and dangerous. As stumbling soldiers and lumbering tanks hit their beach, the Germans shot into them with enfilading fire from machine-gun nests and from heavy artillery deep-sunk in concrete emplacements up on banks which must be stormed, and that right speedily, lest the successive waves of ground troops find no standing room on the crowded beaches. No time to dig fox holes. Up the narrow ravines toward the cliffs our men instantly charged, ravines and gullies filled with murderous booby traps, barbed wire, the German fire-storm and death.

Four landings came on in one great drive, two British, two American. They were spaced widely over sixty miles of the northern shore line of the Contentin Peninsula, and toward the eastern end of it from near Caen, capital of William the Conqueror while duke of Normandy and before he had crowned himself king of England, thence westward approximately two-thirds of the way to the port of Cherbourg. The British Second Army, soon to have Rommel's tanks launched against it, had a relatively easy time at the start. So likewise was it with the Canadian First Army, the men of Canada penetrating seven miles in one day to Bayeux, Duke William's tapestry town. Lady Luck also smiled on those Yanks who landed farthest west, for swamps rather than frowning cliff confronted them, and they were able to drive inland and make speedy contact with the airborne forces to attack Carentan, a railroad station on the trunk line to Cherbourg.

But it was nip and tuck for those Americans who stormed ashore east of the Vire River. All D-Day the GIs there clung desperately to shallow beachheads, suffering most grievous casualties, and not until late afternoon were they out of deadly peril. On D-Day plus one came reinforcements and with them America's beloved correspondent, Ernie Pyle, who describes the scene: "Submerged tanks and overturned boats and burned trucks and shell-shattered jeeps and sad little personal belongings were strewn all over those bitter sands . . . bodies of soldiers lying in rows covered with blankets, the toes of their shoes sticking up in a line as though on drill."[1]

THE CONTENTIN PENINSULA AND NORMANDY

Six weeks' grueling battle came and went before the northwestern corner of France was wrested from the foe. The Allies were held back by execrable weather, high seas and the lack of harbor facilities; by the character of the terrain, particularly the deep-ditched Norman hedgerows, dense thickets lining roadsides, demarking fields, "horse-high, bull-strong, hog-tight"; by the counterattack of German rocket guns on London and by German panzer divisions in France. Had it not been for their overlordship of the air, our forces would have had a far tougher time of it. As it was, British and American planes rode high, wide and handsome over northern France, demolishing rocket gun emplacements, smashing bridges as far south as the Loire, strafing locomotives, stations, railway lines and motor roads so that the Germans had to move troops by

[1] Ernie Pyle, *Brave Men* (New York, Henry Holt and Company, Inc., 1944), p. 360.

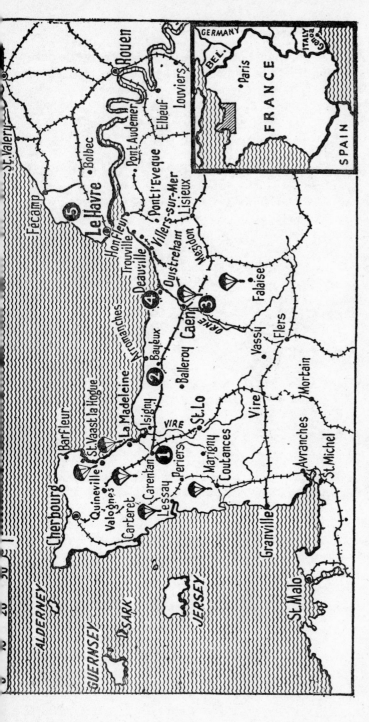

INITIAL ALLIED SUCCESSES FOLLOWING D-DAY AS REPORTED BY THE GERMANS,
JUNE 8, 1944

(Courtesy of the New York *Herald Tribune*)

Parachute symbols show where Nazis said that Allies had landed. A beachhead was reported at Carentan (1), east of which the Allies captured Bayeux (2). Heavy fighting raged at Caen (3), north of which the Allies held another beach at the mouth of the Orne River (4). The Nazis feared a "major bid against Le Havre" (5). Shaded area in insert shows the invasion sector.

night or else detour them long distances, one division, in Holland for instance, reaching the front via Alsace-Lorraine and the railways south of Paris.

A united front once achieved, the first task of the Americans was to split the Contentin Peninsula, thus isolating Cherbourg. That done with speed and dispatch, they pushed on to the city, June 22. Elements of four German divisions within put up one of the hottest defenses of the war; they knew how imperative it was for the Allies to have a harbor; and if there was no chance of holding Cherbourg for the Reich, time might be won in which to ruin it for the Allies. And so for five days the Stalingrad and Cassino scene was reënacted, fighting through house by house, cellar by cellar, street by street, tanks versus tanks, tanks versus pill boxes, tight little pill boxes of reinforced concrete with wicked slits through which machine guns spit, while the heavens were dark with our droning planes. Cave-man war worsened by all modern science.

June 27 Cherbourg surrendered numerous prisoners and a fine harbor, but with its wharves, docks, cranes, buildings and breakwaters so thoroughly wrecked that for many weeks it was of no use to us. As the city lay under American fire, two artificial harbors built in Britain were towed across the Channel in sections and then spliced together. A vital novelty and a well-kept secret. By two weeks after D-Day they were installed in the broad estuary of the Seine. One, close to the American beachhead, could never be used, for a three-day storm demolished it; the other survived the weather, and within its calm waters steel piers ran to shore, said in total length to exceed ten miles. "Through this harbor one million British and American troops had landed in France by the time Cherbourg was captured." The building of those harbors saved months of war. The Germans had been certain that the major Allied landing would take place close to some port. Our hitting their fortified open beaches was thought but a feint, and the real attack to be elsewhere. As matters fell out, by the time they had rushed mobile reserves from northeast France and Belgium, the British and Canadians, their nearest adversaries, had had time to make good their bridgeheads. It was just as well. General Rommel, field commander for the Germans, threw in all he had against these Allied forces, for they were nearer to him than the Americans and their thrust inland the more immediate menace to his communications.

A ding-dong fight for Caen followed, the Tommies driving hard at that Norman city time after time from different angles, the German panzers strongly beating them back and for two weeks with considerable success. But the British finally took Caen. Plunging forward through a sea of mud, they even got four miles beyond. Here they were held down by anti-tank fire and heavy German artillery (July 19).

The Americans had somewhat better luck, forging along on their break-through out of Normandy. Directly after taking Cherbourg they wheeled south heading for the rail junction of St. Lo which, if taken, would serve to seal off German forces in Brittany and on the Atlantic seaboard from German armies based in Paris.

The approaches to St. Lo had to be fought for inch by inch, almost every farmhouse (and they were all made of stone) had been converted into a fortress; and in the omnipresent hedgerows, lining all roads, dividing all fields, the Germans had their machine guns. Out of these hedges they had to be driven, flushed like so many human partridges, by tanks equipped with side-cutters which split the path open for the advancing Yanks. St. Lo was one of the nastiest fights of the entire war. It took us a good month to take the place, a month of heavy casualties, 7,944 American boys being killed and 39,549 wounded. It was worse than D-Day itself.

But by late July, the Americans, the British and the Canadians between them had accounted for 156,000 Germans, of whom 60,000 were prisoners. And, what is more, the Allies held half of Normandy and, out from ruined Caen and blasted St. Lo, were in position to strike hard.

THE RUSH FOR PARIS

July 25 the Americans did so, burst the barriers at St. Lo and, preceded by such assistance from the air as never yet in war had been given ground troops, started what soon became a motorized stampede and victory rush, reminiscent of the trans-France military pageant staged by the wehrmacht in June, 1940.

Once having burst from out their cramped location on Contentin, Yank armor dashed here and there with resistless speed as orders snapped out from headquarters. Turning west we overran Brittany, forcing the Germans into seaports where they stood at bay; curling eastward we cut in between the Germans fronting the British and

Canadians, thus helping to foil a counteroffensive of the wehrmacht; and racing southeast our armored columns headed straight for Paris. We had all the gas and oil we could burn. General Patton in command, driving incessantly full speed ahead, sent probing thrusts of Sherman tanks both north and south as he sped toward the French metropolis. His dirty, sweating, sleep-short tankmen were soon in the streets of Orléans, cutting off German forces in the south of France; almost simultaneously they appeared north of the Seine; one day later the Eiffel Tower was in view of Patton's outposts twenty miles away.

And as this happened the Canadians sweeping eastward toward Rouen, another ancient capital of Normandy, cut off the Germans at Le Havre on the coast; the British Second Army also crossed the Seine and pushed on to the Somme, thirty-four miles distant; and on August 15 an entirely new American army, the Seventh, broke in on the coast of the Riviera.

This new menace to the Germans was made up of troops withdrawn from Italy, some American, some French. Aided by British paratroopers and with strong naval backing, it struck at the Riviera coast between Toulon and the Italian frontier. Terrain was unfavorable but casualties light, some 300 dead after a four-day fight during which a most spacious beachhead was overrun, sixty miles in depth, thirty in width. The Seventh was soon in position to roll back on Italy from the northwest, or to plunge toward Toulon and Marseilles, or to hit north up the valley of the Rhone. And wherever it was ordered to go, it was sure of the assistance of the FFIs (French Forces of the Interior) the Maquis, guerrilla bands of young Frenchmen, poorly armed but knowing well the countryside, enraged by subjection, spoiling for a fight, eager to trap and to kill.

In three short weeks the outlook in the west was revolutionized. In what had been a bare two months earlier a prostrate France, in which no enemy of the Reich dare show his head, Germans everywhere were on the way out, their convoys, tanks and ground troops constantly strafed from the air, escaping over bridgeless rivers as best they might. The wehrmacht still had four armies in France, the First between Paris and the Rhine, the Seventh in front of Paris, the Fifteenth in northern France along the Channel, and the Nineteenth in the south. But the Seventh and Fifteenth were badly shattered, unable to help defend the French capital.

A short time since the Nazi song of annihilation, compulsory in

German schools, sang how all Europe would be in flames when German men expired. Most of it certainly was by this time. Rome, however, had not been put to the torch, nor was that to be the fate of Paris. On August 19 some 50,000 FFIs, abetted by the municipal police, revolted in the invader-emptied city. A remnant garrison resisted until advance units of Patton's army dashed into Paris, then surrendered on August 25. In Paris there had been much loose looting, but of dynamite and destruction there was none, of real damage very little. These were surrender times for invaders.

In Paris the American GIs were kissed freely but their effective pursuit of the Germans never let up. From twenty to fifty miles a day it raced along in a dozen different sectors. The Canadians took Rouen and went past it to the Channel to sew up the German garrison at Dieppe. The British, somewhat farther to the south, recovered Amiens, their headquarters in World War I, continued eastward, eager to seize the launching platforms of rocket guns if they could find them; the American First Army kept rolling along without meeting a foe, past Chateau Thierry, Soissons and Reims of the old war, all the way to an older Sedan. Patton's Third Army, farther south, surged on through Chalons, Verdun, St. Mihiel, and approached Metz; while the American Seventh, advancing up the Rhone, took Grenoble and was fast nearing Alsace, ready for its part on the southern flank of the vast Allied drive for the Rhine. As the crow flies, our tanks were now 350 miles from Cherbourg and close to the German frontier, less than forty days after pouring through the St. Lo funnel, less than three months after D-Day itself. As for the enemy, his overall picture September 1 was summarized by General Eisenhower: "The equivalent of five panzer divisions have been destroyed and a further six badly mauled.... The equivalent of twenty infantry divisions have been eliminated and a further twelve very badly cut up.... Total enemy casualties amount to more than 400,000 killed, wounded and prisoners." The war seemed certain to end in Europe before Christmas.

SOUTHERN AND EASTERN FRONTS

Fast fell the assault elsewhere on wehrmacht legions all through this fateful summer of 1944, in Italy, in the Balkans, in Poland, and in the Baltic states.

Allied invaders were weaker in Italy than elsewhere. Soon after

Rome was taken they had reason to feel that they were the forgotten front. Black death was just as hard to meet in Italy as in Normandy, and the foe confronting us was relatively stronger in numbers and morale, his dislodgement infinitely more difficult. But sweat and toil and hardship on the Roman peninsula was now an old story; whereas D-Day on Norman beaches, the hedgerow fighting, the clash of tanks contending on the broad plains of France—all this was new drama, new characters, new landscapes, the real thing at last, the second front of Russia's pleading and Allied dreams, often postponed, now gloriously fulfilled.

All summer the American Fifth Army under General Clark and the British Eighth under General Leese plugged away at the German defenses, the Americans to the west, mainly along the Tyrrhenian coast, the British at the center and along the Adriatic side. For a short time after passing Rome the pursuit of fleeing German forces was relatively rapid, as the foe was retreating fast to newer and even stronger positions than the Gustav line; once there, it was a different story. The Apennines in northern Italy run south and east of the Po, and that valley the Germans tried to hold to the bitter end, and did. Its fields are one of Europe's major granaries and, with the swastika waving there, Nazi rule could endure in Bavaria, Czechoslovakia, Austria and north Italy, though all the rest of the Reich surrendered. The Po Valley was vital to this citadel of the inner Fortress-Germania, sometimes called "The National Redoubt," and the Gothic line which defended it on the south was defense in depth from Pisa on the Tyrrhenian Sea to Rimini on the Adriatic. At all hazards it must remain German.

The Allied armies had difficulty in reaching even the Gothic line's outer fringes, since Germans in retreat are as skilful as Germans on offensive, and getting rid of land mines takes time. Nevertheless, not until they occupied Siena (July 3) did the Fifth Army again run into hot resistance. Overcoming it, however, they out-flanked the Germans in Leghorn, the port of Florence (July 29), continued more slowly up the coast and took Pisa, September 2, western end of the German defense system.

The American Fifth had a tough time of it; the British Eighth had an even tougher. The little mountains fringing Florence vied with those around Cassino in height and number, and the con-fusedly protracted siege-battling in and around Florence sadly battered Italy's loveliest city. British troops forced an entry there

August 4, the Germans clinging still to strong points within and just north of Florence until August 10. Meanwhile other elements of the Eighth Army, some Polish, some Indian, and in 1945 some Greek, paralleled the American advance on the Tyrrhenian flank by taking Pesaro on the Adriatic Sea, and finally Rimini, on September 21, clawing away at that eastern anchor of the Gothic line, baffled this time not by mountains but by swamps, canals and drainage ditches. The Gothic line bent back a little at both ends, but held in the middle. Whenever the Allies made gains fierce counterattacks threw them back. Owing to the superman Anglo-American rush past Paris in the west and the vast Russian tornado slamming down on Berlin from the east, the world paid little attention to Italy during the second half of 1944. The black eagles of the Teutonic North had been her curse a good fifteen hundred years, and their talon clutch still dug deep in her fairest provinces.

RED RUSSIAN STORM

Despite the glowing victories in the west that summer, one architect thereof, Winston Churchill, kept his sense of proportion. "It is the Russian armies," he told the House of Commons on August 2, "which have done the main work of tearing the guts out of the German army. In the air and on the ocean we could maintain our place, but there was no force in the world which could have been called into being, except after several more years, that would have been able to maul and break the German army unless it had been subjected to the terrible slaughter and manhandling that has befallen it through the strength of the Russian Soviet armies."

This tribute to Russians was well received. Germany not only had ten times as many divisions in the east as in Italy; her troops on the Russian front outnumbered their entire western forces at least three to one. Those eastern German armies the Russians maimed, mauled, broke and destroyed in an endless fury of driving battles from early summer, 1944, to the ripping through of Berlin's defense in April, 1945.

As the western Allies swarmed into Normandy, the Russians were making good their grasp on the Karelian Peninsula, forcing Finland out of the war, paralysing several German divisions in that torn and wasted land. Then, with the opening of the summer offensives, the Red armies struck first and hardest against the Baltic states and East Prussia, for so long as the wehrmacht held on there in strength it was impregnably placed for outflanking any direct Soviet drive on Warsaw and Berlin.

Soon, then, the whole eastern front was ablaze. The First, Second and Third Baltic Armies were out to trap and to destroy thirty German divisions in Lithuania, Latvia and Esthonia. Consummation of this project took months but the shadow of coming Baltic events was clear when Soviet forces reached that sea on August 4, and west of the port of Riga. Meanwhile, three other Russian armies hurtled at the Germans farther west, the First and Second White Russian Armies rushing on into Poland, the Third plunging for East Prussia, cradle of the Teutonic knights of old. Inside of six weeks eastern Poland was taken, the fortress of Brest-Litovsk fell once more, the Reds reached the Vistula both north and south of Warsaw, and its suburbs could be bombed from Russian lines. The Third White Army struck harder going, but it made headway, and pressed now against the East Prussian defenses.

As the Baltic lines bent back and German Poland caved in, the omnipresent Russians opened yet another offensive, this time in the south. All the way from the Carpathians to the Black Sea, the Ukrainian Red armies rolled into action. It was Rumania's turn. By August 29 the Russians were at the Danube's mouth, the Rumanian port of Constanza taken. In two more days they pierced the Galati Gap, pounced on the Ploesti oil fields, broke into Bucharest, the second Axis capital to capitulate. There a palace coup d'état "headed" by boy-king Michael drove the pro-German premier, Antonescu, from office and the bewildered Rumanian army, what was left of it, got orders to turn and fight not Russians but Germans and Hungarians.

With Rumania reversing sides, fifteen German divisions were stuck in the Balkans in even worse plight than those foundered in Finland. Before long all Balkan Nazis were cut off from the Reich except for circuitous routes through Yugoslavia where pro-Russian Marshal Tito was rapidly gaining the upper hand. On September 6 the Red army hit the Yugoslav border and two days later broke into Bulgaria. Politically-minded Bulgar colonels rapidly followed Rumanian precedents, and Bulgaria was at war against Germany by September 9. Even Turkey seemed tempted to throw in her lot on this Balkan anti-German crusade if the Allies would only tempt her more convincingly. Lost now to the Reich's power was the

entire Near East, apart from various garrisons stranded on cut-off
Greek islands, elsewhere in Greece and in isolated German enclaves
of Yugoslavia. Of all the satellites, Hungary alone stood faithful as
conquering Russia kicked in the gates of Fortress Europa from
north, east and south.

WHY THE GERMANS KEPT ON FIGHTING

In September the end was in sight as the front caved in on every
side, and from the air augmenting death came showering down on
German cities, factories and air-fields. Plainly the Reich must yield.
But she would not; and why? Three reasons tell the story: hope,
not altogether fanciful, of secret weapons; hope, more illusory,
that Allied dissensions might split and unbalance their enemies,
lead perhaps to German victory in the field, to win some sort of
compromise peace; and finally not hope but fear; fear of Allied
vengeance and extermination, particularly Russian, and what the
Cossack East might do when once within the Reich; fear at home
of Heinrich Himmler's gestapo, prison camps, and Nazi superthugs
who so far had kept the German people submissive in obedience
and fired to feats of incredible mass energy.

Rumors of secret weapons were now running wild in Naziland,
and never more so than in this war when so many new devices
both for offense and defense proved both feasible and successful.
Long before 1944 Herr Goebbels specialized in such rumors, and
the higher the war-tide rose around the Reich the more he made
use of them. A miraculous new type of submarine, Goebbels said,
would soon wrest the Atlantic from Anglo-American piracy; a new
tank would crunch unscathed through Allied armies; and from the
air new horrors would repay with interest the fiends who bombed
German hospitals and orphan asylums. Some thought that gas
would be released from high altitudes over hostile cities and that
it would be riddled in the air by German bullets to weave a fire
blanket consuming all it touched; others more realistic expected a
new type of bomb, something effective on the atomic weapon's
scale. "Within six months," said an SS propagandist, "all Germans
will know something which for the time being must be kept secret.
You will wake from the dark depressive night. Tomorrow will be
very calm and clear. Everything that threatened and terrified you
will have vanished."

The Allied press sneered and jibed at all these rumors of secret weapons but the British and American governments, knowing full well what their own scientists hard at work were developing in new techniques, were fairly certain that the Germans were doing likewise. As early as April, 1943, the British secret service heard of strange events taking place on a tiny island in the Baltic, and the RAF promptly photographed that island. It was well for Britain that they did so, for the pictures showed what seemed to be an airplane on rails attached to a long ramp, while other pictures showed the ramp with the plane missing. The Germans were experimenting with Hitler's *Vergeltungswaffe,* vengeance weapon, the rocket bomb.

That same month the RAF heavily attacked that island, but a month later British reconnaissance planes discovered a whole series of launching platforms or ramps similar to the Baltic specimen. In fact, land-launched rocket bomb devices were in process of construction in northern France. All pointed toward London, and all that were visible the RAF and the AAF bombed, an action which cost the Allies 450 planes and nearly 3,000 aviators. That attack slowed up the German program which was to start New Year's Day, 1944, with 1,000 rocket bombs; but had to be postponed until June 15 when the first "buzz" shells were launched on the British capital. They came fast and furiously at five to seven miles per minute.

Through June and July some two hundred a day came hurtling down the war-torn air. In some ways it was worse than Goering's great 1940 blitz. Then, at any rate, there was siren warning, bombs came mostly at night with comparative immunity in daytime. Now no one could tell what second of day or night the robot death might strike, or where, for these lethal missives could be aimed only in the general direction of London. Only a few planes had speed enough to overtake the rockets, the new Tempests, Spitfires and Mustangs. Had it not been for radar and innumerable anti-aircraft guns, both British and American, lined thick along the coasts, London would have been pulverized. As it was, not until late August was the new menace curbed. By then the "shooting galleries" caught in air some 90 per cent of the flying death and, shortly after that, capture of the launching sites ended it.

There was still hope of a super-robot launched from farther away and flying at greater speed and higher altitude, a promise actually fulfilled by autumn with the V-2, launched out of occupied Holland.

But Germany then was being so rapidly submerged that the V-2, looking for all the world like a flying telegraph pole, did not get any real testing. The sites were taken too soon.

Always there was chance of a rift between the Allies, an abandonment of the grand alliance by one or another of the three major foes of Germany. Coalitions had always fallen apart and would do so again. A soft peace might then be looked for, the Reich saved from destruction. The best chance for bringing this about was to exploit the latent dread of Communism in Britain and America, and latent Soviet suspicion of the bona fides of the democracies. Once set Churchill, Roosevelt and Stalin by the ears and Germany might get out from under, or for that matter, side with the democracies against Russia or with Russia against the democracies— it made no difference to Hitler.

The prime minister of England showed a queer affection for those moldy kinglets who ruled Italy, Yugoslavia and Greece. Sow suspicion then that the war in the Mediterranean was waged not for fair democracy but to prop up decadent monarchies, whimpering for Allied aid; suspicion also that Russia hated democracy in Poland and intended to kill it there.

In Italy the situation was confusing but British favoritism to the decrepit House of Savoy aroused more antagonism in left-wing circles in Britain and America than it did in Russia; possibly because opposition to the king and to his worthless deputy, the crown prince, was spearheaded primarily by Social Democrats and Liberals, both anathema to pure Communists; possibly because Stalin was indifferent to Italy, regarding that country as beyond the penumbra of Soviet hegemony.

In Yugoslavia any dreams of Allied discord that the Germans might fancy vanished into thin mist as Anglo-American aid shifted from General Mihailovich, formally in command of the Yugoslav Army under the direction of the exiled Yugoslav government in London, to Marshal Tito, victorious Communist-sponsored patriot and partisan. Tito, an ex-garage mechanic, might be a deep, dark Red but he fought Germans with vim, vigor and velocity, which no one could say for the royalist Mihailovich, and when the boy-king Peter spoke up on that side and out of turn in London he was promptly put in his place by the conservative British government, which with the American sent a military commission to assist Tito along the Dalmatian coast and in Croatia.

In Greece as in Italy the British seemed determined to do everything possible for royal authority. The withdrawal of German garrisons there, subsequent to the volte-face of Bulgaria and Rumania to the Allied side, brought civil war to Hellas. The Greek underground, the EAM, had fought the Germans a good three years while King George sat passive in London, as his more conservative supporters did in Cairo and Athens. But the EAM was Red, and found no favor with the British commander in Athens who insisted on their disarming. When they would not, the British intervened with artillery in Greece, and many soldiers of the EAM lost their lives. Just where the responsibility lay for this shooting is not clear, but the publicity resulting from the bloodshed gave rise to hotter opposition in Britain and in America than in Russia, for Stalin had apparently agreed at Teheran that Greece should follow Britain while Yugoslavia, Rumania and Poland followed Russia. Such is power politics.

The exiled Polish government in London was recognized by Britain and America; money had been loaned, Polish soldiers fought in Italy. But Stalin condemned that Polish government as a clique of landlords and loan sharks. The Polish question had been instrumental in dissolving the alliance against revolutionary France in the eighteenth century; it might have a similar result in 1945 if Germany fought bravely on until that year.

Poland was a headache to Washington and to London, and Stalin vented blunt and angry words. He knew what he wanted and would take nothing else, the Polish frontier of 1921 and the establishment of a Communist Polish government in which Communist influence would be dominant.

From the commencement of the war, the London Poles had been anti-Soviet; they had worked like beavers to enlist Poles who were anti-Soviet in a Polish army; they had organized a powerful Polish underground which was anti-Soviet; and with childish naïveté they had swallowed anti-Soviet propaganda tongued by Joseph Goebbels, believing even in the authenticity of Nazi photos which showed the bodies of thousands of Polish soldiers, still clad in Polish uniforms, killed wholesale by the Russians and buried in a common grave.

Stalin had early broken relations with that exiled Polish régime in London, and as his armies scorched Warsaw he set up in Lublin a committee of Polish Communists to whom he proposed to turn over a liberated Poland, which distressed his democratic allies, Britain and the United States.

Then in mid-summer, 1944, as the Russians reached the Vistula, General Bor of the Warsaw underground revolted and defended part of that city for weeks. Fighting the Germans, they clamored for Russian aid. It was not given. The Russians said the rising had been premature; it had been done without Russian approval or knowledge; the Red army for the time being had other objectives than the taking of Warsaw. And so, although it pushed both north and south of Warsaw, it did nothing to relieve General Bor.

Britain was particularly upset. The London Poles had urged Bor to fight on; they had sent Poles to fight for Britain in Italy, and the British in turn sent Bor supplies all the way by air from the Mediterranean. The Germans let Poles out of German prisons; they urged Poles to enlist in the wehrmacht to save Poland from Bolshevism.

Between the intransigent Polish government in exile and the stubborn Stalin, Britain was on the horns of a dilemma and was to stay so. The best Churchill could do was to ask Stalin to receive Mikolajcyk, their Polish premier, in Moscow and persuade the London Poles to despatch their premier to Stalin. Mikolajcyk made the trip twice without result, except that the Polish question was left on ice. It remained a thorny one, and Churchill pleaded with the House of Commons "not to engage in language which would make our task harder." That task was to let Russia have her way and to save face if possible. There was still a war to win and we were winning it, so the Germans gained little from these Polish quarrels.

Last but not least, fear gripped the German heart, galvanized German muscles, sheer terror of what might be if they lay their weapons down. It was not now so much the shrill voice of Goebbels but the black deeds of Himmler which sent shivers down the German spine. A mighty weapon his SS troopers and his gestapo, but a mightier one yet in Germany after July 20, 1944, the day on which the army plot to kill the Führer failed. From that date forward the world heard little that was authentic of Adolf Hitler, for in his name Himmler now ruled the Reich. "The blueblooded swine," the Prussian aristocrats who had tried to save something of Germany by a revolution from within, not only lost their lives, as did those remotely associated with them, but, as matters worsened, a fresh twist was given to the strangler's noose which tightened around the neck of every German who gave voice to doubts about the war or who even was caught with a Swiss or Swedish newspaper.

This terror from within transcended the terror from without. With the foes' forces on all German frontiers, children were ordered out of school, the old out of their armchairs, marched, drilled, put in uniform. The *Volksturm* of Napoleonic days was revived to include all Germans from sixteen to sixty. The last man and boy were rallied that ditches might be dug, mines laid, cities and towns fortified for street-to-street and house-to-house defense. *Festung Europa* was out. The ungrateful continent could look out for itself. Germany would defend her own. If the flat plains of northern Germany were foe-engulfed, then retreat to the stark citadel of Nazidom, the Bavarian Alps! Here, flanked on every side by close-linked mountains, ringed by set defenses, would come the last fight of those to whom death was infinitely better than defeat. Thus were ancient dreams arrayed against air power and machine power, and these soon to include the atomic bomb.

15. HITLER'S LAST STAND

THE Nazi Inner Fortress was shrinking day by day, must be weakening, must be bleeding from every vein of war-power, yet in the northern mists and from out the chemical fogs of air-borne ruin it loomed grim, grey and evil as some great, gaunt timber wolf, cornered for the kill in the last of its granite holds, death in its fangs still and unyielding to the bitter end.

That autumn German resistance hardened—east, south and west. In the far northeast the Russians did not cross East Prussian frontiers until October 18, and then in that lake-studded land of swamp and forest they made but slow headway. Red armies had forced the Vistula barrier, it is true, but Warsaw was German still, as was Cracow in southern Poland, and as long as the latter city held out the approaches to industrial Silesia were relatively safe. Once having cracked the Carpathian defenses, it would seem as though nothing could withstand the sweep of Red armor across flat Hungarian plains, but though Szeged, Hungary's second largest city, fell October 11 it proved impossible in 1944 to capture Budapest, no great distance away.

From Italy, that forgotten front, came word that the Gothic line was being pierced, that Americans soon would reach Bologna, that the British were rounding the foe's eastern flank at Rimini. But prophesies are not facts, and the truth was that the Gothic line stymied the Allies; their victories were rather patrol actions, so minor as hardly to be noted on an ordinary map.

So, too, was it in the west. The German frontier once passed, the Canadians, British and Americans found the going much rougher, due in part to difficulties of transportation. The British captured Antwerp September 4, but since German forces still blocked the exits from the Scheldt, the occupation of Belgium's great seaport was not much help. Almost everything the Allied armies used had to be carried by motor or be flown from a few congested ports hundreds of miles west, and even after British engineers sank a gasoline pipe-line across and under Channel waters the fuel was still far from thirsty tanks. Hitler's Westwall was far more a defense to the Reich than the Maginot line ever could have been to France. It might be, and was, bent in spots by tank rushes, but a defense in depth cannot readily be broken or surmounted.

The Allies were too confident too long of having the Germans on the run; they underestimated the foe's resiliency; the war, they thought, might be forced to a swift finish by outflanking the Westwall far to the north at the extremity of the Siegfried line, where the Rhine River flows sluggishly across Holland through several branches. A way might be opened here to the flat Westphalian plain of western Germany. To strike the enemy in this supposedly weak sector the British First Airborne Division parachuted to earth beyond the Lek River, a tributary of the Rhine. Instantly it was encircled, outnumbered, all but crushed by Nazi forces swarming in like angry wasps. For over a week the Tommies, reinforced constantly by air, put up a brave, heartrending fight. The British Second Army did its best to rescue them and almost succeeded. But only some 1,800 British paratroopers fought their way back across the Lek. The Germans were not done for yet.

This was discouraging, but the steady though costly Allied gains of the autumn might well restore the balance by December. The Canadians, clearing the Channel ports, had conquered Nazi garrisons at Boulogne and Calais, as had the Americans at Brest. British marines, His Majesties Jollies, had forced a landing on Walcheren Island at the mouth of the Scheldt in a daring exploit reminiscent of Tarawa, and with quite commensurate loss of life. The British Second made good its hold on Belgium, and had swept on into Holland. The American First Army, by-passing Aachen, capital of Charlemagne, was well over the frontier, pressing toward Cologne. Patton's Third, retarded by a distinguished defense of an old French fort at Metz by German military cadets, had edged toward the Saar. And the American Seventh, together with a fully equipped French army, had got within striking distance of Belfort near the Swiss corner.

November passed and it was early December. Still the German lines bent backward. The Tricolor flew again over Strasbourg and the upper Rhine was tapped. Patch's Seventh was forcing its way through Alsace. Patton's Third was at the Saar, one bridge across it, with German blast furnaces under American fire. Hodges' First U. S. Army surged forward to the west bank of the Rohr, the only sizable stream between it and Cologne, less than thirty miles away. Farther north Simpson's Ninth U. S. Army and the British Second clawed their way into German areas, and to the far north the Canadians swung up forward ready for a second shot at outflanking the Siegfried line.

Winter was now at hand and the war would not end in 1944. The Allies had moved forward but the most successful of their armies, the American First, had taken four weeks to go twelve miles. Some months earlier Churchill had prophesied that the war would be won by the early spring or early summer of 1945. He now suggested eliminating the adjective "early."

BATTLE OF THE BULGE

Then, December 16, to the amazement of all and to the consternation of many, the fast-fading wehrmacht, like Grundel's dam in the *Beowulf* saga, lashed out at the Americans in one great burst of flame and fury. Behind German lines, unseen by Allied intelligence, the German commander, Von Rundstedt, had gathered his strength, fused a mass of his best fighters, concentered motorized divisions with new tanks, better for this last battle than any the British or American armies had. In a brief order of the day he told his men that their hour had struck, called on them "to achieve the superhuman for Fatherland and Führer." And they almost did.

Out from their Westwall leaped the Germans on a sixty-mile front from south of Aachen into northern Luxembourg, and on they plunged into the Ardennes Forest, the old, old bloody trail which led toward Liege in Belgium, Sedan in France.

The Battle of the Bulge was on, and it raged for weeks, Von Rundstedt caught the Americans off balance. The Allies were hammering hard on a 450-mile front; he hammered harder and hammered through on one of sixty. Once reach Liege on the Meuse, he might strike at Antwerp, drive a wedge between British and Americans, roll back our forces and fuel his thirsty Tiger tanks with American oil. Perhaps do more if fortune favored there.

As it was, he unhinged the American line, isolated and pulverized American regiments, destroyed thousands of our men in the thick, snow-covered forestland of the Argonne; and his armor forced its way fifty miles in, rushing to probe either side of the deep bulge thus created to mark a further break-through.

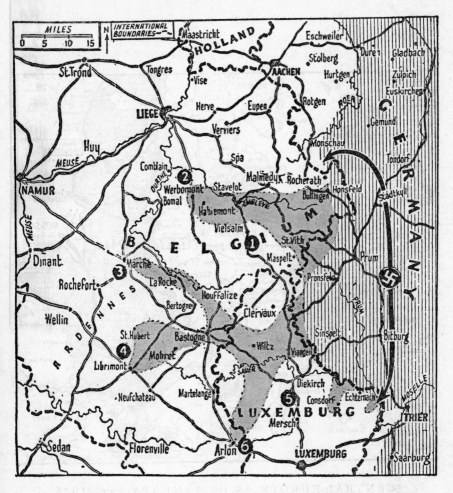

THE BATTLE OF THE BULGE IN ITS EARLY STAGES, DECEMBER 24, 1944

(Courtesy of the New York *Herald Tribune*)

A successful Allied defense in a tank battle between Vielsalm and St. Vith (1) kept the German spearheads that reached Werbomont (2) and the vicinity of Marche (3) from uniting. Enemy forces reached St. Hubert, Librimont and Mohert (4), though an American attack had succeeded in penetrating the southern flank of the enemy north of Mersch (5). The position of the enemy spearhead near Arlon (6) remained the same. Vertical lines indicate Nazi-held territory before the offensive, gray shading the enemy gains reported.

CENTRAL EUROPE AS OF JANUARY 1st, 1945

(Courtesy of the New York *Herald Tribune*. Associated Press map)

Arrows indicate major military moves in Europe in 1944. Shaded areas are Allied territorial gains during that year.

At Christmas the German flood reached its crest, and soon there-after subsided. Many German tanks stalled for lack of gas (they were reported within three miles of our major gas reserve). Time was lost trying to wipe out American enclaves of resistance enclosed by the greater German pocket. Of these, Bastogne has a place in American history. Completely circled by the surging German tide, our men fought round the whole front and held out as aid and munitions reached them by air, and finally paratroopers, without whom they would have died.

From the south Patton dashed with his armor to the rescue of this pocket, as from the north Montgomery came on with the Second British Army. Placed by Eisenhower in command of American troops on the northern side of the bulge, Montgomery hooked up Yanks and Tommies to press on against the German area from that side, as did Patton from the south, and between them they narrowed the base slightly, but enough to be dangerous for the Germans within. An old rule of warfare decrees that a penetration must not exceed one-half the base from which it starts. That base in early January was only the same as the farthest depth, around fifty-five miles. The danger point for Von Rundstedt clearly had been reached. There was even talk of the hunter being hunted, of trapping the Germans, forcing their surrender. The wary Von Rundstedt was not to be caught thus. He extricated both men and armor and by January's end the British and American forces were back pretty much where they had been in early December.

Once again we had underestimated the adversary. GIs cursed loud and long when they found our vaunted General Sherman no match for the German King Tiger tank of sixty-seven tons and eight-inch armor. Having learned their lesson, our generals went more cautiously with their march on Rhine.

EBB TIDE SPEEDS UP

That the Germans hung on thereafter for three months and more was little short of a miracle. Fortress Germania was shrinking now as fast as Fortress Europa had six months before. Finland took her peace from Russia, pledged to intern German divisions left within her lines. The Red armies drove across Finland to attack Germans in northern Norway; they captured Riga and were cutting up the wehrmacht isolated in the northeast; they commenced the invasion

of East Prussia after long probing the frontiers of that iron homeland of iron men; they rolled into Warsaw and were well on the
way to Berlin across western Poland; and reaching the banks of
the Oder opposite Frankfort they came at long last within striking
distance of the Nazi capital. Farther south Czechoslovakia had
been invaded by Red forces; and farther south yet, after by-
passing beleaguered Budapest, Soviet armor drew near Vienna.

Only in Italy did Germans really withstand the adversary. Northern Italy, all but the tip of Norway, Denmark, parts of Finland,
Holland and a few French ports still were held by German soldiers
needed for that last-ditch fight at home, if there was to be one. No
hope gleamed on any horizon. But many were yet to die before
Russians joined hands with Yanks across the Oder, and rigor mortis
officially could be proclaimed.

Futile though further war was, the Nazis kept on with it all
through February, March, April and into May. At ever accelerated
pace the Allies closed and drove in on the doomed Reich. In February closely coördinated blows struck at its heart from both west
and east. The Allies had long been stalled by the little Rohr River
flowing parallel to the Rhine. They were on its banks, but dared not
force a crossing since they knew there were huge dams on its
upper reaches still in enemy hands, and these, once dynamited,
would flood the lower Rohr to a good 1,000 yards in width. The
Germans clung desperately to their dams, their single ace in hole,
and the greater part of February was consumed in mastering the
Rohr Valley. Once done, progress became rapid, German resistance
spotty. Hodges' First Army took Cologne March 6; the American
Ninth, arriving at the Rhine a few day earlier, turned north to
meet Canadians coming south, both armies now behind the Westwall, and by their junction cutting off the retreat of thousands of
Germans. And meanwhile the British Second, storming into Cleves
in the lower Rhineland, headed toward Westphalia.

The west bank of the Rhine was now ours from Cologne north
through Holland, but the Allies had yet to cross the river. The
American First then got a toehold on its eastern shore north of
Cologne March 8, by a rapid dash up the Rhine for the Ludendorf
bridge at Remagen, just as the Germans failed to dynamite it. Patton with the American Third now swept down the Moselle Valley
and, whirling round to his right, drove in behind German forces
which had held him at bay in the Saar. Patton going south met the

advancing U. S. Seventh coming from that direction and the Germans thus cut off surrendered in droves; the Saar was lost; so, too, the Palatinate west of the Rhine; the Westwall ceased to exist and became mere history.

Far north the British fought their way out of Holland onto the Westphalian plain; in the south the French redeemed all Alsace; and now along the whole Rhine River's length British, Americans, Canadians and French threw new bridgeheads over, to cross the swift and beautiful Rhine in almost every conceivable way, using parachutes, pontoons, Bailey bridges, ferrying over in barges, motorboats, "buffaloes," "ducks" and other special craft, many manned by U. S. naval forces. Before March turned to April, Germany collapsed in the west.

So also in the east, and in the south. By early February the Russians were at Frankfort-on-Oder, a city they had taken twice before, once in Frederick the Great's time, once toward the close of Napoleonic days in 1813. The battered rubble of Hitler's capital was fifty miles away, its eastern suburbs but thirty from the Russian front; Berliners saw the flares by night and heard by day the clamor of the guns. But here the Red army paused. In its rapid leap from Warsaw to the Oder, it left behind strong enemy pockets; like Von Rundstedt's bulge, the base of Russia's holding in Germany was too narrow for the depth of penetration. Fifty miles to go, but these fierce with German fortifications. The Russians wanted no Stalingrad in reverse, took no chances. And so, through February and March they widened their base, struck north in East Prussia against Königsberg, hit against Danzig and Stettin, overran Pomerania, drove south to Breslau, and even farther south in Hungary and Austria. Budapest, with more than half its buildings wrecked, surrendered February 13, the third Axis capital to succumb; Vienna, the fourth, held out until April 13.

That same month the end came in Italy. American Mountain Infantry (ski troops long trained in Colorado) at last accomplished what American armor and the Brazilians had been unable to do. By a brilliant demonstration of highly specialized mountain warfare our ski fighters drove out the Germans from their fortified nests on 3,760-foot Mt. Belvedere where they had outflanked the only good road from Florence north to Bologna. The latter city fell April 12, and between Bologna and the fertile lands of Lombardy only foothills intervened. The British Eighth, meanwhile, came circling in from the Adriatic. The Gothic line was erased, the Germans beaten down, a signal for partisans in Genoa, Venice, Turin, Milan, to rise and throw out the Germans. Von Kesselring, next to Rommel Germany's best general, had gone north of the Alps to work military miracles. May 2 his successor surrendered all German troops in Italy and in southwest Austria as well. One day earlier Mussolini was taken near the Swiss frontier, shot, his body and that of a woman hung up by the heels in Milan.

CURTAIN FALLS

Everywhere the twilight of the end was dusking down on Europe's tragedy. The German armies in the west were gone, British and American armies driving at will over Adolf Hitler's superhighways, the British to the north, Americans to the center, and in the south Americans and French. Over half a million war captives were locked in prison pens during the first two weeks of April, and on the 24th Himmler tried to surrender exclusively to the British and Americans. His offer was refused.

May, and in one week more it was over. American armies near Berlin were halted by Eisenhower's orders. It would have been easy for us to have marched straight into the Nazi capital, for our arrival would have been greeted with joy by defenders who dreaded Red devastation. But Hodges' First rested on Elbe bank, leaving, as was right, the war's major honors to the men of the Soviets, who had done most to merit those dread laurels.

Why the German High Command strove still for another week is hard to fathom; the last chance of a last stand had faded with Italian surrender as the American First struck fast across central Germany and two southern American armies and the French forces drove ahead toward Bavaria and Czechoslovakia. No union of last-ditch fighters was possible. All plans were useless, even "planned chaos" was now impossible for the Nazis. Adolf Hitler was perhaps somewhere in Berlin. Power was gone and leadership also.

Berlin, a city dying. The air ministry, the opera house, the vast chancellery of the thousand-year-old Reich-to-be, a blasted shambles. Riots at soup kitchens. Huddled civilians in cellars. The streets a terror by night. The city plastered with Russian shells, British and American bombs. The probing, implacable Red army creeps north and south around the city. Russian tanks crash through barricaded

MILITARY SITUATION IMMEDIATELY PRECEDING
GERMANY'S SURRENDER, MAY 6, 1945

(Courtesy of the New York *Times*)

British troops entered Copenhagen (1). In another liberated country, the Netherlands (2), clashes between Nazis and patriots were reported. Soviet forces captured the islands of Usedom and Wollin and the port of Swinemuende (3). West of Berlin they reduced an enemy pocket (4). Russian attacks south of Moravska Ostrava (5) and east of Bruenn (6) pinched off the eastern end of the Czechoslovak pocket. The American Third Army cut into the Czechoslovak pocket taking Lohm and St. Brunst and drove five miles across the border east of Regen (7). In addition it took Linz and pushed on to Ried (8). The Seventh Army and the French accepted the surrender of German Army Group G (9) in western Austria and southwestern Germany.

MILITARY SITUATION IMMEDIATELY PRECEDING
GERMANY'S SURRENDER, MAY 8, 1945
(Courtesy of the New York Times)

British troops entered Oldenburg (1). In another it visited country the Nether-lands (2), clashes between Nazis and partisans were reported. So far forces captured the Island of Usedom and Wollin and the port of Swinemünde (3). West of Berlin they reduced an enemy pocket (4). Russian attacks south of Stralsund, Greven (5) and east of Dresden (6) pinched off the eastern end of the Czechoslovak pocket. The American Third Army cut into the Czechoslovak pocket taking Linz and St. Pölten and more than twelve miles across the border east of Hecen (7). In addition it took Linz and pushed on to Ried (8). The Seventh Army and the French occupied the remainder of German Army Group G (9) in western Austria and southwestern Germany.

streets. From subways SS men dash out at them from the rear, the death gasp of men already dead.

Goebbels is dead and also, presumably, Hitler—how, a mystery. May 2 the Russians have Berlin, all of it; and farther south where a bridge spans the Elbe Red army men and Yanks on April 26 shake hands, drink together.

German troops in Holland, Denmark and northeast Germany were all surrendered to the British. May 5 and some of our own soldiers were enjoying the view from ruined Berchtesgaden. That day, too, they crossed the Brenner, going south to join the victorious American Fifth coming up from Italy. May 7, and the German High Command surrendered unconditionally. May 9 in Berlin the final papers were signed, the European war was at an end. The Hitler Empire, Europe's most terrific adventure in militarism, had run its course in twelve years. And screened by the fiery ruin of that collapse men plainly saw, from Narvik to Cairo, from Marseilles to Vladivostok, the dim looming greatness of the peoples of Soviet Russia.

16. SUN GODDESS' MIRROR SHATTERED

As weary GIs crunched over the last crest of the Apennines, and rushed the Ludendorf bridge at Remagen, as Canadians and British plunged on through Holland and northwestern Germany, Allied forces in the Far East, brothers-in-arms of a dozen nations, in crawling Burmese jungles, in hot and humid Filipino valleys, on volcanic Iwo Jima and rugged Okinawa paid to the full, both by land and by sea, and at compound interest, Mars' bloody price for the crushing of Japan.

Three years post-Pearl Harbor, and that country still gripped Luzon and Mindanao, the two largest Filipino islands, still was entrenched in China's Yangtze Valley and the better areas of Burma, still lay too far distant from American-held Saipan even for the B-29 to operate with full effectiveness against the Mikado's cities. Stranded enemy units in New Guinea, New Britain and the by-passed islands of the South Seas now had nuisance value only, and the naval strength of Japan was no longer formidable: but her will to war was fierce and grim; and it took two-thirds of a year, plus the atomic bomb, to transmute Samurai bullies into smiling hosts for valiant visitors from overseas.

MANILA RECONQUERED

October 20, 1944, U. S. troops got ashore on Leyte; January 8, 1945, they did likewise at Lingayen Gulf, a hundred miles northwest of Manila on the island of Luzon. The days and weeks between had been taken up with making good our hold on Leyte, in twice defeating the Japanese at sea, in occupying Mindoro Island, north of Leyte, and tiny Marinduque, only ten miles from Luzon's shores and eighty-five miles south of Manila, in constant assault on Japan's shipping, in furious bombardment of Iwo Jima, one of the Volcanic Islands on the route from Saipan to Tokyo, and in air assaults on plane factories and munition works in the rising sun homeland.

By January 1, 1945, no less than 50,000 Japanese dead had been counted on Leyte and resistance there reduced to patrol action in the hills. But enemy forces numbering some 50,000 more still remained in Luzon, and no one knew how many more menaced Mindanao, Panay and the other islands of the archipelago. Our Philippine campaign had just begun.

It had for its next phase the retaking of Luzon. Most fortunately for the United States, enemy air power based there in the last three months had dwindled steadily, for the Japanese had played it all out and for keeps during the Leyte campaign, with swarms of Manila-based planes hurtling south to dash at reckless odds and in vain against our Liberators, Warhawks, Black Widows, navy Hellcats and marine Corsairs. Luzon was strongly held, and should General Yamashita, Singapore's conqueror, hold out in Luzon in 1945 as MacArthur and Wainwright did in Bataan in 1942, a year or more might pass before the mainland of Japan felt the tread of Yank leather.

Since the rising sun flag flew over Corregidor, frontal attack on Manila was out. We had the choice of driving at them from the south—best as far as distance went and best, too, for air coverage—from our land-based planes on Mindoro; or, on the other hand, we could strike in at the Lingayen Gulf and assault Manila from the north—at greater distance but mostly along a broad, flat valley with excellent motor roads admirable for tank war. We chose the Gulf, conveyed thither seven convoys without the loss of a transport, clear proof that Japan no longer could contest the air or the sea.

It was said we surprised the foe; one doubts it, for our large-scale amphibious operations were preceded by three-day bombardment. Opposition was minor, three Japanese motor-boats attacked our fleet and a few swimmers, thrusting explosives ahead of them on poles, abruptly died. That was about all. U. S. General Walter Kruger, German-born American citizen, commanding the American Sixth Army, speedily was landed with all his troops and struck out for Manila.

Yamashita did not set up battle on the open beaches nor in the broad valley; presumably he had neither planes, nor tanks, nor enough matériel to do so. Only when we probed inland to the hills on either side did we meet stiff resistance. There was no evidence of enemy ambush on our main route but Kruger took ample precautions against any surprise as he pressed forward to Manila. By the end of January he was more than halfway there and Clark Field ours once more.

Promptly then came more American landings, one to the west to cut across Bataan and another well southwest of Manila. On February 4, with little loss of life, we were back in the capital of the Philippines. MacArthur had returned. As for Yamashita, his explanation of our conquest was mere face-saving: "At last," he said, "I have MacArthur in my trap. I have been chasing him all over the South Seas and each time he has slipped away from me. This time it will be different, and my pleasure at a face to face meeting will be realized."

Where was that trap? Perhaps the foe had thought to set one in Manila, for fires like those that ruined old Moscow in Napoleon's day broke out everywhere, and in the older sections Japanese soldiers fought to the last from house to house and block to block, while on Corregidor our paratropers had to burn and slaughter the adversary out of his hide-outs one by one. It was a bloody, ghastly business and took a long time, the greater part of February, to clean Manila; the greater part of March and April to retake the seaports and the more important towns in the other islands, to drive the Japanese back into the uplands. How many foemen still were hiding there by middle spring of 1945 was anybody's guess, but a long, nasty campaign yet remained for MacArthur's men, many months of grisly fighting before Yamashita's warriors could be forced to bend the knee.

IWO JIMA

Meanwhile, as bleak silence followed hard upon the battle roar in central Europe and as the cold sun shone through fumes and dust along street after street of roofless German homes, war's crescendo rose higher and higher yet in the Far East. Americans, storming the outlying barrier islands of old Japan, brought the end closer to Hirohito's sacred homeland. The British Fourteenth Army, in a comeback finale, had reconquered Mandalay and Rangoon. And Chinese troops, reclothed, rearmed, victorious at last, struck out viciously against enemy forces in the Celestial Kingdom, ruined

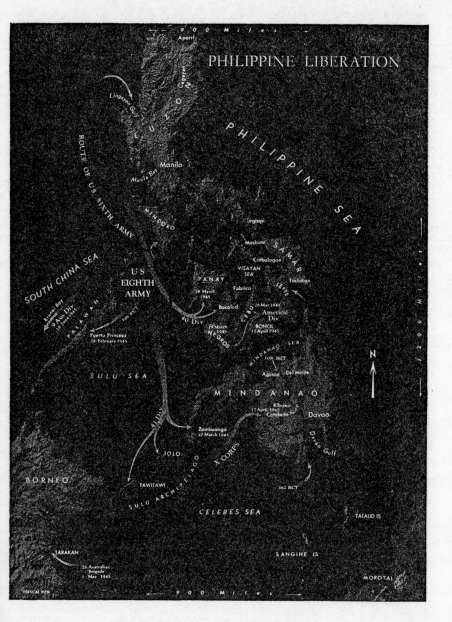

PHILIPPINE LIBERATION

(From General Marshall's Report, *The Winning of the War in Europe and the Pacific.*
Courtesy of the U. S. War Department)

the Japanese north-south corridor, won through to the China coast between Shanghai and Canton.

Our bases in the Marianas—Saipan, Tinian and Guam—were a good thirteen hundred miles from Tokyo, a not impossible distance for the best of our bombers, the B-29. But that round trip to the targets took sixteen hours in good weather, leaving for emergencies less than one hour's margin on gas supply. If the weather was bad, the superfortress was out of luck and out of the war; and even if the weather was fair, there was always danger of attack by Japanese bombers based on Iwo Jima, 600 miles from Tokyo, 700 from Saipan, and on a direct line between them.

Once the United States had Iwo Jima the picture would shift radically; the Americans then would have a fueling depot for returning B-29s; and, what is more, American fighter planes based on Iwo could escort our superforts to the Japanese mainland and thus enable them to fly at low altitudes, engage in precision bombing. Clearly this miserable excrescence of volcanic rock, Iwo Jima, was an American must, "a good rock to have on our side."

Long before we took Manila, long before MacArthur waded in Leyte's surf, the Seventh United States Air Force had been making frequent calls on Iwo, soon plastered with more bombs than even Malta. For seventy-two straight days before we struck to take it, our flyers had dived in and bombed that arena from all sides and every angle in the hope that final casualties might thus be kept low, a hope not realized.

Iwo has been variously described, always in harsh, crude terms. Practically bare of vegetation, it is crusted and heaped with volcanic ash, in some places, particularly along the beaches, soft, miry, treacherous, through which the best of tanks could not plough without wire mats beneath their treads. At the southern end rose 556 feet of rocky Mt. Suribachi, an extinct volcano; at its northern end were cliffs and caves, many of the latter steaming sulphurously from latent subterranean fires; and upon this island battlefield of only eight square miles 23,000 Japanese soldiers held three airfields that meant much both to Nippon and to America. It was a nasty little place for even marines to tackle and, as one remarked, "It ain't like Brooklyn."

An 800-ship armada conveyed 60,000 American marines to the attack, the greatest show in all the history of the United States Marine Corps. D-Day was February 19, 1945, and D-Day minus three, and D-Day minus two, and D-Day minus one the warships had their innings; naval planes skimmed, soared and hovered over Iwo, blasting away at what might be gun implacements; and as they did so our older and slower battlewagons let fly with twelve-inch rifles; while close to shore cruisers, destroyers, and that Pacific all-utility craft of ours, the LCI, "landing craft, infantry." This blast-process, and there had to be lots of it, was called "softening."

The barrage the navy finally threw up on D-Day itself was thick enough and black enough to hide the marines as they hit the beaches. It was said to have broken too high over the defenders but, however that may be, our casualties were heavy indeed, some 20 per cent, and the hardest yet to come.

There was Suribachi to take. Our ships could help but little here; the air force not much more; that volcano had to be skilfully rushed by men on foot, the foe killed out of caves and by hand-to-hand dueling amid the rocks. It was the Devil's Den at Gettysburg 10,000 miles away.

To reach the base of Suribachi and scale it took the leathernecks four days. And even then Iwo was far from won. The Japs still held two of the three air-fields. Pill boxes and block-houses of steel reinforced concrete covered deep with volcanic ash and sand had to be reduced one after another; the foe made full use of their innumerable underground passages; the nasty weather grew nastier; the surf ran high; reinforcements of both men and matériel were hard to get ashore. And even after all three air-fields were won, there were thousands of enemy soldiers holed up in the northern cliffs of Iwo. They died in the last ditch and almost to the last man. There were some suicides and but few prisoners. General H. M. Smith, our marine commander on Iwo, said grimly, "This is the toughest fight we've run across in 168 years." It lasted until March 16. In the American cemetery 4,300 marines are buried.

OKINAWA

On the last lap of his long outward voyage to Japan in 1853, Commodore Perry, U. S. N., paid an extensive visit to the Lew Chew Islands (the Ryukyus of the present day), staying several weeks on Great Lew Chew, the Okinawa of our Pacific war.

Whether those islands then belonged to China or Japan is a matter of doubt, since the islanders paid annual tribute to both powers. Like the Japanese, they gave every evidence of alarm at the approach of Westerners, watched closely Perry's every move, objected violently to Yankee tars sleeping on shore, but ate our "pickled oysters" with avidity. Okinawa was well governed, thickly inhabited and beautifully cultivated, the soil very fertile, doubtless due to the abundance of limestone; altogether a more pleasant place than what we found and left behind us in 1945.

Unlike Iwo, Okinawa is a large island, sixty miles long and varying in width from two to twenty miles. It lies half again as close to the two southern islands of Japan as Iwo does, and has the further advantage of being only 400 miles from China. Formosa is even nearer to the latter country than Okinawa, but 365 miles south of the Ryukyus. If our strategy called first for an invasion of China and subsequently that of Japan, then Formosa would be our best bet. Reverse this, however, and invade Japan first, then Okinawa, quite evidently would be the prize capture. Planes based on it were within easy range of Shanghai in China, Kyushu and southern Honshu in Japan, where heavy industry once was centered. And furthermore, the B-29, if based on Okinawa, could skim the Yellow Sea and the Straits of Shimonoseki and return in safety with fuel to spare.

Easter morning, 1945, and the newly formed Tenth American Army, convoyed and protected by some 1,400 ships and commanded by General Simon Bolivar Buckner III, landed on Okinawa. It looked easy. We had 100,000 men, and we spread across the island to bisect it, scarce hearing a hostile shot. Few suspected then what was to happen, the bloodiest campaign of the whole Pacific war. Eighty-two furious days were consumed to complete it, total American casualties, army and navy together, running to no less than 45,029, while on the other side 90,000 soldiers of Hirohito were killed, 4,000 taken prisoner.

Whether the Battle of the Bismarck Sea, as MacArthur claimed, or that fought for Okinawa was the decisive crisis of the Pacific War may safely be left to the future. The Japanese, however, had no illusions as to the significance of Okinawa. If they lost that island they lost the war, and faced inevitable destruction. It was bad enough to lose Iwo Jima; but that infernal pinpoint in the ocean had only three air-fields, and was much too small to be made our major base. This was not true of Okinawa, much closer to Japan, upon which endless air-fields might be built to harbor thousands of the dreaded B-29s. And Okinawa was built by nature for rugged defense; the southern half, where the capital, Naha, lay was rough and mountainous land, and cut in through its hills wound fortifications equivalent to the Gustav line or the Atlantic Wall, with interlocking and intercommunicating tunnels, caves and pill boxes, a task ahead for GI infantry to test their nerve and guts and sinew to the limit.

At the kick-off of the campaign our marines for once were lucky, for to them fell the comparatively easy assignment of conquering the northern end of Okinawa. That once accomplished, however, marines joined soldiers in driving at Japanese forces ensconced in the south, forces equal in number to the invaders, much less than equal in air power, sea power and matériel but fighting on their own ground. And now it was share and share alike for GIs and leathernecks, day by day running into withering fire whenever and wherever they tried to get on a few yards. And there were many more yards to cover than on Iwo.

This time, too, the American navy felt the death-sting of Nippon's wasp-men. The Japanese plan to concentrate their motor suicide boats on Kerama, seventeen miles from Okinawa, was foiled by our capture of Kerama several days prior to Easter. But the Japanese had a more dangerous threat than that in reserve, the kamikaze, which translated means "divine wind."

Centuries before, Japan, as tradition holds, had been kept inviolate by a divine wind or kamikaze sent by the Sun Goddess, a wind which wrecked the navies of the Mongol conqueror, and now there would be a divine wind, man-contrived, thousands of suicide planes launched at the great American fleet spaced out for miles off Okinawa, an armada inevitably huge in view of the multifarious need of 100,000 men for all the cumbrous supplies and implements of our modern war. The kamikaze planes were of minimum construction, each pilot locked in his cockpit, no armor for the plane, no parachute for the pilot, only brief specific training. Neither pilot nor plane had any perceptible chance to survive.

The kamikaze concept fitted well that older medieval psychology which the Japanese inherit—also their more modern theology. For them, as for Moslems of the earlier centuries, paradise was close at hand; before setting one's course for death, a wonderful party, many drinks, pre-Lethean honors. Kamikaze tactics were an improvement on the banzai charge, for the suicide planes did reach their mark on over 200 of our vessels, sank many a destroyer and small craft, and crippled badly two of our biggest carriers, killing so many bluejackets that in some weeks navy casualties exceeded both those of marines and army.

"One hundred million countrymen: the enemy now stands at our front gate. It is the gravest moment in our country's history." Thus Koiso, Japan's premier, on the eve of Okinawa. But he could do nothing to shake off the black hand of fate that smote Nippon's fighting men on that island. As they lost ground yard by yard, a ministerial crisis ensued at Tokyo and Koiso resigned. His desperate successors ordered the remnants of Japan's navy to Okinawa. Let the kamikaze attack once more with all it had, and in the midst of hoped-for confusion there might be one last chance for Hirohito's war-craft. But the ships of Japan never got to Okinawa. Spotted for them at once by omnipresent scouting planes, our fighter bombers shot out from their flat-tops to the kill, sank two light cruisers, three destroyers, and the battleship *Yamato* of 45,000 tons, Japan's finest. Meanwhile, Russia denounced her ten-year neutrality pact with Japan, ominous indication that the Soviets would attack in Manchuria as soon as they considered it their interests so to do.

The European war ended in May but on Okinawa war continued well into June. Through May the dwindling beleaguered garrison fought grimly as our Tenth Army and the marines edged it back to Shuri Castle in the south, pivotal point in the last defense line. On the way thither stood Sugar Loaf Hill. Time after time the Sixth Marine Division reached that summit only to be blasted off. The Seventy-seventh Division of the Tenth Army had to have six days, not to storm but to hold on to Chocolate Drop, another volcanic butte on the road to Shuri. We were winning because we were killing foes who could not be replaced, some 80,000 of the original 90,000 now being dead. We ruled sea and air. On this island they could only die. And all the while, as our air raids on Japan mounted, our losses in the air were dwindling. Some twenty-six big U. S. carriers, and many more baby flat-tops, now carried the flag in East Asiatic waters, and from them darted swarms of fighter bombers to shoot up the air-fields in southern Japan from whence came the kamikaze planes.

With Iwo's conquest, the B-29 began to come into its own. That plane, far surpassing the old flying fortress in both bombs carried and distance covered, was relatively a newcomer in the Pacific. Its first raid on Japan had been on June 15, 1944, and it did not strike at Nippon again for a month. From then on, the B-29 was more and more frequent over Japan, in greater and greater numbers and with fewer and fewer losses. In March, 1945, for instance, there were ten raids of the B-29 against Japan, and many of them were "large" raids, which meant that about 150 planes participated. In April there were seventeen of these forays, in May thirteen, and many were said to be "very large," which signified the use of 250 at one time, and in a single May raid 400 superforts were sent to smash shipyards, munition plants, factories, and air-fields, and to start devastating fires. All that we needed were more bases, closer to the target, and that meant Okinawa.

Early in June the Tenth Army cracked the Shuri line at last and the battle reached its final stages. Soon the enemy was "to run out of caves and boulders from which to fight and we were nearly out of Japanese to kill." Caught in narrow pockets which all told comprised but twenty square miles, scorched with searing liquid death from flame throwers, they threw themselves over cliffs, waded into the sea to drown, died with gun in hand, and, for the first time in this war, surrendered in appreciable numbers.

"Japanese prisoners" taken hitherto had generally been Korean labor squads hitched to Hirohito's armies or else wounded men caught before they could kill themselves. Now, over 4,000 Japanese soldiers preferred disgrace to death—a good omen for America as the Okinawa campaign closed, June 22, 1945.

BURMA WON BACK

The Japanese were already on their way out of Burma. The colossal and catastrophic defeat in 1942 of the British Empire there, had been well advertised; but the return in triumph of Imperial forces in 1944 and 1945 attracted little notice. The American press, as was natural, laid such emphasis as it gave to the Allied campaign in Burma on the dramatic achievements of our own General Stilwell and his Chinese troops in taking Myitkyina, in effect minimizing rather unduly the assistance rendered by British penetration forces, and underestimating, very decidedly, the stress and strain imposed upon the British Fourteenth Army which had to drive back the main Japanese invaders. That army, during the first half of 1944, not only suffered over 40,000 casualties, but, according to Churchill, "sustained no fewer than 237,000 cases of sickness which had to be evacuated to the rear over the long, difficult communications, and tended in hospitals."

That army, nevertheless, during the first five months of 1945 "liberated" Burma, retook Mandalay, chased the enemy from Rangoon, killed them by the thousands, drove the rest in full retreat toward the Siamese border. And Burma, it is worth remembering, was as large as Germany, with a fighting front in 1945 700 miles long and exceeded in World War II only by the Russian. Here was a country with two enemies to fight—Japan and the climate. Sodden wet, choking dust, malaria, jaundice, dysentery, mud, ticks, a humidity of 95 per cent, and Hirohito's desperate soldiers—a bad land to win.

The American contribution to this southern Pacific victory of 1945 was relatively small. Our concern, and quite rightly, had been with north Burma, to open there communication lines with China. Lend-lease had helped make possible the British comeback of 1945; but planning the final campaign, and the execution of it, was a British Imperial achievement. Statistics tell the tale. Of the ground troops in Burma in 1945, about 250,000 came from Britain, some 470,000 were Indian, 30,000 were from British East Africa, 30,000 from British West Africa. Chinese forces engaged were approximately 125,000 and American troops 25,000. A total of 900,000, possibly more. An array of Imperial strength seldom paralleled, never surpassed.

Kipling's Mandalay was Japan's main base in Burma, and the attack on it had priority for the 1945 campaign which burst forth with speed and fury late in February. General Slim, commander of the Fourteenth British Army, drove at Mandalay from the north and simultaneously rushed a mechanized force south and east for a surprise assault on Meiktila, eighty miles south of Mandalay. While a Sino-American force assisted by British troops drove down from Lashio in the northeast to assist in the siege of Fort Dufferin, an additional brigade was flown intact to support the troops who had won through to Meiktila. Thus it was that when Fort Dufferin fell, May 8, and the Japanese were forced to evacuate the capital city, they found themselves outflanked in the south and overwhelmed in the north. The most severe fighting in Burma ensued, as the Mikado's men tried fanatically to break through to the south. But the line held, and in little over a week Slim's men had killed over ten thousand of the best Japanese troops in Burma, acquired six air-strips in the arid zone about Meiktila, far from mud and monsoons, tons of Japanese war matériel, the top of the railroad Corridor, and Burma's main auto routes, and most important of all, a springboard from which to drive south.

There was still Rangoon to capture, 700 miles down the pestilent valley of the Irrawaddy. Time was precious, for unless Slim took Rangoon before the middle of May the monsoon would block land operations, write finis to war work in the skies. He therefore took the long chance and disregarded his flanks to speed his truck-bearing infantry and tanks on south. All April the adversary did his best to stay that onward rush, but so fast did it crash through that frequently Japanese headquarters only heard of British victories days after they had occurred, and in one instance Slim's tanks "ran down Jap policemen directing traffic at the crossroads."

The terrain now was flat and open, well suited for rapid movement. May 1, and Rangoon was close at hand. From the sea amphibious British landings drove ashore, and British paratroopers dropped down on the lowlands of the Irrawaddy delta. Rangoon was surrounded, north, south and west. The foe had had enough and too much; May 3 he fled. "Slim had beaten the enemy and the monsoon." Japan had suffered her severest worsting on the Asiatic continent.

CHINA REVIVED

Even before Rangoon's fall and the taking of Okinawa, the resilient and tough Chinese were turning past defeat into present victory. Chinese morale was on the upgrade throughout 1945 because of MacArthur's return to the Philippines; the opening of the Ledo Road and the mounting increase in air freight carried over "The Hump"; the tact and support of General Wedemeyer, successor to Vinegar Joe in command of American troops in China; the political and economic reforms of the Kuomingtang, brought about in part by pressure from our adviser there, Donald Nelson, and our ambassador, Patrick Hurley; the wind-up of the Burmese war which released China's best trained army to fight the Japanese in southeast China; and, most of all, the evident intention of Japan to cut losses in the southwest to a minimum and withdraw north of the Yangtze River.

Many thousands of Chinese had earned their living in the Phil-

ippines in days gone by, and no sooner did our flag again fly there
than the Chungking newspapers began to speculate on how long it
would be before the American army landed on China's coast. Before
we headed straight for Japan via Iwo and Okinawa, the chances
seemed excellent that we would strike the foe first through China,
making use of China's one unending capital, manpower, a fact
which made the weakened pulse of Chinese resistance immediately
beat faster.

And it beat still faster as American trucks began to squirm their
way through north Burma hills over the Ledo-Burma highway,
rechristened "Stilwell Road" in honor of the man whose imagination, grit and perseverance had made it possible. "Welcome Hon-
orable Truck Convoy," the banners said, as this new stream of
matériel-in-aid trickled in over the thirsty desert of a half-starved
land. It was only a trickle compared with China's need, some 60,000
tons a month, but as a supplement to what the planes were now
carrying over The Hump it was of real value, and as a psychological
stimulant it was even more.

Also instrumental in reviving China's strength was the reorganization of her army, to a considerable degree "U. S. trained, U. S.
supplied, U. S. supported." General Stilwell and the Generalissimo
did not see eye to eye; both were touchy men and coöperation
lagged. Stilwell's dual job as commander of U. S. troops in China
and as chief-of-staff of Chiang Kai-shek was taken by General
Wedemeyer, who made himself persona grata to that Chinese chief
of state, so that Chinese soldiers were now better fed, better
clothed, better disciplined, and consequently better fighters.

The physical well-being of the Chinese soldier not only reflected
General Wedemeyer's skilful hand but also that of Donald Nelson.
That organizer of victory had gone to China in 1944 on Roosevelt's request to disentangle China's economic woes. He was fairly
successful; red tape was shrunk, if not cut; the banks reduced
interest rates on money spent for production; and wildcat inflation
was checked, at least in part. And what Nelson did for economics,
our Ambassador Hurley was said to have accomplished for political
reform. Acting on his advice, Chiang Kai-shek turned conciliatory
toward Chinese Communists, dismissed his more reactionary advisers, appointed T. V. Soong, his forward-looking brother-in-law,
as premier, reorganized his administration on a semi-democratic
basis. Hurley speedily became the target of those American journal-

ists who had no faith in Kuomingtang; but if the proof of the pudding is in the eating, his influence in China was salutary where the war effort was concerned, and one noted now that crack Chinese divisions, hitherto guarding the north against the Communists, were sent south to join the final offensive there against the Japanese.

That offensive gathered headway throughout the late spring and summer of 1945. The Burmese war once ended, our transport planes were loaded with war-hardened Chinese soldiers hungry for new victories; and from the discomfited adversary in south China not a few were wrested. One by one the United States-built air-fields there were won back and the conqueror's corridor to Indo-China, Thailand and Malaya, for which he had fought so long and upon which he had laid so much stress, was so narrowed by mid-June that he withdrew to avoid capture. And as this happened, the Japanese loosed their grip on Chinese seaports so rapidly that by the end of the month Chiang Kai-shek's men held an unbroken seacoast line of 280 miles north of Hongkong.

ON THE EVE OF HIROSHIMA

Summer, 1945, and Japan was mortally stricken. Her death throes were those of Germany in February, March and April, but with one striking difference; no hostile armies had set foot upon her homeland's soil.

Yet she was done for; the continental conquests shrinking fast, her scattered garrisons over widespread Oceania completely useless; the Australians were depriving her of the oil of Borneo; the converging aircraft of the United States were roasting her cities alive; the American navy conjointly with the planes of the American army were cutting the life-lines to Korea and Manchuria, without which she could not live; and the most imposing armada ever seen on any ocean, mostly American, but joined now by a powerful British squadron, paraded up and down, and down and up her now defenseless coasts, pouring floods of shells on helpless targets.

Invaded Nippon had more to die of and less to fight with than invaded Germany six months earlier. Even before Pearl Harbor, Japan's industrial potential was insufficient for large-scale war; now it was almost nonexistent. Unlike Germany, her domestic resources were few. The food she ate came largely from out the sea or over from the mainland, likewise oil, cotton, iron, rubber. The sea now was death to her, even the fishing boats sunk or driven to hiding.

Even more than Britain, Japan's life depended on ships, and where were they now? Tiny craft still stole stealthily at night Korea-bound, slunk along the China coast, slid slyly into Singapore or rusted at the wharves of Shanghai and Batavia; but the navy which so proudly shattered Imperial Russia's fleet in 1905 was to all intents and purposes erased from this war by Admiral Halsey's raid in July on the Inland Sea dockyards.

During the nine months before Hiroshima our B-29s alone flew over 30,000 sorties, dropped over 169,000 crushing tons on shipyards, air-fields, factories, cities. And this does not count the planes catapulted from our carriers against the enemy, or the four-engined bombers based on Iwo and Okinawa. Now, as resistance dwindled, our bombers flew at low levels, used jellied petroleum to start quenchless fires, and sent scurrying to rural hide-outs the remnant millions of homeless Japan. And even so, we had not reached the peak of this cosmic destruction, for redeployment of the European air forces had scarce begun, and Okinawa air-fields still under construction would launch a thousand more planes per day.

This air assault was deadlier on Japan than on Germany, for the former's economic arteries were more exposed, her far flimsier cities more congested. Almost to the war's end, the German radar and German áck-áck kept functioning. Not so with Japan. She did not have the mechanics, the laboratories, the reserve of technological skill, nor the space that the Nazis could command; her citizens had neither the material nor the skill to make artificial gasoline and synthetic rubber. The Japanese mind, unlike the German, lacked large-scale experience with steel and chemicals, was ill adapted to blue-print buzz bombs and Tiger tanks.

In August the end was near. Japan turned to Russia, besought her aid to approach Britain and the United States. But Stalin, secretly committed to join in Japan's destruction, refused. The United States and Britain dictated unconditional surrender, and to this the Japanese were not willing to subscribe. And so they husbanded their dwindling planes, hid them as best they might, refused combat in the air to the swarming air fleets of the United States, which now struck at rail communications, bridges and ferries rather than at burnt-out factories and slain cities. Bracing themselves against our infantry, soon to storm Nippon's shores, they planned then to bring out their last planes, to renew kamikaze tactics, to kill many thousand Yankees. And they hoped that time soon would come.

Invasion in force had been set for November. It was not necessary, for Hiroshima came first.

HIROSHIMA

July 16 some 300 picked scientists assembled in the New Mexico desert. An experiment was up for testing, the fruit of many years of research, and at a cost of $2,000,000,000.

And this is what the scientists, huddled at safe distance, saw: a great green light, changing color, now purple, now orange, instantaneously expanding, shooting upward in a fifth of a second, higher than Mr. Everest. Then came unbearable thunder. Here at long last was total power, total war, which man himself could wield—"the first cry of the new-born world."

This was the atomic bomb, man-made but of the very stuff of the suns, a bomb equal to 20,000 tons of T.N.T. and with the fullest destructive power of 2,000 B-29s. Prometheus in Greek legend had stolen for us fire from the gods, and for that and other presumptions had been chained to a rock by Father Zeus. Man now, for weal or woe, Prometheus-like, was chained to his own full knowledge of this one central secret of the universe.

August 6 an American plane dropped a single atomic bomb on Hiroshima, a Japanese city and army base with a population upwards of 350,000. Sixty per cent of Hiroshima immediately was no more, dead instantly all those in the doomed area, dying those on the perimeter, "a death no men ever died before."

Two days later Russia declared war on Japan. Stalin had previously agreed to do so. And promptly Russian armies now crossed Manchurian borders.

Three days later a second and deadlier bomb was dropped, this time on the port of Nagasaki, and over an area even larger than at Hiroshima man and everything made by man was obliterated.

On the fourth day of this new world, August 10, Japan offered to surrender and accepted terms four days later.

Before our synthetic Sun-Fire destroyed Hiroshima and Nagasaki so utterly, Soviet entrance on the Far East's last act of world tragedy would have been news of great moment, and Japan's

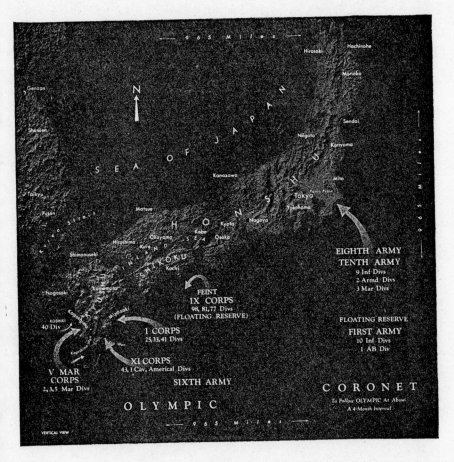

PLANNED ASSAULT ON JAPAN

(From General Marshall's Report, *The Winning of the War in Europe and the Pacific*. Courtesy of the U. S. War Department)

acknowledged defeat would have roused joy entire all through the United Nations. But epoch-making though these facts were, the ghost-shadow of Hiroshima and of Nagasaki eclipsed the Soviet act, damped our joy for peace at last.

It was not that most men opposed the bomb's use; no doubt it shortened the war, saved many thousand lives, Russian, British and American, as well as of Japan's young recruits who would have perished in further battles now impossible. Nor was it wholly horror at what we had done to men that tempered rejoicing among those still capable of thought. There had been too much horror during ten years past for numbed nerves to respond in shock to any new ghastliness. Rather it was a profound sense of awe and fear. Against the energy released by split atoms, how piffling now inventions like gunpowder, the compass, the steam-engine! Out of the laboratory of the chemist-physicist had come this miracled genie, his birth hurried by the clash of arms, the mad roar of battle. His future, what? And our own?

All else was anticlimax in this grim Pacific and Asian war. The Japanese accepted unconditional surrender with but a single suggested reservation—that they might retain their emperor. That was granted provided Hirohito would obey all the orders of our commander of the army of occupation, a concession wine-heady democrats and fire-breathing militarists denounced as fatal error, but one those cognizant of the menacing despair, confusion and chaos inevitably consequent on the collapse of all administrative machinery in Japan's vast empire deemed wise and salutary.

To complete arrangements for the occupation thus suddenly advanced was not easy, and it was September before the American forces landed and MacArthur took over the governance of Japan, final articles of surrender being signed the 2nd of that month on board the battleship *Missouri* in Tokyo Bay.

Thus ended the nightmare of the Greater East Asia Co-Prosperity Sphere. Fortunately the slogan, Asia for the Asiatics, however inducingly presented, had not won the allegiance of the swarming peoples of the Orient. The security of the United States in the Pacific now was doubly secure; but the Far Eastern problems of European imperialism still remained to vex the future of a world where naked power, so far, had won the victory—another nightmare in the making.

POSTSCRIPT

UNIVERSAL peace unbroken had been for centuries the hope of
the rightminded; it had prompted Penn to found his Philadelphia,
an experiment which seemed proof positive to Europeans of the
eighteenth-century enlightenment that the end of the age of iron
was in sight; it had filled men's minds in 1815 and again in 1919,
only to wither with passing years. The Holy Alliance of Tsar
Alexander, crude and mystic, had been one expression of this ideal,
and Woodrow Wilson's League of Nations, aimed at underwriting
peace not simply by discussion but by guarantees, had been
another. That League had failed. Find out the cause, said some,
remove it and proceed anew.

But it was not as simple as that. A war for survival, if it is to be
won, rules out discussion of just what comes after, since all energies
must be devoted to what comes next. To agree on general principles
is relatively easy, to implement and mold them into specific form,
difficult. With this in view, Roosevelt and Churchill signed the
Atlantic Charter of 1941, an ideological flag of merit, but not
legally binding on any nation, and primarily a proclamation of and
for Atlantic powers, as its name implies.

On the larger scale and at best, it was an extra-legal and
uninforcible affirmation of good-will and noble purpose. As such,
it served its authors, encouraging those who, not content to fight for
sheer survival, must first of all persuade themselves that dirty war is
not dirty. It set forth general principles of worth and merit for
future peace conferences to ponder over and to stand by. But it
could and did settle nothing. Soldiers had first to fight, generals to
plan campaigns, statesmen to formulate and to implement agreements concerned not with serene postwar futures but with the
gripping and immediate present. Unless and until the dangers and
the duties of the day were met, there was neither need nor time
for what might later follow.

To be sure, on January 28, 1942, the United Nations made its
debut when an excellent declaration of intent, adherence to the

Atlantic Charter and all it stood for, was signed at Washington by twenty-six nations, subsequently to be adhered to by twenty-one others. But swaddling clothes bound that infant very tightly as Britain, the United States and Soviet Russia guarded carefully the cradle (they still do), admitting later as subordinate and part-time nurses, Chungking China and the Free France of De Gaulle. Not, indeed, until the San Francisco Conference of April, 1945, when delegates from almost all the non-hostile world formulated and agreed upon a United Nations Charter, was that organization much more than an ideological dress uniform in which the big three decked themselves out for popular approval.

Not that history's pages were blank between 1942 and 1945 in that matter of conferences. There were many, at Casablanca, Cairo, Moscow, Teheran, Yalta in the Crimea, and two at Quebec; conferences at Hot Springs, Virginia (food and agriculture); at Bretton Woods, New Hampshire (international finance); Chicago, Illinois (aviation); Philadelphia, Pennsylvania (ILO—International Labor Office); Atlantic City, New Jersey (UNRRA—United Nations Relief and Rehabilitation Administration); and at Dumbarton Oaks, Washington (preparatory for the San Francisco meeting). But to discuss, and to confer, and to draw up resolutions is quite apart from purpose and power to enforce, from men and machinery for enforcement. And not until the end of the European war was in sight could Britain, the United States and Russia well afford the luxury of consulting Mexico and Iran on world affairs as well as oil, to say nothing of running the risk of quarreling with one another either in open or in secret.

The more important of these gatherings, it must be remembered, were not conferences of the United Nations as such, but consultations of two or three larger states on how to win the war. This was true of Casablanca (January 1943), a meeting held between Roosevelt and Churchill with their military and naval staffs in which mention was made of Stalin's inability to attend and assurances given that he had been fully informed of military proposals. It was also true of the first Quebec Conference (August 1943), which was concerned primarily with matters of military strategy in Europe and Asia. In the Cairo Conference (November 1943), Chiang Kai-shek joined Roosevelt and Churchill, and the agenda, as far as published, was confined to war against Japan and how that country was to be stripped after its conclusion, not only of conquests made in the twentieth century but also in the nineteenth. Nothing here, certainly, of any United Nations machinery for governing the postwar world. So likewise with the second Quebec Conference (September 1944), exclusively devoted to considering Anglo-American interests in Eastern Asia, at least as far as we can tell, and certainly as far as announced.

The United Nations, as a group of Allied states, shared in the deliberations of the lesser conferences. But even here the more important rôle in every instance was played by the representatives of the great powers, for it was obvious, that they alone had the strength, financial or otherwise, to make these conferences successful, as for instance, the establishment of an international bank. A state like Yugoslavia whose subscription to the world bank was assessed at $10,000,000, and Ethiopia with an assessment of $3,000,000 could hardly expect to vote on equal terms with Britain, whose contribution was to be $1,300,000,000, or the United States, put down for $3,175,000,000. All of these conferences, however important the matter under discussion, were but architectural drawings for upper stories of a world house, of which the foundations were not yet laid.

To the preliminary planning for laying those foundations we must now betake ourselves.

Some there were, like Walter Lippmann, who wrote learnedly and at times convincingly of a world to come in which it would be well for the Atlantic powers (western Europe and the Americas) to club together for mutual benefit and protection, not strive in the immediate future for world unity or even world federation. Such, however, was not the aim of Roosevelt and Churchill, determined to woo and to win Stalin's coöperation for some kind of international machinery whereby war, if not ended for all time, at least might be postponed to a more distant future.

The two Western warchiefs made some headway in this direction at the Moscow meeting of foreign secretaries (November, 1943) when Britain, Russia, the United States and China affirmed "the necessity of establishing at the earliest practical date a general international organization, based on the principle of the sovereign equality of all peace loving states...." A pledge not only approved but strengthened at Teheran, Persia (December, 1943) when Roosevelt, Stalin and Churchill signed a declaration calling for "a world family of Democratic Nations."

This takes us to Dumbarton Oaks at Washington, where for seven weeks ending October 7, 1944, the representatives of the big three, plus China, threshed out a specific program in accordance with the Teheran pledge.

What emerged was a document with striking resemblance to the projected 1919 League of Nations, providing for a General Assembly in which each state admitted to the privileges of the United Nations should have one vote, and for a Security Council of eleven members, the big three, enlarged to the big five by the inclusion of China and France with permanent membership, the remaining six members to be chosen by the Assembly.

The Dumbarton Oaks plan was presented to Stalin in person by Roosevelt and Churchill at the Crimea Conference held at Yalta (February 1945). Snags were encountered, and compromises made right and left, mainly by the Americans and the British, some open and declared, some secret. As is customary in diplomatic meetings, successes were magnified, failures minimized. Our President's report to the American people clearly indicated that he was not altogether happy with the result, particularly in regard to Poland. Nevertheless, Russia did agree to participate in an ecumenical meeting of all the friendly states, staged for San Francisco, April 1945.

At that city, the infant United Nations came close to dying. Molotov of Russia and Evatt of Australia, the two protagonists at this full-dress gala event, clashed again and again, the former generally winning, holding the better cards, playing them relentlessly; the latter generally losing, but putting up a dogged fight on behalf of real democracy and the lesser nations.

The Russian got what he wanted; he lost two or three minor contests which he could well afford since he was the victor in major ones, not because a majority—or anything like it— of the smaller countries favored the Russian demand, but because Britain and the United States yielded their influence to Molotov's side, persuaded many to vote against their real desire, if not against their convictions. For Britain and America were determined at all cost that their ideological baby, the United Nations, must not perish.

Minor combats were over Poland and the Argentine Republic. Molotov asked admittance for the Lublin Poles as representatives of Poland. To have acceded would have broken the Yalta agreement so barefacedly that the request was refused. He then tried to have the Argentine excluded, on the logical ground that she was a Fascist state. Once more he lost, not because his argument was poor, but because Britain was concerned about her meat deliveries and the United States supported Argentine to placate our string of South American republics.

The Russian victories, however, were outstanding. That country got three votes in the Assembly instead of one, by insisting on and obtaining additional seats for the Ukraine and for White Russia. And, much more important yet, by the constitution of the United Nations as finally adopted, each one of the five permanent members of the Security Council were acknowledged as having a right of absolute veto, not simply in regard to economic sanctions and the use of troops to coerce warlike nations, but also in regard to the peaceful settlement of international disputes.

The San Francisco Conference completed its labors a month before the Nazi collapse and three months before Hiroshima. Had the atomic bomb exploded six months earlier, would the results have been different? Presumably, no. Hiroshima was too much of a shock, still is too much of a shock, for numbed humanity to take in its full significance. Was the Conference a failure? None could say. Its very weakness in time might prove its strength. Certainly it was a disappointment to those enthusiasts who pinned their faith on humanity to learn the lessons of the war before the war was over; and the very fact that Senator Wheeler of Montana and other isolationists voted for the ratification of its labors was not encouraging. Nevertheless, it did give birth to a league of sorts in which some of the technical kinks of the League of Nations were deleted, a league of which both the United States and Russia were actually members—a real accomplishment!

Two months later in July came still another meeting of the big three in Prussian Potsdam; the big three states, that is, not the three big men of whom the world had long been so aware.

Roosevelt was dead. Organizer and architect of victory, F.D.R. would be sadly missed, his dauntless smile no longer seen, his adroit, uncanny political perception no longer discovering a way out of every conceivable impasse, no longer able to turn enemies into fellow-workers if not always into friends.

His place was taken by our new president, Harry Truman of Missouri, living embodiment of that commonwealth as popularly conceived in these United States.

And before Potsdam was over, Winston Churchill, supreme

orator of the Anglo-Americas, victim now of a parliamentary revolution, likewise departed, the place once his taken by Clement Attlee.

Joseph Stalin must have felt the strangeness of such great changes.

Potsdam wisely did little, agreed on the fourfold division of German lands for occupational purposes, granting France a relatively small part to administer, to Russia the lion's share, both of territory to be administered and of reparations to be had, and on the eve of Hiroshima the meeting disbanded, postponing for quieter days and calmer thoughts the political future of Germany.

Italy, Germany and Japan were conquered and the war, or wars, were ended; or were they? There were more to say yes in 1919 than in 1945. The optimistic note of that earlier year was not audible in the latter. The atomic secret once made known, and the master of men all might be neither iron nor Calvary but Portugal or Afghanistan or any other country with a few atomic bombs. The United States had used two of those bombs, had many more on hand, possessed strictly for the time, together with Canada and Britain, the secret of their manufacture. But could the formula be kept secret long? The chances were in the negative.

Mankind was ill prepared to face emergencies of this sort. To most folk they did not seem real, could not be real, must be the freakish dream of some Orson Welles radio program.

Yet certain facts are clearly ascertainable. There is now force enough available to throw a projectile beyond this globe's gravity-magnet to that of another planet. Interplanetary communication is around the corner. And Hiroshima and Nagasaki are right here in plain view, the photographic proof of what took place there in our illustrated periodicals, the awesome sight of that mushroom-shaping emanation to be seen by anyone with the admission price to a movie.

What chance Calvary now? If Kipling's baron had lived to 1946, presumably he would still say, "Iron is master of men all." The One World of Wendell Willkie is but a passing phantasy. So long as national sovereignty exists, great powers are therefore above the law and so long does international anarchy persist. The paper legalisms of the San Francisco Charter put neither check nor rein upon those powers. As for the spirit of world unity, *circumspice*! Russia pledged by Teheran to support democracy, denies it at home, opposes it abroad; the British back in Hongkong, Singapore and Mandalay intend to stay there; the Americans, rejoicing that butter and meat are easier come by, pleased that new tires and autos roll from assembly lines, think less and less about their brothers overseas. From the Urals to the Atlantic, from Norway to North Africa, from Tokyo to Tibet, from the Great Wall of China to the Indian Ocean and the Celebes, the old die of hunger and exposure, and children whose lives have never known decency or peace are growing (if they live) into embittered men and women, the morrow's bread their first concern. Where, said Teufelsdröckh in *Sartor Resartus,* "each, isolated, regardless of his neighbour, clutches what he can get and cries, Mine...." Where likewise "Society, long pining, diabetic, consumptive, can be regarded as defunct...."

To all this perhaps the baron's overlord and his successors would make reply: your indictment though harsh is true. But even so, it is incumbent on us to remember how brief man's history upon this planet, how often in past centuries dim unresolve and bleak despair, hate, jealousy and fear have had the upper hand as man shrank from the terror that flyeth by night and from the pestilence that stalketh at noonday. "The intelligence which has converted the brother of the wolf into the faithful guardian of the flock ought to be able to do something toward curbing the instincts of savagery in man." So wrote Huxley in happier nineteenth-century days. We must now enlarge that same "intelligence," impart to it a wider connotation, intimations and intuitions too deep to fathom, too mystic for word-formulation. It possibly may come to pass that what is now global twilight will deepen into darkest midnight. There is no surety against that. What child stirs now in the womb of the morning we know not; but suffice it unto us to know that eternal inquiry will continue among men concerning the purposes of the Almighty as long as breath remains. By very token of their doing so, ye shall know that they are men.

> Why doth It so, and so, and ever so,
> This viewless, voiceless, Spinner of the Wheel?

Thus the spirit of the pities in Thomas Hardy's epic drama of Napoleonic wars. Hardy's Overworld, his spirits, sinister and ironic, his pities and his recording angels pursue at length their search for an answer to that insistence which echoes through the ages since God made Job. Their reading of life's meaning, not empty of all comfort, may be found in the drama's concluding chorus:

> But—a stirring thrills the air
> Like to sounds of joyance there
> That the Rages of the ages
> Shall be cancelled, and deliverance offered from
>   the darts that were,
> Consciousness the Will informing, till it fashion
> All things fair.[1]

[1] Thomas Hardy, *The Dynasts* (New York, 1904). By permission of The Macmillan Company, publishers.

We will not build "Jerusalem in England's green and pleasant land," or any other land for that matter, and ignore life's major question. It will not down. It cannot be side-tracked. It will persist until time's end. The answer may not be found in life as we know it, and to fret and fume over our nescience avails nothing. Better say meanwhile with Paul, "If after the manner of men I have fought with beasts at Ephesus, what advantageth it me, if the dead rise not?"

READING LIST

ADAMIC, L., *My Native Land*, Harpers, 1943. The tangled skein of Yugoslav politics is somewhat disentangled by a former Slovene and anti-Fascist who regards the Pan-Serbs with disfavor. A fascinating and terrible book.

AGLION, R., *The Fighting French*, Holt, 1943. A French officer fighting under the Cross of Lorraine vividly describes equatorial Africa and the assistance given the British in defeating Rommel.

ARNE, S., *The United Nations Primer*, Rinehart, 1945. Diplomatic conferences in outline form from the Atlantic Charter to the San Francisco Conference.

BARMINE, A., *One Who Survived*, Putnam, 1945. An attack on Soviet policy by a Russian exile who served under Stalin as diplomat, soldier and executive.

BELDEN, J., *Retreat with Stilwell*, Knopf, 1943. An account of the Japanese conquest of Burma.

BOWMAN, P., *Beach Red*, Random House, 1945. Superb description of jungle fighting in blank verse.

BRAILSFORD, H. M., *Subject India*, John Day, 1943. A temperate but leftist analysis of the British raj in India by a distinguished British writer.

BRINES, R., *Until They Eat Stones*, Lippincott, 1945. An experienced newspaper man interned in Manila analyzes Japanese psychology and infiltration tactics.

CARR, E. H., *Conditions of Peace*, Macmillan, 1942. A widely discussed book by an eminent political scientist, praised highly in liberal and conservative circles, roundly denounced by left-wing reviewers.

CHAMBERLIN, W. H., *The Russian Enigma*, Scribner's, 1943. A critical evaluation of the Russian scene, anti-Stalinist in tone.

CHURCHILL, Winston,
While England Slept, Putnam, 1939. Speeches on foreign affairs and national defense, 1932-1938.
Blood Sweat and Tears, Putnam, 1941. Speeches during 1939-1940.
The Unrelenting Struggle, Little, Brown, 1942. Speeches of the preceding year.
The End of the Beginning, Little, Brown, 1943. Speeches of 1942.
On to Victory, Little, Brown, 1944. Speeches of 1943.
The Dawn of Liberation, Little, Brown, 1945. Speeches of 1944.
These six books are a "must" for any student of the war.

CLIFFORD, A. G., *The Conquest of North Africa*, Random House, 1943. The most comprehensive book thus far published on the war in the Lybian desert, from 1940 to Rommel's defeat in 1943.

COT, P., *Triumph of Treason*, Ziff-Davis, 1944. A former minister for aviation in the Third Republic gives the inside story of the Riom treason trials ordered by Hitler.

CURIE, E., *Journey Among Warriors*, Doubleday, Doran, 1943. The distinguished daughter of the discoverer of radium was granted many special privileges by Russian and British officials in Egypt, Russia and Burma. Her book, therefore, on the war in those areas is unusually illuminating.

DAVIES, R. A., and STEIGER, A. J., *Soviet Asia*, Dial, 1942. The economic resources of central Asia and Siberia and the Soviet development of them.

DAVIS, F., and LINDLEY, E. K., *How War Came*, Simon and Schuster, 1942. An account of American reaction to the Second World War from the fall of France to Pearl Harbor.

DULLES, F. R., *The Road to Teheran*, Princeton University Press, 1944. An American scholar reviews Anglo-Russian relations, 1481-1943.

DURANTY W., *U.S.S.R.*, Lippincott, 1944. Somewhat light in vein and anecdotal but worth while on the treason trials just before the outbreak of the war.

EASTMAN, M., *Stalin's Russia*, Norton, 1940. A strong attack on Stalin by a former follower of Trotsky.

EHRENBURG, I., *The Tempering of Russia*, Knopf, 1944. Of utmost value. The author is the Thomas Paine of the Red army, the official propagandist of the Soviets during most of the war.

FORMAN, H., *Report from Red China*, Holt, 1945. Decidedly sympathetic toward the Chinese nationalists, antipathetic toward the Kuomingtang.

GREW, J. C., *Ten Years in Japan*, Simon and Schuster, 1944. Carefully couched in diplomatic language, the U. S. Ambassador to Japan warns Washington breakers ahead.

HAILEY, F., *Pacific Battle Line*, Macmillan, 1944. Excellent reporting of naval engagements during the first half of the war against Japan.

HAMILTON, T. J., *Appeasement's Child*, Knopf, 1943. A highly unfavorable account of the Franco régime in Spain during the early years of the war by the correspondent of The New York *Times* in Madrid.

HAY, Ian, *Malta Epic*, Appleton-Century, 1943. The most authoritative account of the Siege of Malta thus far written.

HERMAN, F., *Dynamite Cargo*, Vanguard, 1943. Dramatic account of the hardships and perils of convoys to Russia around Norway and the North Cape.

IND, A., *Bataan, The Judgment Seat*, Macmillan, 1944. The U. S. intelligence officer of the Army Air Force in the Phillippines describes the futile defense of Bataan Peninsula in 1941-1942.

Infantry Journal, *The Capture of Attu*, 1944. Minute fighting over impossible terrain ably told by many who participated.

Infantry Journal Handbook, *The World at War, 1939-1944*, 1944. Excellent but highly compressed account of military and naval action in all areas to November 1, 1944.

JOHNSON, W., *The Battle against Isolation*, University of Chicago Press, 1944. Based largely on the files of the Committee to defend America by aiding the Allies, this book cannot be said to be impartial. It does, however, contain important materials for any future study.

JOHNSTON, G. H., *Pacific Partner*, Duell, Sloan and Pearce, 1944. Full of local color about the "down under boys" of Australia, their manners, customs, resources, and their "Waltzing Matilda."

KARIG, Commander W. and others, *Battle Report; The Atlantic War*, Rinehart, 1946.

KARIG, W., and KELLEY, W., *Battle Report; Pearl Harbor to Coral Sea*, Rinehart, 1944. Two U. S. Naval reserve officers compile from official and semi-official sources naval operations in the Pacific prior to the Battle of Midway. Should be read in conjunction with Admiral King's three reports.

KING, ADMIRAL E. J., *Our Navy at War*, Three official reports:
Covering combat operations to March 1, 1944, U. S. News, 1944.
Covering combat operations, March 1, 1944 to March 1, 1945, U. S. News, 1945.
Final official report, March 1, 1945 to October 1, 1945, United States, Naval Institute Proceedings, January, 1946.

LASKI, H. J., *Reflections on the Revolution of Our Own Time*, Viking, 1943. A philosophic analysis of contemporary idealogies by a distinguished professor of The London School of Economics and chairman of the British Labor Party. The book is leftist in tendency.

LEE, Jennie, *This Great Journey*, Rinehart, 1942. The courage and resiliency of the British people during the blitz described by a miner's daughter, now a member of Parliament.

LEMKIN, R., *Axis Rule in Occupied Europe*, Carnegia Endowment for International Peace, 1944. Valuable analysis of German law as applied to occupied countries.

LERNER, M., *The Great Offensive*, Viking, 1942. A clear, vivid and comprehensive analysis of fighting on the Eastern front from the summer of 1941 to that of 1942.

LIN YUTANG, *Between Tears and Laughter*, John Day, 1944. A Chinese publicist writes of Western ideas concerning his own country with some humor and considerable bitterness.

LIN YUTANG, *The Vigil of a Nation*, John Day, 1945. China's leading transmitter of Chinese ideals to the Western world writes of his wartime travels and anti-communistic sympathies.

McInnis, E., *The War,* four volumes, published respectively in 1940, 1941, 1943 and 1944, by the Oxford University Press. Written by a Canadian university professor these four books do on a large scale what the Infantry Journal does on a minor one, describing military and naval campaigns in detail.

MacKenzie, D., *India's Problem Can Be Solved,* Doubleday, Doran, 1943. A temperate approach to the problem of India, seen by the author as one involving all the United Nations.

Maritain, J., *Freedom in the Modern World,* Scribner's, 1936. Thoughtful essays by a liberal Catholic philosopher.

Marshall, General George C., *Report of the Chief of Staff of the United States Army,* Simon and Schuster, 1945.

Mears, H., *Year of the Wild Boar,* Lippincott, 1942. An American woman's sensitive account of life in Japan on the eve of the Second World War. Excellent.

Mendizabel, A., *The Martydom of Spain,* Scribner's, 1935. Thoughtful and impartial background of the Spanish Civil War by a distinguished Spanish historian.

Moore, F., *With Japan's Leaders,* Scribner's, 1942. An American officially employed by the Japanese foreign office as counsellor thumb-sketches a number of Japanese statesmen.

Moorehead, Alan, *Don't Blame the Generals,* Harpers, 1943. Excellent, vivid journalism of the Lybian war, the fall of Tobruk and Rommel's invasion of Egypt.

Robinson, P., *The Fight for New Guinea,* Random House, 1943. Graphic account of the difficulties encounted by MacArthur in the early stages of the New Guinea campaign.

Robson, R. W., *The Pacific Islands Handbook,* 1944, Macmillan, 1945. Statistical information concerning islands in the Pacific, their resources, peoples and government. Many excellent maps.

Rolo, C. J., *Wingate's Raiders,* Viking, 1944. The unique story of Britain's unique general who invented new methods of jungle fighting and who did so much to reconquer Burma.

Romulo, Colonel C. P., *I Saw the Fall of the Philippines,* Doubleday, Doran, 1942. A graphic and vivid account of the fighting on Bataan by a colonel on General MacArthur's staff.

Root, W. L., *Secret History of the War,* 2 vols., Scribner's, 1945. The title is a misnomer but the two volumes are useful as a summary of many fairly well-authenticated facts.

Salter, C., *Try out in Spain,* Harpers, 1943. The writer preserves an even keel between Fascist and Communist in describing the Spanish Civil War.

Sayers, M., and Kahn, A. E., *The Great Conspiracy,* Little, Brown, 1946. A pro-Stalin book as its subtitle, "The Secret War against Soviet

Russia" suggests. Amply documented but to be read with great caution.

SCHUMAN, F. L., *Europe on the Eve, 1933-1939*, Knopf, 1940. The ablest account thus far available of the diplomatic background of the Second World War.

SCHUMAN, F. L., *Night over Europe*, Knopf, 1941. European diplomacy, 1939-1940, microscopically examined.

SCHUMAN, F. L., *Soviet Politics at Home and Abroad*, Knopf, 1946. Perhaps the ablest book yet to appear in defense of Soviet policy. The picture is overdrawn.

SEYDEWITZ, M., *Civil Life in Wartime Germany*, Viking, 1945. Replete with quotations from German newspapers. Most valuable.

SHERROD, R., *Tarawa*, Duell, Sloane and Pearce, 1944. A magnificent tribute to the United States Marine Corps. A superb, terse and unadorned account of the conquest of Tarawa.

SMEDLEY, A., *Battle Hymn of China*, Knopf, 1943. A history of China's woes from 1931 to 1941, warmly sympathetic to Chinese Communists, bitterly antagonistic to the Kuomingtang.

SMYTH, H. D., *Atomic Energy for Military Purposes*, Princeton University Press, 1945. The official report of how the atom bomb was manufactured in the United States.

SNOW, E., *Asia*, Random House, 1941. An American correspondent draws on his long experience in China to survey the chaos brought to that country by the war.

SNOW, E., *People on Our Side*, Random House, 1944. Reports on the aspirations of Russians, Chinese and Indians. Somewhat leftist in point of view.

SNOW, E., *Red Star Over China*, Random House, 1938. A remarkably graphic account of the migration of Chinese Communists from Southeastern to Northwestern China.

STETTINIUS, E. R., Jr., *Lend Lease for Victory*, Macmillan, 1944. An exceedingly valuable and statistical study of lend-lease aid to the Allied world, 1941-1943.

STOWE, L., *They shall not Sleep*, Knopf, 1944. An analysis of what the Burmese, Indians, Chinese and Russians think about the war and what they hope to gain from it.

TABOUIS, G., *They Called Me Cassandra*, Scribner's, 1942. The foreign editor of a well-known Paris newspaper, personally acquainted with every Frenchman of political importance in the years immediately antecedent to the war, gives an intimate and breezy description of their aims, acts and character.

TOLISCHUS, O., *Through Japanese Eyes*, Reynold and Hitchcock, 1945. A source book of quotations from Japanese militarists and nationalists.

TOLISCHUS, O., *Tokyo Record*, Reynold and Hitchcock, 1943. Diary of The New York *Times* Tokyo correspondent in the year 1941.

TREGASKIS, R., *Guadalcanal Diary*, Random House, 1943. The summer of 1942 on Guadalcanal and the magnificent fight of the United States Marine Corps to retain their foothold on that island.

WALLER, G., *Singapore Is Silent*, Harcourt, Brace, 1943. How the Japanese swarmed down the Malay Peninsula and overcame Singapore.

WHITE, L., *The Long Balkan Night*, Scribner's, 1944. The jacket truthfully states that "this fascinating account combines the thrills and chills of a hair-raising detective story with a detailed analysis of the Balkan states before and during the war."

VOYETEKHOV, B., *The Last Days of Sevastopol*, Knopf, 1943. Thrilling story of the siege of Russia's Black Sea port.

Index

Admiralty Islands, United States invasion of, 301

Africa, the Ethiopian war, 35-41; the Libyan campaigns, 144-158, 160-163, 244-245, 248-249; the East African campaign, 147, 150-152; United States landings in Algiers and Morocco, 245; the Tunisian campaign, 250-252

Albania, 14, 72, 127, 130

Aleutians, 237-238, 287, 292-293

America First Committee, the, 196-199, 210, 214

Anti-Semitism, in Nazi ideology, 18; in the United States, 198, 214-215; extermination of Polish Jews, 273-274

Antonescu, 129, 335

Anzio, 323-324

Argentina, 194, 201, 369-370

Atlantic Charter, 212-213, 366

Attlee, Clement, 371

Auchinleck, 155-156, 162

Australia, 120, 223; the army in Crete, 139-141; the army in North Africa, 153-154; Battle of the Java Sea, 232; strategic importance and defense of, 233-236, 239; reverse lend-lease to the United States, 234; the New Guinea campaign, 289-291, 301-302; invasion of Borneo, 362

Austria, annexation by Germany, 62-63

Badoglio, Pietro, 40, 41, 257-259

Balkan states. See specific countries.

Baltic states, Russian interest in, 75-76, 82-83, 318; see also specific countries

Bataan, defense of, 224-226

Battle, of Flanders, 95-98; of France, 98-100; of Britain, 111-118; of the Atlantic, 118-119, 141; of Smolensk, 168-169; of Moscow, 170-

171; of Stalingrad, 184-186; of Macassar Straits and the Java Sea, 231-232; of the Coral Sea, 235; of Midway, 237-238; of the Bismarck Sea, 291; of the Bulge, 344-345

Belgium, 88, 343; threats and invasion, 93-94; surrender to Germany, 95, 97; the Battle of Flanders, 96-97; during the Nazi occupation, 270

Beneš, Edouard, 66-67, 70

"Blut und Boden," Nazi doctrine, 18

Blum, Léon, 48, 101, 103, 265

Bonnet, Georges, 70, 197

Borah, William, on American intervention, 190-191

Boris of Bulgaria, 132

Borneo, the Japanese invasion, 231-232; the Australian invasion, 362

Brazil, 196, 201

Bulgaria, 126; reoccupation of Dobruja, 128; becomes German satellite, 132; volte-face to Allied side, 335

Burma, defense and fall, 229-231; Wingate's counterthrust, 296-297; Allied successes, 1944, 310-314; retaken by the Allies, 358-360

Burma Road, 122, 217, 230, 295, 310-312, 361

Canada, 14, 120, 191

Carol of Rumania, 127-129

Cassino, 322-324

Chamberlain, Neville, 52, 61, 63, 65, 88, 191, 197; conferences with Hitler, 66-69; policy toward Russia, 74-77; resignation, 92

Chang Hsueh-liang, 25; kidnapping of Chiang Kai-shek, 55

Chiang Kai-shek, 23-24, 59, 297, 367; hostility toward Chinese Communists, 53-55, 56, 307-310; kidnapped by Chang, 55; disagree-

ference to war, 79, 81-82, 87-89; fighting in Norway, 91-92; the Battle of Flanders, 95-98; Dunkirk, 97-98; position after Dunkirk, 107-111; and the French Fleet, 110-111; Battle for Britain, 111-118; the RAF, 111-112, 114, 117-118, 139-140; air attack on London, 112-114; air attack on the seaports, 114; the heroic people of, 115-116; the Royal Navy, 118-119, 140-141; battle for the Atlantic, 118-119, 141; reasons for aiding Greece, 126, 131, 136; the Greek campaign, 137-138; the Cretan campaign, 138-141; relations with Iraq, 142; situation at start of African campaigns, 145-146; defeat of the Italians in Libya, 146-149; defeat of the Italians in East Africa, 150-152; Rommel's first advance into Egypt, 152-154; first counteroffensive against Rommel, 155-158; Rommel's second advance into Egypt, 160-163; aid to Russia, 180-181, 186; closing of the Burma Road, 217; war with Japan and early losses, 222-223; loss of Malaya, Singapore, and Burma, 227-231; defeat in the Dutch East Indies, 231-233; landing on Madagascar, 240; Indian policy, 240-241, 296; Rommel's final retreat from Egypt, 244-245, 248-249; the Tunisian campaign, 250-252; the Sicilian campaign, 254-256; relations with Badoglio's government, 257-259; the Italian campaign, 259-261, 321-324, 332-334, 346-348; air war on Germany, 278-281; the Burma campaign, 310-314, 358-360; preparations for D-Day, 324-327; D-Day and the campaign in France, 327-332; rocket-bomb attacks on, 337; policy in Italy, Yugoslavia, and Greece, 338-339; Battle of the Bulge, 344-345; the final drive against Germany, 346-349; position in the United Nations Organization, 367

Esthonia, 14, 75, 82-83, 318, 335

Ethiopia, war with Italy, 35-40; significance of Fascist victory, 61; final defeat of the Italians, 150-152

Fascism, growth in Italy, 15-17; significance of victories in Ethiopia, Spain, and China, 61; in Poland, 70; in France, 101; in Rumania, 128-129; in Greece, 130; in the United States, 197-198; "abolished" in Italy, 257

Finland, 14; Russian demands on, 83; war with Russia, 83-85; aid from abroad, 85-86; capitulation, 85; renewal of Russian war, 167, 170; United States sympathy for, 191-192; second peace with Russia, 320, 345

France, 19; policy in the Ethiopian war, 37-41; policy in Spanish Civil war, 47-48; 50-51; Germany's reoccupation of the Rhineland, 62; policy toward Czechoslovakia, 64-69; Polish alliance, 72; relations with Russia after Munich, 74-77; declaration of war on Germany,78; reasons for defeat, 79, 101-106; indifference to war, 81-82, 87-89; the Battle of Flanders, 95-98; the Battle of, 98-100; surrender, 100; armistice terms, 101; the French Fleet, 110-111, 201, 248; conditions during Nazi occupation, 264-267; the Allied landings and the relief of Paris, 327-332; the Maquis and the FFI, 331; position in the United Nations Organization, 367; see also Free French and Vichy France.

Franco, General Francisco, 45-49, 122

Free French, in Syria, 142-143; in East Africa, 150; at Bir Hacheim, 161-162; permission to Allies to occupy New Caledonia, 235; in North Africa, 246-247; see also France

French Indo-China, 59, 217-219, 307, 362

Freyburg, General Bernard, 139, 163

Gallup poll, on the destroyer exchange, 200; on aid to Britain, 206

Gandhi, Mohandas K., 21, 240, 296

Giraud, General Henri Honoré, 249-250, 254

Germany, effect of depression on 9-10; growth of nationalism in, 17-19; participation in Spanish Civil

lease policy, 121, 203-204; aid to Russia, 180-181, 186; public opinion before Dunkirk, 188-194; repeal of the arms embargo act, 189-191; reaction to the invasion of Norway and the Low Countries, 192; The White Committee and The America First Committee, 195-199; the exchange of destroyers for British bases, 199-200; drift toward war, 199-215; the Selective Service Act, 200-201, 213; and the French Fleet at Martinique, 201, 246; reaction to the triple alliance, 202-203; the lend-lease debate, 203-211; the Atlantic patrol, 211, 213-214; occupation of Greenland and landing of troops in Iceland, 212-213; sinking of the *Greer* and the *Reuben James*, 214; reaction to Hitler's invasion of Russia, 213; the Japanese attack on Pearl Harbor, 215, 220-222; relations with China and Japan before Pearl Harbor, 216-220; loss of Wake and Guam, 222; defense and fall of the Philippines, 223-227; defeat in the Dutch East Indies, 231-232; the battle of production, 236-237; the Battle of Midway, 237-238; landings in Algiers and Morocco, 245; relations with the French in North Africa, 246-248; the Tunisian campaign, 250-252; the Sicilian campaign, 254-256; relations with Badoglio's government, 257-259; the Italian campaign, 259-261, 321-324, 332-334, 346, 348; air war on Germany, 278-281; victories in the southwest Pacific, 288-291, 301-302; the Aleutian campaign, 292-293; invasion of the Gilberts, 293-295; development of amphibious craft, 298-299; advance toward the Philippines, 1944, 298-307; B-29 raids on Japan, 303, 357-358, 363; the Burma campaign, 310-314, 358-359; preparations for D-Day, 324-327; D-Day and the campaign in France, 327-332; Battle of the Bulge, 344-345; the final

drive against Germany, 346-349; landings in the Philippines and liberation of Manila, 350-352; invasion of Iwo jima and Okinawa, 353-358; development and use of the atomic bomb, 364; the surrender of Japan and Allied occupation, 365; position in the United Nations organization, 367
Uruguay, 201

Vandenberg, Arthur H., on American intervention, 190, 192, 208
Vichy France, policy in Syria, 142; policy in Indo-China, 217-218; policy in Madagascar, 240; relations with the Allies in North Africa, 246-250; during the German occupation, 264-267; *see also* France
Victor Emmanuel, forms government with Badoglio, 257-259

Wainwright, General Jonathan, 227
Wake Island, Japanese attack on, 222
Wavell, Sir Archibald Percival, 131, 138, 145-149, 153-155, 296
Wedemeyer, General, 360-361
Weygand, General Maxim, 96, 98, 100, 103, 247, 265
Wheeler, Burton K., on American intervention, 191, 196, 207, 210-211
Wilhelmina, of the Netherlands, 94, 268
Willkie, Wendell, 195, 207; on American foreign policy, 199-200, 203; on lend-lease, 205-206, 209
Wingate, General, 312; in Ethiopia, 151; in Burma, 296-297
White, William Allen, 195-196, 200
White, Committee, the, 195-196, 200
Woolton, Frederick, 116-117

Yugoslavia, 126, 335; as Czechish ally, 65; internal dissension, 133-134; rejection of German terms, 133; defeat by Germany and dismemberment, 134-135; Civil war, 136; partisan warfare, 316, 338
Yamashita, Tomoyuki, 351-352